When the Son of Man Didn't Come

# When the Son of Man Didn't Come

A Constructive Proposal on the Delay of the Parousia

Christopher M. Hays in collaboration with
Brandon Gallaher, Julia S. Konstantinovsky,
Richard J. Ounsworth OP, and C. A. Strine

Fortress Press
*Minneapolis*

WHEN THE SON OF MAN DIDN'T COME
A Constructive Proposal on the Delay of the Parousia

Copyright © 2016 Fortress Press. All rights reserved. Except for brief quotations in critical articles or reviews, no part of this book may be reproduced in any manner without prior written permission from the publisher.
Visit http://www.augsburgfortress.org/copyrights/ or write to Permissions, Augsburg Fortress, Box 1209, Minneapolis, MN 55440.

Cover image: The Empty Throne (Second Coming of Christ). Detail from the mosaic of the Dome of the Baptistery of the Arians. Sixth century CE. Early Christian.
Cover design: Tory Hermann

Library of Congress Cataloging-in-Publication Data
Hardcover ISBN: 978-1-4514-6554-9
Paperback ISBN: 978-1-5064-2547-4
eBook ISBN: 978-1-4514-6963-9

*For the Church.*

# Contents

| | | |
|---|---|---|
| | Foreword | ix |
| | Acknowledgments | xi |
| | Abbreviations | xv |
| | Primary Sources | xvii |
| 1. | Introduction: Was Jesus Wrong About the Eschaton?<br>**Christopher M. Hays** | 1 |
| 2. | Prophecy: A History of Failure?<br>**Christopher M. Hays** | 23 |
| 3. | Reconceiving Prophecy: Activation, Not Prognostication<br>**C. A. Strine** | 39 |
| 4. | The Delay of the Parousia: A Traditional and Historical-Critical Reading of Scripture: Part 1<br>**Christopher M. Hays and Richard J. Ounsworth OP** | 59 |
| 5. | The Delay of the Parousia: A Traditional and Historical-Critical Reading of Scripture: Part 2<br>**Christopher M. Hays** | 79 |

6. Negating the Fall and Re-Constituting Creation: An Apophatic Account of the Redemption of Time and History in Christ   109
   **Julia S. Konstantinovsky**

7. Divine Possibilities: The Condescension of God and the Restriction of Divine Freedom   147
   **Brandon Gallaher and Julia S. Konstantinovsky**

8. Divine Action in Christ: The Christocentric and Trinitarian Nature of Human Cooperation with God   175
   **Brandon Gallaher and Julia S. Konstantinovsky**

9. Liturgy: Partial Fulfillments and the Sustaining of God's People   211
   **C.A. Strine, Richard J. Ounsworth OP, and Brandon Gallaher**

10. Our Method: Reflections on Our Hermeneutical Principles and Collaborative Practices   241
    **Christopher M. Hays and C.A. Strine**

11. Conclusion: A Fourfold Response to the Delay of the Parousia   253
    **Christopher M. Hays**

    Bibliography   269
    Index of Names   291
    Index of Subjects   295
    Index of Ancient Writings   299

# Foreword

Many years ago, after publishing an essay on "The Delay of the Parousia," I contemplated writing a book on the subject. It seemed to me a topic of considerable exegetical, historical, and theological importance, but one that had rarely been given the sustained attention it deserved. All too often, scholars in the various theological disciplines have accepted, without much examination, the following simplistic narrative: Jesus and the first Christians expected the end to come soon; it did not; the Church accommodated itself to this disappointment by making itself more at home in the world for the indefinite future; and now, modernity combines with non-fulfilment to make the imminent expectation incredible. There are all kinds of things wrong with this narrative. But there are also serious problems with apologetic approaches that seek, above all and at any cost, to exempt Jesus from being mistaken about the timing of the end.

I never wrote such a book, and in the meantime, nor did anyone else. It has remained a book waiting to be written until five young scholars in a variety of theological disciplines, collaborating in what must have been an exciting process of discussion and writing together, produced the book that is now before you. When I call it a book that was waiting to be written, I do not mean that anyone could have predicted the ways in which these scholars have tackled the topic; only that the topic is one of such wide-ranging significance that it is really surprising no one has tackled it on such a scale before. What I find especially pleasing is that this book treats the subject with the theological seriousness it demands. The fact that the five authors are experts in different disciplines (which are deployed in complementary ways) and draw on an ecumenical diversity of traditions (which also turns out to be a convergence of traditions) is entirely appropriate to the topics they address.

This is no place to anticipate their arguments and conclusions, which range from the nature of biblical prophecy to the doctrine of divine immutability. Anyone who thinks that the delay of the parousia is a minor issue will certainly be persuaded to think again, as will anyone who has made it a reason for not taking biblical eschatology seriously.

Richard Bauckham
Emeritus Professor of New Testament Studies
University of St. Andrews, Scotland, UK

# Acknowledgments

This volume represents four years of collaborative work by the Oxford Postdoctoral Colloquium on Eschatology. As a group, we are grateful to Oriel College, Keble College, Christ Church, and Blackfriars Hall for hosting our various meetings (not to mention, supplying the tea and biscuits). We also want to express our thanks to Dr. Simon Podmore and Dr. Christian Hofreiter; as members of the colloquium during its first year, they contributed great energy and insight to the early stages of our reflections and helped launch us in a fruitful direction. Furthermore, we are very much in debt to the many university seminars that invited us to present portions of our research as we developed and honed our thesis: St. Mary's College Scripture and Theology Seminar, University of St Andrews; the Biblical Studies Research Seminar of King's College London; the New Testament/Modern Theology Joint Seminar of the University of Oxford; the Biblical Studies Colloquium of Fuller Theological Seminary; the Biblical Studies Seminar of the University of Nottingham.

Christopher M. Hays is obliged to the British Academy for their generous postdoctoral fellowship, which created space for him to pursue this and numerous other research projects. He also thanks the Biblical Seminary of Colombia for the teaching relief that allowed him to complete the editing of the volume. Finally, he is grateful to his wife, Michelle, for her unflagging love and support.

Brandon Gallaher is immensely grateful to the British Academy for help with this project (and so many others) through a postdoctoral fellowship. He is indebted to the Faculty of Theology and Religion, University of Oxford; to Regent's Park College, who have supported him over many years; and to Keble College, where his work on the project began. This project was inspired and encouraged at all points by Prof. Paul Fiddes and Metropolitan Kallistos Ware, who have been models of an ecumenical, sympathetic, and synthetic approach to theology. Thanks are due to Fr. Maximos of Simonopetra (Prof. Nicholas Constas) for sharing his translations of Maximus the Confessor with the author. The key last stages of this work were completed while he was a Visiting Scholar at the School of Theology, Doshisha University (Kyoto, Japan) (thanks to CISMOR and Prof. Katsuhiro Kohara). But most of all, he is thankful to his wife, Michelle, for her long-suffering and patient love with his never-ending academic peregrinations, physically and spiritually.

Julia Konstantinovsky wishes to express her thanks to the British Academy for their generous support during her postdoctoral fellowship, which enabled her to develop this and other research projects. She owes a particular debt of gratitude to Dr. Mark Edwards for his continued support throughout the various stages of work on this book, and in particular, for reading and providing invaluable advice for chapter 6. She also expresses her appreciation to Prof. Johannes Zachhuber for his encouragement and expertise in regard to this project. Her family and friends receive her heartfelt gratitude for being there for her every step of the way.

Richard J. Ounsworth OP wishes to record his deepest thanks to his Dominican brothers in Oxford and elsewhere for their loving and prayerful support and fellowship, and for innumerable stimulating conversations. He thanks his family for their unfailing love, and his academic colleagues and friends, not least Christopher M. Hays, for their urgent encouragement to persevere in scholarship.

Casey Strine is indebted to Dr. Richard Pratt, Mr. Christopher Caudle, and Dr. Bill Fullilove, from whom he learned his approach to prophecy and eschatology and with whom he shared many hours of beneficial conversation about the topic. The views expressed in the book on this topic are Strine's, and the errors and peculiarities remain his; but any positive contribution the material on predictive prophecy makes would not have been possible without their teaching and helpful critiques. Strine benefited from the support and input of various colleagues, including David Lincicum, Grant Mackaskill, Christopher B. Hays, Sarah Apetrei, and Jane Heath. Special thanks are due to Prof. Walter Moberly, who offered a sympathetic ear and insightful feedback at a key stage in the process. Strine also owes his thanks to Michael Pogue for reading and commenting on various drafts of his material. Finally, Strine's participation in this project would not have been possible without the support and encouragement of his wife, Amanda, for whom and to whom he is immensely grateful.

# Abbreviations

Works of ancient authors are cited according to the abbreviations listed in the *SBL Handbook of Style*. Most secondary literature is cited according to the *Chicago Manual of Style*, 16th edition, although critical editions are cited in abbreviated form. Citations of standard series and reference works use the following abbreviations.

ACO    *Acta Conciliorum Oecumenicorum*. Edited by E. Schwartz et al. Berlin: De Gruyter, 1914–.

ANF    *Ante-Nicene Fathers: The Writings of the Fathers Down to A.D. 325*. Edited by Alexander Roberts and James Donaldson. 2nd ed. 10 vols. Peabody, MA: Hendrickson, 1994.

BDAG    Bauer, W., F. W. Danker, W. F. Arndt, and F. W. Gingrich. *Greek-English Lexicon of the New Testament and Other Early Christian Literature*. 3rd ed. Chicago: University of Chicago Press, 1999.

CCC    *Catechism of the Catholic Church*. 2nd ed. Washington, D.C.: United States Catholic Conference/Libreria Editrice Vaticana, 1997.

CCSG    Corpus Christianorum, Series Graeca. 81 vols. Turnhout: Brepols, 1977–.

CCSL    Corpus Christianorum, Series Latina. 201 vols. Turnhout: Brepols, 1953–.

CD    Barth, Karl. *Church Dogmatics*. Edited by T.F. Torrance and G.W. Bromiley. Translated by G.W. Bromiley. 13 vols. Edinburgh: T&T Clark, 1936–77.

COS    *The Context of Scripture*. Edited by William W. Hallo and K. Lawson Younger, Jr. 3 vols. Leiden: Brill, 2003.

DS    Denzinger, Heinrich, and Adolf Schönmetzer. *Compendium of Creeds, Definitions, and Declarations on Matters of Faith and Morals*. 43rd ed. San Francisco: Ignatius, 2012.

| | |
|---|---|
| FC | *The Fathers of the Church: A New Translation.* 120 vols. Washington, D.C.: Catholic University of America Press, 1947–. |
| GNO | *Gregorii Nysseni Opera.* Edited by Werner Jaeger, Hermann Langerbeck, Heinrich Dörrie, and Hadwig Hoerner. 60 vols. Leiden: Brill, 1952. |
| L&N | Louw, J.P. and Eugene A. Nida. *Greek-English Lexicon of the New Testament: Based on Semantic Domains.* 2 vols. New York: United Bible Societies, 1988. |
| L-S | *A Greek-English Lexicon.* Edited by H.G.R. Liddell and H.S.J. Scott. 9th ed. Oxford: Oxford University Press, 1996. |
| LCL | Loeb Classical Library. Cambridge, MA: Harvard University Press, 1911–. |
| LW | Luther, Martin. *Luther's Works.* 55 volumes. Edited by J. Pelikan and H. Lehman. St. Louis: Concordia, 1955–75. |
| NPNF1 | *The Nicene and Post-Nicene Fathers: First Series.* Edited by Alexander Roberts and James Donaldson. 2nd ed. 14 vols. Peabody, MA: Hendrickson, 1996. |
| NPNF2 | *The Nicene and Post-Nicene Fathers: Second Series.* Edited by Alexander Roberts, James Donaldson, Philip Schaff, and Henry Wace. 2nd ed. 14 vols. Peabody, MA: Hendrickson, 1996. |
| PG | Patrologia Graeca. 166 vols. Paris: Imprimerie Catholique, 1857–66. |
| PL | Patrologia Latina. 217 vols. Paris: Imprimerie Catholique, 1844–55. |
| PTS | Patristische Texte und Studien. 69 vols. Berlin: De Gruyter, 1964–. |
| Str-B | Strack, Hermann L., and Paul Billerbeck. *Kommentar zum Neuen Testament aus Talmud und Midrasch.* 5 vols. Munich: Beck, 1922–28. |
| SC | Sources chrétiennes. 572 vols. Paris: Cerf, 1943–. |
| SG | *The Summa Contra Gentiles of St Thomas Aquinas.* Translated by the English Dominicans. New York: Benziger Brothers, 1924. |
| ST | Thomas Aquinas. *Summae Theologiae.* 5 vols. Translated by the English Dominicans New York: Christian Classics, 1981. |
| TD | Balthasar, Hans Urs von. *Theo-Drama: Theological Dramatic Theory.* Translated by Graham Harrison. 5 vols. San Francisco: Ignatius, 1988–98. |
| TDNT | *Theological Dictionary of the New Testament.* Edited by Gerhard Kittel and Gerhard Friedrich. Translated by Geoffrey W. Bromiley. 10 vols. Grand Rapids: Eerdmans, 1964–74. |
| WA | Luther, Martin. *D. Martin Luthers Werke: Kritische Gesamtausgabe, Weimarer Ausgabe.* 127 vols. Weimar: Hermann Böhlaus Nachfolger, 1883–1993. |
| WSA | *The Works of Saint Augustine. A Translation for the 21st Century.* 46 vols. New York: New City, 1990–. |

# Primary Sources

### Biblical texts

All English quotations of biblical and apocryphal texts, unless otherwise noted, are from the *New Revised Standard Version with Apocrypha*. Greek and Hebrew citations are based on the following texts.

*Biblia Hebraica Stuttgartensia*. Edited by Karl Elliger and Willhelm Rudolph. 5th revised ed. Stuttgart: Deutsche Bibelgesellschaft, 1997.
*Novum Testamentum Graece*. Edited by Eberhard Nestle and Kurt Aland et al. 27th revised ed. Stuttgart: Deutsche Bibelgesellschaft, 2006.
*Septuaginta*. Edited by Alfred Rahlfs and Robert Hanhart. Revised ed. Stuttgart: Deutsche Bibelgesellschaft, 2006.

### Jewish texts

Citations and quotations of Jewish literature are based on the following texts, unless otherwise indicated.

*The Babylonian Talmud*. Edited by I. Epstein. 34 vols. London: Soncino, 1935–59.
*The Dead Sea Scrolls Study Edition*. Edited by Florentino García Martínez and Eibert J.C. Tigchelaar. 2 vols. Leiden: Brill, 1997–98.

*The Midrash Rabbah.* Edited by H. Freedman and Maurice Simon. 2nd ed. 10 vols. London: Soncino, 1951.

*The Mishnah.* Edited and translated by Herbert Danby. Oxford: Clarendon, 1933.

*The Old Testament Pseudepigrapha.* Edited by James H. Charlesworth. 2 vols. Garden City, NY: Doubleday, 1983–85.

## Greco-Roman texts

All citations and quotations of classical literature refer to the editions of the Loeb Classical Library, unless otherwise indicated.

## Sources from Church History

Citations of Church historical sources depend on the following standard translations, unless otherwise indicated.

Calvin, John. *Institutes of the Christian Religion.* 2 vols. Edited by John McNeil. Translated by F. Battles. Philadelphia: Westminster, 1960.

Calvin, John. *Calvin's Commentaries.* 22 vols. Baker: Grand Rapids, 1984.

Luther, Martin. *Luther's Works.* 55 volumes. Edited by J. Pelikan and H. Lehman. St. Louis: Concordia, 1955–75.

*The Ante-Nicene Fathers: The Writings of the Fathers Down to A.D. 325.* Edited by Alexander Roberts and James Donaldson. 10 vols. Peabody, MA: Hendrickson, 1994.

*The Apostolic Fathers: Greek Texts and English Translations of Their Writings.* Edited and translated by J. B. Lightfoot and J. R. Harmer; second ed. by Michael W. Holmes. Grand Rapids: Baker, 1992.

*The Nag Hammadi Library in English.* Edited by James M. Robinson. 3rd ed. San Francisco: HarperSanFrancisco, 1990.

*The Nicene and Post-Nicene Fathers: First Series.* Edited by Alexander Roberts and James Donaldson. 2nd ed. 14 vols. Peabody, MA: Hendrickson, 1996.

## PRIMARY SOURCES

*The Nicene and Post-Nicene Fathers: Second Series.* Edited by Alexander Roberts, James Donaldson, Philip Schaff, and Henry Wace. 2nd ed. 14 vols. Peabody, MA: Hendrickson, 1996.

# 1

# Introduction: Was Jesus Wrong About the Eschaton?

## Christopher M. Hays

You are not supposed to be starting this book right now. Life, as we know it, is supposed to have ended. At least, according to Harold Camping.

### Apocalypse... Now?

In the spring of 2011, Harold Camping became a household name. Former president of Family Christian Radio in California and host of the show "Open Forum," Camping used his significant communications network to advertise his calculation that on May 21, 2011, Jesus would return to rapture the faithful and judge the world. His listeners responded in droves, donating tens of millions of dollars to spread the apocalyptic word through books and pamphlets in no fewer than 75 different languages.[1] Five thousand billboards sprang up across the USA, proclaiming "Judgment Day May 21," and emblazoned with a yellow seal of faux-authentication which certified the prediction: "The Bible Guarantees It."

This was not Camping's first attempt at rapture prognostication. A couple of decades earlier, his book *1994?*,[2] published by a vanity press called *Vantage*, anticipated that the end of days would likely occur in September of the eponymous year. That set of dates enjoyed rather better circulation than did the ciphers he had adduced in the 1970s and 1980s, but even the interest in Camping's 1994 forecasts paled in comparison to the enthusiasm he generated in early 2011.[3]

In contrast to Camping's previous apocalyptic auguries, the 2011 campaign did some serious damage. People sold their homes, pulled their children out of school, and liquidated all their assets to support the end-of-the-world evangelization effort. This time around, disturbed listeners attempted—and sometimes succeeded at— committing suicide. A Taiwanese man launched himself from a building to avoid the imminent cosmic upheavals; a California mother attacked her young daughters with box cutters before opening her own throat in terror of the tribulation.[4] The atheists sneered; the orthodox shook their heads. And the sun came up on May 22, 2011.

Undaunted, Camping denied that his prophecies had failed entirely. Instead, he explained to his stunned adherents that the judgment had begun *spiritually*, and that things would get properly wrapped up in five months. In his own words,

> Indeed, on May 21 Christ did come spiritually to put all of the unsaved throughout the world into judgment. But that universal judgment will not be physically seen until the last day of the five month judgment period, on October 21, 2011. . . . Thus we can be sure that the whole world, with the

---

1. Robert D. McFadden, "Harold Camping, Dogged Forecaster of the End of the World, Dies at 92," *New York Times*, December 17, 2013.
2. Harold Camping, *1994?* (New York: Vantage, 1992).
3. Sarah Pulliam Bailey, "Harold Camping, Radio Host who Predicted World's End, Dies at 92," *Religion News Service*, 2013.
4. McFadden, "Harold Camping."

exception of those who are presently saved (the elect), are [sic] under the judgment of God, and will be annihilated together with the whole physical world on October 21, 2011, on the last day of the present five months period. On that day the true believers (the elect) will be raptured. We must remember that only God knows who His elect are that He saved prior to May 21.[5]

Of course, October 21, 2011, came and went. Occupy Oakland took over the US news-cycle as police tear-gassed protesters. Justin Bieber released a Christmas album. People forgot about Camping, who died on December 15. Family Christian Radio remains on the air.

But this will happen again.

It will happen again because, despite the Gospels' statements that "concerning that hour or day, no one knows"[6] (Matt. 24:36//Mark 13:32), the New Testament is emphatic that Jesus will return. Soon. In fact, that imminent return is at the epicenter of Christian hope. To some degree, Camping came by his deeply misguided predictions honestly, because the Bible—from the Prophets through the Gospels and into the Apocalypse—is littered with prognostications and prophecies and timelines. From the time of Jeremiah, the Israelites started counting down to the eschaton, excitedly anticipating the end, having their hopes dashed, rewinding the clock and starting again (see chapter 2, pp. 24–33). Accordingly, some could even try to argue that Camping has a respectable prophetic pedigree. Perhaps the real problem with the Parousia is not that the Campings of the world keep predicting it, but that Christians still expect it. Perhaps the basic issue is just that the Son of Man did not come when he was supposed to, back in the days of the apostles.

After all, Jesus had promised his disciples, "Truly I tell you, there are some standing here who will not taste death until they see that the kingdom of God has come with power" (Mark 9:1). He assured

---

5. Harold Camping, "What Happened on May 21?," http://www.familyradio.com/x/whathappened.html. This page has since been removed by Family Christian Radio, although extracts remain available on many other websites.
6. All English translations of the biblical text derive from the NRSV, unless otherwise indicated.

them, "Truly I tell you, this generation will not pass away until all these things have taken place" (13:30)—"all these things" apparently including reference to the "Son of Man coming in clouds with great power and glory". In light of that promise, he adjured them again and again, "keep alert . . . keep awake . . . keep awake" (Mark 13:33–37), for "truly I tell you, you will not have gone through all the towns of Israel before the Son of Man comes" (Matt. 10:23).

But Jesus did not come back. His coming, his Parousia, was *significantly* delayed. As we will see, the fact that "this generation" *did* pass away before the Son of Man returned created concerns for some early Christians. But in successive centuries, the Church found a way to move ahead, cycling between promises that Jesus' return was just around the corner[7] and a more tranquil contentment with the fact that the religion was doing well, wherever its founder might be. On the margins, cranks and "prophets" kept leading laity into the wilderness to await Jesus' return, but the respectable clergy and the proper scholars moved on, and for the most part, set aside that irksome delay of the Parousia, patiently nodding their heads and intoning the truisms that "no one knows the hour or the day" and "with the Lord a day is like a thousand years" (2 Pet. 3:8). Jesus's apocalyptic buzz grew increasingly soft . . . until Johannes Weiss kicked the hornet's nest in 1892.

## Resurrecting the Apocalyptic Prophet: Johannes Weiss and Albert Schweitzer

If anyone can be identified as touching off the modern critical-eschatological debate, it is Johannes Weiss. The previous decades of Jesus scholarship had been especially preoccupied with issues of supernatural (miracles, the virgin birth, the resurrection, etc.) and source-critical (favoring either the depictions of the Synoptics or of John's Gospel) sorts. But Weiss's little book *Die Predigt Jesu vom Reich Gottes* reframed historical Jesus scholarship in terms of the

---

7. For a droll survey of failed Christian apocalyptic predictions, see Bart D. Ehrman, *Jesus: Apocalyptic Prophet of the New Millenium* (Oxford: Oxford University Press, 1999), 4–18.

eschatological expectation of Jesus, correcting the scholarly neglect of the subject which had characterized the century following the posthumous publication of Reimarus' *Wolfenbüttel* fragments (1787). Albert Schweitzer vividly described the experience of the reader who has slogged through liberal nineteenth-century Jesus studies and finally arrives at Johannes Weiss. In Schweitzer's inimitable words, such a scholar feels like "an explorer who after weary wanderings through billowy seas of reed-grass at length reaches a wooded tract, and instead of swamp feels firm ground beneath his feet; instead of yielding rushes he sees around him the steadfast trees."[8]

As the volume title indicates, Weiss placed the proclamation of the kingdom of God back at the center of Jesus' preaching, and that kingdom kerygma, for Weiss, was irreducibly eschatological. While this observation is now commonplace for seminarians, among Weiss's predecessors that point had been quite obscured.[9] Weiss argued that Jesus internalized the expectation of the kingdom's imminent arrival and conventional history's end—an end for which Jesus prepared by casting out demons, even though he did not conceive of himself as the active founder of that kingdom.[10] Nonetheless, Jesus also believed that in the eschaton, he would be the Messiah and Son of Man in a heavenly and exalted sense.[11] The ultimate significance of Weiss's landmark work is that it obliged all subsequent Jesus scholars to make a basic decision between an eschatological and a non-eschatological Jesus.

Nonetheless, Weiss's insights may not have proven quite so decisive had not Albert Schweitzer so successfully won over the academy to this eschatological Jesus. Schweitzer too claimed messianic self-consciousness for Jesus, but by his reconstruction, Jesus knew himself to be far more than a mere "herald" of the kingdom, someone

---

8. Albert Schweitzer, *The Quest of the Historical Jesus: First Complete Edition*, trans. W. Montgomery, et al. (Minneapolis: Fortress Press, 2001), 198.
9. See further the editors' introductory comments in Johannes Weiss, *Jesus' Proclamation of the Kingdom of God*, trans. Richard Hyde Hiers and David Larrimore Holland, Scholars Press Reprints and Translations (Chico, CA: Scholars Press, 1985), 2–7.
10. Ibid., 74–81.
11. Ibid., 114–20, 27–29.

announcing the kingdom without bringing it about.[12] Schweitzer argued that Jesus considered himself to be the agent of the kingdom, who even tried to force the hand of God toward the final consummation.[13] Sadly, as Schweitzer's Jesus took a leap of faith into the arms of the eschaton, he was caught by the beams of the cross, and died forsaken by a God who did not thereafter bring about the kingdom.

> There is silence all around. The Baptist appears, and cries: "Repent, for the Kingdom of Heaven is at hand." Soon after that comes Jesus, and in the knowledge that He is the coming Son of Man lays hold of the wheel of the world to set it moving on that last revolution which is to bring all ordinary history to a close. It refuses to turn, and He throws Himself upon it. Then it does turn; and crushes Him. Instead of bringing in the eschatological conditions, He has destroyed them. The wheel rolls onward, and the mangled body of the one immeasurably great Man, who was strong enough to think of Himself as the spiritual ruler of mankind and to bend history to His purpose, is hanging upon it still. That is His victory and His reign.[14]

This grim tale, along with Schweitzer's five-hundred-page Feuerbachian critique of every previous liberal life of Jesus, largely silenced the guild... at least for a while.

The details of Schweitzer's reconstruction did not carry the day, but together with Johannnes Weiss, he fixed eschatology as a crucial axis for contemporary historical Jesus research. Today, there are three basic positions on the issue.

### Rejecting the Apocalyptic Prophet: The Jesus Seminar

In the late 1980s and early 1990s, it became fashionable to reject Schweitzer's eschatological Jesus *tout court*. The Jesus Seminar argued that all the apocalyptic-eschatological material ascribed to Jesus is historically spurious. Exemplified by people such as Robert Funk,[15]

---

12. Schweitzer, *Quest*, 326.
13. Ibid., 349–50.
14. Albert Schweitzer, *The Quest of the Historical Jesus: A Critical Study of its Progress from Reimarus to Wrede*, trans. W. Montgomery (London: A&C Black, 1910), 368–69. Intriguingly, this stirring comment only appeared in the early editions of Schweitzer's *Quest* and was subsequently removed.

Stephen Patterson,[16] and J.D. Crossan,[17] the Seminar explained that Jesus was originally a disciple of John the Baptist, who was indeed an apocalyptic and eschatological prophet.[18] Jesus, they said, broke away from John and preached a present kingdom, the apprehension of God's divine governance over the world in a new and inclusive community.[19] Nonetheless, after Jesus' death, his disciples wanted to capitalize on the momentum of the Jesus movement, and so they reconceived their (unresurrected) master as a miracle worker and reintegrated him into the eschatological-apocalyptic framework that Jesus himself had rejected.[20]

The perspective generally endorsed by the Jesus Seminar incited quite the media frenzy, and some even spoke (prematurely, it turns out) of the "collapse of the apocalyptic hypothesis."[21] This perspective has, however, fallen on rather hard times, in particular, for methodological reasons. While fellows of the Jesus Seminar are not monolithic in their approach,[22] they tend to share key common elements. Especially important is their reliance upon the *Gospel of Thomas*[23] and upon John Kloppenborg's stratigraphy of Q. *Thomas* is notoriously non-apocalyptic in its orientation. Q does include

---

15. See e.g. Robert W. Funk, *Honest to Jesus: Jesus for a New Millennium* (San Francisco: HarperSanFrancisco, 1997), 68–70, 145–46, 66–69, 254–55.
16. See Stephen J. Patterson, "The End of Apocalypse: Rethinking the Eschatological Jesus," *Theology Today* 52 (1995): 29–58.
17. See e.g. John Dominic Crossan, *The Historical Jesus: The Life of a Mediterranean Jewish Peasant* (San Francisco: HarperCollins, 1991), 227–60.
18. Obviously, there are distinctive features of the works written by different representatives of the Jesus Seminar. Here, we want only to highlight common traits and typical rebuttals thereto without trying the readers' patience with extensive critique of a paradigm whose popularity has already been waning for some years.
19. Crossan, *Historical Jesus*, 261–98.
20. Funk, *Honest to Jesus*, 241–56.
21. Patterson, "End of Apocalypse," 41.
22. Crossan, for example, places a great deal of importance of his so-called "Cross Gospel" (rearranged from bits of the *Gospel of Peter*), the Egerton Gospel, and the *Gospel of the Hebrews* (Crossan, *Historical Jesus*, xxviii–xxxiii, 427–29), a methodological decision that has not been enthusiastically received by many. Marcus Borg, a member of the Jesus Seminar who was early in signaling his skepticism about the apocalyptic Jesus, constructs his argument in a rather different manner (see e.g. Marcus J. Borg, "An Orthodoxy Reconsidered: The 'End-of-the-World Jesus'," in *The Glory of Christ in the New Testament: Studies in Christology*, ed. L.D. Hurst and N.T. Wright (Oxford: Clarendon, 1987), 207–17; Marcus J. Borg, *Jesus in Contemporary Scholarship* (Valley Forge, PA: Trinity Press International, 1994), 47–90; his proposal has been discussed in detail by Dale C. Allison, *Jesus of Nazareth: Millenarian Prophet* (Minneapolis: Augsburg Fortress Press, 1998), 113–22.
23. To which the Seminar tends to assign quite an early date.

apocalyptic sayings, but Kloppenborg has proposed the existence of multiple layers of Q, of which he claims that the earliest (dubbed Q1) is devoid of eschatological expectations.[24] A Jesus built primarily from *Thomas* and Q1 can be easily purged of apocalyptic peculiarity.

Critiques of Crossan, Funk, and Patterson are numerous,[25] and rather than engage in an exercise of pale imitation, it is merely necessary to echo some of the high points of those criticisms. To begin with, Q1 and the *Gospel of Thomas* are not sturdy pillars with which to erect a thesis. There is a good deal of skepticism about the viability of extracting multiple strata of Q, let alone the methodological circularity involved in determining what elements belong to which layer.[26] So also, it is probably fair to say that dating *Thomas* earlier than Mark is very much a minority position,[27] and even if one were to date the former gospel early, it is clear that *Thomas* is aware of and opposed to the apocalyptic construal of Jesus (*Gos. Thom.* 3, 18, 37, 113)—a fact which actually *confirms the prior existence* of that construal.[28]

Moreover, the construction of a "sapiential" Jesus *sans* apocalyptic expectation requires the marginalization of the witness of Mark's Gospel (e.g. Mark 8:38–9:1; 13:1–37), Paul (e.g. 1 Thess. 4:13–18), Luke (e.g. Luke 12:35–59), Matthew (e.g. Matt. 25:1–46), and even John's Gospel (5:28–29), insofar as all of these texts depict Jesus as an apocalyptic and eschatologically-oriented prophet. So, adapting Mark Twain's pithy adage, reports of the apocalyptic Jesus' demise have been greatly exaggerated.

---

24. See e.g. John S. Kloppenborg, *Excavating Q: The History and Setting of the Sayings Gospel* (Edinburgh: T&T Clark, 2000).
25. For example, Dale C. Allison, *Constructing Jesus: Memory, Imagination, and History* (London: SPCK, 2010), 116–36; Allison, *Millenarian Prophet*, 122–36; cf. Ehrman, *Jesus*, 128–39.
26. See further, Allison, *Constructing Jesus*, 118–25.
27. For a history of recent research on the subject, see Nicholas Perrin, "Recent Trends in *Gospel of Thomas* Research (1991-2006): Part 1, The Historical Jesus and the Synoptic Gospels," *Currents in Biblical Research* 5, no. 2 (2007): 183-206.
28. See Allison, *Millenarian Prophet*, 124; Allison, *Constructing Jesus*, 125–34.

## Reconceiving the Apocalyptic Prophet: N.T. Wright

N.T. Wright has suggested a second approach,[29] which many people have received with great enthusiasm because it respects the canonical form of the text while addressing the awkward synoptic texts (e.g. Mark 9:1//Matt. 16:28//Luke 9:27; Mark 13:30//Matt. 24:34//Luke 21:32; Matt. 10:23) that appear to presage imminent and cosmic judgment.[30] Wright argues that Jesus' florid apocalyptic language in Mark 13:24–37 (and parallels) refers not to fantastic earth-rending, time-stopping events, but to sociopolitical upheavals, as was typically the case when such language was used by the Old Testament prophets.[31] Accordingly, in the Olivet Discourse, Wright's Jesus does not prophesy the imminent consummation of the kingdom, but rather, the judgment of Israel through mundane[32] means. Wright also interprets the various Gospel texts[33] referring to the coming of the Son of Man as allusions to Dan. 7:13, which are to be understood as describing the heavenly enthronement of Jesus after his death.[34]

---

29. R.T. France also argued a very similar line to Professor Wright's, but departed from Wright by contending that Mark 13:32–37 shifts focus from the destruction of Jerusalem to the second coming of Christ; see R. T. France, *The Gospel of Mark*, New International Greek Testament Commentary (Grand Rapids: Eerdmans, 2002), 541–43. Insofar as Wright's view is only increasing in popularity, the present discussion will focus on his *oeuvre*.
30. We are most grateful to Professor Wright for taking the time to engage in a generous dialogue with us in response to a conference version of this argument (also entitled "When the Son of Man Didn't Come"), given at the Scripture and Theology Seminar of St Mary's College at the University of St Andrews in December, 2011.
31. N.T. Wright, *Jesus and the Victory of God*, Christian Origins and the Question of God 2 (London: SPCK, 1996), 354–58; also Wright, *The New Testament and the People of God*, Christian Origins and the Question of God 1 (London: SPCK, 1992), 333. It bears note that in the Old Testament, the language of cosmic destruction can indeed be applied to the mundane overthrow of a single city or nation, as in Ezek. 32:7; Amos 8:9; Zeph. 1:15. Still, it has been argued that this very motif aims to apply language of final destruction proleptically to mundane events that prefigure that destruction; Edward Adams, "The Coming of the Son of Man in Mark's Gospel," *Tyndale Bulletin* 56, no. 1 (2005): 56. For the purposes of the present investigation, it suffices to highlight simply that the same cosmic destruction language was also used in the Second Temple era to describe the ultimate consummation (see below, p.11 and p. 13n43).
32. To be clear: when the adjective "mundane" appears in this chapter, it is meant in the etymologically proper sense of "this-worldly", and not in the more popular sense of "banal". Likewise, identifying events as "mundane" is not intended to deny the divine agency/sovereignty operative in the events, but only to separate the sociopolitical events in question from the sorts of cataclysmic disasters and supernatural phenomena that are (we contend) narrated in the prophetic and apocalyptic texts examined in this book.
33. E.g. Mark 13:26–27: "Then they will see 'the Son of Man coming in clouds' with great power and glory. Then he will send out the angels, and gather his elect from the four winds, from the ends of the earth to the ends of heaven."

Finally, Wright explains that when the Gospel texts correlate the "coming of the Son of Man" with visions of cosmic destruction, they intend to denote through apocalyptic tropes that the destruction of Jerusalem was to be understood as vindicatory evidence that Christ had, after the crucifixion, been enthroned at God's right hand.[35] Wright has no intention of denying the future return of Christ to resurrect the dead unto judgment and recompense; he simply distinguishes that Parousia from the New Testament texts with clearly delimited references to the first century. The attraction of Wright's reading is that it constitutes an orthodox interpretation of the text by a premier New Testament scholar that preserves the fulfillment of Jesus' time-specific prophecies within the first century.

Wright's thesis has, however, come under fire, particularly from Edward Adams. First, Adams has pointed out that Jesus' allusion to Dan. 7:13 via his comments about the "coming of the Son of Man" does not need to be construed in terms of a heavenly ascension or vindication, even if that does seem to be indicated by Dan. 7:13.[36] In fact, the first time the language of the coming of the Son of Man appears in Mark, the directionality is from heaven to earth, and not the other way around.[37] Mark 8:38 warns the disciples not to shrink from their fidelity to Jesus, lest they be punished in the final judgment: "Those who are ashamed of me and of my words in this adulterous and sinful generation, of them *the Son of Man* will also be ashamed *when he comes* in the glory of his Father *with the holy angels*." This text is fascinating for a couple of reasons: in the first place, it describes the Son of Man coming in judgment, rather than ascending in vindication; in the second place,

---

34. Wright, *Jesus*, 361, 512–15; cf. *People of God*, 291–97. See also France, *Mark*, 342–43, 500–501.
35. Wright, *Jesus*, 343–46, 362–65, 510–19.
36. Adams explores the way that Dan. 7:13 is interpreted in *4 Ezra* 13 and *1 Enoch* 37–71, showing that in these texts, Second Temple Jewish interpreters read Dan. 7:13 messianically and without adopting Dan. 7:13's trajectory from earth to heaven; Adams, "Coming of the Son," 44–48.
37. Mark 8:38 combines allusions to Dan. 7:13 and Zech. 14:5, the latter of which provides the notion of God's coming in judgment, while Daniel 7 is simply the source of the Son of Man language. *4 Ezra* 13 shares the same motif, describing the coming of a man riding the clouds from heaven who came to earth to inflict judgment. Edward Adams, *The Stars Will Fall From Heaven: Cosmic Catastrophe in the New Testament and its World*, vol. 347, Library of New Testament Studies (London: T&T Clark, 2007), 148–53; "Coming of the Son," 48–52; Alexander N. Kirk, "Yes, 'A Human Figure Flying Downwards on a Cloud': A Response to N.T. Wright and R.T. France on Mark 14:62" (paper presented at the Society of Biblical Literature International Meeting, London, June 2011).

the Gospel's very next verse (Mark 9:1, "Truly I tell you, there are some standing here who will not taste death until they see that the *kingdom of God has come with power*") clarifies that the coming of the kingdom of God in power—apparently, an event concurrent or identical with the Son's coming in judgment—will occur before the disciples have all died. Thus, contrary to Wright's assertion that it is most natural to read the allusion to Dan. 7:13 in Mark 13:26 as a reference to Jesus' heavenly ascent and vindication, Mark 8:38 has already shown that the Evangelist understood Jesus' "coming" in terms of final judgment at the consummation of the kingdom.[38]

This understanding seems to be corroborated in the other Synoptic Gospels. The parallel texts Luke 12:40//Matt. 24:44 certainly seem to think that the coming of the Son of Man refers to Jesus' return in judgment (so also Matt. 25:31), especially in light of the ensuing parable in which the Lord returns to reward his faithful stewards and punish the unfaithful (Luke 12:45-46//Matt. 24:50-51).[39] Similarly, in Luke 18:8, Jesus asks, "When the Son of Man comes, will he find faith on earth?" This inquiry, concluding the parable of the Importunate Widow, quite explicitly identifies the occasion of the Son of Man's *imminent* coming as the vindication of and provision of justice for the elect over against the wicked: "Will [God] delay long in helping [the just]? I tell you, he will quickly (ἐν τάχει) grant justice to them" (Luke 18:7-8).

Furthermore, Adams has shown that Second Temple Jewish apocalyptic texts often use cosmic destruction language (of the sort found in the Old Testament prophets) for the purpose of describing

---

38. The third place in Mark's Gospel where one encounters "the Son of Man coming" is in 14:62, Jesus' declaration that the High Priest "will see the Son of Man seated at the right hand of the Power and coming with the clouds of heaven." This text presents challenges for Wright's thesis that the destruction of the Temple vindicated Jesus, insofar as the High Priest and most of those present would not have been likely to live to see the Temple's destruction in 70 CE. Noting parallel texts in the Wisd. of Sol. 5:1-7 and *1 En.* 62:1-3, Alexander Kirk has argued convincingly that Jesus' statement "You will see the Son of Man seated at the right hand of the Power and coming with the clouds of heaven" refers to the final judgment, in which the resurrected Sanhedrin would witness Jesus' exaltation as the eschatological judge; Kirk, "Flying Downwards".
39. In fact, Matthew is the only Gospel to use the term παρουσία, and his association of the word with the final judgment is clear (Matt. 24:3, 27, 37, 39); Anthony C. Thiselton, *The Last Things: A New Approach* (London: SPCK, 2012), 103.

global, eschatological catastrophes,[40] and not only to refer to mundane sociopolitical events, the likes of which Wright emphasizes.[41] Consider, for example, the first chapter of 1 Enoch.

> The God of the universe, the Holy Great One, *will come forth* (ἐξελεύσεται) from his dwelling. And from there he will march upon Mount Sinai and appear in his camp emerging from heaven with great power.... Mountains and high places will fall down and be frightened. And high hills shall be made low; and they shall melt like honeycomb before the flame. And the earth shall be rent asunder; and all that is upon the earth shall perish. And there shall be a *judgment upon all,* (including) the righteous. And to all the righteous he will grant peace.... Behold he will arrive with *ten million of the holy ones* in order to execute judgment upon all. He will destroy the wicked ones.... (*1 En.* 1.3–9)

Here, the language of cosmic destruction is coupled with the universal judgment, in a text which fascinatingly connects that destruction and judgment with the "coming forth" of the Holy One with myriads of angels.[42] This confluence of images is of obvious relevance to the Olivet Discourse, in which the cosmic destruction precedes the "coming" of the Son of Man with his "angels" (Mark 13:24–27).

One also sees this cosmic destruction language applied to the final judgment in the *Testament of Moses,* in which God comes forth from heaven; the sun, moon, and stars go dark; and the earth is shaken.

> Then his kingdom will appear throughout his whole creation. Then the devil will have an end.... For the Heavenly One will arise from his kingly throne. Yea, *he will go forth* from his holy habitation with indignation and wrath on behalf of his sons. And *the earth will tremble, even to its ends shall it be shaken*. In the high mountains will be made low. Yea, they will be shaken, as enclosed valleys will they fall. The *sun will not give light. In the darkness the horns of the moon will flee*. Yea, it will be broken into pieces. It will be turned wholly into blood. Yea, even *the circle of the stars will be thrown into disarray*. (*T. Mos.* 10.1, 3–5)

---

40. See the detailed study in Adams, *Stars Will Fall,* 52–100.
41. Making reference especially to *4 Ezra* 11–12, *2 Baruch* 35–40, *Sib. Or.* 3.669–701, and Josephus, *B.J.* 6.288–300; N.T. Wright, *Paul and the Faithfulness of God,* Christian Origins and the Question of God 4 (London: SPCK, 2013), 170–74.
42. Angels also accompany God in the final judgment scene described in *1 En.* 102.1–4.

Adams has adduced a number of further examples of the same phenomena.[43] These texts show clearly that the language of cosmic destruction by no means requires an exclusively mundane sociopolitical referent. The scope of the envisioned destruction needs to be determined by the context in which the cosmic destruction imagery appears.

Returning, then, to Mark's Gospel, the immediate context of Jesus' comments about the coming of the Son of Man seems to indicate that Jesus has in mind the consummation of the world as well as the destruction of Jerusalem. The fact that in Mark 13:31, Jesus says that "heaven and earth will pass away" suggests that Mark 13:24–27 includes a view toward the eschatological (that is to say, final) and catastrophic judgment of all humanity.[44] This is not to deny that the events of Mark 13:5–23 refer to the events leading up to the destruction of Jerusalem in 70 CE; surely, they do. It is simply to say that Mark 13 assumes that the final judgment will be shortly preceded by the destruction of Jerusalem.[45]

On closer examination, it seems that Wright's key arguments are rather more vulnerable than they might appear at first glance. Mark's previous usage of the "coming of the Son of Man" language (Mark 8:38) seems to indicate a reference to coming from heaven to earth in judgment at the consummation of the eschaton, and not ascent in vindication after the resurrection. Likewise, the cosmic destruction language of Mark 13:24–27 cannot be limited to a trope for mundane national judgment; Second Temple interpreters frequently use that motif to describe eschatological consummation and Mark 13:31 seems to militate against an attempt to limit 13:24–27 to the events of the first century. So, for all its undeniable merits, it remains to be seen if Wright's reading of Mark 13 (and parallels) will carry the day.

---

43. *1 En.* 83.3b–5; 102.1–3; 1 QH 11.19–36; *Sib. Or.* 4.175–78; *2 Bar.* 32.1; *Apoc. Zeph.* 12.5–8; Adams, *Stars Will Fall*, 96–98; cf. Allison, *Millenarian Prophet*, 160–62.
44. Adams, *Stars Will Fall*, 161–64; "Coming of the Son," 57–59.
45. So also Thiselton, *Last Things*, 100–102.

## A Terminological Excursus

Before moving ahead with our history of research, a brief moment of linguistic clarification is in order due to some unfortunate confusion in the use of the words *apocalyptic* and *eschatological* among scholars. This language is tricky, not least of which because the guild's understanding of *apocalyptic* has changed greatly over the past century, and also because in popular usage, the words have taken on further (and historically inaccurate) significances (as any Hollywood disaster film trailer will attest). *Apocalyptic* denotes, in the first place, the revelation of heavenly realities which give the seer insight into present and future earthly affairs; this literature quite often utilizes fantastic pictures of monsters and cosmic destruction to describe sociopolitical affairs, which may or may not be concomitant with the cessation of world affairs as we know them.[46]

*Eschatology*, by contrast, refers etymologically to the study of the "last things" (ἔσχατα), but insofar as the New Testament itself modifies the scope of the *eschaton* owing to its authors' belief that Jesus only began the end, it is entirely legitimate to talk about *eschatology* in terms of things that happened two thousand years ago, or in terms of things that Christians believe will happen in the future. On top of this, there are live debates about whether or not the consummation of the eschaton should be conceived of in terms of the "end of the world" or in terms of a reordering of the creation that is significant but contiguous with the creation in which we currently live. Apocalyptic literature can be eschatological in either of these senses, or it can be non-eschatological. Eschatology can be apocalyptic, but it need not be. Then, there are all sorts of questions about what is "literal" and what is "metaphorical". Consequently, scholars often feel that they are talking past one another, using the same words to say quite different things.

A good many of the printed disagreements between N.T. Wright, Edward Adams, and Dale Allison (see further below) address these

---

46. Cf. Christopher Rowland, *The Open Heaven: A Study of Apocalyptic in Judaism and Early Christianity* (London: SPCK, 1982), 23-29, 47-48; John Barton, *Oracles of God: Perceptions of Ancient Prophecy in Israel after the Exile* (London: Darton, Longman and Todd, 1986), 218.

terminological issues.[47] Without attempting to create further confusion by proposing our own definitions, it is necessary to specify that we have made an effort to be intentional in our usage. For example, we use *apocalyptic* in the sense(s) proper to the (admittedly diverse) ancient genre and we speak of the *eschatological consummation* to denote the return of Jesus, the resurrection of the dead, and the final judgment.

## Reasserting the Apocalyptic Prophet: Dale Allison and Bart Ehrman

As representatives of the third approach to eschatology in recent historical Jesus scholarship, Dale Allison[48] and Bart Ehrman[49] have argued that the apocalyptic language attributed to Jesus can be neither discarded as a secondary accretion to his kerygma, nor exclusively referred to sociopolitical affairs. Instead, Ehrman and Allison take the bull by the horns, affirming with Schweitzer that Jesus expected the imminent eschatological consummation and that he was wrong.

The arguments these scholars have proposed to defend their construal are compendious and formidable. Still, the length of their works reflects not any obscurity in their readings of the biblical evidence so much as the erudition of those whose perspectives they oppose.

In brief, Allison and Ehrman defend the Synoptic Gospels' ascription to Jesus of the key sayings on the imminence of the Parousia (Mark 9:1//Matt. 16:28//Luke 9:27; Mark 13:30//Matt. 24:34//Luke 21:32; Matt. 10:23).[50] They point additionally to the various "woes" that Jesus pronounces against his contemporaries (Matt. 23:13-36//Luke 11:42-52; cf. Luke 6:24-26), to his declaration that he came not to bring peace, but "a sword" (Matt. 10:34-36//Luke 12:51-53), to his teachings about the eschatological harvest,[51] and to his repeated injunctions to

---

47. Most recently, see the comments in Wright, *Paul*, 167-75.
48. See especially Allison, *Millenarian Prophet*, 1-171; Allison, *Constructing Jesus*, 31-220.
49. Ehrman, *Jesus*, 125-62, 83-219.
50. Allison, *Millenarian Prophet*, 149-50.

"alertness" and discerning the present time (Luke 12:35-48, 54-56; Matt. 24:42-25:13). All these texts converge to support the thesis that, irrespective of the non-specification of the precise date of the eschatological consummation, Jesus did seem to think that these events were coming rather soon. Thus, Allison says,

> Whatever one makes of Mk 9:1; 13:30; and Mt 10:23, one must come to terms with the parables that advise people to watch for the coming of the Lord or the Son of Man, with the pronouncements of eschatological woes on contemporaries, and with the miscellaneous complexes that either announce or presuppose that the final fulfillment of God's saving work is nigh. Those who dissociate Jesus from imminent eschatological expectation need to show us not only that all of this material comes from the church but additionally that it misrepresents what Jesus was all about. They have not done so.[52]

Ehrman additionally underscores the significance of Jesus being (in some way) a successor to the proclamation of John the Baptist and the predecessor (and inspiration) to the early Christians. John prophesied the imminent arrival of the kingdom of God, complete with the judgment that attended it (Matt. 3:1-12; Luke 3:1-17). The Christian leaders that followed Jesus made no bones of their imminent expectation of Jesus' return to resurrect the dead and consummate the eschaton (thus, e.g. 1 Cor. 7:29-31; 1 Thess. 4:13-18; Rev. 22:20). That being the case, it seems eminently logical that the figure who links the Baptist and the New Testament writers would share with them the basic conviction in the proximate arrival of the final judgment and restoration.[53]

Finally, Allison and Ehrman point out that the New Testament bears redactional evidence of an intra-Christian struggle with Jesus' non-return.[54] Luke 9:27 takes the edge off of Mark 9:1, for example, by removing the phrase "having come in power" ($\dot{\epsilon}\lambda\eta\lambda\nu\theta\nu\tilde{\iota}\alpha\nu$ $\dot{\epsilon}\nu$ $\delta\nu\nu\dot{\alpha}\mu\epsilon\iota$) from Jesus' utterance, "there are some standing here who will not taste

---

51. Matt. 13:24-30; Mark 4:2-9//Matt. 13:2-9//Luke 8:4-8; *Gos. Thom.* 9, 57; cf. the functionally similar trope of the net in Matt. 13:47-50.
52. Allison, *Millenarian Prophet*, 150-51.
53. Ehrman, *Jesus*, 137-39.
54. Allison, *Millenarian Prophet*, 165-69; Ehrman, *Jesus*, 130-31.

death before they see the kingdom of God [having come in power]." This revision slightly lowers the bar of fulfilment, allowing the reader more easily to identify moments such as the Transfiguration and Pentecost as "partial fulfillments" of Jesus' prophecy (on which, see further chapter 4, pp. 72–74, and chapter 6, p. 131). Similarly, Luke 22:69 recognizes the difficulty of Jesus' declaration to the High Priest, "you will see the Son of Man seated at the right hand of the Power, and coming with the clouds of heaven" (Mark 14:62), insofar as the High Priest would certainly have died before Luke's Gospel was written; as such, he simply avers "from now on the Son of Man will be seated at the right hand of the power of God"—a statement which he then confirms for his readers with the vision of Stephen in Acts 7:55–56.

So also, Luke 19:11[55] and John 21:22–23[56] make clear that the disciples and members of the first Christian community expected that Jesus would return quite soon to consummate the kingdom, perhaps almost "immediately" (as Luke 19:11 indicates) or at least, before the Beloved Disciple died. This indicates that, however much Jesus may have inaugurated the kingdom of God, many of those around him continued to expect a more complete fulfillment, and soon. "Jesus' prophecies were not originally construed as metaphors fulfilled in his ministry or in the time thereafter. That came only with subsequent, apologetical exegesis."[57]

As such, Ehrman and Allison seem to conclude (or at least imply) that if one is to find meaning in Jesus' life and teachings, such meaning ought not to be thought to reside in an affirmation of Jesus' own central eschatological message. By their readings, it appears that Jesus' essential proclamation, "The time is fulfilled and the Kingdom of God is near" was simply mistaken.

It might come as a surprise to readers to hear that the authors of this volume—all of whom regularly affirm the Nicene Creed's declaration

---

55. "He went on to tell a parable, because he was near Jerusalem, and because they supposed that the kingdom of God was to appear immediately."
56. "So the rumor spread in the community that this disciple would not die. Yet Jesus did not say to him that he would not die, but, 'If it is my will that he remain until I come, what is that to you?'"
57. Allison, *Millenarian Prophet*, 166.

"He will come again in glory to judge the living and the dead, and his Kingdom will have no end"— agree in large measure with Allison and Ehrman's construal of Jesus' prophetic and imminent eschatological expectation (with exception of the views summarized in the preceding paragraph). As critical scholars, this strikes us as simply good exegesis and responsible history. As Christian theologians, however, we appreciate that this critical research creates some serious dogmatic problems.[58]

## The Theological Problems with a Failed Apocalyptic Prophet

At the risk of stating the obvious, the principle problem with saying that Jesus was wrong about his imminent expectation of the consummation of the eschaton is that *the imminence of the kingdom of God was central to Jesus' message.*[59] As much is basically the thesis statement of what is surely the earliest canonical Gospel: "The time is fulfilled and the Kingdom of God is near; repent, and believe in the good news" (Mark 1:15). It is one thing for Jesus to be wrong or ignorant about a matter on which he does not comment (for example, germ theory or the finer points of nuclear physics), or even on a matter peripheral to his kerygma (say, the size of a mustard seed relative to that of a begonia or an orchid; cf. Matt. 13:31-32), but it is quite another thing for him to be wrong concerning the thing he cares most about—the essence of the message the Evangelists handed on. If Jesus was wrong about that, does that not eviscerate the Christian construal

---

58. Naturally, Allison and Ehrman draw very different theological conclusions from their similar critical understandings of Jesus' message. Ehrman is a self-proclaimed agnostic with no current commitments to the Christian faith, whereas Allison is an ordained elder in the Presbyterian Church (USA). Between his *Jesus of Nazareth: Millenarian Prophet* and *Constructing Jesus*, Allison published a smashing and short book called *The Historical Christ and the Theological Jesus* (Grand Rapids: Eerdmans, 2009), which is a good deal more theologically constructive than *Jesus of Nazareth* would have led one to anticipate; moreover, the final paragraphs of all three of his Jesus books are nothing short of stirring. We would do well to remember that, however much exegesis influences theology, there is no one-to-one correspondance between the ways one reads a text and the theology that one embraces. As this book hopes to show, the process is a great deal more rich than that.
59. The ideas (and some turns of phrase) in this section owe much to Dr. Christian Hofreiter, an early member of our colloquium whose expertise was invaluable in shaping our thoughts. We are grateful to him for allowing us to use his insights in this chapter.

of Jesus as Messiah, teacher, and God? Does error here not undermine the plausibility of our future hopes?

A great many people who have no allegiance to Christian orthodoxy concede that Jesus is a great moral teacher. But why should such a concession reasonably be made? If Jesus' teachings on discipleship are generated by his expectation of the kingdom of God, and the kingdom of God did not materialize, then why is it reasonable to salvage his ethical message? How can he be a credible moral teacher if the basis of his morality is a delusion?

More pointedly for orthodox Christians, how can we delude ourselves into thinking that Jesus somehow speaks for (and *as*) God if his basic message was wrong? If the beloved Son in whom the Father was supposedly well-pleased was mistaken about his essential kerygma, should we really continue to believe that God favored Jesus as much as the Evangelists claim? Should we even give earnest consideration to the suggestion that he is one and the same being as the deity that is putatively in control of the fate of the world?

If the basic message of Jesus was wrong—wrong in a way that might ostensibly falsify the Church's Christology—then how can anyone presume to find "salvation" through faith in him? More pointedly, why are people living and dying in hopes of being received into the kingdom of heaven when the terms of that offer seem to have expired nineteen centuries ago? With such (post-)eschatological knowledge, can we still maintain that the Christian hope has a meaningful referent outside its existential implications, i.e. beyond the call that we should live *etsi deus daretur*, *as if* the dead were to be raised, *as if* a just judge would one day put things to rights?

If Jesus' prophecy about the timing of the kingdom's coming was not fulfilled, then isn't this Christianity thing really just all wrong?

## Volume Outline

In the following chapters, we propose to explain that, even though Schweitzer, Allison, and Ehrman are essentially correct that Jesus prophesied the consummation of the kingdom of God (judgment, resurrection, punishment, and reward) to occur within striking distance of his earthly ministry (certainly within several decades), this should not be thought to undercut Christian hope. On the contrary, *it is our thesis that the delay of the Parousia is entirely consonant with the way ancient prophecy works and with the operations of the God that Christians worship.*

To demonstrate this point, we will first show (chapter 2) that Jesus' eschatological prophecies were, in fact, only the latest in a long series of prophetic non-fulfillments, partial-fulfillments, and deferrals. This observation might compound Christian anxiety, rather than alleviating it, but it is a necessary initial step in a longer process. Though the history of partial fulfillments and deferral may strike modernist readers as falsifying the prophecies altogether, that supposition derives from a basic failure to understand the nature of Judeo-Christian prophecy. While prophecy does entail an element of prognostication, it is perhaps more fundamentally a ministry of *activation*, of telling what God intends to do to people, given that they behave in a certain way, *for the purpose of motivating them to a course of action which might confirm or avert that prophecy* (chapter 3). For this reason, unfulfilled prophecies are not failed prophecies; sometimes, unfulfilled prophecies are successful prophecies, because prophecy is often conditional. Likewise, partially fulfilled prophecies are sometimes the only appropriate outcomes of morally inconsistent or mixed actions on the parts of the addressees, and yet, in their partial fulfillment, they sustain the forward march of the faithful, like stepping-stones across the river of sacred history (chapter 4).

In light of these observations about the conditional nature of prophecy, the non-consummation of the eschaton that Jesus prophesied is not the problem that this chapter's previous section (pp. 18–19) made it out to be. Quite the contrary, Jesus' prophecies can themselves be understood as conditional. In fact, that supposition is borne out by the witness of the New Testament and patristic authors themselves, who interpret the events following Jesus' death as partial fulfillments of prophecy, and as deferrals of ultimate fulfillment appropriate to the conditionality of Jesus' proclamation (chapter 5).

We go on, thereafter, to demonstrate that this dynamic of prophetic conditionality, deferral, and partial fulfillment is, in fact, deeply contiguous with the sort of God that is the object (and subject) of Christian theology, and with a Christian view of how salvation history unfolds under the sovereignty of that God.

In relation to the stepping-stones argument elaborated in chapter 4, we draw on the apophatic theology of the ancient Church to discuss the distinctions between divine and human experiences of time. We argue that the partial realizations of the kingdom of God do not merely foreshadow the eschaton, but are, in fact, the in-breaking of the eschaton, as God heals the crippled linearity of human historical time (chapter 6).

The next step is to embed the exegetical argument about the contingency of the Parousia's timing (from chapter 5) in a robust theological framework. This requires initially that we articulate a traditional Trinitarian theology that explains God's essence in terms of a pure act of love between the persons of the Trinity. Such an account of God's essence explains how the immutability of God is not threatened by God's engagements with and reactions to human decisions, even to the extent of diverging from a previously prophesied action (chapter 7).

Thereafter, we continue our theological explanation of the deferral of the eschaton by articulating the way in which God has, in fact, *committed* himself to consummating human history in a manner that graciously entails the *cooperation of humans*. The pro-Chalcedonian dyothelite understanding of the hypostatic union—as well as the story of incarnation, resurrection, and ascension—supports the account of the delay of the Parousia adduced in chapter 5, because it shows that God has chosen to cooperate in his body the Church with human wills and actions to bring about the end. But the inverse is also true: lack of human cooperation can defer the return of Christ. Thus, orthodox Christology confirms our exegetical case by showing that eschatological deferral is proper to the character of God himself and to the way God has bound himself to consummate the kingdom (chapter 8).

The self-sacrificial natures of the Trinity and of kenosis underscore the ways in which God deigns and delights to cooperate with those whom he loves. Thus, our argument's next step is to reflect on the ways in which the people of God throughout history have recognized God's redemptive action on their behalf and have participated in that restorative work through Jewish and Christian liturgies (chapter 9). We will explain how these liturgies bear witness to and bind together the narratives of God's people throughout the ages, how they reflect and are used by God to instantiate the linkages between heaven and earth, and how they sustain and propel the people of God toward the final consummation.

The penultimate note to be sounded in this volume will be a methodological one (chapter 10). As this brief outline has already revealed, the theological method utilized in this book incorporates historical criticism, canonical and final-form exegeses, patristic studies, constructive theology, and Christian liturgical reflections (*inter alia*). In a methodologically-obsessed profession, we would be remiss not to explain how we did what we did. Most monographs would insert such comments at about the present juncture of the volume. But since the proof of the pudding is in the eating, we chose not to share the recipe until our readers decided that they liked the dessert.

A few final pages (chapter 11) of the book will draw the whole argument together. Therein, we elaborate the way that our exegetical and doctrinal arguments reinforce one another, and we conclude with a *Maranatha*.

# 2

# Prophecy: A History of Failure?

## Christopher M. Hays

### Introduction

What if Jesus was wrong? Blunt though it be, this is the question we are left with after the last chapter's survey of historical Jesus scholarship (chapter 1, pp. 4–18). Having maneuvered through the exegetical intricacies of Jesus scholarship, we concluded that Jesus did indeed prophesy his second coming and the consummation of the kingdom of God sometime within a generation of his preaching. But the years after his ascension turned into decades and centuries, and insofar as we long ago laid to rest the apostles, it is now difficult to skirt the conclusion that Jesus' prophecy did not come true. This is not a point that Christians can afford to gloss over.

After all, Christians proclaim in Jesus the arrival of the long-awaited "Prophet like Moses" foretold in Deuteronomy (Deut. 18:15–17; cf. Acts

3:22; 7:37). That being the case, we cannot overlook the fact that almost immediately, Deuteronomy explains how to judge between a true and a false prophet: "If a prophet speaks in the name of the Lord but the thing does not take place or prove true, it is a word that the Lord has not spoken" (Deut. 18:22). The penalty for failing this litmus test was nothing short of death (Deut. 18:20).

We believe this problem is too grave to ignore. Christian hope is shot through with the expectation of Christ's second coming, and Jesus himself identified the return of the Son of Man as the climactic moment of all redemptive history. It would be a disservice to the people of God not to communicate the poignancy of this problem upfront. For the health of the Christian faith, those most keenly aware of the Church's problems should be among her ranks, serving as effective defenders of that faith against the most informed of detractors. We, the authors, believe, after much research and deliberation, that a compelling and indeed edifying explanation can be given regarding the problem of the delay of the Parousia. It is precisely because of that confidence that we will devote this chapter to providing a sharp critique of the Christian hope in the Parousia.

We will do so first by narrating the commonplace historical-critical belief that the half millennium prior to Jesus' advent was riddled with failed prophetic promises. Then, we will turn to the New Testament and show that the canonical epistles and Apocalypse also evince a belief that Jesus was to return in glory in a very short time period, likely within the first century itself. These views, though routine in historical-critical scholarship, also present poignant challenges to Christian hope in the Parousia, and any compelling account of Jesus' deferred return would need to give serious attention to them. In that spirit, allow us now to play the adversary of Christian prophetic hope.

### The Failure of Jeremiah's Prophecy of Seventy Weeks

There is a distressing bitterness to the idea that Jesus was just wrong about his proclamation. But this problem is hardly a novelty of Christian hope; prophetic failure is deeply rooted in Jewish tradition.

To anyone who has paid close attention to the history of Jewish eschatological hope, the awkward silence and chagrined mumbling that follow prophetic failures should sound familiar. Perhaps no Scriptural tradition so helpfully illustrates this embarrassing phenomenon as Jeremiah's prophecy that the exile would last seventy years (Jer. 25:8–14; 29:10–14). This line of prophetic tradition commends itself to us because it is testable—either the exile does end after seventy years, or Jeremiah was wrong. But in addition to being conveniently explicit, Jeremiah's promise of the return from exile is arguably the paradigmatic Old Testament prophecy of restoration.[1] What's more, in his capacity as a prophet of destruction and subsequent restoration, Jeremiah may be seen as a model for the Gospels' portrayals—especially, perhaps, Matthew's portrayal—of Jesus' prophetic ministry, with his own prophecy of the destruction of the Temple akin to Jeremiah's "Temple sermon" (Jer. 7:1–15).[2] Thus, if we are exercised about the reliability of Jesus' promises of subsequent restoration, Jeremiah's quite specific prediction would provide us with an important and telling precedent.

> Therefore thus says the Lord of hosts: Because you have not obeyed my words, I am going to send for all the tribes of the north, says the Lord, even for King Nebuchadnezzar of Babylon, my servant, and I will bring them against this land and its inhabitants, and against all these nations around; I will utterly destroy them, and make them an object of horror and of hissing, and an everlasting disgrace. . . . This whole land shall become a ruin and a waste, and these nations shall serve the king of Babylon seventy years. Then after seventy years are completed, I will punish the king of Babylon and that nation, the land of the Chaldeans, for their iniquity, says the Lord, making the land an everlasting waste. (Jer. 25:8–9, 11–12)

> For thus says the Lord: Only when Babylon's seventy years are completed will I visit you, and I will fulfill to you my promise and bring you back to this place. For surely I know the plans I have for you, says the Lord, plans for your welfare and not for harm, to give you a future with hope. . . . I will restore your fortunes and gather you from all the nations and all the

---

1. Joseph Blenkinsopp, *A History of Prophecy in Israel* (Louisville, KY: Westminster John Knox, 1996), 135.
2. Ross E. Winkle, "The Jeremiah Model for Jesus in the Temple," *Andrews University Seminary Studies* 24, no. 2 (1986): 155–72; cf. ch. 3, p. 52 and ch. 5, pp. 85–86.

places where I have driven you, says the Lord, and I will bring you back to the place from which I sent you into exile. (Jer. 29:10-14)

So, Jeremiah prophesied that Babylon would conquer Judaea and rule the Israelites and their land for seventy years, after which God promised to restore them. But did things turn out as planned? Not exactly. The Old Testament is littered with texts trying to account for the way in which subsequent history *did not* line up with Jeremiah's timeline. Initially, the biblical authors needed to explain why the exile began to wind down too early; then, they had to reverse their tactics and explain why restoration from exile was taking too long; and finally, some of them just threw up their hands and denied that the prophesied restoration was ever even inaugurated (however abortively or impartially). In short, the Hebrew Bible seems a veritable cacophony of voices trying to explain why things did not turn out as Jeremiah had prophesied. For a sample of this confused prophetic "witness," we need only lend an ear to Zechariah, Ezra-Nehemiah, and Daniel.

## Zechariah, Ezra, and the Early Fulfillment of Jeremiah's Seventy Years

Admittedly, if one were simply to read the prophet Zechariah, without knowing much about Israelite history, Jeremiah's prophecy might appear to fare reasonably well. "In the second year of Darius" (Zech. 1:7)—i.e. around 519 BCE, 68 years after the invasion of Judah—Zechariah preached to the exiles and predicted the imminent fulfillment of this prophecy.

> Then the angel of the Lord said, "O Lord of hosts, how long will you withhold mercy from Jerusalem and the cities of Judah, with which you have been angry these seventy years?" Then the Lord replied with gracious and comforting words to the angel who talked with me. So the angel who talked with me said to me, Proclaim this message: Thus says the Lord of hosts; I am very jealous for Jerusalem and for Zion. . . . Therefore, thus says the Lord, I have returned to Jerusalem with compassion; my house shall be built in it, says the Lord of hosts, and the measuring line shall be stretched out over Jerusalem. Proclaim further: Thus says the

Lord of hosts: My cities shall again overflow with prosperity; the Lord will again comfort Zion and again choose Jerusalem. (Zech. 1:12-17)

This prediction is repeated and intensified in chapters 7-8, set two years later (see especially Zech. 7:4). So, Zechariah expected the restoration of the Israelites to occur rather shortly after the completion of seventy calendar years. This all seems very neat.

Still, the neatness of Zechariah's calculation glosses over a rather significant point. Jeremiah did not just say that the exile would last seventy years; he said that the *Babylonian* exile would last for seventy years. But Babylon's reign proved rather more ephemeral than Jeremiah had anticipated. The other Old Testament documents credit the liberation of Judah to the Lord's anointed, Cyrus, and not Darius (Isa. 44:28-45:1; 2 Chron. 36:20-21; Ezra 1:1); Cyrus defeated Babylon in 539 BCE, only 48 years after the fall of the Jerusalem Temple. And it was *Cyrus* who first sent the Israelites back to Jerusalem with instructions to rebuild the Temple (Ezra 1:2-4; 2 Chron. 36:2-23), a mere half century after the Temple's destruction. One might say that history unfolded ahead of schedule, pre-empting Jeremiah's prophecy. Even if we were so generous as to calculate the beginning of the exile from the first deportation in 597 BCE, then the exile appears to have lasted sixty years—still a decade short of the prophetic mark. Things are not so clean as they appear at first glance.

The editor of Ezra is aware of this problem, so he has to scramble a bit. Ezra makes the case that the end of the seventy years is marked not simply by the return to Jerusalem, but the *completion* of the Temple's reconstruction (on this point, Ezra's interpretation is compatible with the predictions of Zech. 7:1-8:23, where it is the return of *the Lord* to Zion that is about to take place). Thus, the first five chapters of Ezra are dedicated to explaining how the exiles returned to Jerusalem, only to have their restoration interrupted, waylaid for the duration of Cyrus' rule (Ezra 4:1-23). It is only under Darius that the Temple reconstruction can be resumed, explains Ezra (Ezra 5:1-6:11).

Ezra tells us that rebuilding of the Temple was completed "in the sixth year of the reign of King Darius" (Ezra 6:15), seventy-two years after the invasion of Judea. In this, Ezra and Zechariah adopt a fairly literal reading of the seventy years, and in so doing, they shove aside the pesky fact that Cyrus's decree came ahead of schedule.

## Ezra-Nehemiah and the Late Fulfillment of Jeremiah's Seventy Years

But just as soon as the editor of Ezra-Nehemiah seems to have accounted for the premature beginnings of the restoration, he has to make a complete about-face and explain why the restoration from exile had been so sluggish! Even seventy years after the invasion of Judea, things still hadn't come together as Jeremiah had prophesied. Jeremiah 29:10–14 (cf. 25:11–12) promised that after the seventy years, God would return the Israelites from exile and restore their fortunes. But it is not as if *all* the Israelites had returned to the Promised Land by the time the Temple had been rebuilt. Only a portion of the Israelite population hobbled back to Judaea under Cyrus's decree (Ezra 2:1–65). When Ezra's ministry began around 458 BCE, a solid 130 years into the exile, he was still only leading a modest contingent of Israelite exiles to Jerusalem (see Ezra 8:1–20), and even then, their travel required the gracious permission of King Artaxerxes (Ezra 7:11–28). A dozen years after that, Nehemiah undertook his ministry (Neh. 2:1–10), and he too lamented that the exile was far from over (Neh. 1:1–11). Thus, in about 446 BCE, some 141 years after the destruction of the Jerusalem Temple, Nehemiah was still in Persia; the walls of Jerusalem lay in ruins; and those who had supposedly escaped captivity remained "in great trouble and shame" (Neh. 1:3). To compound matters, Nehemiah 5:14–15 reveals that, in the years prior to Nehemiah's appointment as the governor of Judah, Nehemiah's predecessors had been exploiting and oppressing the Israelite residents. To put it mildly, the restoration of Israel after seventy years that Jeremiah promised had proven an overstatement; God's "plans to prosper them and not to harm them" (Jer. 29:11) were not coming to pass as advertised.

So, the editor of Ezra-Nehemiah had to back-pedal. Although he wanted to read the prophecy of Jeremiah as being fulfilled in more-

or-less literal, chronological terms, he was obliged to see 515 BCE as the beginning of a fulfillment that remained quite incomplete even seventy additional years later. The editor of the book, summoning a pitiably quixotic optimism, seemed to hope that, with men such as Ezra and Nehemiah at the helm, Israel might steer a course toward complete restoration. But then again, writing sometime in the fifth or fourth century, perhaps he could get away with being so sanguine.[3] Later authors, however, found Ezra-Nehemiah's interpretation to be less than credible.

### Recalculating Jeremiah's Seventy Years Altogether

The author of Dan. 9:1–27 was one such discerning interpreter of prophecy. He rejected the opinion of 2 Chronicles, Ezra, Nehemiah, and Zechariah that God had made good on Jeremiah's promise, and instead, he tried to re-calibrate the prophetic timeline.

Most critical scholars think that the author of Daniel 9 wrote in the second century, during the reign of the mad Seleucid Antiochus IV (175–163 BCE, thus a date of 167–164 BCE for Daniel 9).[4] The author of Daniel 9 (henceforth "Daniel") did not accept Ezra-Nehemiah's reading of Jeremiah, because, from where he was sitting, life was a disaster. The Jews who made it back to Palestine in the previous centuries never regained national autonomy, but were simply vassals shuffled from one kingdom to the next, like orphans in the foster system of imperial history. In this respect, Daniel did agree with Nehemiah's lament that "we are slaves to this day" (Neh. 9:36). Even the semi-tolerable pseudo-freedoms they had been tossed by rulers such as Darius and Artaxerxes had given way under the reign of Antiochus "Epiphanes." That demented pagan tyrant turned their Temple into a shrine to Zeus, defiling the sacred precincts with the blood of slaughtered swine and compounded his villainy by compelling the pious to participate in the

---

3. On the dating of Ezra-Nehemiah, see Hugh G. M. Williamson, *Ezra-Nehemiah*, Word Biblical Commentary, vol. 16 (Waco: Word, 1985), xxxiii–xlviii, esp. xxxv–xxxvi.
4. John E. Goldingay, *Daniel*, Word Biblical Commentary 30 (Dallas: Word, 1998), 237–38; John J. Collins, *Daniel: A Commentary on the Book of Daniel*, Hermeneia (Minneapolis, MN: Fortress Press, 1993), 61, 360.

blasphemous offerings, on pain of vile tortures and excruciating deaths. From this vantage point, Jeremiah's prophecy seemed nothing short of a cruel illusion. So, the author of Daniel 9 made a counter-claim to that of Jeremiah and Ezra-Nehemiah, and said that God had revised his plans.

The author adduced a new prophecy to supersede the previous schema. He alleged that back in the mid-sixth century, the "historical" Daniel had also been expecting the fulfillment of Jeremiah's prophecy in terms of seventy literal years. So, being one of the exiles himself and praying "in the first year of Darius" (Dan. 9:1), Daniel questioned how much longer it would be before Jeremiah's prophecy was fulfilled. Alas, the archangel Gabriel told him that it would, in fact, be seventy sevens—seventy lots of seven *years*. The extra wait notwithstanding, Gabriel promised that after 490 years, Israel's fortunes would surpass all previous expectations: there would be "everlasting righteousness" (Dan. 9:24). Even though Gabriel admitted that the last several years of the 490 would be undeniably ghastly, he promised that in the end, it would all be worth it.

The overall effect of the 490-year timeline outlined in Daniel 9 was to put the contemporary situation of the author's community into eschatological perspective, such that the community's suffering under Antiochus Epiphanes was understood as the tail-end of a much longer story, which (the author thought) would soon be concluded.

Still, even with the significant extension in the prophetic timeline that the author of Daniel contrived to help deal with the appalling deeds of Antiochus Epiphanes, history did not deliver the kind of good news for which he hoped.[5] Even within the book, one observes a growing nervousness about the accuracy of this prediction that motivates a recalibration of the prognosis. As events made the prediction more tenuous, the author of Daniel 12 created some

---

5. The timeline is "contrived" because, as Anderson explains, one is forced to squeeze 490 years into a span of 423 years or less (starting from 587 BCE and spanning to 171, 167, or 164 BCE, as interpreters variously do). For detailed discussion of these difficulties, see Robert A. Anderson, *Signs and Wonders: A Commentary on the Book of Daniel*, International Theological Commentary (Grand Rapids: Eerdmans, 1984), 110–18, especially 115–16; cf. Collins, *Daniel*, 400–401; Fishbane, *Biblical Interpretation in Ancient Israel*, 479–89, especially 483–87; see further ch. 4, pp. 12–12.

ambiguity by linking the final three and a half years—the last half-week of the seventy weeks—to two different events, namely, the rededication of the Jerusalem temple and "the end" (i.e. the culmination of all things that would come sometime after the temple was restored). In this way, Daniel 12 builds some elasticity into the prediction (cf. Dan. 8:14). Although Daniel 12 offers this cagey qualification, soon enough, all the prognostications in Daniel succumbed to history and disappointed hopes; Daniel's seventy weeks of years, stretched well beyond the mathematical and chronological tearing point, lay limp atop the wreckage of prophetic history.

## Judaism's Habit of Relocating Prophecy

Daniel was not alone in picking up a bit of unfulfilled prophecy and refashioning it to bolster the religious and nationalist hopes of his contemporaries. The *Habakkuk Pesher* (found among the Dead Sea Scrolls) and *4 Ezra* (a book of the Old Testament Apocrypha, also called *2 Esdras*) exemplify this tendency (or capacity) to relocate the referent of prophecy.

Way back in the seventh century BCE, Habakkuk had prophesied that God would send the Babylonians to punish the evil rampant in his day. Several hundred years later, in Qumran, an enthusiastic sectarian cherry-picked Habakkuk's comments about the Babylonian exile, and applied them to his own era, to the Romans (whom he calls the "Kittim") and to his own Jewish adversaries in the late first century BCE.[6] The author of the *Pesher* may well have felt that the approach was veritably invited by Habakkuk, who said, "For there is still a vision for the appointed time; it speaks of the end, and does not lie. If it seems to tarry, wait for it; it will surely come, it will not delay" (Hab. 2:3).

The "end" in question for the prophet Habakkuk was probably the *beginning* of the Babylonian conquest, which would finally bring divine judgment on the previously unpunished wickedness rampant in

---

6. See further William H. Brownlee, *The Midrash Pesher of Habakkuk: Text, Translation, Exposition with an Introduction*, Society of Biblical Literature Monograph Series 24 (Missoula, MT: Scholars, 1979), 23, 95–98.

Judaea. But the pesherist recast the time and content of the supposed "end" in a manner that differed extravagantly from what Habakkuk had envisioned, indeed averring the "end" was an eschatological and final judgment which would, in fact, take place in the pesherist's own proximate future (1 QpHab VII 1-14). He adduced the following interpretation of Hab. 2:2-3: "the last time will be long in coming but will excel all that the prophets predicted, because the mysteries of God are wonderful" (1 QpHab VII 7-8). The pesherist recognized that the marvels promised by the prophet Habakkuk (e.g. the end of the nations' abuse of the righteous and the filling of the earth with the knowledge of the glory of the Lord; see Hab. 2:15) had not yet occurred. But the pesherist asserted that a delay in fulfillment was no reason to discount the prophecy; such unexpected turns were part and parcel of the mystery of God.[7] Of course, the "Kittim" not only stuck around for several centuries, but also succeeded in rooting the Jews out of their own holy city and scattering them from the holy land for nearly two millennia. The hopes of the pesherist were disappointed. If nothing else, history provides such disgraced prophets with ample company.

A similar process of prophetic re-interpretation occurs in *4 Ezra*, an apocryphal text which re-works Daniel's vision of the four beasts coming out of the sea. The four hideous creatures of Dan. 7:1-28 symbolize the great empires of the era, no doubt terminating with a reference to the reign of Antiochus Epiphanes.[8] *4 Ezra* 11:1-46, however, narrates a vision of another beast—something of a mutant eagle with three heads and twelve wings—which *4 Ezra* 12:10 identifies with the fourth beast of Daniel 7. This symbolic shuffling is significant because *4 Ezra* is a document from the first century CE, composed in order to animate pious Jews living under Roman dominion.[9] Thus, for *4 Ezra*, the great eagle (and Daniel's fourth beast) refers not to the Seleucids, but to the *Romans*. One can see that *4 Ezra* reinterpreted the referents of Daniel 7's four beasts in a way that allowed him to

---

7. Ibid., 115-17.
8. Goldingay, *Daniel*, 176-81; Collins, *Daniel*, 299, 320-21.
9. See Michael E. Stone, *Fourth Ezra: A Commentary on the Book of Fourth Ezra*, Hermeneia (Minneapolis: Fortress Press, 1990), 9-10, 363-66.

apply biblical prophecy to his own day, and further, to supplement that prophecy with new visionary ornaments in order to fashion an apocalyptic encouragement for his co-religionist contemporaries.

From a critical perspective, it seems that the authors of Daniel 9, the *Habakkuk Pesher*, and 4 *Ezra* 11–12 are doing the same thing: they identify a previous prophecy that did not seem to come true, excise that prophecy from its historical context, and apply it to their own time, animating the hopes of their generation by promising the prophecy's fulfillment in the near future. One might surmise that this kind of breakdown in prophecy would (should?) have disillusioned the Jews, but that was not the case. Subsequent generations were happy to uproot the promises of these books and to adduce fulfillments to those prophecies in their own eras.[10] Thus, the non-fulfillment of Daniel's prophecies was not seen as a cautionary tale. Rather—owing especially to the flexibility afforded by their symbolism—Daniel's visions simply provided allegorical and numerical fodder for would-be prophets and eager apocalypticists.

## The Failure of Prophecy in the New Testament

Prophetic revision is nothing new. The highly selective use of texts by Harold Camping and others has ancient parallels. Indeed, the New Testament carefully chooses to ignore preceding material in its eschatological thinking as well. The New Testament, for instance, promises an ever-superior eschatological kingdom and refuses to see the non-arrival of that kingdom as reason to despair of its coming. The generating center of New Testament eschatology is, of course, the

---

10. Christian interpreters have proven themselves equally adept at this process. For patristic examples, see e.g. William Adler, "The Apocalyptic Survey of History Adapted by Christians: Daniel's Prophecy of 70 Weeks," in *The Jewish Apocalyptic Heritage in Early Christianity*, ed. James VanderKam and William Adler, *Compendia Rerum Iudaicarum ad Novum Testamentum* (Minneapolis: Fortress Press, 1996), 217–38; Roger T. Beckwith, *Calendar and Chronology, Jewish and Christian: Biblical, Intertestamental and Patristic Studies*, Arbeiten zur Geschichte des antiken Judentums und des Urchristentums 33 (Leiden: Brill, 1996), 272–75. One common topic of speculation is how current political and economic events are the referents of prophecies from Daniel and related passages in Revelation. For a contemporary example, see the discussion of the European Union by Grant Jeffrey, *Prince of Darkness: Antichrist and the New World Order* (Colorado Springs, CO: WaterBrook, 1994), 112–24.

kerygma ascribed to Jesus. But as we have already seen (ch. 1, pp. 15–18), Jesus promised the establishment of the kingdom of God within a generation. This prediction fared no better than other Jewish ones, as there was a mass exodus from Jerusalem around the time that most of Jesus' generation expired.

## Paul

Yet, in the middle of the first century, the Apostle Paul himself, lacking the benefit of hindsight, thought that the end had drawn nigh, that the second coming of Christ in judgment was just around the corner. He encouraged the Corinthians to radically re-orient their conduct and perspective because the world, as they knew it, would very soon cease to exist.

> The *appointed time has grown short* (ὁ καιρὸς συνεσταλμένος ἐστίν); from now on, let even those who have wives be as though they had none . . . and those who buy as though they had no possessions, and those who deal with the world as though they had no dealings with it. For the present form of this world is passing away. (1 Cor. 7:29–31)

Paul thought there had been a significant enough *change* in the proximity of the Parousia that the Corinthians should make major alterations to their lifestyles.[11]

The epistle to the Romans evinces a similar perspective. "You know what time it is," he says, "how it is now the moment for you to wake from sleep. For salvation is nearer to us now than when we became believers; the night is far gone, the day is near" (Rom. 13:11–12; similarly, see Phil. 4:5). On the one hand (as conservative commentators have hastened to underscore), the linearity of time means that the church would necessarily be "nearer" to the second coming than when they converted, irrespective of how far off the Parousia might be. On the other hand, an interval of 1,900 years certainly is hard to square

---

11. Richard A. Horsley, *1 Corinthians*, Abingdon New Testament Commentaries (Nashville: Abingdon, 1998), 106; cf. Joseph A. Fitzmyer, *First Corinthians: A New Translation with Introduction and Commentary*, Anchor Bible 32 (New Haven: Yale University Press, 2008), 313, 17.

with the assertion that "the night is far gone, the day is near," even allowing a good deal of flexibility in the metaphor.

Indeed, it is on the basis of his expectation of Jesus' imminent return that Paul promises the Romans, "The God of peace will *shortly* (ἐν τάχει) crush Satan under your feet" (Rom. 16:20). Paul aims to animate the piety and integrity of the Romans with the encouragement that they will not have to endure Satan's attacks much longer, insofar as the final judgment of Satan would soon vindicate the Roman believers.[12] Still, had the Roman Christians known that they would not witness Satan's overthrow before they all died, Paul's promise would have proven a cold comfort.[13]

In brief, Paul's exhortations in 1 Cor. 7:29-31 and Rom. 13:11-12, 16:20 invoke and indeed logically depend upon his assumption that Christ will return within the lifetimes of at least some of his contemporaries. But, to be frank, the terminology of *soon*, *quickly*, and *near* seems today to be impossible to reconcile with the fact that two thousand years have elapsed. Even if one wants to construe Paul's expectation of the nearness of the end relative to the entire length of the exile, the return of Christ has proven to tarry three-times longer than the exile itself did. That's nearly twice the interval between Jesus and the Davidic monarchy. "Soon" it was not. No amount of appeal to imminence and uncertainty can account for the fact that the delay of Christ proportionally dwarfs the entirety of the exile.

---

12. Ernst Käsemann, *Commentary on Romans*, trans. Geoffrey W. Bromiley (London: SCM, 1980), 362-63, 418-19; James D. G. Dunn, *Romans 9-16*, Word Biblical Commentary 38B (Dallas: Word, 1998), 905, 907; cf. Robert Jewett, *Romans: A Commentary*, Hermeneia (Minneapolis: Fortress Press, 2007), 821-24.
13. Similarly, in 1 Thess. 4:15, Paul speaks in such a way that implies an assumption that he and some of his audience will be alive at the second coming; so F.F. Bruce, *1 and 2 Thessalonians*, Word Biblical Commentary 45 (Dallas: Word, 1998), 99. Of course, the expression "we who are alive, who are left until the coming of the Lord, will by no means precede those who have died" does not promise that Paul will remain living at that juncture, even though as much is the most natural reading of the text. Still, by the time Paul wrote 2 Cor. 4:14, he seems to have moderated his expectations a bit.

## Revelation

Paul was not the only New Testament author to be premature in promises of the world's end; the book of Revelation seems to have been similarly embarrassed. In the 17th chapter of John's Apocalypse, the seer has a vision of a woman riding on a beast with seven heads and ten horns. The woman is a great whore, drunk on the blood of the saints, and across her forehead is scrawled the moniker "Babylon" (Rev. 17:1-4). She is a thinly veiled cipher for Rome, in which the seer (writing late in the first century CE) perceived the culmination of Satan's forces in the world. An angel interprets the seer's vision of the beast, explaining:

> The seven heads are seven mountains on which the woman is seated; also, they are seven kings, of whom five have fallen, one is living, and the other has not yet come; and when he comes, he must remain only a little while. As for the beast that was and is not, it is an eighth but it belongs to the seven, and it goes to destruction. (Rev. 17:9-11)

Thus, he confirms that the woman represents Rome, the city on seven hills.

The angel further exploits the imagery of the seven heads by averring that they also refer to rulers of the empire. He explains that the seer and his contemporaries are living in the time of one of the final kings, represented as number six in the sequence. They can expect but one or two more kings to come before the great Roman Empire is shattered (Rev. 17:15-18:24) and the final wicked ruler, along with his client kings (represented by the ten horns), is struck down by Jesus at his Second and Terrible Coming (Rev. 19:11-21).[14] Like Daniel before him, the seer portrays the final consummation of all things as just a stone's throw in the future, just on the horizon, just a ruler or two down the road. Little did he know that after Domitian (or whoever

---

14. For further details on this passage, see David E. Aune, *Revelation 17-22*, Word Biblical Commentary 52C (Dallas: Word, 1998), 945-51; cf. G. B. Caird, *A Commentary on the Revelation of St. John the Divine*, Black's New Testament Commentaries (London: Adam & Charles Black, 1966), 215-21. Some of the complexity in this text may well owe to successive redactional emendations, each aimed toward extending the promised deliverance of the text a few more steps into the future; in this respect, the redaction history of Revelation 17 may have a good deal in common with that of Daniel 12.

the seer's contemporary emperor may have been), more than three dozen emperors would ascend and topple from Rome's throne, after which Diocletian would take his turn and start beheading Christians all around the Mediterranean.

## 2 Peter

Nonetheless, as time went on, the Church had to resign itself to the fact that, though they had scattered the seeds of the kingdom, the only fruit they had harvested were eschatological lemons. Undaunted, they set about to make lemonade. Thus, the author of 2 Peter challenged those made skeptical by the non-occurrence of the eschaton.

> But do not ignore this one fact, beloved, that with the Lord one day is like a thousand years, and a thousand years are like one day. *The Lord is not slow about his promise, as some think of slowness, but is patient with you, not wanting any to perish, but all to come to repentance.* But the day of the Lord will come like a thief, and then the heavens will pass away with a loud noise, and the elements will be dissolved with fire, and the earth and everything that is done on it will be disclosed. (2 Pet. 3:3–4, 8–10)

Here, one can see that the door of the second coming was swung wide open and left ajar, so that Christ could walk through in his own good time. But walk through it, 2 Peter insisted, he will. No amount of delay could sour the anticipation. And so, Christian eschatological hope fell in lock-step with the interpretive strategies of their Jewish predecessors, expecting the end at any moment, irrespective of the myriad of reasons Christians had to give up their eschatological optimism.

## Concluding Summary

This chapter has sought to investigate the dynamics of prophetic deferral, outlining how the non-appearance of Jesus' prophesied second coming is simply part and parcel of a longstanding pattern of failure seen already in Jewish prophecy. Most historical-critical investigation of Jewish and Christian prophecy concludes that prophecies often fail. What can be said then of Jews and Christians is that they have a resilient ability to ignore the stark disparity between the claims of these texts and subsequent historical events. Prodigious in their capacity for "cognitive dissonance," they continue to defer the sublime consummation of all things while generating limitless imaginative excuses for the delay, irrespective of fact that the non-occurrence of the eschaton has now provided serious grounds on which to impugn the credibility of their hope.

As noted at the beginning of this chapter, we have aimed here to state the case against Christian eschatological hope in the sharpest terms possible. To that end, we have spared no rhetorical expense, for we do not desire to leave room for the accusation of besting a mere straw-man. In the aftermath of this historical-critical bombardment, the commonplace Christian approach to the delay of the Parousia lies in ruins. What then can be built from this rubble?

3

# Reconceiving Prophecy: Activation, Not Prognostication

## C. A. Strine

If we take the preceding assessment seriously—and there is little reason to think we should not—then the notion of Christian hope lies before us, demolished and in disrepair. Among this rubble is the raw material from which we shall seek to refashion a foundation for Christian hope and to provide a different approach to the delay of the Parousia.

### The Majority Hermeneutic for Prophetic Prediction

To start, it is necessary to highlight a key presupposition that underlies the various traditional and critical approaches to the delay of the Parousia surveyed in chapters 1-2: when Jesus spoke about the imminent arrival of the kingdom of God, he aimed to describe accurately the future events surrounding his return as the exalted Messiah. Said differently, interpretation of the relevant passages starts from the controlling premise that in order to make sense of the New Testament eschatological proclamation, one must consider how events subsequent to the promise of the Parousia have fulfilled those predictions. This hermeneutical approach to predictive prophecy takes for granted that when a prophet or prophetess speaks about future events, they intend to describe what they believe will actually happen in the future. Perhaps this is an obvious point, but it is essential to expose this notion in order to proceed.

This approach—what we will call the *majority hermeneutic* for predictive prophecy—finds its biblical basis in the way that the book of Deuteronomy delineates the role of the prophet. The topic arises first in Deut. 13:2-6 (ET 13:1-5), where the prophet or dreamer of dreams is declared "false" if they attempt to persuade the people to follow other gods. The severity of this conduct is specified by its punishment—namely, the death of that person, an act that "shall purge the evil from your midst" (Deut. 13:6).

Not satisfied that this will put fine enough a point on the issue, Deut. 18:15-22 takes it up again, albeit in the context of a discussion about the various officials who will govern Israel. This passage explains that in the future, YHWH will raise up one (or more) prophet(s) such as Moses to speak on God's behalf with the community. This divine messenger, like Moses, deserves the community's obedience; however, should any prophet who takes up this mantle "speak in [YHWH's] name a word that I have not commanded" (Deut. 18:20), they shall be punished by death. The text immediately poses the community's logical question: how does one know when a prophet has spoken something YHWH has *not* commanded? And here lies the crux of the issue: "If a prophet speaks in the name of the Lord but the thing does not take place or prove true, it is a word that the Lord has not spoken" (Deut. 18:22).

This Deuteronomic or majority hermeneutic re-emerges whenever the question of "true" and "false" prophecy occurs,[1] not just in antiquity but also in contemporary scholarship. Indeed, this view underlies the three major critical analyses of the Parousia outlined in chapter 1 (pp. 6–18). The Jesus Seminar thinks it has excised this problem altogether by dissociating Jesus from any sort of eschatological proclamation; in reality, the Seminar has simply passed the buck to the disciples, who they seem to view as "expendable"—to borrow a Hollywood mobster expression. N.T. Wright's proposal is attractive for various reasons, but perhaps none is more alluring than its potential to provide an avenue by which this Deuteronomic criterion is met while simultaneously accounting for what is, at a minimum, a peculiar earthly manifestation of the predicted events. Dale Allison and Bart Ehrman both evaluate Jesus' prophecy by applying the Deuteronomic criterion. In the end, one might wonder why scholars have not adopted the role of Deuteronomic judge and jury, throwing out any case for hope in the erroneously prophesied *parousia*!

However ubiquitous the majority hermeneutic may be in modern scholarship, it did not enjoy such hegemony in antiquity. Indeed, when one locates the prophetic texts of the Old and New Testaments in their ancient Near Eastern and early Jewish contexts, there also emerges a rather different approach that is frequently overlooked by contemporary scholars. This minority hermeneutic for interpreting predictive prophecy receives its most explicit biblical exposition in the book of Jeremiah.[2]

---

1. On the potential problems with the categories of "true" and "false" prophecy in antiquity, see Matthijs de Jong, "The Fallacy of 'True and False' in Prophecy Illustrated by Jer 28:8-9," *JHS* 12, no. 10 (2012): 1–29.
2. The basis for the minority hermeneutic in the Old Testament has been outlined previously in a little-known essay by Richard L. Pratt Jr., "Historical Contingencies and Biblical Prediction," in *The Way of Wisdom: Essay in Honor of Bruce K. Waltke* (Grand Rapids: Zondervan, 2000), 180–203 (esp. 183–90). Though we both disagree with Pratt on various critical and doctrinal issues and also significantly develop his position by including evidence from many non-canonical texts that he does not address, his argument has provided our project with a vital conceptual stimulus, and for that, we are most grateful.

## The Minority Hermeneutic for Prophetic Prediction

Jeremiah is portrayed as the Deuteronomistic prophet *par excellence*.[3] It is, therefore, noteworthy that the book bearing his name engages in a dialogue with Deuteronomy on this issue. To anticipate what follows, Jeremiah indicates that some predictive prophecy is *not* meant to come true. It advances this view—with conscious knowledge of Deuteronomy's opposing position—in two steps.[4]

Jeremiah 18:1-11 explains that YHWH reserves the right to change course even after the prophet who speaks on God's behalf predicts either blessing or cursing. Phrased another way, God may decide not to do the ill foretold if the people repent, or conversely, to withhold a foretold blessing if the people do evil in God's sight (cf. Ezekiel 18 and 33).

Jeremiah introduces the issue by employing the familiar biblical images of God as a potter and human nations as clay vessels (cf. Isa. 29:15-24; 45:9-13, 64:7-11; Rom. 9:19-33):

> The word that came to Jeremiah from the Lord: "Come, go down to the potter's house, and there I will let you hear my words." So I went down to the potter's house, and there he was working at his wheel. The vessel he was making of clay was spoiled in the potter's hand, and he reworked it into another vessel, as seemed good to him.
>
> Then the word of the Lord came to me: Can I not do with you, O house of Israel, just as this potter has done? says the Lord. Just like the clay in the potter's hand, so are you in my hand, O house of Israel. At one moment I may declare concerning a nation or a kingdom, that I will pluck up and break down and destroy it, but if that nation, concerning which I have spoken, turns from its evil, I will change my mind about the disaster that I intended to bring on it. *And at another moment I may declare concerning a nation or a kingdom that I will build and plant it, but if it does evil in my sight, not listening to my voice, then I will change my mind about the good that I had intended to do to it.* (Jer. 18:1-10)

---

[3]. For a recent and extended discussion, see Mark Leuchter, *Josiah's Reform and Jeremiah's Scroll: Historical Calamity and Prophetic Response*, Hebrew Bible Monographs 6 (Sheffield: Sheffield Phoenix, 2006).

[4]. Cf. J. Todd Hibbard, "True and False Prophecy: Jeremiah's Revision of Deuteronomy," *JSOT* 35 (2011): 339-58.

This programmatic statement is illustrated by Jeremiah 26, one of two chapters in the book that depicts Jeremiah proclaiming YHWH's looming judgment against the Jerusalem Temple (cf. Jeremiah 7). This passage asserts, *pace* Deuteronomy, that a successful prophet is precisely the one who does *not* see his prediction come to pass.

Jeremiah 26 alerts the reader to the centrality of interpreting predictive prophecy at its outset with a brief recollection of Jeremiah 18's conceptual approach (vv. 2-3). Afterwards, it recounts that the priests, the prophets, and all the people condemn Jeremiah to death (vv. 7-9) because of his prediction of doom upon the Jerusalem Temple. Even though it must be inferred from the text, the plain implication is that the crowd is so astonished by this message that they think Jeremiah can be convicted under the guidance of Deut. 13:2-6, where a prophet leads the people to follow other gods! This is accentuated by Jeremiah's defense, which only reasserts that he speaks for YHWH (v. 12), and therefore, invokes the more complex criteria of Deut. 18:15-22. The people must now reconsider their verdict. This momentary hesitation provides the dramatic pause necessary for the book to make its viewpoint explicit, which it does through a speech offered by the elders of the land:

> And some of the elders of the land arose and said to all the assembled people, "Micah of Moresheth, who prophesied during the days of King Hezekiah of Judah, said to all the people of Judah: 'Thus says the Lord of hosts,
> Zion shall be ploughed as a field,
> Jerusalem shall become a heap of ruins,
> and the mountain of the house a wooded height.'
> Did King Hezekiah of Judah and all Judah actually put him to death? Did he not fear the Lord and entreat the favor of the Lord, and did not the Lord change his mind (וינחם) about the disaster that he had pronounced against them?" (Jer. 26:17-19)[5]

Among the fascinating features of this passage, its invocation of the prophet Micah (cf. Mic. 3:12) raises the stakes of the debate by

---

5. This passage is all the more notable because it is the only explicit quotation of one prophetic book by another in the Hebrew Bible.

suggesting that Jeremiah is far from the only authoritative prophet who predicted doom with the hope of being wrong. The book of Jeremiah, it is clear, believes that there is great peril in slavishly following the majority—or Deuteronomic—hermeneutic to prophetic prediction.

Considering these texts, Robert Carroll, the distinguished exegete of Jeremiah, concludes:

> The interpretation of prophecy is not simply a matter of asking "what actually happened?" (*wie es eigentlich gewesen*) in relation to what the prophets said—they were not weather forecasters charting the immediate future but men attempting to shape the destiny of the community. They were not only concerned with the likelihood of certain events but with why they were happening and the ways in which the community should respond to such possibilities. The criteria of Deuteronomy provided for a falsification paradigm of prophecy whereas prophecy was a much more complex affair altogether. Part of their proclamation was that certain events would happen because of conditions in the community; they were not providing information about the future so much as a critique of the community's current activities.[6]

In order to appreciate that this debate is more than an internecine Deuteronomistic feud, it is imperative to show how closely Jeremiah mirrors the attitude toward prophetic prediction taken more broadly in the ancient Near East.

## Ancient Near Eastern Attitudes to Prophetic Prediction

Matthijs de Jong has demonstrated that ancient Near Eastern prophecy shares four features:[7] (1) prophets encouraged their audiences in times of emergency and gave them support in times of trouble; (2) the gods used prophets to present their claims to the people; (3) as guardians of the well-being of the state, prophets harshly denounced threats to the

---

6. Robert P. Carroll, *When Prophecy Failed: Reactions and Responses to Failure in the Old Testament Prophetic Traditions* (London: SCM, 1979), 187-88.
7. Matthijs de Jong, "Biblical Prophecy—A Scribal Enterprise. The Old Testament Prophecy of Unconditional Judgment considered as a Literary Phenomenon," *VT* 61 (2011): 39-70. It is important to bear in mind, as de Jong does, that prophecy is a phenomenon that lies within the overarching practice of divination, which is common elsewhere in the ancient Near East despite being largely absent in the Hebrew Bible.

existence of the state, whether external or internal; and (4) prophets warned the people about the disasters planned by the gods, *with the express purpose of averting them*.[8]

Expanding upon the final feature, de Jong writes that when a prophet spoke:

> The threat was to be taken seriously, the right action carried out so that the disaster would be averted. If the predicted outcome was successfully averted, this did not make the prophecy false. On the contrary, a prophet protecting society by revealing a threatening disaster was doing his job well. For this was among the tasks of all diviners, including the prophets: to reveal the plans of the gods, either *to encourage or to warn their audience*.[9]

Because of the focus of his article, de Jong attends to predictions of disaster; nonetheless, the corollary is contained within the concept: some predictions were meant to encourage the audience to embrace behaviors that would ensure the arrival of foretold blessing or victory.

De Jong mentions the Babylon Inscription of Esarhaddon tangentially, and this text illustrates the point well. The inscriptions recall that Babylon's destruction was adumbrated through evil omens, which the peoples' persistent misappropriation of temple property did nothing to avert; but after the city is destroyed, favorable omens and astronomical phenomena prophesy the future restoration of Babylon. These omens appear, according to the text, after Esarhaddon has "learned the fear of the gods."[10] It is, ultimately, Esarhaddon's rebuilding of the city's temples and refurbishment of the divine statues that motivates the gods to return to the city and exalt it among the nations. Royal propaganda notwithstanding, the inscription enshrines the concept that foretold blessing arrives if and when it activates faithful conduct from its human audience. That is to say, the divinatory indication that blessing is possible encourages the behavior desired by the gods so that it can be realized.[11]

---

8. Ibid., 48–50.
9. Ibid., 49–50; cf. de Jong, "The Fallacy of 'True and False' in Prophecy," 4.
10. Rykle Borger, *Die Inschriften Asarhaddons, Königs von Assyrien* (Graz: Im Selbstverlage des Herausgebers, 1956), 17, episode 12, version B. For a more recent study of Esarhaddon's inscriptions, see Erle Leichty, *Royal Inscriptions of Esarhaddon, King of Assyria (680-669 BC)*, RINAP 4 (Winona Lake: Eisenbrauns, 2011), esp. 193–201.

Lena-Sofia Tiemeyer has argued along the same lines in an article that explores a few predictive texts in the Deuteronomistic History.[12] Tiemeyer finds further evidence for the conditionality of prophetic predictions outside the Assyrian divinatory texts. She discusses the *Shamash Hymn* and highlights that the text describes Shamash both as a god who sends people an omen that cannot be changed (ll. 127–29, 151–2), and also, as one moved to mercy by the supplication of those same people (ll. 163–4).[13] Tiemeyer contends this same view appears in the *Poem of the Righteous Sufferer* (also known by its ancient name, *Ludlul bel nemeqi*):[14] this text portrays a sufferer who prays to his goddess, seeks helps from a diviner, and speaks to a dream interpreter, all in hopes of turning away the divine wrath he is experiencing. Tiemeyer concludes that this "supports the idea that there is a connection between future predicted omens and the attempt to revoke it [*sic*] by rituals and prayer."[15]

All these examples underscore the provisional nature of prophetic predictions. Such statements did not amount to a claim to know an inevitable future in the ancient Near East. Perhaps the better analogy than prophet as fortune-teller is of prophet as concerned parent: like the mother who warns her child against crossing a street without regard for traffic or extols the benefits of healthy eating, so also does the prophet frame the likely outcome of obedience to or disregard for divine instruction by vividly depicting the probable future consequences. This is not to deny that the prophets claimed (and indeed, believed) their message to be a revelatory word from a deity,

---

11. See J. A. Brinkman, "Through a Glass Darkly: Esarhaddon's Retrospects on the Downfall of Babylon," *JAOS* 103 (1983): 35–42. Another indication that predictive prophecy was understood conditionally is the so-called "*atbash*" code in this text: the original prediction that Babylon would lie in ruins for seventy years is, by the reversal of the two cuneiform symbols used to write seventy, converted into 11 years. In this case, the motivation for the exile's abbreviation is unprompted divine mercy, but the concept that a prediction is not a hard and fast map for events remains nonetheless.
12. Lena-Sofia Tiemeyer, "Prophecy as a Way of Cancelling Prophecy – The Strategic Uses of Foreknowledge," *ZAW* 117 (2005): 329–50.
13. For an English translation, see "The Shamash Hymn," translated by Benjamin R. Foster (*COS* 1.117: 418–19).
14. For an English translation, see "The Poem of the Righteous Sufferer," translated by Benjamin R. Foster (*COS* 1.153: 486–92).
15. Tiemeyer, "Prophecy," 342–43.

for these messages are presented and received as far more than educated guesses. Still, the function of the prophet's statements about the future is primarily intended to underscore the consequences for continuing to defy the deity rather than to outline an unavoidable course of events.

Since the evidence that de Jong and Tiemeyer compile stretches across time and place in the ancient Near East, one might come to regard the so-called minority hermeneutic of Jeremiah 18 as the ancient *norm* and Deuteronomy 18 as the anomalous text.[16] Irrespective of how one resolves that question, the preceding evidence warrants concluding that predictive prophecy was widely recognized as conditioned by human response in ancient Israel and Judah.

## Old Testament Support for the Minority Hermeneutic

Perhaps, by now, the plot of the book of Jonah has come to mind. This prophet—no doubt a comic figure in a comical book, but surely one with a serious point—demonstrates the prevalence of the belief that the prophet's real task was to change society's behavior and not to prognosticate future events accurately. The basic outline of Jonah is well-known: when God commands Jonah to "[g]o at once to Nineveh, that great city, and cry out against it for their wickedness has come up before me" (Jon. 1:2), the prophet flees in the opposite direction. Why? Because Jonah understands that his proclamation of impending divine judgment will provoke the king, the people, and even the animals to fast in sackcloth and ashes with the hope that "God may relent (שוב) and change his mind (נחם); he may turn away from his burning anger so that we shall not perish" (Jon. 3:9). The result is precisely that: YHWH spares Nineveh (Jon. 3:10). Jonah is not pleased by this turn of events, expressing his disgust with all the sophistication of an aggrieved teenager ("Isn't this just what I said when I was still in my own country?" Jon. 4:2a) before offering a despondent opinion that "I would rather die than live" (Jon. 4:3b).

---

16. Indeed, this is what de Jong concludes ("The Fallacy of 'True and False' in Prophecy," 26–29).

Hyperbolic self-pity aside, it is noteworthy that the book of Jonah explains that YHWH is willing to withhold predicted judgment by reference to a central confession of divine character: "That is why I fled beforehand to Tarshish. For I know that you are a compassionate and gracious God, slow to anger, abounding in kindness, renouncing punishment" (Jon. 4:2b, *JPS*). It is plain that the book of Jonah sees the conditionality of prophetic prediction as a *logical corollary to the core attributes of Israel's deity*, not some indication of capriciousness or fickle thinking on YHWH's part.[17] It is entirely logical that some predicted events do not come to pass because God is exceedingly merciful (see also chapter 8, pp. 194-95).

Rather less familiar by comparison to Jonah, the book of Joel is equally demonstrative in its insistence about the conditionality of prophetic prediction. This "problem child of Old Testament exegesis"[18] is hard to pin down on many fronts, but there is no argument that it twice depicts the carnage of divine judgment that will accompany the day of the Lord (Joel 1:2-4; 2:1-11).[19] In both cases, the book specifies the proper response to this prophetic vision: rather than accept this fate, the people are called to lament in public their previous conduct and to amend their behavior so that YHWH might void the announcement of punishment (Joel 2:11b-14; cf. 1:8-15):

> For great is the day of the LORD, and it is most terrible—who can endure it?
>
> "Yet even now"—says the LORD—"Turn back to me with all your hearts, and with fasting, weeping, and lamenting, rend your hearts rather than your garments. Turn back to the LORD your God: for he is gracious and compassionate, slow to anger, abounding in kindness, and one who relents from punishment." Who knows[20] but he may turn and relent (נחם),

---

17. Cf. James L. Crenshaw, *Joel: A New Translation with Introduction and Commentary*, Anchor Bible 24C (New York: Doubleday, 1995), 144.
18. John Barton, *Joel and Obadiah: A Commentary*, Old Testament Library (Louisville, KY: Westminster John Knox, 2001), 3, quoting Adalbert Merx.
19. Barton, *Joel and Obadiah*, 14.
20. The question "who knows" (מִי יוֹדֵעַ) occurs in several relevant passages: Joel 2:14, Jon. 3:9, as well as 2 Sam. 12:22, which is treated below. For a discussion of its broader use in the Hebrew Bible, see James L. Crenshaw, "The Expression *Mî Yôdēa'* in the Hebrew Bible," *VT* 36 (1986): 274-88.

and leave a blessing behind as a meal offering and drink offering to the LORD your God? (Joel 2:11b–14, JPS)

Here, Joel is a perfect complement to Jon. 3:9.[21] Whereas Jonah emphasizes that YHWH relents and does not do what was predicted, Joel 2:14 imagines that repentance turns potential judgment into a great blessing. Thus, Joel goes on to describe the gift of abundant grain and wine that supplies for the cultic celebration of God's mercy upon the people.

Back on more familiar ground, the call of the prophet Isaiah expresses the same view toward the potential result of predictive prophecy. During the prophet's vision of the enthroned Lord, Isaiah is given a confounding task:

> And he said, "Go, say to that people: 'Hear, indeed, but do not understand; see, indeed, but do not grasp.' Dull that people's mind, stop its ears, and seal its eyes—lest, seeing with its eyes and hearing with its ears it also grasp with its mind and repent (ושב) and heal (ורפא) itself." (Isa. 6:9–10, JPS)

Commentary on this passage is dominated by debate about the theological ramifications of God hardening the people's heart.[22] Without disregarding the importance of that issue, its prominence obscures the concept upon which the prophet's task is predicated: the passage presumes that the public declaration of the community's transgressions will lead to repentance. It is the probability of that outcome that requires the *extraordinary* measure of YHWH's drastic, indeed supernatural, intervention *to keep it from happening*.[23]

With these examples in mind, it seems appropriate to trace the role of the minority hermeneutic in later Jewish texts.

---

21. Ibid, 23.
22. See *inter alia* Brevard S. Childs, *Isaiah*, Old Testament Library (Louisville, KY: Westminster John Knox, 2001), 49–60. Craig A. Evans, *To See and Not Perceive: Isaiah 6:9-10 in Early Jewish and Christian Interpretation*, JSOTSup 64 (Sheffield: JSOT, 1989), helpfully traces the interpretation of this text through the early rabbinic and patristic period.
23. The Isaianic vocabulary of repenting (שוב) and healing (רפא) is distinct from the preference in Jonah and Joel to speak of relenting (נחם). Yet, it is clear from the use of רפא elsewhere in Isaiah (e.g. Isa. 19:22; 53:5; 57:18) that the meaning of these terms is essentially synonymous.

## The Minority Hermeneutic in Early Judaism

As further evidence that this approach to predictive prophecy remained influential in the Second Temple and post-biblical eras, one can point to the Babylonian Talmud tractate *Sanhedrin* and the *Sibylline Oracles*. These two texts, being very different in genre and content, suggest that a wide range of groups adopted the minority hermeneutic for predictive prophecy.

The final chapter of *Sanhedrin* includes a discourse on when the Messiah will return. In the midst of a winding discussion, which begins by asking about the "seven year cycle at the end of which the son of David will come" and continues through various interpretations of Deut. 32:36 (Indeed the LORD will vindicate his people/have compassion on his servants/when he sees that their power is gone/neither bond nor free remaining), the following views are noted:

> Rab said: All the predestined dates [for redemption] have passed, and the matter [now] depends only on repentance and good deeds. (*b. Sanh.* 97b)

> R. Alexandri said: R. Joshua b. Levi pointed out a contradiction. It is written, in its time [will the Messiah come], whilst it is also written, I [the Lord] will hasten it! (Isa. 60:22)—if they are worthy, I will hasten it: if not, [he will come] at the due time. (*b. Sanh.* 98a)

Observe that Sanhedrin attests both the idea that the end of the ages *depends on repentance and good deeds,* and also, that this *time might be hastened*—that the eschaton might be brought forward—by a certain pattern of human behavior. Both these ideas shall reappear in due course when we explore the relevant New Testament texts. For now, it must suffice to note that rabbinic interpreters were aware that the fulfillment of prophetic prediction depends upon human behavior, and, furthermore, that they felt free to employ that notion in order to encourage the people of God to behave in a particular fashion.

It is also valuable to note that Sanhedrin is not alone in espousing this view. The Babylonian Talmud exposition of the Mishnaic tractate *Yoma* 8:8 adopts a similar viewpoint, discussing how human action relates to future eschatological hope. It contains this remark:

> R. Jonathan said: Penitence is great, so that it brings the redemption, as it is written [Isa. 59:20]: "But unto Zion shall come the redeemer, and unto those who return from transgression in Jacob," which means, Why is the redeemer come? Because Jacob has returned from transgressions. (b. Yoma 86b)

Here, the minority hermeneutic guides a rabbinic interpretation of Isa. 59:20 and provides the opportunity to connect faithfulness to God with the realization of the prophetic hope for the onset of God's kingdom.

Turning to a very different text and milieu, the *Sibylline Oracles* provide further evidence for the role of the minority hermeneutic. Book four of the *Oracles*—widely regarded as the product of two stages of composition, with the initial material originating in the Hellenistic period and the later content emerging from Jewish circles around 80 CE[24]—employs the schema of ten ruling generations (six Assyrian, two Median, one Persian, and finally, the Macedonian empire), to which Rome is added as the eleventh; this periodization culminates in the end of the ages. After the text inveighs against impious Jews and the vicious Roman Empire, it declares that God takes note of this behavior and waits with growing anger to judge iniquity—a judgment described at great and graphic length. But there remains a way to stave off this cataclysm:

> Ah, wretched mortals, change these things, and do not lead the great God to all sorts of anger, but abandon daggers and groanings, murders and outrages, and wash your whole bodies in perennial rivers. Stretch out your hands to heaven and ask forgiveness for your previous deeds and make propitiation for bitter impiety with words of praise; *God will grant repentance and will not destroy*. He will stop his wrath again if you all practice honorable piety in your hearts. (*Sib. Or.* 4.162–70)

It is hardly surprising now to find that the concept that underlies the call for repentance is the assumption that future events are neither determined by past behavior alone nor by the content of predictive prophecy, but by the response of people to God's message.[25]

---

24. An attribution that owes to the focus on the predicted disasters as punishment for the destruction of Jerusalem (*Sib. Or.* 4.136).

Though other texts might also be discussed, these two demonstrate that the minority hermeneutic for predictive prophecy is operative across the ancient Near East and plays an important role in Jewish thinking over the course of many centuries. It is, therefore, justifiable to conclude that the understanding of predictive prophecy as conditioned by human response remained plausible and active throughout the first few centuries of the Common Era.

### Early Christian Adoption of the Minority Hermeneutic

Of course, for this approach to be relevant for the present question, it must have exerted influence on the authors of the New Testament. Greco-Roman prophecy is not the same as Jewish eschatological prophecy, to be sure, although it is noteworthy that Greco-Roman oracles were also conditional on some occasions.[26] Nevertheless, the primary rationale for applying the minority hermeneutic to Jesus' eschatological prophecy is the evidence that Jeremianic conceptions of prophecy influenced Jesus and the earliest Christian communities. A full treatment of the relevant New Testament texts is the topic of the next chapter, but it is sensible to note here just how influential Jeremiah is for the Gospels' portrayal of Jesus' prophetic activity.

No reasonable scholar denies that early Christian communities knew both Deuteronomy and Jeremiah. But, more specifically, scholars have argued that Jeremiah provides an important model for at least the Synoptics' depictions of Jesus as prophet.[27] The preeminent example is the way in which Jesus' cleansing of the Temple serves as the

---

25. It also bears mentioning that *1 En.* 83.3–10 includes a vision of cataclysmic cosmic destruction ("*I saw in the vision the sky being rolled down and snatched and falling upon the earth. When it fell upon the earth, I saw the earth being swallowed up into the great abyss, the mountains being suspended upon mountains, the hills sinking down upon the hills, and tall trees being uprooted and thrown and sinking into the deep abyss*" (*1 En.* 83.3–4)), apparently of the eschatological and final sort, to which Enoch is told to respond by praying that God might change his mind ("*Rise and pray to the Lord of glory, for you are a man of faith, so that a remnant shall remain upon the earth and that the whole earth shall not be blotted out.*" (*1 En.* 83.8)).
26. David E. Aune, *Prophecy in Early Christianity and the Ancient Mediterranean World* (Grand Rapids: Eerdmans, 1983), 60–61, cf. 237–40. For example, "When you honor Leto's son Phoebus [Apollo] and Zeus Patroios, you will receive fame; then fasten your shackles here on the tree" (ibid., 60).
27. N.T. Wright, *Jesus and the Victory of God* (London: SPCK, 1996), 166, 184–85, 417–24; cf. Korinna Zamfir, "Jeremian Motifs in the Synoptics' Understanding of Jesus," in *Prophets and Prophecy in Jewish and Early Christian Literature*, eds. Jozef Verheyden, Korinna Zamfir, and Tobias Nicklas,

proximate cause for his trial and crucifixion. "Like Jeremiah," remarks N.T. Wright in discussing this account, "Jesus constantly runs the risk of being called a traitor to Israel's national aspirations" and is tried "not least as a false prophet."[28] The overlap between Jesus' actions at the Temple and Jeremiah 26 is simply too great to be coincidental. It follows logically, then, that the authors of the Gospels were not only aware of the Jeremianic approach to predictive prophecy, but were pleased to call it to mind with their own texts.[29] Given the substantial evidence for the prominence of this approach to interpreting predictive prophecy in the ancient Near East and early Judaism, there is strong justification for applying this minority hermeneutic to the New Testament's eschatological proclamation.

This approach to eschatological prophecy is also to be found among the most influential early Christian writers (see also chapter 5, pp. 84, 99-101#). For example, the Fathers revealed their belief in the variability of the final judgment when calling for the *acceleration* of the eschatological timetable. Tertullian—whose *Apology* vaunted the role of Christians in deferring the final judgment—finds occasion in his exposition of the Lord's Prayer to take exception with others who pray that the end be delayed, rather than expedited:

> How do some pray for some protraction of the age, when the kingdom of God, which we pray may arrive, tends unto the consummation of the age? Our wish is, that our reign be hastened, not our servitude protracted. Even if it had not been prescribed in the Prayer that we should ask for the advent of the kingdom, we should, unbidden, have sent forth that cry, hastening toward the realization of our hope. . . . Nay, Lord, Thy kingdom come with all speed—the prayer of Christians, the confusion of the heathen, the exultation of angels, for the sake of which we suffer, nay, rather, for the sake of which we pray! (Tertullian, *Or.* 5; ANF 3:683; PL 1, pp. 1159-60)

---

Wissenschaftliche Untersuchungen zum Neuen Testament 286 (Tübingen: Mohr Siebeck, 2010), 139-76.
28. Wright, *Jesus and the Victory of God*, 166.
29. On this method of alluding to antecedent texts in the New Testament, see Richard B. Hays, *Echoes of Scripture in the Letters of Paul* (New Haven, CT: Yale University Press, 1993) and Steve Moyise, *Evoking Scripture: Seeing the Old Testament in the New* (London: T&T Clark, 2008).

A similar idea is present in the writings of Cyprian of Carthage (*Mort.* 18; *ANF* 5:473; PL 4, p. 595), indicating that this approach was not an isolated one in patristic writing on the Parousia.

## Is All Prophetic Prediction Historically Inaccurate?

By this stage, an important question will likely have materialized in the mind of the reader: does the minority hermeneutic for prophetic prediction rule out the possibility that a predictive prophecy might simply be fulfilled in the way the prophet foretells? No systematic answer to this question is given in the Old Testament, which comes as small surprise, given its characteristic lack of interest in such schematic thinking. There is, nevertheless, at least one narrative that suggests that future fulfillment of putatively conditional prophetic prediction is possible.

In the long national history that stretches from Deuteronomy through the books of Joshua, Judges, Samuel, and Kings, there is no more prominent human character than King David. A man of grand accomplishments, he is no stranger to deep tragedy either. Of course, the text makes it plain that his misfortune is connected to his own choices. The paradigmatic example of this action-consequence theology is the story of David's initial encounter with Bathsheba (2 Samuel 11–12), conspicuously identified as the "wife of Uriah" (2 Sam. 11:3). This narrative is known for its characterization of David's moral failures and for its ultimate resolution in the birth of Solomon, who succeeds David as king of Israel. It is also familiar because of the clever parable that Nathan, prophet of the royal court, uses to bring David to recognize his transgressions. Here, we encounter another text like Jonah, one that assumes the minority hermeneutic to predictive prophecy in its narrative substructure.

Nathan's parable about a rich man who steals a poor man's lamb (2 Sam. 12:1–4) provokes David to pronounce judgment upon "the man who has done this." Narrative tension reaches its peak when Nathan declares to David, "you are the man!" (2 Sam. 12:7) Afterwards, the prophet applies David's unsolicited verdict to the king's own situation, explaining that there will be much violence within his family, that David himself will be spared, but that the unborn child conceived as a result of his rendezvous with Bathsheba will die. David reacts to this prediction not with sorrowful and passive fatalism, but by snapping into action: he seeks God by fasting for seven days, during which he eschews the trappings of royalty. To the amazement of his servants, when David finds out that the boy has indeed died, he remains calm, washes himself, and returns to his routine. His peculiar behavior elicits this exchange:

> Then his servants said to him, "What is this thing that you have done? You fasted and wept for the child while it was alive; but when the child died, you rose and ate food." He said, "While the child was still alive, I fasted and wept; for I said, 'Who knows? The Lord may be gracious to me, and the child may live.' But now he is dead; why should I fast? Can I bring him back again? I shall go to him, but he will not return to me." (2 Sam. 12:21-23)

David explicitly invokes the minority hermeneutic when he recognizes the possibility that his fasting and weeping might persuade God to relent from the punishment announced by the prophet Nathan. And yet, even the penitence of King David is not enough to forestall this tragedy.

On this basis, one can conclude that at least the Deuteronomistic tradition[30]—where the issue of how to approach prophetic prediction is treated most directly—simultaneously viewed predictive prophecy as conditioned by human response while also accepting that a genuinely pious turn might not preclude a prophetic prediction from coming to pass. Adopting the minority hermeneutic is not equivalent to offering an ethical *carte blanche* that allows one to persist in the belief that events will transpire as they hope, regardless of past behavior. The person who acknowledges the conditionality of prophetic prediction does not believe repentance is some sort of magical spell that prohibits God from acting in an undesired way.[31]

---

30. Regarding the question of how the succession narrative in 1-2 Samuel relates to the Deuteronomistic tradition, see C. A. Strine, *Sworn Enemies: The Divine Oath, the Book of Ezekiel, and the Polemics of Exile*, BZAW 436 (Berlin: Walter de Gruyter, 2013), 134–39.

There is much more to say about how the minority hermeneutic reframes interpretation of the New Testament statements about the Parousia and the coming of the eschaton, not to mention how this approach to prophecy impinges upon theology proper, especially the issue of divine foreknowledge. Rather than offer an all-too-brief (and therefore, ill-fated) statement on those issues here, we take them up in detail in the second part of this volume (chapters 6-8). Chapters 4-5, however, explore how the minority hermeneutic enables a fresh, constructive reading of key passages about the Parousia in the New Testament. The fruits of that exegesis allow us to introduce a theological concept that complements our exegetical approach: partial fulfillment of predictive prophecy. These partial fulfillments—cases in which the blessing or curse predicted does not occur to the full extent suggested in the original prophetic statement—play the role of providing a series of "stepping stones" that support Christian communities and individuals as they traverse the stream of history and move toward its consummation. Prior to proceeding in that endeavor, it is sensible to offer a brief summary of the ground just covered.

## Concluding Summary

This chapter began with the rather mundane observation that critical explanations for the delay of Parousia presume that when Jesus spoke of his return, he believed that future events would occur *as he foretold*, indeed, *only as he foretold*. A priori, this approach defines the veracity and success of prophetic prediction by measuring it against how subsequent events have or have not corresponded to its content. Deuteronomy epitomizes this view, contending that the faithful people of God were given this model in Moses and shall also find it in the prophets like Moses, who follow him (Deut. 18:15-22).

That majority, Deuteronomic, or one might say *Mosaic*, hermeneutic stands in tension with the evidence from across the ancient Near East, throughout the Old Testament, and in subsequent Jewish and Christian

---

31. Cf. Hans Walter Wolff, *Joel and Amos*, Hermeneia, trans. Walter Janzen, Sean D. McBride, and C. A. Muenchow (Philadelphia: Fortress Press, 1977), 49-50.

interpretation that prophetic predictions are conditional and that their occurrence or non-occurrence is contingent upon human responses to the prophet's words. No less prominent a figure than Jeremiah exemplifies this model. The importance of this minority, one might call it *Jeremianic*, hermeneutic is revealed by the crucial role it plays in numerous Old Testament texts, such as Isaiah's call, Jonah's conflict with the Lord, and even the narrative of David's sin with Bathsheba.

No doubt, the view expressed in Jeremiah 18 and applied in Jeremiah 26 is part of an inner-biblical deliberation with the historically accurate "prophet like Moses" described in Deut. 18:15-22. The plurality of early Jewish and Christian statements about prophetic fulfillment reflects the reality of that intra-canonical tension. Still, both communities enshrined the divergent statements in their authoritative scriptures. As historical critics, we recognize this issue, and as theologians, we intend, in due course, to comment on what it means to hold the two together (cf. chapter 5, pp. 103-7).

At this stage, it is vital to emphasize the main point of this chapter: the biblical evidence indicates that in order to understand predictive prophecy, we need to read prophecy with a hermeneutic of *activation*, not one of *prognostication*. Because the eschatological proclamation attributed to Jesus is predictive prophecy, it requires this approach too. The intent of Jesus' public declarations was not simply to provide *foreknowledge* of the future. Rather, by offering a graphic depiction of the blessing or torment likely to follow from present conduct, these messages sharply framed how individual and communal action was *forming* the future. Predictive prophecy is an invitation to affect divine action. Or, as the great Jewish theologian Abraham Heschel (1907-72) phrased it, "This is the mysterious paradox of the Hebrew faith: The All-wise and Almighty may change a word that He proclaims. Man has the power to modify his design. . . . The call of anger is a call to cancel anger."[32]

---

32. Abraham J. Heschel, *The Prophets* (New York: Harper & Row, 1962), 286.

It remains, then, to query how various intervening historical contingencies[33] affect the unfolding of the eschatological proclamation. That is to say, it is necessary to ask how did the New Testament authors think that human actions could influence the occurrence or *non-occurrence* of those events foretold in the Gospels and Epistles. In answering this question, we shall argue a viewpoint that is neither unprecedented nor unduly idiosyncratic: the Gospels and Epistles depict a kingdom that is irreducibly ethical in nature, addressing what it means to live as an individual and in community under the dominion of God. What makes our argument unique among contemporary scholarship is our contention that those ethical instructions are the criteria that qualify the eschatological predictions. Perhaps the extent to which the community that identifies itself with Jesus incarnates those ethical ideals is the criterion upon which God will decide whether to persist in his intent to bring the eschaton, or draw back from that declaration. Indeed, chapters 6–9 argue that our beliefs about God and our actions are intimately interconnected. God has become one of us for us in Jesus; and in the Church, which continues Jesus Christ's work in this age, God cooperates with the people of God to bring about the eschaton. In short, we shall argue in all that follows that eschatology is ethical, and vice versa, for Christians, ethics are intrinsically eschatological.

Prior to that, it is now necessary to apply the understanding of prophecy outlined in this chapter to the New Testament texts relating to the Parousia.

---

33. This phrase, which so succinctly encapsulates the critical interpretive idea, is taken from Pratt, "Historical Contingencies," 183.

# 4

# The Delay of the Parousia: A Traditional and Historical-Critical Reading of Scripture: Part 1

Christopher M. Hays and Richard J. Ounsworth OP

In chapter 2, we grappled with Jeremiah's prophecy about Babylon's seventy years (Jer. 29:10–14), meeting head-on the problem of deferred prophetic fulfillment illustrated in the afterlife of Jeremiah's prophecy. Entitled "Prophecy: A History of Failure?", that chapter adopted a highly critical, even hostile, posture, and offered an uncharitable assessment of Jeremiah's veracity. Indeed, we pointed out that Ezra and Nehemiah contain ample information to demonstrate that everything did not occur as Jeremiah had expected, and we shone a harsh light on the way Daniel radically extended Jeremiah's timeline into a far distant future, an extension which nevertheless did not result in harmony between rhetoric and events. In the same spirit, chapter 2 questioned Paul and the Synoptics. They claimed that in Jesus' ministry and second coming, there would transpire the fulfillment of all that Jeremiah and Daniel (*inter alios*) had foretold. Yet, the second coming receded beyond their grasp.

In chapter 3, we began to take back lost territory. There, we demonstrated that historical critics are frequently premature in pronouncing the failure of Old Testament prophecy because their negative assessments fail to appreciate the conditional character of prophetic speech. With that context now established, it is possible for us to offer a defense of the Christian belief in the Parousia, delay included.

Our argument will unfold across the next two chapters by fusing together two interpretative and theological insights. These arguments are mutually balancing, rather than free-standing; yet, for clarity, we have chosen to elaborate them over the course of two chapters, allowing a metaphorical "deep breath" between steps in our argument.

The first strategy, elaborated here in chapter four, is traditional: we stress the ways in which the Old and New Testaments recognize partial fulfillments of prophecies, even when the progress of history does not yield all that the prophet had proclaimed. These partial fulfillments, we explain, act as redemptive-historical "stepping-stones" that support the hopes of God's people and provoke their penitence throughout history.

The second strategy applies the historical-critical insights regarding the conditional nature of prophecy, articulated in chapter 3, to Jesus' prophecies about the timing of the Parousia. Thus, in chapter 5, our argument is straightforward: because Jesus' statements concerning the consummation of the kingdom of God are prophecies, they must be understood as conditioned by peoples' responses to those prophecies. Not only is there strong historical precedent for this from the ancient world, but we will show that the New Testament also advocates this view of the timing of Jesus' Parousia.

The separation and sequencing of the arguments across chapters 4 and 5 correspond to the division of material in chapters 2 and 3. Whereas it was necessary to outline rigorously the "failures" of the prophetic predictions in the Old and New Testaments prior to reframing the concept of what predictive prophecy is, it is likewise necessary to examine the positive contribution of the traditional approach to adducing partial fulfillments of prophetic proclamations before building upon the crucial, but nevertheless limited, explanatory power of that approach to explaining the delay of the Parousia. The context of partial fulfillments—which sustain hope, exhibit God's mercy, and yet do not resolve the dilemma of prolonged delay—is essential to understanding the innovative interpretive move to read various New Testament passages through the lens of prophetic conditionality.

Through all of this, the theologically astute reader will recognize that our exegesis inherently raises doctrinal questions on the nature of God and God's interaction with the world. Chapters 6 through 8 will demonstrate how historical and systematic theology reinforce and vindicate the exegetical moves made in these chapters. For now, however, we must ask for patience regarding those matters. The perceived problem of the Parousia's delay is, in the first place, biblical, so the epicenter of our solution is exegetical, though we strive never to disregard the equally important radiations from that epicenter that necessitate the discussions of hermeneutics and doctrine in the latter half of this book.

## Partial Fulfillments as Redemptive-Historical Stepping Stones in the Old Testament

As we begin to make something of a defense of the biblical prophecies, let us emphasize that we have not the slightest desire to downplay the ways in which the putative prophetic fulfillments fell short of what the prophets foretold. We quite understand why this disparity between what was prophesied and what transpired has caused many other critical scholars to view these prophecies as some combination of failed and fraudulent. And yet, for all of the common ground we share with other critical scholars in our assessment of the degree to which actual history failed to align with prophetic hopes, we do not share the common negative critical assessment of the veracity of these prophecies.

## Partial Fulfillment is Not Failure

The dominant critical construal of these prophecies as "failures" falters insofar as it focuses excessively on what did not occur as prophesied, while dismissing what did transpire in accordance with what the prophet foretold. People tend to treat prophecy's legitimacy in an all-or-nothing fashion: either the prophet is vindicated by the complete fulfillment of the prophecy, or he is proved false by any degree of non-fulfillment. This binary approach, however, skews the evaluation of a prophecy's truthfulness in favor of the nay-sayer, insofar as it does not countenance the value of partial fulfillments of prophecy.

This all-or-nothing view of prophetic truth, which fails to consider the ways in which prophecies are partially fulfilled, bespeaks the degree to which critical scholars are influenced by a Mosaic understanding of prophecy, which emphasizes only the roles of God and the prophet. If the prophecy does not come true, then they conclude that the prophet must not speak for God. If, however, our view of prophecy is informed also by the Jeremianic construal of prophecy, our evaluation of a prophecy's truthfulness needs to account for more factors, insofar as Jeremiah emphasizes not only the role of God and the prophet, but also the agency of the addressees of the prophecy, in evaluating a prophecy's veracity. Since prophecy can be conditional, its outcome depends in character and degree on the response of the people; a prophecy's fulfillment might well be partial, or indeed, not even transpire, without the prophecy itself being falsified. If the prophet foretells blessing for the people, conditional on their piety, and the people respond with rebellion, the only way in which God's truthfulness in the prophecy can be vindicated is by the non-occurrence of the prophesied blessing. If, however, only some of the people respond with holiness and justice, then the only way in which God's truthfulness in the prophecy can be vindicated is by the partial occurrence of the prophesied blessing. In other words, the Jeremianic account of prophecy, which attends to the role of the prophecy's human addressees more than does the Mosaic account of prophecy, legitimates and requires attention to the partial fulfillment or non-fulfillment of prophecy as evidence of God's truthfulness in that prophecy. Our evaluation of conditional prophecies must take into account varieties and degrees of fulfillment and non-fulfillment if we are to maintain a belief in God's integrity and the role of human agency in history.

Our previously dim verdict on Jeremiah's prophecy of seventy years needs, thus, to be re-examined in this light. So, let us consider that history once more.

### The Partial Fulfillment of Jeremiah's Seventy Years

As we already saw, Jer. 29:10-14 prophesied that God would restore Israel from exile after the seventy years of Babylon's dominion over them was complete. "In the second year of Darius" (Zech. 1:7)—i.e. around 520/519 BCE, sixty-eight years after the invasion of Judah and destruction of the Jerusalem Temple—Zechariah predicted the imminent fulfillment of this prophecy (Zech. 1:7-17). This prediction is repeated and intensified in chapters 7-8 of Zechariah, set two years later. Ezra and the Chronicler fall in line and identify the restoration of Israel with the rebuilding of the Temple (Ezra 1:1-3; cf. 2 Chron. 36:20-23); that work was completed "in the sixth year of the reign of King Darius" (ca. 515 BCE), about 72 years after the exile (Ezra 6:15). Frankly, that initial fulfillment is rather remarkable, especially when one bears in mind that a number such as "seventy years" should certainly be taken as a round figure.

To be sure, the Israelites' homecoming was not easy, nor did it transpire immediately for all the people (Ezra 8:1-20; Neh. 2:1-10), as we noted in chapter 1. And yet, both Ezra and Nehemiah explain that those who returned from exile were still transgressing God's law in a variety of ways. Upon arriving in Jerusalem sixty years after the Temple had been rebuilt, Ezra finds that the Israelites had been intermarrying with foreigners in great numbers (Ezra 9–10), which was a great affront to Ezra's ethno-centric sensitivities. The book ends on a deeply ambivalent note, listing ca. 100 names of those who had married foreign women, but agreed to put them away; this does not include the names of those who refused to divorce their wives and send away their children (10:7-8)! It is not clear from Ezra whether this guilty remnant will escape God's renewed wrath (Ezra 9:10-15).

Nehemiah gives an even less heartening account of the Israelite's response to being delivered from exile. The rebuilding of the walls coincided with a season of famine, during which many Israelites had to borrow money to buy food and to pay taxes; in order to secure those loans, they put up their homes and fields as deposits. Unfortunately, the bad yield of crops meant that they were incapable of repaying their debts, such that they were losing their land and being forced to surrender their children as slaves to the creditors.[1] This was precisely the sort of economic oppression that got the Israelites and Judaeans kicked out of the land decades earlier.[2] Nehemiah 9 is an extended account of the people's confession of sin and expression of resolution to reform themselves. Nonetheless, this confession and resolution seems to have availed for little, since Nehemiah 13 reveals a litany of continuing sins: the people were still intermixed with foreigners (13:1-3); the priest in charge of the Temple chambers had turned one of the sacred rooms into an apartment for a relative (13:4-9); the Israelites had failed to tithe and the Levites had abandoned their ministry because they were being deprived of their provisions (13:10-14); people were working on the Sabbath (13:14-22); and the Jews (even one descendent of the high priest!) were still intermarrying with foreigners (13:23-29). By ending the book with this catena of violations, the author expresses his own grave misgivings about the

---

1. Neh. 5:1–13; H.G.M. Williamson, *Ezra; Nehemiah*, Word Biblical Commentary 16 (Waco: Word, 1985), 237–38.
2. Amos 2:6–8; 8:4–6; Zech. 7:8–11; Isa. 5:8–13.

future fate of Israel. And insofar as it was the transgression of the Law that first brought God's judgment upon the Israelites, it should not be surprising that persistent rebellion would radically slow their restoration from exile.

In short, Ezra and Nehemiah identify the return of exiles from Babylon and Persia, as well as the rebuilding of the Jerusalem Temple and wall, as partial fulfillments of Jeremiah's prophecy, demonstrating God's faithfulness to Israel. Nonetheless, the books detail persistent sin and intransigence amidst the people—transgressions of the sort that might not only slow, but even reverse God's restoration and require their renewed castigation.

Writing some generations later, the author of Daniel 9 confirms the worst fears of Ezra and Nehemiah. Daniel calls out to God for mercy, for an end to exile (Dan. 9:1–19), in spite of the fact that the current generation has followed in the steps of their forefathers in iniquity (Dan. 9:16). But God sends Gabriel to deliver disappointing news to Daniel. Because of the people's unflagging rebellion, even after the experience of divine castigation and exile, God is obliged to extend their time of subjugation. The angel explains that the duration of Jeremiah's seventy-year exile is to be multiplied by a factor of seven; the exile is now fated to persist seventy weeks of years, 490 years (Dan. 9:20–27). This is not, however, simply an arbitrary extension of Israel's punishment. Leviticus 26:14–26 warns the Israelites that, if they do not hearken to the castigations God brings upon them in response to their wickedness, God will multiply his punishment seven-fold. As such, the seven-fold multiplication of the length of the exile was to be expected in response to Israel's persistent disregard of God's Law and warnings through the prophets.

Ezra, Nehemiah, and Daniel all bear witness to the fact that during and after exile, many Israelites continued to rebel against God; alongside the heartening piety of men such as Ezra and Nehemiah and countless anonymous Israelites, there persisted the same sorts of wickedness that got the Israelites exiled in the first place. What was God to do? In faithfulness to the prophecy of Jeremiah and in keeping with the humble and penitent response of part of the nation of Israel, God began to bring them out of Babylon, partially fulfilling his promises to his people. And yet, in faithfulness to his own justice, in keeping with the warnings and stipulations of Leviticus, and in reaction to the unflagging sinfulness of part of the nation of Israel, God was obliged not to complete the restoration from the exile, but to extend the experience of exile for many of the people, until true righteousness and justice were finally restored (Dan. 9:24).

No doubt, the events of history could have been evaluated differently; Ezra, Nehemiah, and Daniel see the salvation-historical glass as "half-full" because of their confidence in God. They contend that Jeremiah's prophecy did not fail, but that it was partially fulfilled. In fact, one might say that the very partiality of that fulfillment was, in fact, the only way in which Jeremiah could be vindicated as a true prophet, insofar as a complete fulfillment of a conditional prophecy to which the people responded with incomplete obedience would itself belie God's self-revelation and warnings. In the light of Israel's partial repentance and partial intransigence, partial fulfillment of Jeremiah's conditional prophecy is the only way that the prophecy could be proven true.

### Stepping Stones: The Positive Roles of Partial Fulfillments

Still, we should not be so preoccupied with providing a rear-guard for the prophets, explaining why their prophecies were *only partially* fulfilled, that we lose sight of the fact that they *were* partially *fulfilled*. Zechariah, the Chronicler (2 Chron. 36:22–23), Ezra, and Nehemiah were not deceptive in how they appropriated the seventy-year prophecy for their own time, but rather, perceived partial fulfillments of that prediction. The Israelites did return to the land from exile, they did rebuild the Temple and the wall; they did experience divine provision for their needs and preservation from their enemies. Ezra, Nehemiah, and the Chronicler celebrate these fulfillments of prophecy, however partial, because they undergird the hope of the people of God that the rest of the prophecy would also come to pass.

These claims about fulfillment are not incompatible with a contention that Daniel too offers a legitimate interpretation of the same prophecy: Daniel agrees with Ezra and Nehemiah in seeing the continued plight of Israel as the result of her own sinfulness.[3] While Daniel postpones the further fulfillment of the earlier prophecies, he also expresses intensified expectation for what that fulfillment might entail (Dan. 7:24: "everlasting righteousness"!). These biblical texts can be read as complementary rather than conflicting. The Old Testament canon narrates the Israelite return from exile as an initial and partial fulfillment of a prophetic promise, which demonstrates the authenticity of Jeremiah's prophecy as well as God's faithfulness to his promises. Still, the Old Testament books also point forward to a greater and more profound fulfillment of prophecy, re-animating the commitment of the people of God.

Prophetic fulfillment, whether partial or complete, corroborates the warnings and exhortations of the Law and the Prophets, vindicates the power and integrity of the God for whom they speak, and enlivens future hope that God will bring to pass all that he has purposed and promised. Partial prophetic fulfillment supports the exiled and oppressed people of God, helping them press forward in righteousness and hope as they look forward to the ultimate restoration of the kingdom to Israel.[4]

For these reasons, it might be helpful to think of partial fulfillments of prophecy as "stepping stones" across a broad and churning river, small isles of security and solidity amidst turbulence. The image is apt insofar as it combines the roles of prophecy in: 1) sustaining present hope and 2) enabling God's people to move forward. In the former sense, stepping stones keep one aloft amidst the flow of the current; in the here and now, the knowledge that God has long made good on

---

3. Similarly, Zechariah underscores that God exiled the Israelites because of their injustice in disregard of the Law and the prophets (Zech. 7:9–14); likewise, immediately after promising that God will restore the Israelites, Zechariah warns them not to slip back into injustice (Zech. 8:14–17).

4. Of course, to those who do not share the prophets' paradigm, this will simply look like special pleading. Any time a worldview (be it Marxist, Muslim, or Modernist) has to deal with apparently countervailing evidence, it will appear to engage in just such an act of special pleading. The question is whether or not the countervailing evidence seems sufficient to overwhelm the explanatory power of the worldview.

the promises and prophecies help sustain the faith of his people. In the latter sense, stepping stones enable one to traverse the water's expanse, to make progress through history in a way that pleases God and is faithful to his purposes, sometimes treading gingerly, sometimes hopping and slipping, and sometimes leaping from one moment of justice and righteousness to the next, until we finally reach the firmness, safety, and breadth of the distant shore.[5]

This stepping-stones image is thoroughly consonant with biblical statements on eschatology, especially in the Old Testament prophetic books. In his book *Oracles of God*, John Barton has pointed out that, in addition to being used to speak of *imminent* expectations about the end or goal of history, the idea of "eschatology" has a different, broader sense. This aspect of Old Testament eschatology emphasizes that

> history ... has an end goal which will one day arrive, and the path towards which passes through various distinct phases or epochs. In this sense "eschatological" interpretations of history can be distinguished from cyclical interpretations, as well as from those which refuse to see any pattern, consistency, or direction in the historical process....[6]

Our proposal asserts that the patterns the biblical authors discern are shaped by the final eschatological end of history for which they long; this image of the "end" is stamped, more or less firmly, more or less obviously, into the particularities of history, and one's ability to observe these repeating patterns sustains the belief that the partial fulfillments of earlier predictions will act as "stepping stones" for the people of God making their way toward that final end. We will discuss the role of patterns and types in salvation history further in chapter 9 (pp. 212, 227–35).

## Stepping Stones and the New Testament

The Jewish people of God were sustained and borne along by the partial fulfillments of God's prophetic words to Jeremiah and Daniel, by those

---

5. See further ch. 6, p. 131 and ch. 9, pp. 223–27.
6. John Barton, *Oracles of God: Perceptions of Ancient Prophecy in Israel after the Exile* (London: Darton, Longman and Todd, 1986), 218.

stepping stones, through successive imperial transitions. Finally, during the reign of the Roman emperor Tiberius (Luke 3:1), another prophet arose and proclaimed that the restoration of the kingdom to Israel, the fulfillment of the prophecies, was indeed at hand. Like all the prophets before him, John the Baptist urged the Jews toward repentance and righteousness in preparation for the coming of the Messiah, lest they once again incur judgment at God's hand, rather than the promised blessing (Mark 1:1-8; Matt. 3:1-12; Luke 3:3-14).

In some ways, John the Baptist is much like Zechariah, standing at the cusp of the long-awaited fulfillment. Similarly, the authors of the Synoptic Gospels are rather akin to the editor of Ezra and Nehemiah, identifying the significant fulfillment of prophecy, and deferring further consummation to the future. While the Synoptic authors are certain of the ultimate consummation of things, they also are like Ezra-Nehemiah in expressing the way that God's people, in their stubborn rebellion, might still cast a spanner in the redemptive-historical works, deferring the end yet further.

It is increasingly (though not universally) recognized by Jesus scholars of various stripes that Jesus believed that in his ministry, God was beginning to bring about the kingdom,[7] and that the completion of all that had been promised was imminently to be accomplished through Jesus' own person. In his teachings and deeds, Jesus and the Synoptic authors perceived the fulfillment of eschatological and Messianic prophecies (Mark 1:14-15; Luke 4:16-21; 7:20-23). Even in the preaching and miracles of a man who remained at best a regional celebrity in his own life, the end had begun, the Gospels proclaim. And yet, notwithstanding dissonance with contemporary expectations, Jesus and the Synoptic authors also emphasize repeatedly that the ultimate consummation, the restoration of the Kingdom of Israel, the judgment of the wicked, and the vindication of God and his righteous

---

7. Gerd Theissen and Annette Merz, *The Historical Jesus: A Comprehensive Guide*, trans. John Bowden (London: SCM, 1998), 256-61; George Eldon Ladd, *The Presence of the Future: The Eschatology of Biblical Realism* (London: SPCK, 1974), 110-14; N.T. Wright, *Jesus and the Victory of God*, Christian Origins and the Question of God 2 (London: SPCK, 1996), 226-43; James D.G. Dunn, *Jesus Remembered*, Christianity in the Making 1 (Grand Rapids: Eerdmans, 2003), 426-65.

people, remains to come, though it be soon.[8] So, the parables of Jesus liken the kingdom of God to a mustard seed, leaven in a lump of dough, seeds sown among differing soils, wheat among tares. Like a tiny seed that would become a great plant, the small beginnings of the kingdom did not belie its cosmic claims (Matt. 13:31-32//Mark 4:30-32//Luke 13:18-19). Like a pinch of yeast buried in dough, though the tiny kingdom might appear to have been swallowed up, yet it would rise again and spread throughout all things (Matt. 13:33//Luke 13:20-21). Like seeds falling on different soils, the kingdom would arouse differing responses in different souls (Matt. 13:1-9, 18-23//Mark 4:1-9, 13-20//Luke 8:4-8, 11-15). And like wheat growing up among weeds, the members of God's kingdom would, for a time, coexist with the members of Satan's, until a day on which all would be reaped (Matt. 13:24). In other words, Jesus claimed that the prophecies had been fulfilled, but only partially; nonetheless, the evangelists invoked those partial fulfillments in order to galvanize repentance and righteousness in expectation of the final end (Matt. 4:13-17; Luke 24:44-48; Acts 2:16-38). In that sense, the partial fulfillments of prophecy in Jesus' life and ministry, his first coming, become stepping stones, holding God's people aloft as they stride forward toward his second coming.

We could enumerate any number of places in which this dynamic is operative in the ensuing sections of this chapter. For the sake of brevity, however, we will mention only a few of the texts in which events in the earliest days of the Jesus-movement were adduced as stepping stones to the second coming, as partial fulfillments of what was prophesied, in order to support the message of Jesus and undergird the progress of God's people in history.

## Aside: Against Synchronizing Chronologies

Before this next step, however, allow us a brief comment on prophetic chronologies. It is worth noting that the New Testament authors do not

---

8. George Eldon Ladd, *A Theology of the New Testament*, rev. ed. (Grand Rapids: Eerdmans, 1993), 114-21; Theissen and Merz, *Historical Jesus*, 253-56; Dale C. Allison, *Jesus of Nazareth: Millenarian Prophet* (Minneapolis: Augsburg Fortress Press, 1998), 129-51; Allison, *Constructing Jesus: Memory, Imagination, and History* (London: SPCK, 2010), 31-55, 190-204; Dunn, *Jesus Remembered*, 406-36.

show interest in aligning the coming of Christ with Daniel's seventy weeks—making them curiously exceptional to the first-century rule. As we mentioned in chapter 2 (pp. 29–30), modern critical scholars often identify the beginning of the seventy weeks with the beginning of Jeremiah's seventy years, thus placing the seventieth week sometime in the near future for those living under the reign of Antiochus Epiphanes. The Essenes, by contrast, dated the seventy weeks from the return from exile, and, because their dates differ from those of modern scholars, anticipated the end of the seventy weeks to occur between 3 BCE and 2 CE. Pharisaic computations pushed the date even later, depending on their own political leanings; thus, they suggested dates ranging from 68–70 CE (the First Jewish-Roman War), to ca. 117 CE (the Alexandrian Revolt), or ca. 131–38 CE (in the ballpark of the Bar Kochba Rebellion). Third-century Christians also got in on the action, trying to line up the conclusion of the sixty-ninth/seventieth weeks with either Jesus' birth or the fall of Jerusalem—and later generations of Christians have added their two cents.[9]

For many Christians, it is a source of comfort that one can, with a bit of jiggery-pokery, line up the conclusion of Daniel's seventy weeks with the events of the incarnation and apostolic era (especially if one favors a loose reckoning of the numerology). But the New Testament authors do not seem to have been taken with this speculation on Daniel 9, and neither are the present authors. The better part of the past chapter emphasized the ethical contingency of prophetic fulfillment, such that even a critical dating of the completion of the seventy weeks to the reign of Antiochus Epiphanes should not be conceptually difficult to surmount.

Moreover, Christians operate from the decisive assumption that Jesus' life and death mark the inauguration of the kingdom of God. Given that assumption, debating the alignment of Jesus' advent with Daniel's seventy weeks seems akin to asking on D-Day whether the

---

9. This sketch of various Jewish and Christian chronological computations derives from the far more detailed and rigorous treatment of Roger T. Beckwith, *Calendar and Chronology, Jewish and Christian: Biblical, Intertestamental and Patristic Studies*, Arbeiten zur Geschichte des antiken Judentums und des Urchristentums 33 (Leiden: Brill, 1996), 260–75.

Allied forces had deposited their declaration of war with The Hague in accordance with the statutes laid out in the 1907 "Convention Relative to the Opening of Hostilities": all the Allies cared about was that the tide of the war had finally and decisively turned in their favor. The fact that the New Testament writers do not bother much with Daniel's seventy years seems to indicate that they were of a similar mind, and as a result, the present authors are not much vexed about Danielic calculations either.

### Synoptic Stepping Stones to the "Coming of the Son of Man"

In the first chapter of this volume (pp. 15–18), we argued that the "coming of the Son of Man" in the Olivet Discourse (and parallels) does indeed refer to the eschatological return of Jesus in judgment. Without wanting, in any way, to deny the yet-future referent of that prophecy, we should note that the Gospel authors made a variety of efforts to adduce at least initial, partial fulfillments to this coming. These fulfillments are a "foretaste" of the coming consummation of the eschaton. For example, all the Synoptic Gospels place the promise that "there are some standing here who will not taste death before they see the Son of Man coming in his kingdom" (Matt. 16:28; cf. Mark 9:1//Luke 9:27) directly before the story of Jesus' transfiguration (Matt. 17:1–13; Mark 9:2–13; Luke 9:28–36). Of course, on that mountain, Jesus does not judge all of humanity as he will do in the eschaton, but he does appear as a radiant heavenly being, "in the glory of his Father" (Matt. 16:27), corroborating his claim that he can and will come again in that glory and mete out the promised rewards and castigation according to people's deserts. So, the transfiguration provides an initial and partial fulfillment of Jesus' promise, a foretaste of the kingdom, one that offers the disciples a stepping stone leading toward the prophecy's ultimate fulfillment in the Parousia.

Let us take another example, this time in keeping with N.T. Wright's understanding of the "coming of the Son of Man" statements. Wright's now-famous association of the coming of the Son of Man with Jesus' resurrection and ascension is based on a contextually sensitive reading of Dan. 7:13.[10] The reference to Dan. 7:13 is clearest in the Markan and Matthean versions of Jesus' trial before the High Priest, when Jesus asserts, "From now on you will see the Son of Man seated at the right hand of Power, and coming with the clouds of heaven" (Matt. 26:64, cf. Mark 14:61-62). Within the context of Matthew (in contrast to the Markan parallel; cf. ch. 1, p. 11n38), with its temporal qualifier "from now on (ἀπ' ἄρτι)," the vindication to which Jesus refers is mostly likely his resurrection and ascension.[11] In other words, Matthew may well have been looking for the fullness of the Son of Man's coming in Jesus' eschatological return, but he does seem to consider Jesus' resurrection to be a stepping stone toward that consummation.

### Stepping Stones to the Joel's "Day of the Lord"

When we compare the Synoptic Gospels, we are afforded glimpses into the way that later Gospel authors built on and worked with the insights of their sources in unpacking how the prophesied "coming of the Son of Man" came to partial fulfillment in the early days of the Jesus movement. For example, beginning with the earliest canonical Gospel, the reference to the coming of the Son of Man in Mark 13 (vv. 24-27) includes an allusion to Joel 2:10 (as well as to Isa. 13:10, 34:4; Joel 4:15-16) and its enumeration of the cosmic disturbances which will accompany the "Day of the Lord"; we have already argued that Mark 13 refers the fulfillment of Joel 2 to the Parousia of Jesus (which Mark did not anticipate would be distinct from the destruction of Jerusalem; see chapter 1, p. 13 and chapter 5, p. 81n6).[12]

What is interesting, though, is that the Third Gospel's parallel to the Olivet Discourse (Luke 21:25-26) actually mutes the similarities to Joel 2:10; nonetheless, Luke refers explicitly to the text of Joel 2:28-32 in Acts 2:17-21, when Peter preaches on the day of Pentecost. In Joel

---

10. See chapter 1, p. 9; Wright, *Jesus and the Victory of God*, 360-65, 524-28.
11. R. T. France, *The Gospel of Matthew*, New International Commentary on the New Testament (Grand Rapids: Eerdmans, 2007), 1027-28; Donald A. Hagner, *Matthew 14-28*, Word Biblical Commentary 33B (Dallas: Word, 1998), 800; cf. Wright, *Jesus and the Victory of God*, 360-65, 642-43.
12. On partial fulfillment in Mark 13, see especially the excellent comments of Anthony C. Thiselton, *The Last Things: A New Approach* (London: SPCK, 2012), 101-2.

2:28–32, alongside descriptions of eschatological cosmic disturbances, the prophet avers that the Spirit of the Lord will be poured out on all flesh in the last days. In Acts, Peter explains the glossalalic happenings of the day of Pentecost with reference to Joel 2:28–32, notwithstanding the fact that the apparent pneumatological phenomena of that day were not accompanied by any celestial irregularities. By this token, it seems that Luke, writing a couple of decades after Mark, is offering Pentecost as a stepping-stone to the Parousia.[13] The partial fulfillment of Joel's prophecy is taken as proof that the rest of the foretold judgment was also at hand, such that Peter can, on the basis of the flurry of tongues in the Christian community, summon his Jewish audience to repentance in order to avert God's judgment (Acts 2:37–40).

### Stepping Stones and the Three Comings of Christ in John 14

The Fourth Gospel does the most to integrate hopes of Jesus' final coming with the partial fulfillments of that promised return. In John's fourteenth chapter, Jesus speaks of his coming in three different ways.[14] At the beginning and end of that chapter, Jesus promises that after his departure from the world, "I will come again and will take you to myself, so that where I am, there you may be also" (John 14:3; cf. 14:28). This is a simple enough reference to the Parousia (cf. John 21:22–23).[15]

In the middle of the dialogue, however, Jesus promises "I will not leave you orphaned; I am coming to you. In a little while the world will no longer see me, but you will see me; because I live, you also

---

13. Likewise, Luke 9:27 softens Mark 9:1 ("There are some standing here who will not taste death until they see the kingdom of God after it has come with power"), by eliminating the phrase "after it has come with power." This elimination creates more space for Luke's inaugurated but non-consummate construal of eschatology.
14. We would like to thank Prof. Edward Adams for pointing out the relevance of this text to our thesis.
15. Andreas J. Köstenberger, *John*, Baker Exegetical Commentary on the New Testament (Grand Rapids: Baker Academic, 2004), 427; J. Ramsey Michaels, *The Gospel of John*, New International Commentary on the New Testament (Grand Rapids: Eerdmans, 2010), 771–72; Raymond E. Brown, *The Gospel According to John: Introduction, Translation, and Notes*, Anchor Bible 29B (London: G. Chapman, 1971), 628; D.A. Carson, *The Gospel According to John*, The Pillar New Testament Commentary (Leicester: Intervarsity, 1991), 489.

will live. On that day you will know that I am in my Father, and you in me, and I in you." (John 14:18-20). Here, Jesus presages his *post-resurrection appearances* to the disciples, when he would "come" to the disciples and be "seen" by them, even though remaining unknown to the world (cf. Acts 10:40-41).[16] At the end of the Gospel, John continues to characterize the resurrection appearances as occasions on which Jesus "came" to the disciples again (John 20:19, 26).[17]

In the next paragraph of John 14, the Evangelist adds another layer to the comings of Christ, clarifying a third and more abiding way in which Jesus would be present with his followers:

> Those who love me will keep my word, and my Father will love them, and we will come to them and make our home with them. Whoever does not love me does not keep my words; and the word that you hear is not mine, but is from the Father who sent me. I have said these things to you while I am still with you. But the Advocate, the Holy Spirit, whom the Father will send in my name, will teach you everything, and remind you of all that I have said to you. (John 14:23-26)

So, the third time Jesus speaks of his coming, Jesus explains that both he and the Father will be coming and abiding with them in the person of the Holy Spirit. In this proto-Trinitarian sense, John explains that Jesus is already with us.

Thus, in one chapter, John speaks of the future coming of Jesus in three senses: the Parousia, the resurrection, and the descent of the Holy Spirit. The sum total of this discourse is to promise the disciples that, after he has ascended to the Father, Jesus will come again to gather the disciples to him. In the meantime, however, the disciples will enjoy a preview, a foretaste, of his coming, as they know him to

---

16. Carson, *John*, 501-2; Michaels, *John*, 786.
17. Some commentators have argued that John 14:18-20 also refers to the coming of the Holy Spirit, as do verses 16-17, 23-27; Köstenberger, *John*, 439; Brown, *John*, 644-47. This is a plausible reading as well, although Carson has argued that the specific references to "that day" (v. 20) and "seeing" make more sense in relation to the resurrection appearances, because of which the disciples know that Jesus was vindicated and that they too will live in the resurrection (Carson, *John*, 501-2). It is logical for a comment on Jesus' resurrection and ascension to occur at this point in the discourse, since it is his departure from the world that is prerequisite for the coming of the Spirit (v. 16). Still, even if one favors Köstenberger and Brown's interpretation, the fact that Jesus' resurrection appearances are also described to as "coming" means that the three-fold sense of the coming of Christ remains present in John's Gospel as a whole, if not specifically in chapter 14.

be resurrected and as he and the Father come to them in the Holy Spirit. This latter sense of coming is, thus, a partial fulfillment of the prophesied and promised coming, and yet, as a partial fulfillment, the coming in the Holy Spirit enables the disciples to obey Christ's commandments, to abide with him, and ultimately, to proceed along the way to the Father until Christ comes finally and fully (John 14:6, 21, 24).

## Summary

The Four Gospels and Acts all speak of the arrival of the promised kingdom of God in two senses: present and future. Even as they look forward to the future coming of Christ, in Jesus' transfiguration, resurrection, and ascension, and in the sending of the Spirit, the New Testament authors perceive a partial fulfillment of the final prophesied end. Those partial fulfillments represent progress toward the ultimate end and serve as hope-sustaining stepping stones to bear God's people forward. Thus, the New Testament authors preserve their future hope in very similar ways to the Old Testament writers.

Allow us to make a concluding caveat about this notion of "stepping stones". We are keen to distinguish this idea of stepping stones from the futurist eschatology of American dispensationalism, which takes great delight in the production of timelines and colorful wall-charts laying out a detailed future sequence for world religio-political events. When we speak of stepping stones, we do not imply belief in a fixed progression of events set to unfold as soon as the divine hourglass is flipped. Rather, the sorts of events that we see as expressing and sustaining Christian hope and the emergence of the kingdom of God are those articulated in the moral teachings of the Gospels ("Behold, the Kingdom of God is among you"; Luke 17:21) and the liturgical and missional life of the Church; we will discuss this further in chapters 8 (pp. 197–205) and 9 (pp. 239–40). Our estimation of the eschatological future is one in which divine action cooperates much more dynamically with human agency than is countenanced by the nigh-deterministic prognostications of popular writers such as Tim LaHaye and Jerry Jenkins. Indeed, as the ensuing chapter will show, New Testament authors affirmed a similar cooperative contingency in their understandings of the dynamics of the eschatological denouement.

# 5

# The Delay of the Parousia: A Traditional and Historical-Critical Reading of Scripture: Part 2

## Christopher M. Hays

As is no doubt obvious to many readers, when we spoke about stepping stones in the previous chapter, we essentially said what the Church always has about the way that the kingdom of God has broken into the present age. Whether one uses the language of "already and not yet" or "inaugurated eschatology" or the "presence of the Kingdom," it is nothing new to contend that the kingdom has arrived in partial ways that point and bear us onward toward the consummation of all things. Insofar as the present authors are not much taken with faddish iconoclasm, this precedence strikes us as a good thing.

## The Limits of Traditional Approaches

Nonetheless, we recognize that this notion of stepping stones does not deal sufficiently with some truly tricky passages of the Gospel, those which seem to put a clock on the second coming. But we are not trying to give the reader the slip. Indeed, while the stepping-stones strategy has canonical and church-historical precedent, we still do not think it accounts for all of the textual data pertaining to the eschatological consummation.

Furthermore, we do not want to deny the textual evidence that Christians have traditionally adduced to counter critical charges about the delay of the Parousia. Jesus did seem to have anticipated that the space between his initial ministry and the final consummation would feel disconcertingly long, that it would feel like a delay.[1] Jesus also took pains to prevent people from trying to calculate the timing of his return; he makes it clear that nobody, not even he himself, knows the precise day or moment in which he will come again in glory.[2] The specific prognosticatory forecasting of Harold Camping and his ilk was excluded from the beginning. Instead, we encounter a myriad of injunctions toward watchfulness and readiness predicated precisely on the uncertainty of the timing of Jesus' return.[3] All these Gospel themes need to be duly countenanced by those addressing the delay of the Parousia.

But how much wiggle-room does this really give the New Testament interpreter? The Olivet Discourse, and its parallels, may well allow for some room between, as it were, the budding of the fig tree and the onset of summer—that is, between the Fall of Jerusalem and the consummation of all things—but two thousand years? Surely that is beyond the pale of the metaphor. After all, Jesus promised to complete this epoch of cosmic history before all of his disciples succumbed to

---

[1]. Luke 12:38; Matt. 24:48//Luke 12:45; Matt. 25:5; one might well ascribe some of these texts and comments to the Evangelists rather than to Jesus (cf. Luke 19:11; John 2:19–22), but it seems more likely to the present authors that the Evangelists drew out Jesus' comments on delay than that they made them up out of whole cloth.
[2]. Matt. 24:36//Mark 13:32; Matt. 25:13; Luke 12:46; so also in 1 Thess. 5:1–2; Acts 1:7.
[3]. See e.g. Mark 13:33–35; Luke 12:35–40//Matt. 24:32–34; Luke 21:34–36; Matt. 25:1–13.

death;[4] he *delimited* the timing of the consummation of the eschaton. Jesus may not have fixed a precise date for the second coming, but he did set outer limits on the timing of his return! And history sauntered past those chronological boundaries a long, long time ago.

To be quite frank, the Synoptic Evangelists do not provide an answer to this problem . . . but in their day, they did not need to do so. After all, when they wrote there were still people alive who had sat at Jesus' feet, who were among the generation that supposedly would not expire before Jesus' return.[5] So, the non-return of Christ was not yet a problem they needed to solve. In fact, it stands to reason that the Synoptic authors would have written with renewed confidence in the return of Jesus. After all, Jesus had indicated that the Fall of Jerusalem would presage his arrival; Mark's Olivet discourse (which the present authors think *predates* the city's overthrow in 70 CE) could be thought to imply that Jerusalem's sack and Jesus' return would occur in reasonably quick succession. Matthew and Luke do a bit of editorial work to allow for slightly more space between Jerusalem's fall and the coming of the Son of Man,[6] and yet, they still seem rather sanguine that the end is not far off. But again, as long as there remained survivors from the first generation of disciples, the problem of the delay of the Parousia had not reached critical mass. After all, they had clear dominical pronouncements that Jesus would return before the first generation died out.

---

4. Mark 9:1//Luke 9:27//Matt. 16:28. Similarly, Matt. 10:23; and Mark 13:30//Luke 21:32//Matt. 24:34. See argumentation in ch. 1, pp. 15–18.
5. Among the last surviving members of the first generation of Jesus' disciples were John the Elder and one Aristion. Papias seems to have met Aristion and John the Elder while they were still alive (Eusebius, Hist. eccl. 3.39.4; notice the use of the present tense λέγουσιν), perhaps ca. 90 CE; for detailed argumentation, see Richard Bauckham, *Jesus and the Eyewitnesses: The Gospels as Eyewitness Testimony* (Grand Rapids: Eerdmans, 2006), 15–21. For further comments on the last generation to remember the eyewitnesses of the apostles, see Markus Bockmuehl, *Seeing the Word: Refocusing New Testament Study*, Studies in Theological Interpretation (Grand Rapids: Baker Academic, 2006), 180–87; ibid., *The Remembered Peter: In Ancient Reception and Modern Debate*, Wissenschaftliche Untersuchungen zum Neuen Testament 262 (Tübingen: Mohr Siebeck, 2010), 22–29.
6. Consider the Synoptic parallels to the Olivet discourse. Whereas Mark 13:24 reads "But *in those days*, after that suffering, the sun will be darkened...", Matt. 24:29 drops the comment "in those days" and clarifies "*Immediately after* the suffering of those days the sun will be darkened . . . ." Luke (assuming the Farrer-Goulder-Goodacre hypothesis) then softens the chronological link even more; he eliminates the phrase "after the suffering of those days" and vaguely says "and there will be signs in the sun and moon . . . ." See also ch. 4, pp. 72–74.

By 90 or 95 CE, however, the Christian hope seemed more misplaced; that first generation could not have survived much longer.[7] So, the question arose, "What about those 'clear dominical pronouncements'? What about the promise that Jesus would return before the first generation died?" The questions are even more pointed after a now 1,900-year lapse. However unspecific Jesus was about days, hours, and minutes, he did broadly (i.e. generationally) delimit the time of his return in glory, to consummate the kingdom and judge the world. But that eschatological consummation is now way overdue. We are way past appealing to fuzzy scheduling. It's time to grasp the nettle: how do we explain the fact that Jesus did not return in glory within the timeframe he prophesied?

The answer is simple: *it was a prophecy. And prophecies are conditional.*

## The Delay of the Parousia as a Consequence of Conditional Prophecy

The problem that we have with Jesus' "failure" to return in the first century is that we have failed to understand the genre of the prophetic utterance. As explained in chapter 4, prophecy was not simple foretelling; although prognostication is part of the work of the prophet (as we saw in the "Mosaic" definition of prophecy), prophecy is about a good deal more than prognostication. The goal of prophecy is to address God's people about the state of their lives and worship, to encourage or to rebuke them by (inter alia) telling them what blessings await fidelity and what punishments await infidelity. But what actually does occur in the future is more often than not dependent upon the response of the people to the prophet; God is quite within his rights to renege on what the prophet foretold, depending on how the people responded. Since Jesus was a prophet (and we believe a great deal more than that as well!), we should not overlook the conditionality native to his prophetic utterances.

---

7. Cf. Richard Bauckham, *2 Peter, Jude*, Word Biblical Commentary 50 (Dallas: Word, 1998), 158.

## Jesus and the Ethical Contingency of the Eschaton

Our explanation, then, of Mark 9:1//Matt. 16:28//Luke 9:27 (and other texts like them) does not consist of redefining what it means to "taste death" or to see the "Kingdom come." We will not be reconstruing the significance of "generation" (Mark 13:30//Luke 21:32//Matt. 24:34) or what is entailed by the "coming of the Son of Man." Instead, we are reframing what it means for Jesus to "prophesy," on the basis of how prophecy works throughout much of Scripture and the ancient world.

Jesus' prophecy about the time of the end was not "wrong" because the veracity of his prophecy did not depend simply upon whether or not the end came. His prophecy about the timing of the end assumed that the people would respond rightly to his instructions about how to act in light of God's impending judgment. After all, Jesus' prophecies regarding the time of the end are all followed by imperatives to the disciples, demanding that they proclaim the good news to all the nations (Mark 13:10//Matt. 24:14); bear witness to Jesus fearlessly under trial (Mark 8:38//Matt. 10:32-33; Mark 13:11//Luke 12:14-15//Matt. 10:19-20); be ethically and existentially awake and alert (Mark 13:33-37//Matt. 24:42-45; Matt. 25:1-13). Insofar as people did not respond properly (as evidenced by the myriad of ethical rebukes contained in the New Testament epistles and the letters to the seven churches in Revelation 2-3), one might aver that it is not only understandable, but necessary that the end not occur within the prophesied time-frame.

At this point, the reader may well object that our explanation, though consonant with how prophecy works elsewhere in Scripture, is simply not derived from the Synoptic Gospels themselves. The Evangelists do not explicitly state that the prophecies in question were conditional. Even if we can understand why, at the time of their writing, they did not yet need to "hedge their bets," do the Gospels back up our hypothesis? While we have already seen that not all prophecies state their conditionality upfront (indeed, doing so would undermine the force of the prophecy), might we be accused of offering a plausible "out" which is nonetheless bereft of Scriptural confirmation? Are we just making a "guess" without any explicit biblical corroboration?

We don't think so. Jesus himself gives indications that the timing of his coming is not only hidden, but even somewhat flexible. In the Lord's Prayer, for example, the disciples are enjoined to pray, "May your kingdom come (ἐλθέτω) and may your will (γενηθήτω) be done on earth as it is in heaven" (Matt. 6:10; cf. Luke 11:2). But Jesus had already made quite clear that he was bringing about the kingdom . . . so how should we understand the intention of these imperative verbs? Insofar as God had long since purposed to bring about the kingdom and to instantiate the perfect observance of his will on earth just as in heaven, it seems that these imperatives reflect the variability of the timing in which God's kingdom and will would be consummated on earth. When Jesus' disciples prayed the Lord's Prayer (and likewise, when Paul and his churches cried out "Maranatha [Our Lord, come!]"; 1 Cor. 16:21; cf. Rev. 22:20), they may well have been asking that the kingdom come sooner than it might otherwise do.

Some of the Church fathers seemed to interpret the Lord's Prayer in precisely this way. For example, Cyprian of Carthage inquires,

> Why, then, do we pray and ask that the kingdom of heaven may come, if the captivity of earth delights us? Why with frequently repeated prayers do we entreat and beg that the day of His kingdom may hasten (*ut acceleret dies regni*; cf. 2 Pet. 3:12), if our greater desires and stronger wishes are to obey the devil here, rather than to reign with Christ? (Cyprian, *Mort.* 18; ANF 5:473; PL 4.595)

By alluding to 2 Peter 3 in parallel to the Lord's Prayer, Cyprian explains that the petition for the coming of the kingdom is a request that the Lord may return sooner than he otherwise would have done. One encounters the same perspective in Tertullian. In his treatise *On the Lord's Prayer*, the Father of Latin Christianity connects the second and third petitions of the *Paternoster* ("Your Kingdom come, your will be done"; Matt. 6:10) with the cries of the martyrs ("How long, O

Lord...!") beneath the altar in Revelation 6:10 (Tertullian, *Or.* 5; *ANF* 3:683; PL 1.1261-62; cf. chapter 3, pp. 53-54).

In the same vein, when Jesus tells his disciples that "this gospel of the kingdom will be proclaimed throughout the whole world as a testimony to all nations, and then the end will come" (Matt. 24:14; cf. Mark 13:1), he reveals that the timing of the consummation of the kingdom depends on human actions and obedience.[8] In Protestant evangelical circles, this passage is read within a framework that assumes that the timing of the end is fixed, but the text itself suggests no such a thing. Consider likewise Jesus' exhortation in the Olivet discourse, "Pray that your flight [from Jerusalem] may not be in winter or on a Sabbath" (Mark 13:18; cf. Matt. 24:20). Insofar as the Olivet Discourse in Mark seems to link the flight from Jerusalem with the events immediately preceding the Coming of the Son of Man (cf. above, p. 81n6), this exhortation to pray regarding the timing of the flight reveals an assumption that the dates of the last things are not fixed.

Furthermore, we would argue that Jesus conceived of his ministry in at least partially Jeremianic terms (cf. chapter 3, p. 52), in which case, one ought to take seriously the possibility that Jesus also would have understood the fulfillment of his prophecies to be conditional in the Jeremianic sense. After all, Jesus' denunciation of the Temple establishment is paralleled by—and indeed, modeled on—Jeremiah's Temple sermons (Jer. 7:1-15; 26:12-15). Moreover, when cleansing the Temple Jesus explicitly cites the *first* of Jeremiah's Temple sermons (Jer. 7:11 in Matt. 21:13//Mark 11:17//Luke 19:46). So also, in Matthew, Jesus' invectives against the scribes and Pharisees are conjoined with a lament over Jerusalem, the common element between the denunciations being that all parties are indicted for killing the prophets sent to them (Matt. 23:34-39; cf. Luke 11:49-51; 19:41-44). This passage is significant insofar as Matthew's phraseology evokes the *second* of Jeremiah's Temple sermons (Jer. 26:12-15, as well as Jer.

---

8. Thus, Luke 13:6-9 indicates that God had already restrained his wrath upon Israel once in order for her to come to repentance and bear fruit.

22:5), in which Jeremiah is about to be put to death by the Temple leaders and warns them that they "will be bringing innocent blood upon yourselves and upon this city" (Jer. 26:15).[9] Even more intriguing is the fact that precisely that same paragraph (Jer. 26:12-15) delineates the explicitly conditional nature of Jeremiah's prophecy of the Temple's destruction: "Now therefore amend your ways and your doings, and obey the voice of the Lord your God, and the Lord will change his mind about the disaster that he has pronounced against you" (Jer. 26:13). Insofar as Matthew modeled Jesus' prophetic denunciation of the Temple establishment on the ministry and sermons of Jeremiah, and in light of the fact that the second of Jeremiah's Temple sermons hangs upon the conditional nature of Jeremiah's prophecy, it seems likely that Matthew (and perhaps, even Jesus himself) would have apprehended the contingency of prophetic foretelling. And if that be the case, then there would be little reason to think that Matthew or Jesus would deny that Jesus' own prophecies possessed a similarly contingent character.

In addition to Jesus' own implications about the variable timing of his Parousia, other New Testament texts explicitly affirm that the timing of the consummation of the eschaton could be (and was) delayed as a consequence of human action. The return of Christ and the final judgment are said to have been deferred because of the insufficiency of human repentance. In other words, they corroborate our contention that Jesus' prophecies about the timing of the end were conditional. We will examine a few New Testament texts that aver quite plainly that God can and has altered the timing of the consummation of the eschaton (whether viewed from the perspective

---

9. Ross E. Winkle, "The Jeremiah Model for Jesus in the Temple," *Andrews University Seminary Studies* 24, no. 2 (1986): 163-71; cf. Donald A. Hagner, *Matthew 14-28*, Word Biblical Commentary 33B (Dallas: Word, 1998), 675; R. T. France, *The Gospel of Matthew*, New International Commentary on the New Testament (Grand Rapids: Eerdmans, 2007), 884. Similarly, when Jesus asks the disciples "Who do people say the Son of Man is?", Matthew's disciples reply by saying "Some say John the Baptist, but others Elijah, and still others *Jeremiah* or one of the prophets" (Matt. 16:14). Matthew is unique in inserting the reference to "Jeremiah," indicating a sharp apprehension of the parallels between the ministries of Jeremiah and Jesus as prophets of the Temple's destruction; see Winkle, "Jeremiah Model," 155-58, 72; France, *Gospel of Matthew*, 616-17.

of Jesus' return, the final judgment, the new creation, or the vindication of the righteous) in response to human behavior.

It is the thesis of this book that the timing of the consummation of the kingdom of God is contingent upon the behavior of mortals. We do not deny that Jesus prophesied his return in glory and wrath within the first century; we do not deny the certainty of that return. We simply deny the fixity of that timing. And so do the New Testament authors.

## 2 Peter 3

We begin with 2 Peter, one of the latest New Testament documents, and thus, one of the texts one would expect to feel the poignancy of the eschatological delay most acutely. Two Peter lends itself so naturally to this debate because it responds explicitly to precisely the question with which we are occupied: the non-occurrence of the eschatological consummation.[10]

> First of all you must understand this, that in the last days scoffers will come, scoffing and indulging their own lusts and saying, "Where is the promise of his coming (ἡ ἐπαγγελία τῆς παρουσίας αὐτοῦ)? For ever since our ancestors died, all things continue as they were from the beginning of creation!" (2 Pet. 3:3-4)

The "scoffers" mentioned by the author of 2 Peter (henceforth, just "Peter") seem to be skeptics living late in the first or early in the second century who were well aware of the traditional Jewish expectation of divine judgment. The apparently perpetual deferral of the expected consummation seems to have stretched their credulity and amounted to reasonable grounds for gainsaying that expectation altogether.[11] The delay of this consummation would only have been

---

10. Cf. August Strobel, *Untersuchungen zum eschatologischen Verzögerungsproblem: Auf Grund der spätjüdisch-urchristlichen Geschichte von Habakuk 2,2 ff.*, Supplements to Novum Testamentum 2 (Leiden: Brill, 1961), 96-98; Gene L. Green, *Jude & 2 Peter*, Baker Exegetical Commentary on the New Testament (Grand Rapids: Baker Academic, 2008), 316-18; pace Charles H. Talbert, "II Peter and the Delay of the Parousia," *Vigiliae Christianae* 20, no. 3 (1966): 137-45; A. L. Moore, *The Parousia in the New Testament*, Supplements to Novum Testamentum 13 (Leiden: Brill, 1966), 151-56.
11. While it is more common for interpreters to identify the παρουσία in question with the παρουσία of Jesus, the pronoun αὐτοῦ in 2 Pet. 3:4 is ambiguous. Edward Adams has argued convincingly that the scoffers were taking issue specifically with the non-fulfillment of Old Testament expectations; Edward Adams, "Where is the Promise of His Coming? The Complaint of the Scoffers in 2 Peter

made more poignant for the Christians in Peter's community who identified Jesus' promised Parousia as the occasion of that eschatological judgment and destruction (v. 4; cf. 2 Pet. 1:16),[12] especially if they reflected on the fact that Jesus had foretold that the end would come before his disciples ("the fathers"?[13]) all died.

By the end of the first century, it seems that a number of Christians were feeling uncomfortable with the non-occurance of the eschatological consummation, and that different Christian leaders felt obligated to take action to control attendant disbelief in Jesus' second coming.[14] We already saw (above, p. 81n6; chapter 4, pp. 72-74) the ways that Matthew and Luke took steps to tone down Jesus' teachings about the eschatological consummation (Luke 22:69), and how the Third and Fourth Gospels both chastened readers who were under the impression that the Parousia already should have occurred (Luke 19:11; John 21:22-23). Apparently opposing the same sort of challenges, *1 Clement* (c. 95-97 CE) says:

> Wretched are the double-minded, those who doubt in their soul and say, "We heard these things even in the days of our fathers, and look, we have grown old, and none of these things have happened to us." ... Truly his purpose will be accomplished quickly and suddenly, just as the Scripture

---

3.4," New Testament Studies 51, no. 1 (2005): 106-22. This is not to drive a wedge between the παρουσία of Jesus and the παρουσία of the Old Testament God; it is clear from 2 Pet. 1:16 that the author would identify the παρουσία of Jesus as the coming of God in eschatological judgment and consummation.

12. Παρουσία had become a Christian technical term akin to the older Jewish "Day of the Lord" (*TDNT* 5:865-66). In Matthew 24, the παρουσία entails not only the coming of the Son of Man, but also, the end of the age (Matt. 24:3). Paul sees the παρουσία of Jesus as the time in which believers will be resurrected (1 Thess. 4:15; 2 Thess. 2:1) and earthly powers will be destroyed (1 Cor. 15:23-24; 2 Thess. 2:8, 19; 3:13; 5:23). James describes the παρουσία of the Lord as the time of judgment of the wicked and vindication of the righteous sufferers (James 5:7-8). While 2 Peter focuses on Jesus' παρουσία as the occasion for eschatological judgment, there is no reason to think that he separated that judgment from the reign of Jesus (quite the contrary, see 2 Pet. 3:13) and resurrection of the dead we see associated with the παρουσία in other New Testament writings.

13. While the expression "the fathers" typically refers to the patriarchs in Jewish writings, most commentators have discerned a reference to the original disciples in 2 Pet. 3:4; see e.g. Bauckham, *2 Peter, Jude*, 290-91. This suggestion has been disputed by Edward Adams, whose emphasis on the larger and general problem of the non-occurrence of Jewish eschatological hopes would make a reference to the patriarchs much more natural at this juncture; Adams, "Where is the Promise," 111-14; cf. Charles Bigg, *A Critical and Exegetical Commentary on the Epistles of St. Peter and St. Jude*, second ed., International Critical Commentary (Edinburgh: T&T Clark, 1902), 291.

14. As we can see in texts like *1 Clem.* 23.3-5; *2 Clem.* 11.2-12.1; Herm. *Vis.* 3.9.9; *Sim.* 9.14.2; 10.4.4. See further Martin Werner, *The Formation of Christian Dogma: An Historical Study of its Problem* (London: Adam & Charles Black, 1957), 40-48.

also testifies: "He will come quickly and not delay; and the Lord will come suddenly into his temple, even the Holy One whom you expect." (*1 Clem.* 23.3, 5)

Peter responds to the scoffers with a pair of complementary rebuttals. First, he eschews their assertion that "all things continue as they were from the beginning of creation" (v. 4); Peter's argument is basically: "that's what Noah's neighbors said, and look how it worked out for them." After all, the supposed stasis of the world since the beginning was interrupted by the Great Flood (Gen. 6:9–8:13), which is a type of the coming destruction of the world (vv. 5–7).[15]

Peter's second rebuttal disputes the basic notion that God is as sensitive to historical time as are humans. Invoking Ps. 90:4, Peter retorts that "with the Lord one day is like a thousand years, and a thousand years are like one day" (v. 8).[16] The scoffers assumed that the anticlimactic years following death of the fathers loudly bespoke divine indifference; Peter counters that God's actions are not strictly circumscribed by years and lifespans, as are our own.

> But do not ignore this one fact, beloved, that with the Lord one day is like a thousand years, and a thousand years are like one day. The Lord is not slow about his promise, as some think of slowness, but is patient (μαχροθυμεῖ) with you, not wanting any to perish, but all to come to repentance. (2 Pet. 3:8–9)

Were the allusion to Ps. 90:4 a free-standing rebuttal, Peter might appear to be making a somewhat flat-footed defense of God's tardiness. But v. 8 would be better conceived of as the first part of a parry-thrust combination, swatting the scoffers' rhetorical foil to the side so that Peter can lunge at the heart of their argument. The real payoff of Peter's allusion to Ps. 90:4 is that it demonstrates that God has all the time in the world to accomplish his goals.[17] Temporary obduracy on

---

15. See further Sam Meier, "2 Peter 3:3-7: An Early Jewish and Christian Response to Eschatological Skepticism," *Biblische Zeitschrift* 32, no. 2 (1988): 255–57.
16. Against the notion that the allusion to Ps. 90:4 (so e.g. Daniel von Allmen, "L'apocalpytique juive et le retard de la parousie en II Pierre 3:1–13," *Revue de theologie et de philosophie* 16(1966): 261–62) was intended to invoke a six-thousand year timeline for human history, see Bauckham, *2 Peter, Jude*, 306–10.

humanity's part does not derail God's plan, but can be accounted for by God's dynamic mercy (see also chapter 8, pp. 194-95).

Peter explains that God has delayed the prophesied judgment for a very specific purpose: to give people time to repent. The delay is not a matter of neglect or impotence; it is a matter of patience: "The Lord is not slow about his promise, as some think of slowness, but is patient (μακροθυμεῖ) with you, not wanting any to perish, but all to come to repentance" (v. 9). God is patient with sinners so that they might repent and avoid his wrath.[18] This point is so important to Peter that his closing exhortation repeats it: "regard the patience of our Lord as salvation (μακροθυμίαν σωτηρίαν ἡγεῖσθε)." In other words, Peter affirms the conditional character of the timing in which the Parousia was prophesied to occur.

Peter is not being creative in saying that God has deferred the final judgment in order to bring people to repentance. As we saw in chapter 3 (pp. 42-52), Jews long before and long after him would make precisely the same argument, explaining that God delayed his judgment of the wicked out of patience[19] and in order to provide time for repentance.[20]

> But you are merciful to all, for you can do all things, and you overlook people's sins, so that they may repent. (Wisd. of Sol. 11:23)

---

17. It bears emphasizing that Psalm 90 has an eschatological function in the final form of the Psalter itself. As Gerald Wilson maintains, Book IV of the Psalms (Pss. 90-106) is a response to the despondency that prevails at the end of Book III (Pss. 42-89). Psalm 89 concludes with the probing question brought about by the exile: "Lord, where is your steadfast love of old, which by your faithfulness you swore to David?" (v. 49). This question prompts the emphatic response of Psalm 90 that the Lord has always been a refuge for the people. Next, the enthronement psalms (Pss. 93-99) declare that YHWH is king (Ps. 93:1; 96:10; 97:1; 99:1). As the Psalter moves toward its climax in Book V, there are the psalms of ascent (Pss. 120-32), taking the audience on pilgrimage to the Jerusalem Temple; similarly, the concluding hymns of praise (Pss. 145-150) celebrate YHWH's victory. Heard in this editorial context, Psalm 90 is the first note in a movement that proceeds from a tone of exile and despair to one of enthronement and triumph in association with God's reign. See Gerald Wilson, *The Editing of the Hebrew Psalter*, SBLDS 76 (Chico, CA: Scholars, 1985), 139-228, especially 207-19.
18. See further *TDNT* 4:386-87; Richard Bauckham, "The Delay of the Parousia," *Tyndale Bulletin* 31 (1980): 19-28.
19. See e.g. *2 Bar.* 12:3-4; 21:20-21; 24:2; 48:29; 59:6; 85:8; *4 Ezra* 3:30, 7:33, 72-74, 134; *1 En.* 60.4-6, 25; 1 Pet. 3:20; *m. 'Abot* 5:2; see further Bauckham, "Parousia", 14-19; Str-B 3:775.
20. Wisd. of Sol. 11:23-24; 12:10; *Qoh. Rab.* 7:15; see further Bauckham, "Parousia", 11-14; Strobel, *Verzögerungsproblem*, 90-91; Str-B, 3:78.

> For it is an especial property of God to offer his good things freely and to be beforehand with men in bestowing gifts upon them, but to be slow in bringing evil on them. . . . God does not visit with his vengeance even those who sin against him, immediately, but that he gives them time for repentance, and to remedy and correct their evil conduct. (Philo, *Leg.* 3.34 [§105–106])[21]

Many Jews believed that, true to his character as "a God merciful and gracious, slow to anger (μακρόθυμος)" (Exod. 34:6-7),[22] the Lord delays to judge the wicked in order that they might repent. Even the pagan philosopher Plutarch averred very much the same thing when he disputed with materialist Epicureans.[23] It seems that Peter's only innovation is to invoke this idea as a Christian, claiming that Jesus would be the one to bring about God's judgment.

The Church fathers recognized the merit of this perspective, and continued to explain the deferral of the eschatological judgment as an expression of God's patience toward those who had not yet repented.

> Go and speak to all people, in order that they may repent and live to God, for the Lord in his compassion sent me to give repentance to all, though some, because of their deeds, do not deserve to be saved. But being patient, the Lord wants those who were called through his Son to be saved. (Herm. *Sim.* 8.11.1)[24]

Nonetheless, patience should not be confused with a lack of resolve, either in other Judaisms[25] or in the letter of 2 Peter. Peter denies that the deferral of the final judgment permits indifference to or agnosticism about the return of Jesus; instead, he reasserts the

---

21. Translation from *The Works of Philo: Complete and Unabridged*, trans. C.D. Yonge, rev. ed. (Peabody, MA: Hendrickson, 1993).
22. See further *TDNT* 4:376; Green, *Jude & 2 Peter*, 328–29; J.N.D. Kelly, *A Commentary on the Epistles of Peter and of Jude*, Black's New Testament Commentaries (London: Adam & Charles Black, 1969), 362–63.
23. Plutarch, in his essay "On the Delays of Divine Vengeance," responds to the Epicureans (who disputed that notion that the gods, if they exist, are involved in human affairs) by saying that God restrains wrath in order to show "gentleness and magnanimity" and to "make room for repentance; and for those in whose nature vice is not unrelieved or intractable, he fixes a period of grace" (Plutarch, *Mor.* 551B-D). Thus, the Jewish explanation for the delay in God's wrath has pagan counterparts.
24. See further Justin, *1 Apol.* 28; *Clementine Hom.* 9.19.1; 16.20; cf. Ignatius, *Eph.* 11.1.
25. *TDNT* 4:377; Green, *Jude & 2 Peter*, 328.

certainty of the eschatological judgment, and uses that very eschatological certainty to motivate Christian ethics.[26]

> But the day of the Lord will come like a thief, and then the heavens will pass away with a roar, and the heavenly bodies will be burned up and dissolved, and the earth and the works that are done on it will be exposed. Since all these things are thus to be dissolved, what sort of people ought you to be in lives of holiness and godliness, waiting for and hastening the coming of the day of God. (2 Pet. 3:10-12).

So, eschatology stimulates ethics. But note that Peter does not conclude with an injunction to holiness. Rather, he says, "What sort of people ought you to be in lives of holiness and godliness, waiting for and hastening the coming of the day of God (σπεύδοντας τὴν παρουσίαν τῆς τοῦ θεοῦ ἡμέρας)" (2 Pet. 3:11-12).

Peter proclaims that lives of holiness and godliness can actually expedite (σπεύδω) the Day of the Lord; believers can make the day of the Lord happen sooner.[27] So, eschatology not only stimulates ethics, but ethics stimulate eschatology; the two are mutually reinforcing. And this makes good sense; if Peter believes that the eschaton is delayed so that people can repent from wickedness, it stands to reason that lives of holiness would expedite the eschaton. The kingdom has not been fulfilled, Peter says, because you are slothful, so strive diligently to expedite the coming of the kingdom of God.[28] Repentance is at the core of this gracious divine-human synergy at work in the Church.[29]

---

26. Peter appropriates Jesus' image of the thief (v. 10a), and, true to all other New Testament instances of the trope (Matt. 24:43//Luke 12:39; 1 Thess. 5:2, 4; Rev. 3:3; 16:15), he utilizes it to underscore simultaneously the certainty of the coming of the Lord and the unexpected timing of that day.
27. The word σπεύδω can have bear either a transitive or an intransitive sense. The intransitive sense can be rendered "seek eagerly, strive after"; the transitive significance is reflected in translations such as "to cause to happen soon," "to hurry up," "to promote" (Euripides, *Iphigenia among the Taurians* 201; Homer, *Iliad* 236; Herodotus, 1.38; Aeschylus, *Suppliants* 599; L&N 68.80; LSJ ad loc). Reflecting the latter usage, Sir. 36:6 urges God to expedite the exercise of his wrath: σπεῦσον καιρὸν καὶ μνήσθητι ὁρκισμοῦ, "hasten the time and remember your oath" (Sir. 36:6 LXX; 36:10 ET). Only the transitive significance of σπεύδω seems plausible in 2 Pet. 3:12 (so also L&N 68.80), considering that Peter has already cited lack of repentance as the cause of the Parousia's delay (v. 9, cf. 15).
28. As we saw in chapter 3 (pp. 50-51), other Jewish and Christian writers often spoke of God hastening the time of the eschatological consummation (Isa. 60:22; 2 Bar. 20.1-2; 54.1; 83.1; LAB 19.13; Barn. 4.3); they also affirm that people's righteous behavior can accelerate the arrival of God's kingdom (b. Sanh. 97b, 98a; Yoma 86b; 2 Clem. 12:6). See further Bauckham, *2 Peter, Jude*, 325; Strobel, *Verzögerungsproblem*, 92-93; Green, *Jude & 2 Peter*, 334; Kelly, *Peter and Jude*, 367.

What is more, Peter does not see his perspective as idiosyncratic. We already mentioned the solid Jewish precedent for Peter's assertion that a dearth of repentance had stayed the occurrence of the Day of the Lord, but Peter does us one better; he avers that Paul would back his play.

> Strive (σπουδάσατε) to be found by him at peace, without spot or blemish; and regard the patience of our Lord as salvation (τὴν τοῦ κυρίου ἡμῶν μακροθυμίαν σωτηρίαν ἡγεῖσθε). So also (καθὼς καὶ) our beloved brother Paul wrote to you according to the wisdom given him, speaking of [these things][30] (περὶ τούτων) as he does in all his letters. (2 Pet. 3:15–16)

The grammar of this clause indicates that "these things" concerning which (περὶ τούτων) Paul spoke are both the need to pursue holiness (v. 14) and the fact that God practices patience in restraining judgment in order that more might be saved (v. 15). Little reflection is needed to recall texts in which Paul summons people to holy and blameless living.[31] But even Paul (whose emphasis on divine sovereignty has, at times, been construed as deterministic) affirms that God's deferral of the final judgment is intended to provide time for repentance, a point made in no less auspicious a canonical location than the Epistle to the Romans.[32]

### Romans 2:3–4

In the second chapter of Romans, Paul warns his Christian audience (significantly Jewish in constituency) that they, like the pagans, can also be judged for evil deeds should they, like the pagans, fail to repent in good time.

> Do you imagine, whoever you are, that when you judge those who do such things and yet do them yourself, you will escape the judgment of God? Or

---

29. Very much in the spirit of 2 Peter, in chapter 8 we will lay out six other sorts of ethical activity (worship, mission, ecumenism, social justice, asceticism, and contemplation; see pp. 197–208) by which Christians can cooperate with God in Christ in expediting the eschaton.
30. The NRSV is insufficiently precise when translating περὶ τούτων as "of this".
31. Cf. Kelly, *Peter and Jude*, 371–72; Bauckham, *2 Peter, Jude*, 330.
32. While Rom. 2:3–4 may not have been the Pauline text that the Peter had in mind in 2 Pet. 3:16, it simply serves to show that Peter was not taking baseless liberties in calling Paul to his aid.

do you despise the riches of his kindness (χρηστότητος) and forbearance (ἀνοχῆς) and patience (μακροθυμίας)? Do you not realize that God's kindness is meant to lead you to repentance? (Rom. 2:3-4)

Judgment is certainly coming, Paul warns his interlocutor, and in failing to repent for sinful deeds "you are storing up (θησαυρίζεις)[33] wrath" to be doled out on the last day (v. 5). In that light, Paul urges his audience to repent from their sins.

The explicitly stated premise supporting Paul's imperative is that the interval between people's sinful praxis and the final judgment is intended to serve as a window for repentance. Out of kindness, forbearance (ἀνοχή), and patience, God has withheld his judgment for a time, in order that people might repent.[34]

Ἀνοχή, meaning "forbearance" or "restraint", is a key word, clarifying that God has not abandoned his wrath, but has staid his final judgment patiently in order that his mercy might have more scope for exercise.[35] This idea is well-attested in Jewish and Christian writings.[36] Paul makes a similar assertion later in Romans, explaining:

> God, desiring to show his wrath and to make known his power, has endured with much patience the objects of wrath (ἤνεγκεν ἐν πολλῇ μακροθυμίᾳ σκεύη ὀργῆς) that are made for destruction; and ... he has done so in order to make known the riches of his glory for the objects of mercy, which he has prepared beforehand for glory—including us whom he has called, not from the Jews only but also from the Gentiles. (Rom. 9:22-24)

Once again, Paul explains that God has chosen not to punish the wicked (though they well deserve it), in order to allow time for further peoples, both Jew and gentile, to receive his mercy (cf. Rom. 11:25). Even though God would be justified in judging the wicked immediately, he restrains himself in order to show mercy to even more people.

---

33. Just as 2 Pet. 3:7 says the heavens and earth are being "stored up (τεθησαυρισμένοι) for fire," so also Paul says that impenitent humans store up wrath. Both aver that the judgment is inexorable, even though it has been deferred until other purposes can be accomplished.
34. So also Strobel, *Verzögerungsproblem*, 198-99; Robert Jewett, *Romans: A Commentary*, Hermeneia (Minneapolis: Fortress Press, 2007), 201; cf. chapter 3, pp. 42-54.
35. *TDNT* 3:359-60.
36. See e.g. Str-B 3:77 and *Ep. Diog.* 9.1; Ign. *Eph.* 11.1.

Obviously, Paul wrote at a time when many of the first disciples were still alive; Paul was not yet in a bind about the non-return of Jesus. As such, his discussion focuses on God's deferral of the final judgment more generally. Nonetheless, insofar as the last judgment and the Parousia were events conjoined in Paul's mind, Peter was quite right to see Paul as an ally in addressing the delay of the Parousia beyond the death of the first generation of Christians. Indeed, Cyprian of Carthage put Romans 2 to the same use:

> Although [God] has revenge in His power, He prefers to keep patience for a long while, bearing, that is to say, mercifully, and putting off, so that, if it might be possible, the long protracted mischief may at some time be changed, and man, involved in the contagion of errors and crimes, may even though late be converted to God. . . . [Here follow citations of Ezek. 27:32; Mal. 3:7; Joel 2:13] Which, moreover, the blessed apostle referring to, and recalling the sinner to repentance, sets forward, and says: . . . [Here follows a citation of Rom. 2:4–6] He says that God's judgment is just, because it is tardy, because it is long and greatly deferred, so that by the long patience of God man may be benefited for life eternal. Punishment is then executed on the impious and the sinner, when repentance for the sin can no longer avail. (Cyprian, *Pat.* 4; *ANF* 5:485; PL 4.624B–C; cf. *Test.* 35)

Even though the notion of eschatological delay with a view toward maximizing repentance was a minor stream in Pauline thought, Romans 2 and 9 show that such a theme was not antithetical to the apostle's strong belief in divine sovereignty over human history.

### Revelation 6–7, 9

These Pauline texts make clear that belief in divine, wrathful sovereignty is not at odds with seeing the delay of the eschaton as an expression of divine patience. The book of Revelation has an apocalyptic perspective that is every bit as deterministic as what we find in the Pauline canon; nonetheless, Revelation joins Paul and 2 Peter in describing the delay of the eschatological consummation as an expression of divine forbearance. As Richard Bauckham has argued,[37]

---

37. Bauckham, "Parousia," 28–36.

the Apocalypse's accounts of the seven seals and the seven trumpets highlight precisely this dynamic.

The seven seals of Revelation 6–7 and the seven trumpets of Revelation 8–9 are not to be thought of as earth-shaking travesties to happen in the final days before the return of Christ. Quite the contrary, they are symbolic representations of God's preliminary works of judgment throughout the Church age;[38] while anticipating God's ultimate wrath, the seal and trumpet judgments only harm a portion of the earth and its populace (Rev. 6:8; 8:12). These partial punitive acts demonstrate that God is not idle about or indifferent to the earth's present wickedness; still, he withholds his final judgment a little while longer. By contrast, the seven bowl judgments of Rev. 15:1—16:21 represent God's complete and final act of destructive judgment; they are "the last, for with them the wrath of God is ended" (Rev. 15:1).

In the interim between God's proleptic and consummate judgments, the fifth seal is broken (Rev. 6:9-11). There, under the altar in heaven, the Seer witnesses martyred saints crying out for vindication. The martyrs express indignation at the fact that, from their perspective, the judgment seems to have delayed, and so they cry out "how long will it be before you judge and avenge our blood on the inhabitants of the earth?" (6:10-11).[39] While the slain saints are provided consolation, being clothed in white and freed from suffering in the intermediate state (6:11; 7:9-17), they are told that they must wait "a little longer" (ἔτι χρόνον μικρόν; Rev. 6:11) before the final judgment does come.[40]

On the contrary, the seven trumpets show that the partial judgments (which anticipate, but forestall the final bowl judgments) also create

---

38. G.K. Beale, *The Book of Revelation: A Commentary on the Greek Text*, New International Greek Testament Commentary (Grand Rapids: Eerdmans, 1999), 370-71, 472-73.
39. Tertullian connects the martyrs' cry with the petition of the Lord's Prayer "your Kingdom come" (Matt. 6:10): "Our wish is, that our reign be hastened.... Even if it had not been prescribed in the Prayer that we should ask for the advent of the kingdom, we should, unbidden, have sent forth that cry, hastening toward the realization of our hope. The souls of the martyrs beneath the altar cry in jealously unto the Lord.... [Rev. 6:10]" (Tertullian, *Dom. or.* 5; ANF 3:683).
40. One of the deterministic features of the book of Revelation occurs here, as the martyrs are told to wait "until the number would be complete both of their fellow servants and of their brothers and sisters, who were soon to be killed" (Rev. 6:11). On the role of the numerum martyrum in Revelation 6, see Rainer Stuhlmann, *Das eschatologische Maß im Neuen Testament*, Forschungen zur Religion und Literatur des Alten und Neuen Testaments 132 (Göttingen: Vandenhoeck & Ruprecht, 1983), 154-63.

space in which sinners might come to repentance (9:20–21). Nonetheless, in intriguing contrast to 2 Peter and Romans, the Apocalypse is not sanguine about the wicked repenting during this interval before the final consummation. If anything, the hard-heartedness of the wicked in the face of God's warnings only heightens their culpability. Of course, this does raise the question of whether or not Revelation categorically excludes the possibility of such people repenting under God's proleptically punitive hand. Does the Seer opine that the harrowing threats of his vision are to be totally ineffectual, as if the trumpets represent a divine fool's errand? Or are the foreboding auguries of the text in fact rhetorical devices intended to move the wicked towards repentance?

Perhaps the Wisdom of Solomon (chapters 11–12) can shed some light on this subject. When Wisdom discusses God's forbearance toward the Israelites,[41] it construes God's patience and preliminary judgments as mechanisms intended to bring the holy people to repentance. By contrast, when Wisdom describes God's patience toward the Canaanites,[42] it denies that they ever would repent. In other words, we witness within Wisdom the same tension that exists between 2 Peter and Revelation; the delay of the judgment offers people the chance to repent, while the wicked are said not to mend their ways. While one might see this contradiction as insuperable, the present authors would suggest that these texts collectively present us with a tension which is native to the doctrine of God's electing grace, and should be preserved, rather than allowing one side (predestination) to overwhelm the other (free will). This subject will be addressed at greater length in the chapter 8.

---

41. Wisd. of Sol. 11:23: "you overlook people's sins, so that they may repent"; Wisd. of Sol. 12:2: "you correct little by little those who trespass . . . so that they may be freed from wickedness and put their trust in you."
42. Wisd. of Sol. 12:10: "But judging them little by little you gave them an opportunity to repent, though you were not unaware that their origin was evil and their wickedness inborn, and that their way of thinking would never change."

## Acts 3:19-21

In order to balance out the more deterministic side of the New Testament canon, we turn finally to the Acts of the Apostles. In the book's third chapter, we encounter an evangelistic speech by Peter, who adjures the Jerusalemites:

> *Repent* therefore, and turn to God so that your sins may be wiped out, *so that* (ὅπως ἂν) *times of refreshing may come* from the presence of the Lord, and *so that he may send the Messiah* appointed for you, that is, Jesus, who must remain in heaven until the time of universal restoration that God announced long ago through his holy prophets. (Acts 3:19-21, NRSV with minor adjustment by the author)

Here, Peter urges the Jerusalemites to repent[43] in order that (ὅπως ἂν)[44] the eschatological consummation might come to pass. In other words, repentance is a precondition of the second coming of Christ.[45]

Peter specifically states after the Jews repent and are forgiven their sins, "times of refreshing" (καιροὶ ἀναψύξεως)[46] will come, and God will send Jesus, the Messiah. Until that time, Jesus remains in heaven; but when he returns, he will bring about the "universal restoration" (ἀποκαταστάσεως πάντων) which the prophets had long foretold.[47]

In other words, the eschatological consummation was delayed until the second coming of the Messiah, this time to a penitent and righteous people. Although perhaps surprising to twenty-first-century ears, we have already seen that many Jews believed "that the End would come

---

43. On repentance and eschatology in Acts more generally, see John T. Carroll, *The Return of Jesus in Early Christianity* (Peabody, MA: Hendrickson, 2000), 30-33, 40-45.
44. In vv. 19-20, Luke uses the subordinating conjunction ὅπως ἂν followed by a pair of parallel aorist subjunctive verbs ἔλθωσιν . . . καὶ ἀποστείλῃ. In every Lukan occurrence of this construction, it expresses purpose (Luke 2:35; Acts 15:17; see also BDAG 718).
45. So also Ernst Haenchen, *The Acts of the Apostles: A Commentary*, trans. Bernard Noble, Gerald Shinn, and R. McL. Wilson (Oxford: Basil Blackwell, 1971), 208.
46. The καιροὶ ἀναψύξεως most likely refer to the era of peace in the world to come, insofar as they appear to parallel the "times of the restoration of all things" (χρόνων ἀποκαταστάσεως πάντων) which will accompany the Messiah's return. Consider the similar expression in m. 'Abot 4:17: "Better is one hour of רוּחַ קוֹרַת [cooling of spirit] in the world to come than the whole life of this world." See further 4 Ezra 11:46; TDNT 9:664-65; Haenchen, Acts, 208, ft. 8; Joseph A. Fitzmyer, *The Acts of the Apostles: A New Translation with Introduction and Commentary*, Anchor Bible 31 (New York: Doubleday, 1998), 288; Richard I. Pervo, *Acts: A Commentary*, Hermeneia (Minneapolis: Fortress Press, 2009), 108.
47. Mal. 4:6; Isa. 62:1-5; 65:17; 66:22; Fitzmyer, *The Acts of the Apostles*, 289.

only after the repentance of God's people";[48] this assumption was also the driving force in the preaching of John the Baptist (Mark 1:2-8; Matt. 3:1-12; Luke 3:3-17). So it seems that Peter has simply taken up the common Jewish belief that the Messiah would only come after the nation had repented, and then applied it to the return of the Christian Messiah. This was a logical corollary of Jesus' statement that the end would not come until the gospel was preached to all peoples (Matt. 24:14): the climax of the ages was being held at bay until people repent. Therefore, repent.

## Summary

While 2 Peter, Paul, Revelation, and Acts address distinct issues with slightly different emphases, they share in common the conviction that God has withheld the consummation of the eschaton so that people can repent. Romans 2:3-4 underscores the need to repent lest one be judged, and makes God the key agent in the timing of the End. Acts 3:19-21 emphasizes the importance of repentance so that people can enjoy the Kingdom, and makes humans the key agents in the timing of the End. Revelation avers that failure to repent heightens the culpability of those who are warned to turn from their wicked ways. But 2 Peter still holds out hope, explaining to sinners that the end has been deferred in order that they might repent, and urging believers to pursue holiness in order that they might hasten the arrival of their Lord. Still, different occasional and theological emphases notwithstanding, all these authors would explain the delay of the eschatological consummation in basically the same way: it is God's merciful patience to sinners, granting them more opportunities for repentance.

---

48. Bauckham, *2 Peter, Jude*, 312; see also *T. Jud.* 23.5; Str-B 1:599-601.

## Confirming the Thesis: The Conditional Timing of the Parousia in the Church Fathers

Lest it seem that the present authors are engaged in an exercise that has more to do with modern ingenuity than with historical Christian orthodoxy, it bears emphasizing that our thesis is not a twenty-first-century innovation. Through a combination of historical-critical analysis of prophecy and old-fashioned biblical exegesis, we have *recovered* a reading that was prominent in the early Church. A number of pre-Constantinian Christian texts reveal the belief that the timing of the final judgment was alterable. These Fathers believed that the eschatological consummation could be delayed or hastened by the *piety, prayers, and penitence* of God's people.

Justin Martyr, for one, explains that the last judgment was delayed because God was concerned to provide time for further *repentance*. "For the reason why God has delayed to do this, is His regard for the human race. For He foreknows that some are to be saved by repentance, some even that are perhaps not yet born." (Justin Martyr, *1 Apol.* 28; ANF 1:172). This is very much the argument made in 1 Pet. 3:9: God delays the Parousia because he anticipates that more sinners will repent.

This expectation of future repentance is complemented by a belief that the culmination of the eschaton has been retarded by the *intercession* of Christians. So, Tertullian explains, "We pray, too, for the emperors, for their ministers and for all in authority, for the welfare of the world, for the prevalence of peace, for the delay of the final consummation."[49] Similarly, Aristides affirms, "To me there is no doubt but that the earth abides through the supplication of the Christians."[50] These apologists, in defending the merits of Christianity to an empire uncertain of the religion's acceptability, did not shy away from the bold claim that the prayers of Christians held back the floodgates of God's wrath.

---

49. Tertullian, *Apol.* 39; ANF 3:46; PL 1.532A; so also *Apol.* 32; ANF 3:42–43; PL 1.447B–448A.
50. Aristides, *Apol.* 16.6; ANF 9:278; critical Syriac edition and French translation in B. Pouderon and M.J. Pierre, *Aristide: Apologie*, Sources Chrétiennes 470 (Paris: Cerf, 2003), 246–47.

This argument was paralleled by the affirmation that the presence of *virtuous Christians* restrained God's holy fury. Justin contends that

> God delays causing the confusion and destruction of the whole world, by which the wicked angels and demons and men shall cease to exist, because of the seed of the Christians, who know that they are the cause of preservation in nature. Since, if it were not so ... the fire of judgment would descend and utterly dissolve all things (Justin Martyr, *2 Apol.* 7; ANF 1:190; PG 6.456A).

Comparable sentiments are expressed by Clement of Alexandria (*Quis div.* 36; ANF 2:601; PG 9.641A-B) and Tertullian (*Apol.* 32; ANF 3:42-43; PL 1.509A).

Moreover, as we saw in chapter 3 (p. 53), some of the Fathers shared the view of 2 Pet. 3:12 that the eschatological timetable could be *accelerated* (Tertullian, *Or.* 5; ANF 3:683; PL 1.1261-62; Cyprian, *Mort.* 18; ANF 5:473; PL 4.595A). It may seem odd to invoke Tertullian in this connection in *De oratione*, insofar as his *Apologeticus* (cited above) vaunted the role of Christians in deferring the final judgment. One might argue that this inconsistency in Tertullian's emphases (corresponding to the difference between the pagan Roman readers of the *Apologeticus* and the Christian audience of *De oratione*) evinces a slightly disingenuous bit of rhetorical maneuvering, but for our purposes, it suffices to underscore that both texts turn on the assumption that the timing of the prophesied final judgment could, in fact, be altered in response to human actions.

It should not seem odd to us that the Church Fathers express opposite impulses regarding the timing of the Parousia—on the one hand, praying for its acceleration, and on the other hand, pronouncing its deferral. These countervailing emphases derive from the New Testament's divergent eschatological comments, as the canonical texts speak alternately of the hastening (1 Pet. 3:12; Acts 3:19-21; Matt. 6:10; 1 Cor. 16:21; Rev. 22:20) and delay (1 Pet. 3:9; Rom. 2:3-4; 9:22-24) of Jesus' return. Salient for our present purposes, however, is the fact that all these patristic writings reflect a belief in the variability of the eschaton's timing, which is to say, they demonstrate a widespread assumption about the *conditionality of eschatological prophecy*. In short, this chapter's proposal regarding the delay of the Parousia would have resonated with a number of the Church Fathers.

## Conclusion

It is time to bring our biblical argument full circle. Jesus came preaching the kingdom of God, and in his words and deeds, his followers perceived the dawning of that long-awaited age in which God would be recognized as King over Israel and all the nations. But the kingdom of God did not arrive in all of its epic eschatological glory during the ministry of Jesus. Nonetheless, Jesus had delimited the timing of his return in glory to consummate the kingdom of God, prophesying that he would bring all things to completion before the first generation of his disciples died. And so, Jesus' followers went forth undaunted, spreading Jesus' proclamation further abroad, and drawing inspiration from the fulfillment of prophecy that they had already witnessed. The Gospels and Acts portray various moments within the life of Jesus and of the early Church as partial fulfillments, proleptic instantiations of the final consummation, stepping stones that fostered hope in and helped sustain the presence of the kingdom.

For a while, the appeal to stepping stones sufficed for the members of the Jesus movement, and in many important ways, it still suffices. After all, Christians awaiting the Parousia continue to take heart in the apostolic witness to the transfiguration and resurrection of Christ. Likewise, the presence of the Spirit of God should animate the hope and foster the work of the Church in expectation of the second coming. Moreover, insofar as the holiness, righteousness, and repentance of humanity play roles in expediting the return of Jesus, we can assert that these stepping stones do, in some way, succor and speed the Parousia, countering the delay of Christ's return that resulted from human indolence and impiety. Stepping stones, both those described in the text of Scripture and those experienced in the liturgical and missional life of the Church (see chapter 8, pp. 197–99 and chapter 9, pp. 223–27), are integral to sustaining Christian hope between the two comings of Christ.

In that light, this chapter's invocation of the conditional nature of prophecy is not presented as an alternative to stepping stones, but as a complementary apostolic answer to the specific question of why, centuries after the last of Jesus' disciples expired, Jesus' prophecy remains unfulfilled. As we saw in chapter 3, the fulfillment of prophecy was often contingent upon the reaction of the addressees to the prophetic pronouncement. Jesus prophesied his return to vindicate his faithful witnesses, to bless penitent believers, and to punish his recalcitrant enemies. But when the Jewish and gentile nations did not respond sufficiently to the witness of his messengers, God chose to defer the complete fulfillment of the prophecy.

Consequently, the New Testament authors called sinners to repentance, affirming the certainty of the Parousia of Christ, and indeed, urging believers to lives of holiness so that that coming might occur soon. Even today, we remain in much the same place, as God has deigned to stay his hand a little while longer, that we might repent. We live in a magnetically-charged era of salvation history, suspended between the poles of God's just wrath upon humanity's evil and God's merciful patience on souls which might yet come to repentance. This tension between justice and mercy has generated the delay of the Parousia; we witness this tension in the revelatory moments of Christ's prophecy of his second coming and of 2 Peter's explanation of his delay. Indeed, we abide in this tension in our own proclamation and prayer, as we call the lost to repentance in light of Jesus' coming, as we thank God for his forbearance in waiting a little while so that sinners like us might repent, and as we nonetheless pray *Maranatha*.

### Embracing Tension: An Antinomic Hermeneutic

Before we step forward from our exegetical grappling with this topic, a word is in order about our hermeneutic.[51] The word *tension* has cropped

---

51. A more detailed account of our interpretive approach will be offered at the end of this book, in ch. 10.

up repeatedly in this book thus far, perhaps to the chagrin of some. *Tension* is a favorite word of theologians, as it allows us to bring divergent perspectives into interaction. By *tension*, we mean generally the epistemological state of paradox where two equally necessary but opposite truths are both upheld, although these truths (being in opposition) are in an apparent clash or logical contradiction. They, therefore, need to be held together through an act of faith with one truth counterbalancing and qualifying the other, indeed, living in and through its other in a ceaseless dialectic or antinomy. *Tension*, we hope to show, is ultimately in the service of wonder at God's truth that defies our normal categorization and binaries.

Still, we are also aware that *tension* can be a lazy word. Sometimes, it is a slippery term that allows us blithely to overlook complete inconsistency in an argument. Sometimes, *tension* is a big tent under which we can gather together a bunch of disparate ideas without working out exactly if or how they fit together. We want to avoid these rhetorical abuses. In light of the general definition given above, we would do well to comment on the sorts of tensions we think are operative in this discussion of the delay of the Parousia, and to clarify the nature of those tensions.

We would suggest that there are three different tensions operating here, one nested inside the other, like Russian matryoshka dolls. First, the heart of our inquiry has been the tension between Jesus' prophecy that he would come again in glory before the first generation of his disciples expired, and the fact (evident within the canon and still poignant in the twenty-first century) that he has not returned; it is the apparent contradiction between delimitation and delay. We have seen that the New Testament canon itself accounts for that dissonance by explaining that humanity's repentance had been insufficient, such that God deferred the Messiah's return in judgment and glory until more people would turn from their sins and glory in God's mercy.

The reason this explanation is arguably more than an *ad hoc* excuse for Christ's non-return is that Jesus' promise of his return was a prophecy, and thus, nestled inside of a second canonical tension between what we have called Mosaic and Jeremianic notions of prophecy. The Mosaic construal of prophecy focuses on the occurrence or non-occurrence of what was prophesied; the Jeremianic construal emphasizes the role of prophecy in calling for a response from humanity, and protects God's right to alter his actions, depending on the response of his people. Some might want to discard one (or both) of these notions of prophecy on the grounds of their apparent contradiction. But the two can be reconciled in our sense that they are opposite truths about how revelation works and together they illumine the diversity of divine action. In the case of Jeremiah's prophecy of the restoration of God's people from exile, we believe that the various twists and turns of history which resulted from human intransigence and divine machination will eventually issue in the vindication of Jeremiah's prophecy in Mosaic terms: God's people will eventually be brought back from exile.

This second tension, between Mosaic and Jeremianic accounts of prophecy, is ultimately embedded in a third and quintessential tension: the paradox of divine providential sovereignty and free human responsibility. Indeed, our discussions up to this point have brushed up against this problem repeatedly. Mosaic prophecy leans toward the providential side of the paradox, while Jeremianic prophecy emphasizes the role of free human actions. This tension, this nisus of paradox, this apparent contradiction, has been the hub of countless debates over the past millennia, in large part because it is a tension native to the distinct voices of the canon.

When you get down to the bottom of the issue, what you find is that these nested tensions in Christian theology derive from two sources. First, they derive from the source of revelation itself, Jesus Christ, who, as the incarnate Son of the Father, embraces any number of tensions in a difference-in-unity between opposites from the uncreated and the created, to spirit and flesh, to divinity and humanity.[52] Second, they come from the diversity of the canonical witness. Quite simply, the Bible appears to be making contradictory affirmations. The question

---

52. See further ch. 6, pp. 139–42, and ch. 8, pp. 195–97.

is then how one responds to these "contradictions." Some of course will relativize or marginalize one set of voices out of deference to the principle of non-contradiction; at times, perhaps that is the appropriate way forward. Nonetheless, for readers who do not share our religious perspective, we recognize that any attempt to salvage revelatory insight from texts that appear woefully discordant might seem deluded. But those who worship the Christian God might have reason to dissent from such a conclusion, on the very basis of how we understand the nature of God.

Christians, after all, believe in a God who far transcends the bounds of our world, whose essence and operation are only known to us at all because God has chosen to make himself known in Jesus Christ. That being the case, we should perhaps pause before assuming that two paradoxical statements are, in fact, incompatible. Conflict between texts might be suggestive of a more profound reality than is articulated by either individual text. It may just be that the paradoxical voices of Scripture point us toward a truth about God that transcends our created finitude (see further chapter 6, pp. 121-23, on theological *apophasis*). Is it not to be expected that God's essence and operations cannot be confined by the categories of our immanent existence? Is it not necessarily the case that the Unmoved Mover would exist and move in a different way than all derivative movers? If so, then we who seek to know the revealed God should seize Scriptural tensions as potential windows, wormholes, theophanies, apocalypses, glimpses of the divine life beyond the constructive-analytical ken of the created being. Paradoxes are not always liabilities to be shirked; sometimes, they are revelations to be embraced.

As such, the approach of this book, which capitalizes on Scriptural polyphony, might be categorized as an *antinomic hermeneutic*. "Antinomy" is another word for paradox; it denotes a situation in which reason drives the philosopher to two convictions that are apparently incompatible. Sometimes that incompatibility means that the philosopher has missed a step along the way. And sometimes that paradox is the entryway to things yet unknown. Insofar as the antinomies we are examining seem to have arisen from a canon of Scripture, which we believe to be true, we are eager to lay hold of them. If a tension is truly biblical, and thus, revelatory, we do not want to neutralize it, for it is in revelatory antinomy that Christian theology, and Christian life, will thrive.

# 6

# Negating the Fall and Re-Constituting Creation: An Apophatic Account of the Redemption of Time and History in Christ

## Julia S. Konstantinovsky

> I pray that [my life] will end up in the unshakeable home
> Where lives the bright union of the Trinity,
> By whose faint reflection we are now raised up.[1]

### Introduction

Exegetical and historical-critical considerations dominated the previous chapters' discussions of the delay of the Parousia. We saw that prophetic statements are better understood as "activating" human

---

1. Gregory of Nazianzus, *Concerning his own life*, lines 1947–49, in Gregory of Nazianzus, *Autobiographical Poems*, ed. and trans. Caroline White, Cambridge Medieval Classics 6 (Cambridge: Cambridge University Press, 1996), 89–116.

response, inviting repentance and change of heart, and not exclusively as calendric "prognostications" about future turns of human fortunes. To complement that idea, we explained that prophecies are revelations of God which help transform human history into a history of salvation; they are stepping stones toward the ultimate Theophany of the Lord's second coming. We will now continue to develop our argument by tackling the "eschatological problem" from another interpretive angle—that of *theologia negativa*, or *apophatic theology* in early and pre-modern Christian theologies

This chapter aims to demonstrate that early apophatic theologies contribute in a powerful and fresh way to today's discussions about eschatology. Classical pre-modern theologies have potent understandings of the doctrines of creation, the fall, and especially, the incarnation, the latter being at once the remedy for the fall and the completion of the divine creative act.[2] These doctrinal formulations view the eschaton as integral to the dramatic unfolding of creation and redemption; the eschaton is understood as the close and the annulment of the fallen temporal condition and the inauguration of the creaturely eternality with God. Classical theology, in other words, understands the eschaton as the completion of the act of creation. The advantages of this approach for our project are significant: it enables one to see the eschatological problem as part of the larger narrative of creation and redemption, while also providing a better grasp of our *own* state of alienation from true knowledge and from our authentic self. From this realization, it follows that the eschatological problem urgently awaits its resolution in *our own* lives first, before God comes "down" and makes all things new.

This chapter proceeds in three major stages. Part 1 establishes some features of negative theology in the thought of key Western and Eastern pre-modern Christian thinkers, such as Origen, Basil the Great, Gregory of Nyssa, Gregory of Nazianzus, Evagrius Ponticus, and Augustine—so-called "patristic writers." In the course of discussing these pre-modern theologians, we challenge some common assump-

---

2. See the "It has been accomplished" of John 19:30.

tions about the kind of theology apophasis is, demonstrating that among pre-modern Christians the purely "negative" (*apophatic*) strategy was regarded as insufficient; negation, therefore, formed one part of a synergetic structure that included the "affirmative" (*cataphatic*) discourse. The two modes of thought and speech complement and enhance each other in this view. Furthermore, we maintain that early Christian theological negations are inseparable from theological affirmations, constituting far more that experimentations with the poetics of language. The statements are, by contrast, direct engagements with metaphysics and the dilemmas of Christian life. Negative theological language was—and is—grounded in particular ontologies, christological insights, and views of human knowledge and final salvation.

Enabled by this epistemological shift, the ensuing sections of the chapter proceed to study aspects of traditional Christian theology in the cataphatic-apophatic perspective. Part 2 examines the Christian doctrine of the fall,[3] identifying its profound ramifications for the limitations of human understanding and for the nature of time itself. With the distortion of time and knowledge in sharp relief, Part 3 elaborates an apophatic Christology that begins to articulate how fallen humanity and history are being restored in Christ.

In the conclusion, we suggest possibilities for extending the use of traditional apophasis for further theological and eschatological engagements. Inasmuch as apophasis undergirds such characteristics of God as the freedom of God's action in Christ, the present chapter prepares the ground for the discussion of the radical divine freedom in chapter 7 (pp. 163–65).

## Part 1: Apophatic Theology

Since apophatic theology is frequently misunderstood in Western Christian discourse, it seems appropriate to launch this chapter with a brief primer on apophasis.

---

3. On ancient and early modern conceptions of the fall, see Peter Harrison, *The Fall of Man and the Foundations of Science* (New York: Cambridge University Press, 2007), 7–10.

## Apophasis: Establishing the Parameters

Conceived broadly, *apophasis*—the Greek word for "negating" or "turning away from speech"—is an intellectual strategy of refusing to "jump the gun" by making inflated or overly self-assured epistemological claims. Christian theological apophasis, known often by the Latin *via negativa*, is an epistemological stance that reminds us that God is not an object of speculation, but the transcendent one who makes himself known. Thus, theological apophasis attempts to relate to God, his engagements with the world, and his eschatological revelations of himself in a manner appropriate both to our human condition, and also, to his majesty, transcendence, and utter freedom (see further chapter 7, pp. 158–67).

In a more restricted sense, the term *apophasis* often denotes specific turns of phrase that pre-modern Christian writers liked to use when speaking of God. Thus, they named what God is *not*, rejecting attempts to "circumscribe" and "crowd" him by relying excessively on affirmative statements about what he *is*. There is, however, a broader sense to early Christian apophaticism—one that engages not with language alone, but with aspects of divine and created existence. Philosophy and philosophical theology hold that there is a "correspondence between language and the world language is about."[4] Apophatic and cataphatic theologies pursue this purpose: to make finite language correspond to the infinity of the divine greatness and our eschatological restoration in it. This characteristic is why apophatic theologies are directly relevant to the problem of the delay of Parousia. There are, moreover, different kinds of theological apophasis, pre-modern and modern. While all Christian apophatic theologies manifest an interest in the human condition and issues of our (eschatological) restoration, they have distinct anthropologies, which underscore their dissimilar understandings of the fall, Christology, and the eschatological fulfillment.

---

4. M. J. Loux, "The World of Universals," in *Metaphysics: Contemporary Readings*, ed. M.J. Loux, Routledge Contemporary Readings in Philosophy (New York: Routledge, 2001), 9.

## NEGATING THE FALL AND RE-CONSTITUTING CREATION

When we consider broader senses of theological apophasis and cataphasis, early Christianity presents itself as apophatically oriented in all the major helices of metaphysical inquiry: the human nature and the ordering of its faculties, divine grace and natural knowledge, typology and history, creation and salvation, and time and eternity. Early Christian theologies, then, tend to appear apophatic throughout, in the particular sense in which early Christians utilize this kind of metaphoric language as they approach *all* realities—divine and created—from apophatic perspectives, which, to them, is the only "sure sign of an attitude of mind conformed to truth."[5] Within these intellectual parameters, "apophatic" becomes the definition of "true" theology, while the lack of the negative approach to reality is seen as reducing theological vision to mere secular philosophy and atheism.[6] In this broader sense of apophasis, therefore, the early Church can be seen as according an apophatic treatment to life's every domain, upholding apophatic doctrines of God and creation, an apophatic anthropology, and an apophatic vision of the *eschata*.

Inasmuch as pre-modern apophasis treats of the realities of the ultimate and its relation to human nature, the early Church itself can be seen as eschatological in orientation. Consequently, even when it does not overtly discuss the events of the second coming and the stages of the eschatological fulfillment, the apophatic theology of the early Church is eschatological in outlook. Aspects of apophasis in reflections of individual thinkers and Church councils dominate the theological scene, West and East, through the long Late Antiquity and into the early Middle Ages.

### Negations and Affirmations about God

The early Christian theological negation (*apophasis*) forms one unified whole with the theological affirmation (*cataphasis*). Ancient Christians can be seen using the two forms of theological language to tell the story

---
5. Cf. Vladimir Lossky, *The Mystical Theology of the Eastern Church* (Crestwood, NY: St Vladimir's Seminary Press, 1976), 39.
6. Ibid.

of our meta-historical origin and our spiritual ascent. Apophasis and cataphasis are about the story of a soul's rediscovery of possibilities of knowledge and of progress to God. As such, apophasis relates to experiences of contemplation, *theoria*.[7]

Ancient Christian accounts of theological language often attach more value to the vocabulary of negation than to that of affirmation. Thus, Dionysius the Areopagite (late fifth century) holds negative statements (ἀφαιρέσεις), which describe what God is not, to be superior to affirmations (θέσεις) about him.[8] For example, when we attempt to describe God in positive terms as good, wise, and powerful, this would be incorrect, strictly speaking, because the Creator surpasses all things in the world, including the qualities of being good, wise, and powerful. To other early Christian contemplative writers, such as Gregory of Nyssa (fourth century CE), ascribing properties to God as one would to natural things (in terms of their qualities and their position in space and time) amounts to prying into the being of God by substituting "a false likeness" and "an idol" in the place of the true God.[9] Gregory of Nazianzus (fourth century CE) likewise expresses the need for negation in discourse about God, claiming that while it is difficult to think adequately about God, "to define Him in words is impossible."[10] It is more constructive, therefore, to converse using theological negations, rather than affirmations, because discussions couched in negative terms correspond better to the state of human knowledge—or lack thereof—about transcendent things. This is so on account of God's divine infinity, absolute freedom, and complete and utter transcendence. To say that God is "beyond everything"[11] is to

---

7. Further on contemplation, see chapter 8, pp. 205–8.
8. Dionysius the Areopagite, *Mystical Theology* 1.3 (PG 3.1000–01). For a critical edition of Pseudo-Dionysius the Areopagite, see *Corpus Dionysiacum*, ed. Beate Regina Suchla, Günter Heil, and Adolf Martin Ritter, 2 vols. (Berlin: De Gruyter, 1990–91). For an in-depth introduction to Dionysius's theology of the mystery of the unknowable God and its place within the Byzantine apophatic tradition, see Andrew Louth, *Denys the Areopagite* (London, New York: Continuum, 1989/2002).
9. Cf. Lossky's account of Gregory of Nyssa, *Against Eunomius* 10 (PG 45.828); Lossky, *Mystical Theology*, 33. For an authoritative source on Gregory of Nyssa's anthropology and theology of creation, see Johannes Zachhuber, *Human Nature in Gregory of Nyssa: Philosophical Background and Theological Significance* (Leiden, Brill, 2000).
10. Gregory of Nazianzus, *Oration* 28.4(=*Theological Oration* 2.4) (PG 44.1028D; SC 250.106): "Θεὸν νοῆσαι μὲν χαλεπόν, φράσαι δὲ ἀδύνατον," paraphrasing Plato, *Tim.* 28c.

affirm that he does not belong to any class of beings at all, but is supremely beyond beings and being, and in his choices, is not conditioned by created considerations of any kind. "My thoughts are not your thoughts, neither are your ways my ways, declares the Lord" (Isa. 55.8). God's utter freedom and transcendence make it impossible for the human mind to understand him and render it preferable to discuss him by abstraction from all things.[12]

Nonetheless, unlike some instances of modern apophasis, ancient Christian theological negation is something more than a denial of the possibilities of knowledge. In aspiring to surpass the concepts of created being, apophasis has the purpose of elevating the mind to the realms of the uncreated. There is a sense, then, that apophasis proceeds from negating to affirming. This is manifested by the kind of biblical "theophanic" themes early Christian negative theology typically employs. Couched in the language of poetry and analogy, these are affirmative accounts of the mysterious God, who, in series of concealments and uncoverings, reveals himself to humans according to the measure of their receptivity.

## Theological Cataphasis

As we have already indicated, early Christian negation is not a position of skepticism, denying the possibility of knowledge of God. On the contrary, by stripping away positive notions, apophaticism aims to elevate the mind beyond the created realm and to lift it to an encounter with the supremely free God, who is not constrained by anything at all, but reveals himself to us freely, how and when he chooses. This is the case with the preparatory *theophanies* seen by humans. These theophanies are stepping stones toward the final consummation, and especially so, with regard to the timing of the Lord's second coming.

---

11. Cf. Dionysius the Areopagite, *Divine Names* 2.10 (PG 3.648C): ὑπερουσίως ἁπάσης οὐσίας ἐχρημένη; *Corpus Dionysiacum*, 1:134.
12. Cf. John Damascene (eighth century), *The Orthodox Faith* 1.4 (PG 94.800A–B; SC 535.148).

Negative theology is thus balanced out with positive constructions. Theological cataphasis begins with what apophasis proscribes: attributing names and properties to God drawn from the multiplicity of created beings and properties of things. It is, thus, legitimate to hold that God is "sun, star, and fire, water, wind, and dew, cloud, ... stone, and rock [and] that He is all,"[13] because there is a real sense in which God is present in all the things that he made, just as the artist is present in his art. This enables a two-fold revelation. Even though Dionysius might overall prefer "bodiless" (ἀσώματα) terms such as "love" and "super-essential being" for the powers and characteristics of divinity, he nevertheless labors the point that God *can* be described by all things he made.

How is God reflected in creation? At this point, early Christian metaphysics becomes a little complex, but the essence of the idea is lucid. God's reflection in creation comes about through what early Christians called "the *logoi* (λόγοι) of beings." The theology of the *logoi* of beings and of being is especially elaborated in the thought of Origen, Evagrius Ponticus, and Maximus the Confessor, and we will engage with it further in chapters 7 and 8 (pp. 155–57 and 179–85). For now, it is sufficient to note that these *logoi* are, so to speak, the tiny divine "sparks" that are "inscribed" or encoded within the very fabric of the cosmos. By looking at the *logoi*, humans come to know both created beings and God as their "Creator, wise, provident and judge."[14]

These *logoi* possess a double identity. In one sense, they are the traces of God's "fingers" on the created beings. In another sense, they are the principles of the cohesion of the universe itself; they are what makes cosmos out of chaos. As we shall see in chapter 7 (pp. 167–70), these *logoi* represent divine possibilities from which God can choose

---

13. Dionysius the Areopagite, *Divine Names* 6 (PG 3.596C); *Corpus Dionysiacum*, 1:119. English translation: *Pseudo-Dionysius: the Complete Works*, trans. Colm Luibheid (New York: Paulist, 1987), 76.
14. Evagrius Ponticus, *Scholion* 8 on Psalm 138:16 (PG 12.1661); translation of the *scholion* in Julia S. Konstantinovsky, *Evagrius Ponticus: the Making of A Gnostic*, Ashgate New Critical Thinking in Religion, Theology, and Biblical Studies (Farnham: Ashgate, 2009), 56. See likewise Luke Dysinger, *Psalmody and Prayer in the Writings of Evagrius Ponticus*, Oxford Theological Monographs (Oxford: Oxford University Press, 2005), 172–73. No published English translation of all the *scholia* on the Psalms exists at present.

to act as he wills in his free life of perfect love. Through these *logoi*, God "lives" in his creation; thus, we can affirm qualities and things about God because the creatures that contain the *logoi* resemble God in aspects of harmony and luminosity. Cataphasis both activates this resemblance and enables our knowledge of it.

Positive theology is not merely the more "verbose element in theology."[15] Cataphatic theology asserts not only likenesses but also dissimilarities, so that what one affirms, one can then take away and go beyond: "God is like a stone, and yet He is greater than a stone, because He made it." Similarly to negations, therefore, positive statements about God are expressive of the reticences and silences of language used wisely,[16] when the believer begins to know him who escapes knowing and whom she desires to see. Here, the cataphatic coheres with the apophatic so that we cannot tell one from the other, with the result that they come together in prayer to him who is above all in his loving freedom:

> Trinity!! Higher than any being, any divinity, any goodness! . . . Lead us up beyond unknowing and light, up to the farthest, highest peak of mystic scripture, where the mysteries of God's Word lie simple, absolute and unchangeable in the brilliant darkness of a hidden silence . . .[17]

Early Christian theological mysticism, then, manifests these "twin pressures of language,"[18] allowing the two strategies to complement one another and to form complicated self-subverting utterances[19] that are cataphatic *apophases* and apophatic *cataphases*. Through the use of the bizarre and the paradoxical, imagery of light and darkness, presence and absence, play, sex and family life, affirmation (in the words of Denys Turner) is "linguistically *overburdened*,"[20] and so,

---

15. Citing Denys Turner's insightful *The Darkness of God: Negativity in Christian Mysticism* (Cambridge: Cambridge University Press, 1995), 20.
16. Cf. the "learned ignorance" of Nicholas of Cusa (15th century), *De docta ignorantia*; Nicholas of Cusa, *Complete Philosophical and Theological Treatises of Nicholas of Cusa*, 2 vols., trans. and ed. Jasper Hopkins (Minneapolis: Arthur J. Banning, 2001).
17. Dionysius the Areopagite, *Mystical Theology* 1 (PG 3.997A-B). English translation, 135.
18. Turner, *Darkness of God*, 22.
19. Cf. ibid., 21.
20. Ibid., 20.

transcends all "normal" and "sensible" cultural orthodoxies and all discourse of plain speech and respectability—reaching out into progressively more radical negation in quest of a positive contemplation. Through negation, the mind denies all connections between temporal things in the world, and between things in the world and atemporal intelligible realities. It then negates and transcends itself. Finally, using the language of dissociation as an intellectual springboard, the mind "reaches out" further and into a contemplative union with God "in the brilliant darkness of a hidden silence...."[21]

What we have in this theological project, therefore, are exemplarist cosmological elaborations of Eph. 3:10, especially the theology of "the manifold wisdom of God as manifested in creation." In this way, there is a fusion of a specific form of Christian natural theology with a theology of revelation.

## Apophasis and Cataphasis: A Road to Reality?

To see how this discussion relates to our eschatological problem, it is worth bearing in mind that the early Christian cataphatic apophasis is meant to be a "road to a reality." Early Christian descriptions of apophatic mystical experiences, such as those of Dionysius and the Nazianzen, purport these experiences to be real. They are said to arise from contemplation (*theoria*); authors recording the contemplative experiences emphasize that these are authentic, transformative, metaphysical events with an extra-mental reality of their own, beyond the purely neurological brain-event.

Yet, how are these experiences real? For one thing, mystical apophatic accounts that depict these experiences seem contrived and make no good common sense. But in mystical texts, negations do not negate and neither do affirmations affirm; both are mysterious, self-subverting, incomplete, and forever changing. In these accounts, nothing can be taken for granted and all our "normal" conceptions of space-time and reality are challenged. In particular, the human sense

---

21. Cf. Dionysius the Areopagite, *Mystical Theology* 1 (PG 3.997A–97B).

of direction and of chronology crumbles: in a mystical apophatic account, we cannot tell whether we are moving back or forth chronologically, into the past or on to the future, because the accounts are expressed in a timeless non-directional present. The very "arrow of time"[22] seems called into question.

All of this, plainly, is weird.

Nevertheless, apophatic accounts are real in a different sense of the term. To the early Christians, the contemplative language of apophasis and the experience of *theoria* are not independent, but "enmeshed and relative" to the metaphysics they presuppose, inclusive of the radical atemporality of divine eternity in which they are grounded. It would be flawed to treat them in any other way. An analogy that springs to mind is with Einstein's theory of the relativity of space and time, which are not independent and absolute, but instead, form "part of a unified whole" and "together participate in the cosmic evolution."[23] In a somewhat similar manner, theological apophasis and cataphasis (along with the revelatory experiences they represent) are not unchangeable and rigid, but relative to the entire fabric of the created universe and the uncreated divine activity in it.

More specifically, the reality of apophatic and cataphatic theologies rests on the principle of a connection and gracious commensurability between the self and God, as well as between the cosmos and God. Patristic writers term this connection "participation" in God. As descriptions of mystical encounters accentuate, the mysteriousness of these "events" of contemplation arises from the irresolvable paradoxes of being, whereby we perceive the "vision" of a divine nonlinear eternality and our own (fleeting) "eternal moment," without quitting our temporality. Every such "eternal moment" is, in fact, an

---

22. Cf. Arthur Eddington, *The Nature of the Physical World* (Cambridge: Cambridge University Press, 1928). This is a classic account of our perception of reality as highly orderly whereby things unfold in time in a certain direction: from the past to the future and not the other way around.
23. Cf. Brian Greene, *The Fabric of the Cosmos: Space, Time, and the Texture of Reality* (London: Penguin, 2005), 9–10.

eschatological moment, the eschaton already present, yet not completed.

What we have here, therefore, is a particular inverted logic of transcendence, where cataphatic apophaticism articulates both our spiritual transformation and God's action in lives and selves. Mystical accounts such as these are first-hand reports of a spiritual journey to the transcendent. This highlights one key aspect of early Christian apophasis: its moral dimension. At the heart of the complex apophatic paradox is the ability of ancient Christians to expect that the small temporal self will, at some point, desire to become temporally-eternal and quasi-uncreated.[24] Such was the momentary (as opposed to permanent) transfiguration that the disciples underwent when they saw Jesus change in front of them into a vision of divine glory.[25]

Apophasis and cataphasis in traditional Christianity, therefore, are not merely plays on words. Together, they are a way of life and a point of view characterized by a dual attitude of disengagement and embracing, where the mind strips itself of attachments to things that appear real, but are false, in favor of the realities of the ultimate. Therefore, when we praise apophasis for bringing out the "deconstructive" potential of human thought through the use of apophatic "self-subversion,"[26] we are embracing the self's subversions and deconstructions that occur in the quest of the authentic "I." This is a process comprising voluntary purification (*catharsis*) of life, which traditional Christian theologies term *kenosis*.[27] This is an attitude of transcending *my* "wisdom of this world" (cf. 1 Cor. 3:19) through turning away from my present self and toward the authentic "I" and the divine wisdom within God's creation.[28]

---

24. Cf. Lossky's insights on this in *Mystical Theology*, 33–40.
25. Cf. Mark 9:2–13, a Christological text that gave rise to prolific late-ancient and Byzantine hermeneutical production in the apophatic key, from the "Macarian" corpus in the fourth century to the *Triads* of Gregory Palamas in the 14th century.
26. Cf. Denis Turner, *The Darkness of God*, 8 and 21, respectively.
27. In traditional Christian terminology, *kenosis* signifies voluntary sacrificial "self-emptying" for the sake of another. Christ's kenosis is the essence of the incarnation, and, in return, in order to grasp the reality of Christ's Parousia, we too are to become kenotic in imitation of him. "It is no longer I who live, but Christ lives in me" (Gal. 2:20).
28. Here, the reader will perceive a progressive blending between contemplative and moral language. This anticipates the integrated vision of Christian theology developed further in ch. 8 (pp.

# NEGATING THE FALL AND RE-CONSTITUTING CREATION

The idea, therefore, is that the inverted logic of apophasis brings about alternative modes of awareness, the spiritual contemplative *theoria*, whereby the self comes to see ultimate realities: God "as He is" (cf. 1 John 3:2) and creation as it was first made and will once again be when Christ comes back. In the view of ancient Christians, the ultimate contemplative realities, bizarre as they might appear to the eye of everyday "normalcy," are the selfsame realities of the eschaton.[29] Inasmuch as *theoria* is about foretasting ultimate realities, it is eschatological already *now*. Through it we are given a foretaste of the age to come—another stepping stone toward the consummation of the full Parousia.

## Part 2: The Fall of Humanity and Time

What transpires from this analysis of early Christian apophasis is that, in the view of early Christians, the capacity and incapacity of the mind to know God is grounded in a duality of metaphysical considerations. God is both utterly unknowable (the *deus absconditus*) and completely known (the *deus revelatus*). Likewise, humans are at once incapable of any spiritual knowledge and nonetheless experience contemplative vision.

### Metaphysics and the Limits of Knowledge

Traditional Christianity presents two reasons for the restriction of our possibilities of knowledge and of language. The first consists in our ontological status *qua* creatures *vis-à-vis* the Creator. As created, we

---

197–208), where we will show how the Church's faith, *theoria*, and practice are central to bringing about the coming again of the Lord.

29. Cf. Pseudo-Macarius, *Collection* II.15.38:

> . . . as the body of the Lord was glorified when he climbed the mount and was transfigured into the divine glory and into infinite light, so also the bodies of the saints are glorified and shine like lightning. Just as the interior glory of Christ covered his body and shone completely, in the same way also in the saints the interior power of Christ in them in that day will be poured out exteriorly upon their bodies.

*Pseudo-Macarius: The Fifty Spiritual Homilies and the Great Letter*, trans. and ed. George A. Maloney S.J. (New York: Paulist, 1992), 123. Greek text in H. Dörries, E. Klostermann, and M. Kroeger, *Die 50 Geistlichen Homilien des Makarios*, PTS 4 (Berlin: De Gruyter, 1964).

belong within the structures of existence that ancient Christians term *diastema* (διάστημα), "extension." In contrast to divine non-extended (*adiastemic*) life, creatures *by definition* belong within the created "extension" and are, thus, "extended" beings. That is to say, they are subject to the limitedness of the "extended" spatio-temporal continuum,[30] which is radically *unlike* the "non-extended" divine eternity.[31] The perfect divine eternity is the mode of God's pure, unconditioned, and utterly free love as Trinity. Our knowledge depends upon and is relative to our condition. Our attempts to comprehend metaphysical realities are launched, as it were, from within our spatio-temporal limitations. Humans are unable to see God from within these strictures because we remain "inside" while God is "outside," beyond all time and space, surpassing even the "eternality" of the angelic beings.[32] This ontological gap is the primary reason why God "is not numbered with the things that exist,"[33] why everything in the world is "far removed from and completely foreign to [God]," so that "if God is nature, other things are not nature; but if every other thing is nature, He is not a nature, just as He is not a being if all other things are beings."[34] To Thomas Aquinas (thirteenth century) in the West, divine transcendence is grounded in God's existence as *"being* itself" (*esse ipsum*) and the source of all being. It is solely *in virtue* of God causing things to exist that those things exist at all. But this means that even though God is present with the creation, he is so not as part of the creation. God's own being "remains utterly distinct from all things."[35]

---

30. Cf. Einstein's use of the term in his theory of relativity.
31. Cf. P. Plass, "Transcendent Time and Eternity in Gregory of Nyssa," *Vigiliae Christianae* 34, no. 2 (1980): 181.
32. Cf. ibid., 181.
33. Cf. Evagrius Ponticus (fourth century), *Gnostic Chapters* 2.47 (my translation from the Syriac text).
34. Cf. Gregory Palamas (14th century), *Topics of Natural and Theological Science* 78. For English, see *The Philokalia*, vol. 4, trans. and eds. G. E. H. Palmer, Philip Sherrard, and Kallistos Ware (London: Faber and Faber, 1995), 381.
35. In the words of Aquinas, "unde per ipsam suam puritatem est esse distinctum ab omni esse." *De ente et essentia* (=*On Being and Essence*), c. 4 and c. 5.2; translation adapted by Brandon Gallaher from *On Being and Essence*, ed. and trans. Armand Maurer. 2nd ed. (Toronto: Pontifical Institute of Mediaeval Studies, 1968), 60–61; critical edition: *De ente et essentia opusculum S. Thomae Aquinatis*, ed. L. Baur. Opuscula et Textus: Series Scholastica et Mystica 1 (Aschendorff: Münster, 1926). Cf. *Summa Contra Gentiles* book 1, c. 26; for English, see *The Summa Contra Gentiles of St Thomas Aquinas*, trans. English Dominicans (New York: Benziger Brothers, 1924), 64.

The other reason why God is wholly "other" to the world lies in the world's determination not to know him. This second reason for God's aseity is solely a result of the world's choice not to participate in him. But the world's existence consists in participating in God, and refusal to do so amounts to a descent from being into non-being, or to a reversal of being as was originally conceived in the divine plan for creatures. In synthesizing earlier Christian material, Maximus the Confessor affirms the world's participation in God to be its participation in Christ as Christ's body. The world's voluntary participation in Christ is the full realization of the principle of its being (*logos*)[36] and the goal of deification (*theosis*)[37] toward which the creature's natural movement (*kinesis*) is directed.[38] In this respect, all participations of creatures in Christ as his body are eschatological, whether they are instances of an incomplete inaugurated eschatology (which break into history even as it unfolds, but which do not persist individually for the entire duration of this historical process), or the eschatological fulfillment (which will finally draw history to its close). Nonetheless, the world's refusal to participate in God may be the hallmark of its present historical-temporal condition, its current διάστημα. This distorted "extension" is known in Christianity as the fall. This subject, due to its significance in matters of Christian eschatology, merits special consideration.

### The Fall: Early Christian Conceptions

Especially prior to the tenth century, Christian metaphysics are rooted in conceptions of the biblical account of the fall. For pre-modern Christians,[39] the fall—the alteration of the human condition as presented in Genesis 3—constituted a drastic ontological trans-

---

36. Cf. Maximus the Confessor, *Ambiguum* 7.15 (PG 91.1077C): all things are created "according to their *logos*." All English translations of Maximus' *Ambigua* are from *Ambigua to Thomas*; *Second Letter to Thomas*, CCSG 48 (Turnhout: Brepols, 2009), unless otherwise indicated.
37. Cf. Maximus the Confessor, *Ambiguum* 71.5 (PG 91.1412C).
38. Cf. Maximus the Confessor, notably *Ambigua* 7 and 10.
39. This hold also for early moderns like Luther and Calvin. On Luther's views of the post-lapsarian humanity, see in particular his "Sunday after Christmas"; *Sermons* 111, 226; *Lectures on Galatians*; *Lectures on Genesis 1-5*. For Calvin's view of the fall, see his *Commentary in Genesis*; *Institutes* 2.1–3.

formation. The contrast between the "unfallen" and "fallen" appears to be so radical that some early Christian thinkers speak of an almost complete loss of the original human nature, which early Christians sometimes term "the entire life of wickedness."[40] It is a condition characterized by a universal inbred aversion to virtue, a disposition toward vice,[41] and a departure from the resemblance to the divine prototype.

The fallen departure from the divine image that was God's original paradigm for humanity is also a departure from oneself. Thus, Athanasius characterizes fallen humanity as a humanity that has lost its "original nature," and thus, abandoned itself.[42] Elucidating the great fourth-century Christian ethicist Evagrius Ponticus, Maximus the Confessor maintains that, in the fall, human nature "becomes not the same as itself."[43] Consequently, writers of the so-called patristic tradition believed that the fallen condition raises grave concerns about issues of personhood, in terms of fallen humans' loss of the ability to be true to themselves.[44] In the place of the original authentic humanity, the fall produces a new, terrifying, and false one.

To early Christians and some modern theologians,[45] moreover, the fall has serious epistemological implications. In the words of the philosopher Blaise Pascal (seventeenth century), the fall is a state of mind whereby we only "perceive an image of truth and possess nothing but falsehood, being equally incapable of absolute ignorance and certain knowledge."[46] Pascal here aptly echoes early Christian sentiments that our present existence is a consequence of the primordial fall that drastically impaired the human mind's moral and intellectual powers.

---

40. Evagrius Ponticus, *Scholion* to Ps. 144.20. The completion of this restorative separation comes about only in the eschatological fulfillment.
41. Cf. Maximus the Confessor, *Ambiguum* 8 (PG 91.1104D).
42. Athanasius of Alexandria, *Against the Gentiles*, 8.1. For English, see *Contra gentes and De Incarnatione*, ed. and trans. Robert W. Thomson, Oxford Early Christian Texts (Oxford: Clarendon Press, 1971).
43. Maximus the Confessor, *Letter 2* (PG 91.400D–01A); translation from Andrew Louth, *Maximus the Confessor* (London: Routledge, 1996), 89.
44. Ibid.
45. For the moderns, see especially Sergei Bulgakov, *The Bride of the Lamb*, trans. Boris Jakim (Grand Rapids: Eerdmans, 2002).
46. *Pensées* 1.131, in Blaise Pascal, *Pensées*, trans. A. J. Krailsheimer (London: Penguin, 1966), 65.

One consequence of this impairment is that we are actually unable to "know" the fall—on the logic that the fall was a change from a meta-historical existence to the present temporal-historical condition. That the fall is "situated" outside the boundaries of the historical process has fundamental corollaries with regard to what we can know about the fall and the original creation. The "events" of the fall and the Lord's second coming alike are meta-historical; they are not directly knowable from within the current historical unfolding. Thus, Noble emphasises that "empirical, historical investigation is incapable of taking account of either the *parousia* or the fall."[47] Early Christian expositions of Genesis likewise exhibit a pessimistic account of the consequences of the fall for human knowledge of God, *and of God's second coming.* In other words, this construal of the fall informed early Christian discussions about the grounds of knowledge, the eschaton, and salvation.

### There is Evil in This World, yet God Did Not Make Evil

All pre-modern Christian thinkers (notably Irenaeus, Athanasius, Basil, Gregory the Theologian, Augustine, and Maximus), as well as early modern theologians such as Calvin and Luther, contrast the fallen condition of creation (characterized by the presence of evil and mortality)[48] with the original pristine one. There is evil in this world, yet God did not make it. Neither could evil coexist with the original good, for God was no maker of any contradiction.[49] Humans, in particular, were good and beautiful, because they bore in themselves

---

47. R. J. Berry and T. A. Noble, *Darwin, Creation and the Fall: Theological Challenges* (Nottingham: Apollos, 2009), 119.
48. Speaking of the universal mortality inherent in the present age, Paul describes it as "the body of this death" (Rom. 7:24).
49. On the present state of things whereby evil coexists with the good and, moreover, constitutes a condition for its existence, see Richard Swinburne's discussion in *Providence and the Problem of Evil* (Oxford: Oxford University Press), 166–67. Swinburne maintains that if physical evils were taken away at a stroke,

> then so many opportunities for coping with difficult circumstances would have been removed that many of us would have such an easy life that we simply would not have much opportunity to show courage or indeed manifest much in the way of goodness at all."

The claim here is that in either permitting or bringing about bad states, God enables good states to exist. This, of course, is descriptive of the "secondary" (fallen) state, whereby evil is part of God's

seeds of the divine perfections. For instance, the divine image conveyed the potential to develop humanity in the unfolding cycles (αἰῶνες) of God-fashioned nonlinear benign time, which would result in a perfect resemblance to him (cf. Gen. 1:28). Thus, there was a program of perfection, the Creator's plan A for the world—in the words of Paul Blowers, "the overarching divine plan (λόγος; βουλή)"[50]—which God traced especially upon the human creation: humans were to become his own sons and daughters, and gods (cf. Ps. 82:6: "I said you are gods."), not by nature, but by the grace of adoption.[51] That is to say, humans were to become createdly uncreated. At the end of this progression of perfection, the perfected creation of God would have abided with him unto eternity, where "with him" signifies that humans would have continued to progress eternally and apophatically in their knowledge of God through their participation in his life. After all, in the view of many ancient Christians and pagans, perfection and transformation are only complete when they have no end, so that in perfection, one "still thirsts for that with which [one] constantly filled himself to capacity, and [one] asks to attain as if [one] had never partaken, beseeching God to appear to him."[52]

In the fall, however, the Creator-creature equivalence that makes the knowledge of God achievable broke down, became impossible to practice, and all but vanished. This is how humanity rejected God's original plan for it. This is the present state of the universe that

---

providence. To early Christians, however, evil belongs only within the economy of salvation but not as part of God's original creation.

50. Cf. Paul Blowers, "The Dialectics and Therapeutics of Desire in Maximus the Confessor," *Vigiliae Christianae* 65 (2011): 428.

51. For a treatment of early Christian theologies of salvation as deification, *theosis*, see Norman Russell, *The Doctrine of Deification in the Greek Patristic Tradition*, Oxford Early Christian Studies (Oxford: Oxford University Press, 2004); also Stephen Thomas, *Deification in the Eastern Orthodox Tradition: A Biblical Perspective* (Piscataway, NJ: Gorgias, 2008).

52. Cf. Gregory of Nyssa, Vita Moysis 230 (GNO 7.1); for the English translation, see *Gregory of Nyssa: The Life of Moses or Concerning Perfection in Virtue*, ed. and trans. Abraham J. Malherbe and Everett Ferguson (Kalamazoo, MI: Paulist, 1978), 114. The principle that change is only complete when it has no end-point was adopted into early Christian metaphysics from Plotinus, who, in turn, was correcting the Aristotelian notion of change, *kinesis*, as requiring a completion point. For both Plotinus and the Christians, authentic change is thus not temporal but eternal. See Plotinus, 6.1 [42] 16; and Aristotle, *Eth. Nic.* 1174a14-23; cf. *Metaph.* 9.6. For discussion of Aristotle's and Plotinus's respective notions of change, see Richard Sorabji, *The Philosophy of the Commentators: 200-600 AD: A Sourcebook: Volume 2: Physics* (Ithaca, NY: Cornell University Press, 2005), 61–66.

determines our current state of ignorance, including the obliviousness of the *eschata*. The evil ignorance of the fall, therefore, is itself one of the reasons why, unaware of God's ways, we perceive the Lord's non-coming as perplexing. Yet, in that very instance, through our willful insistence on *our* knowledge and *our* view of how things, physical and metaphysical, ought to be, one might say that we contribute to the deferral of his coming, lest "when the Son of Man comes," he not "find faith on earth" (cf. Matt. 18:8).

As the ancients saw it, the incarnation of the divine Logos as Jesus Christ is the healing medicine for the fallen condition.[53] It enables us, through the commandments of the love of God and neighbor,[54] to re-grow our first "wings of virtue" and once more to "soar up"[55] toward our first knowledge of the Creator, ourselves, and the cosmos. Till those wings sprout, however, our conjectures about God's *eschata* remain a non-apophatic pseudo-knowledge. It is this fallen ignorance that, in the minds of the ancient apophatic writers, would constitute the root of our perplexity at the Parousia's "delay." This is why, Justin Martyr and Irenaeus, Clement and Augustine, Dionysius, Maximus, Luther, and Calvin (and, for that matter, Sergei Bulgakov, Karl Barth, and Hans Urs von Balthasar) all agree that, in our present condition and within this history of ours, what we know of God and his ways, we know apophatically and through revelation.

### The Time Arrow: The Contradictoriness of Fallen Time

Earlier on in this chapter, we mentioned the problem of the "arrow of time."[56] What is it and why does it matter?

The problem of time is a central thread in the present argument about the eschatological dilemma. This is on account of the defining

---

53. Cf. the abundant references in late antique and Byzantine Christian ascetic writers, notably those of the Philokalic tradition, to Christ's work as healing toward the restoration of the original virtue. For example, see Evagrius Ponticus, *On the Thoughts* 3.
54. Cf. Matt. 22:36–40; Mark 12:30-31; Luke 10:27; see further ch. 8, pp. 197–208.
55. Gregory of Nyssa, *Homilies on the Song of Songs*, 15.449 "κατὰ τὴν ἀρχαίαν χάριν ἀνεπτερώθημεν" (*GNO* 6.449); English translation from *Homilies on the Song of Songs*, trans. Richard A. Norris Jr., Writings from the Greco-Roman World 13 (Atlanta: Society of Biblical Literature, 2012), 474–77.
56. See p. 119n22 above.

role time plays in everyday experience and our perception of our grasp of reality. According to this experience, time seems asymmetric, in that it has a direction pointing from past to future, which is how things temporally unfold. Thus, "eggs break, but they don't unbreak; candles melt, but they don't unmelt."[57] And people die, but they don't undie.

There is, thus, a tragic twist to this directionality, because the latter seems fraught with despair on account of the futility of things. Camus's celebrated *Le Mythe de Sisyphe* (1944) illustrates the point. The essay is a response to the underlying problem of temporal existence, namely that life (and time) is absurd in multifarious ways. The greatest absurdity of all, however, is that humans continue to seek abiding meaning where there is none. Therein lies the contradictoriness of life, time, and human expectation: whereas the common expectation is that one eventually discovers an ultimate meaningfulness to things, life and time are directed to non-life and non-time—that is to say, to death understood as complete extinction.

Consequently, at the heart of the problem lies a singular contradiction between the reality of an overarching futility of things that we experience and our more philosophically-optimistic expectations.[58] The latter endure until one discovers "the elusive feeling of absurdity" of such expectations.[59] This, however, does not dispel the sense of a huge puzzle of reality; Sisyphus toils silently on. "Vanity of vanities; all is vanity," as Qoheleth succinctly puts it (Eccl. 1:2 *et passim*).[60]

How can we ever envision breaking free from the chains of this futility? Gaining deeper understanding of the eschatological problem

---

57. Brian Greene, *Fabric of the Cosmos*, 13.
58. On the ultimate futility of the present temporal condition infused with death, see especially Gregory of Nyssa: "At every moment, nature trains itself for death; life that progresses in time is radically inoculated with death. For, since transitory life is driven toward the future without ever finding a resolution vis-à-vis the past, death is what radically follows, in the strictest sense, life's energy." Gregory of Nyssa, *De mortuis* III, 521AB (*GNO* 9.52), cited by Hans Urs von Balthasar, *Presence and Thought: Essay on the Religious Philosophy of Gregory of Nyssa* (San Francisco: Ignatius, 1995), 67.
59. Albert Camus, *The Myth of Sisyphus*, trans. Justin O'Brien (Harmondsworth: Penguin), 17–19.
60. Note also the insight of Pozzo into the futility of the human life: "They give birth astride of a grave, the light gleams an instant, then it's night once more." Samuel Beckett, *Waiting for Godot* (London: Faber and Faber, [1956] 1988), 86.

would, in any case, create a sense of our empowerment in face of the inevitability of history's end. Here, early Christian cosmological speculation, understood as an apophatic mystery, seems to offer a solution that, although non-systematic and dispersed, encourages deeper metaphysical apophatic reflection upon the complex nature of reality. At the very least, this reflection points to serious inadequacies of our perceptions of "classical reality" and can perhaps help reveal baffling aspects of space and time more helpfully than the existentialist tradition from Kierkegaard to Camus[61] has succeeded in doing so far. At the most, it may even inspire one to tackle the problem of existence eschatologically, by becoming actually "ready" to welcome the Day of the Lord itself, when at long last it dawns.

As we have already indicated, in early Christian cosmologies, all created things have an instantaneous beginning. And yet, time as initially created, is mysterious and intimately related to eternity. It is a "movable image of eternity." Its unfolding contains one "never-ending day" (τὴν ἄπαυστον ἡμέραν) in continuity with eternity.[62] This is why Basil emphasizes that time always returns "again in a circle to itself." To Basil, time was made timelessly, for it was made in the day called "day one," not the "first day" (cf. Gen. 1:5, LXX: ἡμέρα μία). Now to Basil, "day one" signifies "a day without evening, without succession, and without end, that day which the psalmist also called the *eighth* day, because it belongs outside this week of time."[63] This, then, is an eternity in which the end is like the beginning and where things "turn back upon" themselves, because in eternity, there is no successive unfolding of any kind.

What Basil means is that this original time, which existed prior to the fall, was in some respect *aionic*, an adjective derived from the Greek αἰών, denoting (according to Basil) "created eternity." Before

---

61. For lineaments of the existentialist tradition, see Jacob Golom, *In Search of Authenticity: Existentialism from Kierkegaard to Camus* (New York: Routledge, 1995); J. Judaken and R. Bernasconi, eds., *Situating Existentialism: Key Texts in Context* (New York: Columbia University Press, 2012).
62. Basil, *On the Holy Spirit* 27.66 (PG 32.192B; SC 17 bis *ad loc.*). English translation from *On the Holy Spirit: St Basil the Great*, trans. Stephen Hildebrand (Yonkers, NY: St Vladimir's Seminary Press, 2011), 106.
63. Basil, *Homilies on Hexaemeron* 2.4.28–29 (SC no. 26 bis *ad loc.*).

the fall, original time was enmeshed in created eternity and was itself like it: time was spacious, benign, and somehow in touch with God's complete timelessness of grace. This flawless divine timelessness is perfectly non-extended divine eternity, what Greek philosophy and ancient Christian writers call ἀΐδιον, meaning "everlasting" (a term reserved for divinity). The first-ordered created time was meant to be "upgraded" to a proper aionic eternity for creatures called the "eighth day," and to continue in touch with the divine uncreated eternity (the ἀΐδιον). Now, the "eighth day" is identical with the "day one." It is also the eschatological "Day of the Lord."[64]

In Basil's (somewhat convoluted) argument, we encounter an early Christian understanding of the eschaton as simply the completion of the act of creation whereby creatures are finally invited into actual (not potential) eternal happiness. Moreover, in this early Christian understanding of temporality, time as initially created is not plainly linear, but complex, multidimensional, non-futile, and non-sinister, in touch with eternity while on the road to eternity. Time is essentially a means to life, not death.

When set side by side with this early Christian understanding of time, it is easy to see how time's present contradictoriness can be accounted for in terms of the fall: what we have is a fallen, damaged, and reduced version of the optimal product. More generally, time's overall character, according to both Basil and Einstein, is not uniform, but flexible, molding or "draping" itself around objects: the passage of time creates the sensation of the movement of an object, and the movement of an object results in the sensation of a passage of time.[65] According to Basil, just like space, time is "coextensive with the existence of the cosmos."[66] Time, therefore, is *not an absolute independent entity*, as Newton thought at the birth of modern science; time

---

64. See Basil of Caesarea's extended excerpt from *Homily 1* on the *Hexaemeron*, cited above. For a detailed discussion of these matters, see Brandon Gallaher, "Chalice of Eternity: An Orthodox Theology of Time," *St Vladimir's Theological Quarterly* 57, no. 1 (2013): 5–35. See also Ilaria L.E. Ramelli, *The Christian Doctrine of Apokatastasis: A Critical Assessment from the New Testament to Eriugena*, Supplements to Vigiliae Christianae 120 (Leiden: Brill, 2013).
65. Cf. Georgios I. Mantzaridis, *Time and Man*, trans. Julian Vulliamy (Waymart, PA: St. Tikhon's Seminary Press, 1996), 3.

is, instead, *relative* to the dimensions of moving objects, a little like what Einstein calls time's relativity to an object's spatial location and gravity. Therefore, in early Christian philosophical writers, the manner of the flow of time, even when it was first made, relates to and depends upon the free choice that beings—especially humans—exercise. Fallen beings, therefore, exist in fallen time. And this is why time, at present, requires redeeming (cf. Eph. 5:16).

Christ's incarnation made all the difference, literally changing the course of time. Fundamentally, the incarnation enabled time to become the means of healing and recovery. The incarnation—and more broadly, God's self-revelatory and redemptive action throughout history—allows this "evil" time (cf. Eph. 5:16) to begin to bring about or push toward the timeless eschaton as an event that is both apophatically mysterious and certain.

This comes about in two ways. In the first place, through the incarnation, the eschaton is allowed to enter time already here in this life. This comes to pass through the Church's prayer to God, its sacraments, and other theophanies, such as the transfiguration. Inasmuch as these "moments" are instances of time connecting with timelessness, they are eschatological and they allow the universe a foretaste of the final consummation (see further chapter 8, pp. 195, 197-98). The change wrought upon time by the incarnation is such that henceforth, every moment of temporal being becomes capable of opening up on to eternity. Yet, these instances of "eternity in time" are occurrences of an eternity that is incomplete. They are but a series of "stepping stones" leading on to the final Day of the Lord.

In the second place, therefore, the incarnation changes time so that, through ever-new successive "stepping stones," time's unfolding is no longer blindly "non-teleological" (as in biological evolution). Rather, time now aims toward the final consummation into a non-temporal, nonlinear, unending personal existence of participation in the divine life.

---

66. Basil of Caesarea, *Against Eunomius* 1.21 (PG 29.560B). English from *St. Basil of Caesarea: Against Eunomius*, trans. Mark Delcogliano and Andrew Radde-Gallwitz (Washington, D.C.: Catholic University of America Press, 2011), 122.

## Part 3: Christ: The One Undivided Mystery of Creation, Incarnation, and Second Coming

Where is Jesus Christ in all this? Surely, Jesus should be at the heart of any discussion of eschatology. "Who do the crowds say that I am?" Luke reports him as asking (Luke 9:18), after which he proceeds to lay the foundations of Christology. It seems justified to maintain that—despite the divergences with regard to tenets of the right belief within the early Church and all the distance separating *us* from *them*—how one understands who Jesus Christ is still determines the kind of eschatology one constructs; this holds across denominations and allegiances, today as it did in the past. Jesus Christ and no other is the ultimate eschatological subject. Eschatological redemption centers upon God and Jesus so that the "last day" is the "Day of the Lord Jesus" (cf. Rev. 22:20).

In much pre-modern Christian reflection, the divine acts of creation, incarnation, and second coming are intimately related as three stages—instances of the one self-same meta-historical divine action with regard to created beings.[67] If the purpose of God's act of creation is to bring beings into existence and that of the incarnation is "to save that which was lost" (Matt. 18:11), then the aim of the second coming is to complete the work of both by bringing about perfect salvation for the universe in the restoration of God's original plan. Who, then, is the Jesus who lived "under Pontius Pilate" and "will come again in glory"?

### Early Christian Perceptions of Jesus Christ

Despite variations in ancient Christian speculation about God, Christ, and salvation, from Christianity's inception, there inhered a certain core set of intuitions that was focused on the person of Jesus Christ.[68]

---

67. See, in particular, Maximus the Confessor's *Ambiguum* 71.5 (PG 91.1412C–D) on the inseparable connectedness of these three divine acts:

> ...when the wise Ecclesiastes... beheld... the vision of what had been truly created and brought into being, he said: *What is this that has been brought into being? It is the same as that which will come into being. And what is this that has been created? It is the same as that which will be created.* He clearly had in mind the first things and the last things, inasmuch as they are the same things and truly exist....

Even though some of these intuitions took centuries to crystallize, they eventually emerged as the mainstream Christian confession of faith: the Church's *theology*. Early Christians saw these tenets as the truth of divine revelation, which reflected some of the pre-eternally abiding aspects of God's very being and nature that God in his benevolence chose to reveal in time and history. In fact, this crystallized theology of revelation arises from the earliest Church's worship and sacraments, indeed going back to what the Church recognized as the words and deeds of Jesus Christ himself. The centrality of the Christ-event in history and to the destiny of the universe is at the heart of these beliefs: that Jesus lived, died, and rose from the dead; that through his life, death, and resurrection, he has showed himself to be the Savior of the world (cf. 1 John 1:14); and that at the end of times, he will without fail "come again in glory, to judge the living and the dead."[69] These beliefs about Jesus Christ developed side by side with the Church's speculation about the mystery of God: that God is one, but also somehow three—Father, Son, and Spirit—and that this is how God reveals himself. The Son is also the preexistent Logos (or Word) of God and the wisdom of God,[70] and it is the Logos and not the Father or the Spirit who became incarnated in human history as Jesus Christ.

*Pace* German Lutheran critical sensibilities, early Christian sources yield little evidence of any "gap"—hermeneutical or factual—between "the Jesus of history" and "the Lord of faith." The Lord of glory and the Jesus of history are one and the same, so that the Lord of glory *is* the Jesus of history. The "Man of Sorrows" of Isaiah 58 is Jesus of Nazareth in these texts. The Lord of glory, who raises the dead and arises from the tomb himself, is the Son of Man, the Son of God, the one Lord Jesus Christ.

---

68. We are not suggesting thereby any primordial state of "orthodoxy" within the earliest Christianity, along the lines that von Harnack envisions in his *Dogmengeschichte* (Tübingen: Mohr Siebeck, 1905). On early Christian beliefs manifesting divergence and variation from their very inceptions, see Walter Bauer, *Orthodoxy and Heresy in Earliest Christianity* (London: SCM, 1972). See also Lewis Ayres, *Nicaea and Its Legacy: An Approach to Fourth-Century Trinitarian Theology* (Oxford: Oxford University Press, 2004).
69. From the Apostles's Creed.
70. For an early articulation of the theologies of Christ as the Wisdom of God and as the Word of God, see Justin Martyr (d. 165 CE), especially his *Dialogue with Trypho the Jew*, ch. 61.

### The Resurrection as a Fact; the Second Coming as a Certainty

The earliest Church equally upholds a literal belief in the resurrection of Jesus Christ, the greatest miracle of all. To obliterate this fact would be to misinterpret early Christian views about the second coming. To maintain that Jesus will come again in glory presupposes that he died, rose from the dead, and ascended to the right hand of the Father. By way of contrast with some twentieth-century liberal Protestant views, the early Church accepts the resurrection as an historical fact, wherein the rising from the dead is understood literally and physically and not as a (mere) psychological experience of the disciples important to their self-understanding. The resurrection of Christ is also a meta-historical act of God, turning the course of history and re-creating things anew. It is from this vantage point that eschatological insights in the early Church can be fruitfully approached. Put simply, for the earliest Christians, Jesus was the preexistent Christ the world had expected because he rose from the dead and because his resurrection bore unmistakable marks of his mastery over life, death, and immortality.

The earliest Christians may have felt disappointed on account of the perceived delay of the Parousia. Nonetheless, while the circumstances surrounding the future eschaton remained to them a mystery requiring an apophatic approach, its factuality was never doubted.[71]

### Jesus' Complete Future Immortality

From a certain point in the fourth century (at the latest), the mainstream Church's beliefs in the resurrection and the second coming rested upon the view that Jesus possessed a complete future immortality, understood in terms of his own eternal co-existence with God and the gift of eternal life that he bestows on those believing in him.[72] That Christ "rose from the dead," "ascended into heaven,"

---

71. For all the variability of the ancient baptismal creeds, they concur in the conviction that Jesus Christ will return without fail.
72. Cf. John 10:28: "I give them eternal life, and they will never perish . . . and no one will snatch them out of my hand."

and "will come again to judge the living and dead,"⁷³ meant that he possessed immortality open upon the future eternity. (From this point on, we shall draw more extensively on later Byzantine cosmological syntheses and we will pay special attention to the work of Maximus the Confessor, "the most daring systematician of his time.")⁷⁴

Jesus was mortal in the sense that he showed himself capable of dying. Yet, his was a death unlike that of "all mortal flesh."⁷⁵ It was fully voluntary and undergone "that the Scriptures might be fulfilled" (cf. John 19:28).⁷⁶ Chosen in freedom, his death was also freely laid aside at the hour of his resurrection. In the words of Scripture, "No man takes [my life] from me, but I lay it down of myself. I have power to lay it down, and I have power to take it again" (John 10:18). To the early Christians and to subsequent (mainstream) Byzantine, Latin, and Syrian theological traditions, this indicated that Jesus was the master of his own death and immortality, and that, moreover, his death was not part of the "natural" necessity of the physical life-and-death cycle that had in its grip all biological life. The ascension story, which early creeds often emphasize, manifests a view that, once risen, he was not to die again but was raised on high, to be seated together with the Father in an eternal future immortality. It was only as possessing a future-oriented immortality that he can be expected to come again in the immortality of the Father.

### Jesus' Complete Pre-Existent Immortality

Furthermore, Jesus Christ is also immortal "towards the past" and possesses a complete pre-existent immortality.⁷⁷ In what constitutes

---

73. From the Creed of Nicaea-Constantinople, 381 CE.
74. Hans Urs von Balthasar, *The Cosmic Liturgy: The Universe According to Maximus the Confessor*, trans. Brian E. Daley S.J. (San Francisco: Ignatius, 1989), 29.
75. Cf. the Byzantine hymn sung at the Great Entrance in the *Liturgy of St. Basil* on the Great Holy Thursday.
76. On the tenet that Jesus' death was both voluntary and transformative for the created order, see especially Maximus the Confessor, *Ambiguum* 5.15 (PG 91.1053C): "By His power He transformed the passions of nature into acts of the will, so that they were not the results of natural necessity, as they are with us, but in His case it was just the opposite."
77. On this subject, see in particular, Simon J. Gathercole, *The Preexistent Son: Recovering the Christologies of Matthew, Mark, and Luke* (Grand Rapids: Eerdmans, 2006).

another paradox, Jesus Christ, who was "crucified ... under Pontius Pilate," predates his own temporal life as Jesus of Nazareth. He precedes chronologically both the prophet David and Abraham: "Before Abraham was, I am" (cf. John 8:58). That he is the Son of God and is sent to the world expresses Jesus' pre-existence (Gal. 4:4). The pre-incarnate Christ is present within the Scriptures and in the world as the wisdom of God (Prov. 8:22-30). Drawing on Jewish-Hellenistic sapiential literature—where Wisdom is personified as the hypostatized wisdom of God, preexistent, creative, and itself divine[78]—Paul identifies Christ with this Wisdom of God (cf. 1 Cor. 1:18-2:16). In fact, Christ preexists the world entirely and absolutely. Christ is "pre-eternal,"[79] meta-temporal and meta-historical, even though he manifests himself in history. As seminal Church councils promulgated, there never was a temporal or other moment that he "was not."[80] Christ eternally shares in the Father's divine absolute non-temporality, where his being is forever constituted by the meta-historical divine present—the "I am" of John 8:58 and Exod. 3:10.

## Christ's Perfect Divine Eternity

In contrast with the interests of the liberal Protestant tradition, Byzantine theologians such as Maximus the Confessor wished to approach the phenomenon of Christ primarily as an atemporal mystery manifested in time. Maximus's philosophical Christology synthesizes previous theologies of Christ (in particular, the views of Gregory of Nazianzus and Dionysius the Areopagite), grounding the early Church's mainstream theology of atonement in the presupposition of Christ's complete non-temporal transcendence according to his divinity, which makes itself known in his perfect incarnation in space and time for the sake of creatures. As co-eternal with the Father, Christ always lives in the non-temporal, non-extended divine "now;"

---

78. Cf. Job 28:20-28; Prov. 8:22-31; Eccl. 1:4-9; 24:3-22; Wisd. of Sol. 7:25-37; Philo, *Leg.* 2.86; *Det.* 115-18.
79. Cf. the Byzantine *troparion* hymn of the Nativity of Christ, where Christ is termed "the pre-eternal God."
80. See the anti-Arian Creed of Nicaea, 325 CE, on the Son's perfect co-eternality with the Father.

ancient liturgies employed apophatic language in an endeavor to lift up the minds of the faithful to this comprehension. Consider, for instance, the following Byzantine liturgical address to God and Christ:

> It is meet and right to sing praises to you, to bless you, to magnify you, to give thanks to you, to worship you in all places of your dominion: God ineffable, unknowable, invisible, incomprehensible, you are the same from everlasting.[81]

The assumption here is that Christ's eternality and co-eternality with God entails his divinity in some real, non-mythologized sense. Christ is the Κύριος, just as God is, a view emphasized by Christian appropriations of the Septuagint.[82] In fact, Jesus Christ is "one of the Holy Trinity."[83]

### Christ the Creator and Eternal Logos

This, to the early Church, necessitates that Christ is the Creator, who co-creates the world with the Father and the Spirit.[84] The author of John 1 describes the Logos as identical with Jesus Christ and as the Creator of the world. As Maximus the Confessor points out, he brings creation into creaturely being out of non-existence.[85] This means that all beings together and each one in particular exist *in virtue* of being created by Christ. Thus, to Paul, Jesus Christ is the creative power of God, himself the Creator: "One is the Lord Jesus Christ, through whom all things, and we are through him" (1 Cor. 8:6). Consequently, Maximus argues, "all the ages of time and the beings within those ages have received their beginning and end in Christ."[86]

---

81. The Offertory (*anaphora*) prayer of the liturgy of St. John Chrysostom.
82. Cf. Rom. 10:12–17.
83. For emphases on Christ's kenotic divinity, see the Acts of the Second Council of Constantinople 553, of which canon 10 reads: "If anyone does not confess that our Lord Jesus Christ who was crucified in flesh is true God and Lord of glory and one of the holy Trinity, let him be anathema" (ACO 4.1). English translation from R. Price, ed., *The Acts of the Council of Constantinople of 533 with Related Texts on the Three Chapters Controversy*, 2 vols., Translated Texts for Historians 51 (Liverpool: Liverpool University Press, 2009), *ad loc.*
84. Even early subordinationist Christologies, such as that of Arius (early fourth century), while holding Christ to be purely a creature, maintained that he co-creates together with the Father.
85. Maximus the Confessor, *Ambiguum* 7.16 (PG 91.1080A): "By His *word (logos) and His wisdom* He [=Jesus Christ] *created* and continues to create *all things*—universals as well as particulars . . ."

To early Christians, Jesus' status as the universe's Creator is manifested through the nature of his engagement with people and beings. Christ relates to things in the world through a relation of love. To traditional Christians, this is a manifestation of his status as divine and the Creator: if it is a feature of divinity that God creates and sustains the world in love, then Christ is authentically divine because of the manner of his engagement with beings in his incarnation. Thus, when later Byzantine hymnography depicts Christ's loving care for the world, it uses analogies of human parenthood, even motherhood.[87] As the mother cares that even her ugly offspring flourish, so the risen and exalted Christ is ever present to bring about "comeliness" from our ugliness. It is the Creator of the universe that became incarnated in the very creation that he made as its Savior; the same Creator and Savior will come again at the end of this present time to "make all things new" (cf. Rev. 21:5).

This Christology, therefore, identifies in its worship, kerygma, and later Byzantine systematizations the suffering Jesus Christ as the divine Logos of God, the pre-eternal Alpha and Omega (cf. Rev. 1:8) of creation, who eternally contains in himself the pre-existent *logoi* of beings.[88] These latter *logoi* are also the dynamic divine possibilities of and for all beings, as chapters 7 and 8 will expound (see pp. 167–70 and 179–85).

This all means that, as the pre-eternal Beginning and End of all things, Christ stands at the heart of history and of its consummation. Epistemologically, then, Christ also resides at the epicenter of any human attempt to understand the so-called delay of the Parousia.

---

86. Maximus the Confessor, *Ad Thalassium* 60 (CCSG 22.75), in *On the Cosmic Mystery of Jesus Christ: Selected Writings from Maximus the Confessor*, trans. Paul M. Blowers and Robert Louis Wilkens (New York: St Vladimir's Press, 2003), 125.
87. See, for instance, Byzantine prayers addressed to Jesus Christ of the Office of the First Hour.
88. Cf. Maximus the Confessor, *Ambiguum* 7.16 (PG 91.1080A). For Maximus's theology of the *logoi*, see especially Andrew Louth, "St Maximos' doctrine of the logoi of creation," in *Studia Patristica: Vol. XLVIII*, ed. J. Baun et al. (Leuven and Paris: Peeters, 2010), 77–84.

## Christ as the Source of Contradiction to "Common Experience"

We have seen that the early Christian picture of Christ, while breathtaking, is also mysterious and riddled with contradictions, particularly with respect to metaphysical binaries such as life and death, time and eternity, space-time and infinity, divinity and humanity. In fact, Christ is the very personification of contradiction in whom all categories of "normality" apparently are inverted. He never does anything "normally" and "straightforwardly," but he acts "para-doxically" (a term which in Greek signifies "beyond plain understanding"). One can never tell from the Gospel narratives whether in a given instance, he acts as God or as man; in fact, Jesus seems to perform human activities divinely and divine ones humanly.[89] Even in his birth, Christ seems to negate the fundamentals of normalcy. He is born, yet through a different mode of birth, enabling motherhood and virginity (the two greatly incompatible statuses) to come together.[90] Finally, his resurrection reverses the "natural" order whereby death irrevocably follows and negates life. In Christ, therefore, two apparently contradictory realities come together and co-inhere in a perfect union, a union-in-difference of two perfect manners of being (divine and created), where the two stand in a creative tension.[91] Discerning this with the eye of faith, we are empowered to act through virtue and through his grace as members of his body. As the measure of all things, then, Christ is the ultimate

---

89. Cf. Maximus the Confessor, *Ambiguum* 5.14: "He also did human things in a way that transcends humanity, demonstrating in an exalted union that the human activity is assimilated to the divine power without being changed."
90. Maximus the Confessor, *Ambiguum* 5.13 (PG 91.1052C–53A):

> "Though [Christ] was beyond being, He came into being, fashioning within nature *a new origin of creation* and a *different* mode *of birth,* for He was conceived having become the seed of His own flesh, and He was born having become the seal of the virginity of the one who bore Him, showing that in her case mutually contradictory things can truly come together. For she herself is both virgin and mother, innovating nature by a coincidence of opposites, since virginity and childbearing are opposites, and no one would have been able to imagine their natural combination."

English from Maximus the Confessor, *On Difficulties in the Church Fathers: The Ambigua*, 2 vols., ed. and trans. Nicholas Constas (Cambridge, MA: Harvard University Press, 2014).
91. See the christological definition of the council of Chalcedon.

source of our biblical hermeneutics, our theological epistemology, our ethics and eschatology.

In bringing these oppositions into unity, however, Christ and his Church are the "sign of contradiction" (cf. Luke 2:34; Acts 28:22), a stumbling block to the gentiles (cf. 1 Cor. 1:23). Because his truth flies in the face of the "verities" of this world, Jesus Christ becomes subject of extreme opposition to the point that this is his distinctive definition.[92]

## Christ the "Contradiction" Unites and Resolves All Contradictions

In our current state of epistemological limitation, our knowledge rebels against the categories of spiritual nonlinear apophatic knowing. We feel the pressures of speaking in orderly linear sequences, just as we wish to see our lives and history as orderly and chronologically sensible. This is the manner in which human thought currently functions, unable to approach the divine or even created realities without reasoning in categories that we "possess" and "order" with our non-apophatic logic. It is this tendency toward linear thinking that startles the mind attempting to conceptualize Christ as eschatological in the sense of being co-eternal with the Father.

But this reorientation of ourselves to Christ presupposes our embracing a state of being in contradiction to the world. The fully realized eschaton comes about if we live it in Christ already within—or better, despite—our current temporality, however contradictory, bizarre, and apophatic that it might be to our so-called "common sense." Modern post-Enlightenment unease regarding the Christ-event and the eschatological problem itself reflects the contradictoriness of the phenomenon of Christ, whereby majesty is inseparable from lowliness.[93] Here, we are to recall once more the point already made regarding the manner of divine revelation as reflected in apophatic speech (see above, pp. 112–18): the paradox of the divine agency and

---

92. Cf. John Paul II, *Sign of Contradiction* (Strathfield NSW, Australia: St. Paul, 1979), 8.
93. See e.g. Phil. 2:16 (KJV): "Who, being in the form of God, thought it not robbery to be equal with God."

# NEGATING THE FALL AND RE-CONSTITUTING CREATION

of the language we use for it. Christ both reveals and conceals himself in the contradictoriness of his manifestations. He is transcendent, and yet, fills all things. He is fully human, and yet, he is one of the three irreducible divine persons indivisibly united. And he will come again to re-constitute his creation (cf. Rev. 21:5).

More pointedly, Jesus is a contradiction to fallen linear existence: Christ generates in himself a perfect union of opposites, reconciling the Creator-creature oppositions which seem so radical within our current historical and biological progression. This is the contradictoriness of Christ's glory and humiliation, the marks of the Lord and those of the servant, life and death, timelessness and "evil" time. Christ is the point where the uncreated and the created in its present state are perfectly united: without confusion and without division, without change and without separation.[94] As Maximus the Confessor stresses in a critical definition, Christ brings together the fragmented contradictoriness of the present created being "between a limit of the ages and limitlessness, between measure and immeasurability, between finitude and infinity, between Creator and creation, between rest and motion. . . ."[95] More profoundly, Christ draws together into harmonious unity in his very person all the confusions, brokenness, and fragmentations of passions, and selfishness that characterize the present manner of existence.[96] Through drawing disparate things together, Christ re-creates them, with the result that in the kingdom, there will be a new existence for creatures: instead of being fallen and temporal, creatures will be redeemed into a completed created eternity (αἰών; see above, p. 129), which Gregory of Nyssa terms the "time" that is "newly contrived."[97] In all this, Jesus Christ presents himself

---

94. Cf. the four *apophatic* adverbs of the definition of Chalcedon (451 CE) describing Christ as the one in whose person the divine and the human natures are perfectly and unconfusedly united (*ACO* 2.1).
95. Maximus the Confessor, *Ad Thalassium* 60 (CCSG 22:75); for English, see Maximus the Confessor, *On the Cosmic Mystery of Jesus Christ: Selected Writings from Maximus the Confessor*, trans. Paul M. Blowers and Robert Louis Wilkens (New York: St Vladimir's Seminary Press, 2003), 125. For a recent treatment of the subject, see Gallaher, "Chalice of Eternity," 5–35.
96. On Maximus's theology of the fall and restoration in Christ, see Melchisedec Törönen, *Union and Distinction in the Thought of St Maximus the Confessor*, Oxford Early Christian Studies (Oxford: Oxford University Press, 2008), 176–82.
97. Gregory of Nyssa, *Easter Sermon 1* (*GNO* 9.290.4-7):

as the grand underlying principle of all being, the only key to unlock the secret of the universe so that we can return to the divine plan. Apophatic reasoning alone can search out ways to relate to this.

To comprehend the coming of the last day, therefore, we need first to restore our true vision of the mystery of Jesus Christ and his redemptive work. Then, the eschatological restoration will be activated in our lives here and now. Appropriately, the etymology of "restoration" suggests a return to a previous condition of health: the moral authenticity of the self turned toward God, πρὸς τὸν θεόν (cf. John 1:1). In "looking for the life of the age to come," our τέλος, therefore, we strive to rediscover our primordial beginning, our ἀρχή, the way we were "before" the evil dawn of history broke:

> Now the resurrection promises us nothing else than the restoration of the fallen to their ancient state; for the grace we look for is a . . . return to the first life, bringing back again to Paradise him who was cast out from it.[98]

## Conclusions

We have seen how ancient apophatic reflections on time, the fall, and Christ generate new space and possibilities for our twenty-first-century debates about the delay of the second coming. These fresh perspectives rest upon assumptions of both ontological-metaphysical correspondences and disjunctures between God and the created, fallen world. In particular, these apophatic metaphysics can enrich reductionist modern discourses about human perceptions of reality and about historical time.

A key contribution of the pre-modern doctrine of the fall is the belief that human reason (not to mention morality) has been hampered. Due

---

> For it was right in the case of him who rules the temporal order by his sovereign power that his works should not necessarily be forced to fit set measures of time, but that the measures of time should be newly contrived for what his works required. . . . For the one who has power both to lay down his life of his own accord and to take it again had power when he wished as creator of the temporal orders not to be bound by time for his actions, but to create time to fit his actions.

English text from *The Easter Sermons of Gregory of Nyssa: Translation and Commentary*, translated S.G. Hall, ed. Andreas Spira and Christoph Klock (Cambridge, MA: Philadelphia Patristic Foundation, 1981), 40–41.

98. Gregory of Nyssa, *De hominis opificio* XVII.2; English translation from *NPNF2* 5.407.

## NEGATING THE FALL AND RE-CONSTITUTING CREATION

to our finitude and fallenness, humans lack the capacity for accurate foresight[99] and our "common perception" of the unfolding temporal sequence is flawed. Much of what humanity now recognizes as "normal" is, in fact, in opposition both to God and God's original creation. Indeed, our treatments of the eschatological problem are symptomatic of our post-Enlightenment views about Jesus Christ that, put side by side with early Christian theologies of the Lord of glory, are often reductive. In traditional Christian views, Jesus Christ is the same "yesterday, today, and forever" (Heb. 13:8); he is utterly beyond all time (χρόνος), eternity (αἰών), and extension (διάστημα) in his divinity. He is the Master of time, for it is not befitting for the Lord of time to be subject to time.[100] It is as the Master and Creator of time that Christ re-constitutes the "old" time anew.[101] Nevertheless, even though Jesus is the Lord of time, he involves himself in the very fabric of current temporal linearity, enabling time's very deficiencies—such as its enmeshment in pain and death—to work for us toward its own completion. This divine involvement in time is omnipotent, yet patient and respectful of our limitations, unfolding as God's desire to revive, complete, and re-create the immortal freedom that is ours (see further chapter 8, pp. 194–97).

But this immortal freedom is not forthcoming to us as skeptical observers deliberating over the "problem of eschatology" *in abstracto*,

---

99. Cf. the causal link Fyodor Dostoevsky establishes in his *Crime and Punishment* (1866) between sin, on the one hand, and the loss of freedom, insanity, and death, on the other.

100. Gregory of Nyssa, "On the Three-day Period of the Resurrection of our Lord Jesus Christ" (*GNO* 9.290-911; trans. S.G. Hall, in Spira and Klock, *Easter Sermons*, 40–41:

> It was right in the case of him who rules the temporal order by his sovereign power that his works should not necessarily be forced to fit set measures of time, but that the measures of time should be newly contrived for what his works required.... For the one who has power both to lay down his life of his own accord and to take it again had power when he wished as creator of the temporal orders not to be bound by time for his actions, but to create time to fit his actions.

101. See Janet M. Soskice's view on the unity of the beginning and the end in traditional Christianity, where man is *a priori* viewed as eschatological:

> Anthropology in the Bible is never wholly separate from eschatology, nor creation from redemption, because "what we will be" is not separable from what we were made to be and what we now are. We should perhaps speak, in the New Testament, of an *eschatological anthropology* in which we are loved, we will love, and we will be made lovely in our Lord Jesus Christ.

Janet M. Soskice, *The Kindness of God: Metaphor, Gender, and Religious Language* (Oxford: Oxford University Press, 2007), 181.

stammering apologetically *vis-à-vis* the twists of scientific progress, or inertly pondering the non-arrival of an unknown Godot.[102] Instead, it will be given to us (and the creation *in toto*) as active participants "groaning as in the pains of childbirth" (Rom. 8:23, *NIV*), as the creation progresses toward rediscovering its ἀρχή and τέλος in Christ. Early Christians described humans as active co-workers with God in the task of bringing this history of the fall to a closure, so as to start anew in the divine created eternity of αἰών. Therefore, despite our current spatio-temporal limitations, if we subject our "normal" sensibilities to divine upheavals, we can contribute to resolving some of the poignant problems of our moment in fallen history, such as the current Christianity-culture détente. By promoting further Christianization of the Christian culture in terms of enabling it to see ways of embracing the *others* as our neighbors, by sanctifying and Christifying every aspect of society so as to discover theological ways of relating to multiculturalism,[103] we can work to open ourselves and the world to a relationship with God, striving together with God to bring about the aionic restoration. On the personal level, this requires people, as God's creatures, to make a theologically apophatic response through a particular, self-emptying manner of life described frequently as the "taking up of our cross."[104] A personal apophasis, a cathartic negation of the self, an individual *kenosis* is required (see further, chapter 8, pp. 202–5).

For us, then, to understand the eschaton and the "delay of the Parousia" in our present state of all the unresolved tensions of existence, we need a certain "graced state of being,"[105] whereby our *natural* history becomes suffused with the eternal presence of the Christ-Logos in it *already now*. But if we require such a state to understand the eschaton, we might even go as far as to say that the Lord's coming is graciously conditioned by his condescension to this very state (see further, chapter 8, pp. 187–93).

---

102. Cf. Beckett, *Waiting for Godot*.
103. Cf. Rowan Williams, "The Judgment of the World," 56.
104. Cf. Matt. 16:24–26; Mark 8:34; Luke 9:23.
105. Blowers, "Dialectics and Therapeutics," 429–30.

# NEGATING THE FALL AND RE-CONSTITUTING CREATION

The eschaton, then, is a divine-human collaborative project already in progress. To paraphrase a contemporary discussion of the unreality of time,[106] the truth of the past and the future is in the eye of the beholder, and for things to be real, they need to stare us in the face here and now as the eternal "present." This dynamic holds for our knowing and embracing the second coming of the Lord Jesus Christ, *whenever it shall occur*. The righteousness and faithfulness of God[107] are the surety of its coming, but our eagerness for it to transform us is immediately relevant as well. An authentic Christian theology of the Parousia, our apophatic anticipation of it, contributes to bringing the Day of the Lord about.

And yet, if the coming of the Lord is dependent on us in terms of our cooperation—or not—with God in Christ through his body, the Church, that means that it may well arrive this very day and hour, or after another 1,000 years. Our responsibility as members of the Church and of as part of God's creation, then, is to endeavor to ready ourselves: "Be watchful and pray, for you do not know the hour when he Son of Man will come."[108] As the following chapter argues (pp. 158-71), in his infinite perfect freedom, God in Christ has before him an innumerable number of creative possibilities for the advent of the eschaton from which he will choose to actualize the possibility that he alone knows is right. He will do this in collaboration with us, his living body. But inasmuch as we await it, the eschaton already inheres in the "presentness" of now—the "now" that knows no eventide.

---

106. For instance:

> Presentness is, in truth, one and the same as being real, and one can only think that past events are real by taking the eternalist view that they are eternally there as presenting themselves, while past and future in relation to other events. Pastness and futurity ... only exist in the eye of a beholder but presentness is the form of beholding itself.

T.L.S. Sprigge, "The Unreality of Time," *Proceedings of the Aristotelian Society*, n.s. 92 (1992): 19

107. Cf. Rom. 1:17 (*NIV*): "For in it [=the Gospel] the righteousness of God is revealed from faith for faith, as it is written, 'The righteous shall live by faith'."

108. From the Byzantine matins of Lent.

# 7

# Divine Possibilities: The Condescension of God and the Restriction of Divine Freedom

Brandon Gallaher and Julia S. Konstantinovsky

We have argued that in order to see eschatology *ethically* and ethics *eschatologically,* it is necessary to have an understanding of God that is both apophatic *and* cataphatic. This theological vision is one in which God is beyond all our conceptions, being simultaneously "the Father of lights with whom there is no variation or shadow due to change" (James 1:17) and the God of new, unforeseen possibilities and promises. The most important of God's commitments to us is that Jesus will come again in glory to establish the kingdom on earth in its fullness. Such a God is lovingly responsive, and, in a manner of speaking, willing to "change his mind" in relation to the actions of his creation for the purposes of the divine economy while remaining wholly self-same. Apophaticism, then, exists in conjunction with, and indeed, is the basis of a cataphatic vision of God as ontological love. In other words, in order to say what we can know of God, we also must confess what we do not and cannot know or understand. Paradoxically, albeit retrospectively, because we understand God to be free, we see that God has room to be reliable. We know that God will fulfil his promises, coming again to us, being true to himself as the One who loves in freedom.

In this chapter, we shall propose a vision of divine Being as act, according to which God's Being, in the purity of its activity, can be responsive to the actions of creation (e.g. its repentance or non-repentance) while remaining the self-same God. We shall then outline an account of God's providence, building on the tradition of divine possibilities in which God is free to act with an infinity of possible "options" before him. To do so, we will establish that key classical theological figures (i.e. Augustine of Hippo, Maximus the Confessor, Gregory of Nyssa, and Thomas Aquinas), and also, significant modern theologians who draw on that tradition (i.e. Sergii Bulgakov, Hans Urs von Balthasar, and Karl Barth) have a vision of the divine Being as utterly dynamic but still unvarying. As a result, they understand that God can be responsive to human mutability by taking humanity's changes into consideration in his actions of love. On this basis, we will explain that God retains the possibility of a world in which Jesus returns immediately following Pentecost, as well as the possibility of a world in which Jesus may return at some distant future, based upon how the Church responds to its vocation to build the kingdom of God on earth.

We will show how these possibilities find their shape and coherence through God's work in Jesus Christ. This salvific work, culminating in the Parousia, is not unilateral; instead, it always and necessarily recapitulates and summarizes all the human bumblings and strivings which contribute to the divine economy of salvation. Jesus' second coming depends on us: God is God for us in Jesus Christ, and God will not act alone; God waits on us and relies on us as his co-workers in history. This chapter argues for the theological plausibility of the idea that God condescends to allow us to participate in bringing about the eschaton in and with Christ. Indeed, we will contend that God binds himself to the possibility of cooperating with humanity in Jesus Christ, whose perfect humanity recapitulates all humanity: past, present, and future.

## A Christocentric Vision of the Divine Being

Theologians tend to respond in one of two ways to the Scriptural depiction of God as a God who can "change his mind." On the one hand, one can say that such "changes" are really only *apparent*, that God only says he changes his mind as a concession to our time-bound reasoning. According to this view, God always knew that creation would, for example, turn from its wicked ways in response to a given prophetic threat of doom; thus, when God says he changed his mind and withdrew a decree of destruction, it would be the case that his eternal, immutable will had always been set on this path in light of his foreknowledge of human action.

There are two problems with this position. First, it does not grant human freedom any true efficacy *coram Deo*. There is no hint of human cooperation with God in Christ under grace, no synergy that allows human activity not only to make a difference in time, but also in eternity. Instead, in this unnuanced reading of divine foreknowledge and predestination—which relies heavily on a particular reading of the Pauline Epistles—all people are foreordained as either "vessels of wrath made for destruction" or "vessels of mercy, which he has prepared beforehand for glory" (Rom. 9:22-23).

Second, this position requires a vision of God as so perfectly self-contained in the immutability of his eternity that even to hint that God might be affected by his creation would make him into something he is not—a creature. Such an austere God who cannot change—while remaining WHO HE IS (cf. Exod. 3:14, LXX)—in light of his creature's response becomes a victim of his own freedom. More gravely, this vision of God is not sufficiently Christocentric: neither does it allow Christ's divine-human activity to be the center of history, the decisive point which *effects* eternity (cf. chapter 6, p. 138), nor does it grant Christ's divine-human activity the efficacy to bend broken, corrupted time and creaturely eternity back to its true foundation in him, in unity with his Father and Spirit.[1] This is an activity in which humans can and do participate in the Church as Christ's living body, filling up what is lacking in Christ's sufferings (Col. 1:24).[2]

Instead of claiming that God's changes of mind are only apparent, in this chapter, we will formulate the doctrine of God on the basis of God's intervention in history through Jesus Christ. Our approach views the divine Being in light of God becoming human for us in Christ: dying, rising, taking all of creation with him to the Father in the ascension, and promising to return in glory to lift up creation to new life.

This approach resembles the *method* of Martin Luther (1483–1546), even if it does not accept all Luther's assumptions or derive the same conclusions. Luther held, as a general rule, that one should avoid as much as possible any question that might carry one to the "throne of the Supreme Majesty."[3] Luther's approach is well-illustrated by his interpretation of Gen. 6:6–8. In that text, God sees the wickedness of humanity and says he is "sorry that he had made man on the earth, and it grieved him to his heart" (Gen. 6:6, KJV2000); God concludes that he will wipe out everything on earth except righteous Noah and those with him (Gen. 6:6–8). Luther claims one should not speculate on the meaning of these things from the perspective of eternity.[4] Still, if one remains intent on such speculation, Luther argues that one must say God, who is unchanging in his eternity, foreknew that creation would act wickedly. When the creature sinned, it means that God, with divine foreknowledge of the creature's action, *allowed* it to act wickedly and permitted it to fall. By permitting the creature to err, God simply allowed the evil intention he foreknew to be enacted, and thereby, confirmed the creature's wickedness. Any talk of changing

---

1. On the distinction between uncreated and created eternity, and between fallen and renewed time, see Brandon Gallaher, "Chalice of Eternity: An Orthodox Theology of Time," *St Vladimir's Theological Quarterly* 57, no. 1 (2013): 7–17.
2. This topic is taken up in detail in ch. 8, pp. 197–208.
3. Martin Luther, *Lectures on Genesis* 6:5–6 (LW 2.44–45; WA 43.293–94).
4. That is, how can God be sorry he made man and grieve in his heart for it, and then change course?

his mind or repenting and grieving is God's way of lowering himself to our comprehension and using simple images, like one would for a child.[5] Thus, Luther concludes that "[i]t is better and safer to stay at the manger of Christ the Man. For there is very great danger in involving oneself in the mazes of the Divine Being."[6]

Luther nevertheless argues that the true will of God's good pleasure is not some unveiled reality of the divine Being to which we can ascend (Rom. 10:5-8; cf. Deut. 30:11-14). Rather it is the "good will" of the gospel (Rom. 12:2) revealed in Jesus Christ: "This is indeed the will of my Father, that all who see the Son and believe in him may have eternal life" (John 6:40; cf. Matt. 3:17; 12:50). This "will of grace" is precisely the "will of the divine good pleasure . . . ordained from eternity and . . . revealed and displayed in Christ."[7] But if this is the case, why cannot one interpret the divine Being in light of the manger of Christ the man? This would be to argue that we can only properly speak of God's Trinitarian Being in the wake of the free kenotic dynamism of Jesus Christ.

Might there be an alternative way to think about the biblical descriptions of God changing his mind? Though we disagree with Luther's account of divine foreknowledge and predestination, his Christocentric methodology is rich, albeit applied too strictly. How, then, can we take something of Luther's own method and apply it to the contemplation of the Divine Being? Is there another theological path when faced with Scripture's insistence that God can, and indeed, does, change his mind in light of human responsiveness to his love as expressed in prophecy?

We maintain that, in light of the knowledge that God has given himself to us utterly in Jesus Christ, it is apparent that God is not a static Being in a negative sense. Not wanting to be left silent about this unutterable God and needing to respect that he has definitively revealed himself in his hiddenness in Christ, we move forward to

---

5. Luther, *Lectures on Genesis* 6:5-6 (*LW* 2.44-45, 47ff.; *WA* 43.294ff.); cf. *The Bondage of the Will* (*LW* 33.42); *Lectures on Jonah* 3:4-10 (*LW* 19.85-90; *WA* 19.234-39).
6. Luther, *Lectures on Genesis* 6:5-6 (*LW* 2.45; *WA* 42.293-94; cf. *LW* 48; *WA* 42.295).
7. Ibid., (*LW* 2.48; *WA* 42.295).

explore this paradox. The mode of the divine Being is, for lack of proper creaturely conception and language to explain it, a *dynamic stillness* beyond all categories of time and eternity. God is both movement and rest.

One helpful analogy here is that of a person balancing. The image of balancing helps to depict how the uncreated God relates providentially to his creation (even if it suffers the fundamental difficulty of any theological analogy, to wit, that God is *not* a human). When one balances, she may appear to be perfectly still; yet, she is making hundreds of small movements, constant incremental adjustments in order to maintain that posture of stillness. Likewise, one can say, albeit imperfectly, that God is unchanging in his posture toward humanity and the rest of creation, but this does not mean that God is entirely static. Rather, to stay perpetually in a fixed posture of eternal and unbending love, bent low toward the creation to which he has bound himself, means God condescends to act and react to what creation is doing, even if God foreknew what his creatures would do before they even acted.

Just such a God can intervene in history by the incarnation while continually upholding history through his Spirit, this God is unchanged in his love despite his creative ability to adapt to our needs. Thus, he can and will return again in glory dependent on our co-operation with Jesus Christ in the Church. God is a God who will be what he will be (Exod. 3:14): he pledges to Israel that he will be its deliverance from its sufferings in Egypt and lead them to a land of abundant life; likewise, he pledges to the Church that in his second coming, he will be its Passing Over—its Pascha—from death to abundant, eternal life.[8] This is God as the God of future hope, of innumerable possibilities, even of the *impossible possibility* of our consummate reconciliation with God in Christ when he will come "with the clouds; every eye will see him, even those who pierced him; and on his account all tribes of the earth will wail. Even so. Amen" (Rev. 1:7). Yet, this God is not simply

---

8. See Melito of Sardis, *Peri Pascha* 103–5; for English, see Melito of Sardis, *On Pascha: With the Fragments of Melito and Other Material Related to the Quartodecimans*, trans. Alistair Stewart-Sykes (Crestwood, NY: St Vladimir's Seminary Press, 2001), 65–67.

a pure Becoming, a sort of divine torrent of Being that one cannot step into and out of twice given its pure movement—akin to Heraclitus' ever-changing river.[9] God is reliable, trustworthy, unchanging in his love, even if describing this love is utterly beyond our mental powers because it changes and adapts itself in response to our finite actions.

Lest this approach seem wholly novel in Christian thinking, the following discussion of Augustine of Hippo, Maximus the Confessor, Gregory of Nyssa, and Thomas Aquinas demonstrates its consistency with seminal theologians that represent the best Christian theological reflection across antiquity and the medieval period.

## Divine Dynamism in the Eastern and Western Traditions

The Christian tradition is united in understanding that God's Being and attributes (goodness, wisdom, etc.) are both properly God because God's will and God's essence are one. It has varied, however, in how it has expressed the relationship between his Being and his attributes. We will argue that God can, without ceasing to be himself, change his actions toward us, depending on our responses. This is a logical extension of the tradition's insistence that God's Being and his action are one dynamic, but unchanging reality. If the Being and the activity of God are one, then, in imitation, human contemplation of God and human ethical activity in the world—whereby we conform ourselves to Christ—are likewise inseparable. Thus understanding the oracles of God (prophecy) cannot be divided from living in thanksgiving according to his law, by faith through grace (activity). This is the case because God's wisdom—conceived as his Being in action, in self-revelation to himself and to us—is pre-eminently practical and only understood as we work with him in bringing about his kingdom which is to come.

---

9. See G.S. Kirk, J.E. Raven and M. Schofield, eds. and trans., *The Presocratic Philosophers: A Critical History with a Selection of Texts*, 2nd ed. (Cambridge: Cambridge University Press, 1993), 194–97 (§§214-16).

## Augustine of Hippo

Augustine (354–430 CE) argued that in God's simplicity, there was no difference between *who* he is (his Being) and *how* he is (his subsistence). To be and to subsist are one and the same; "therefore if the trinity is one being, it is also one substance."[10] Put slightly differently, just as there is no difference between God's substance and his existence, so too there is no difference between what God is (his Being) and what he possesses (his attributes). For instance, God both has life and is life. God is identical with his attributes: "For him existence is not something different from life. . . . For him to exist is the same as to live, to understand, to be happy."[11] The substance of the Being of God is alone of all things immutable—indeed, he cannot change. Therefore, God *truly* can be said "to be" because he does not lose his Being, as does a creature that changes; what a creature becomes is different from what it once was.[12]

It might seem from this that Augustine's idea of the divine Being is purely static. But this is not the case, for the will and the substance of God are one reality. When God wills, he wills all things simultaneously in one eternal act, which is his Being (as in the act of creation). This is different from a mutable creature, which wills one thing now and another thing at another time. Nothing mutable is eternal,[13] and so, God's eternal activity must itself be changeless. But this does not mean it is in any way unresponsive to human changeability and negates human contingency; rather, God's eternal activity, his will as the highest efficient cause, simply takes human changeability into consideration. Knowing the ways of creaturely wills, God providentially and graciously orders free human action without in any way

---

10. Augustine, *Trin.* 7.3.10 (CCSL 50.261; PL 42.943); for English, see Augustine, *The Trinity*, ed. and trans. Edmund Hill, WSA I/5 (New York: New City, 1996), 228.
11. Augustine, *Civ.* 8.6; cf. 11.10; for English, see Augustine, *Concerning the City of God against the Pagans*, trans. Henry Bettenson (London: Penguin, 1987), 307–8; cf. 440–41; for a critical edition, see *La cité de Dieu: Livres I-V*, ed. Bernhard Dombart and Alfons Kalb, trans. Gustave Combes, 2 vols., Bibliothèque augustinienne 33 (Paris: Institut d'Études Augustiniennes, 2012), 2:206.
12. Augustine, *Trin.* 5.1.3; cf. 8.1.2 (CCSL 50.208, 269–70; PL 42. 912, 948); English: *The Trinity*, 190, cf. 242.
13. Augustine, *Conf.* 11.7.9; 11.10.12; 12.15.18 (CCSL 27.198–99, 200, 224–25); for English, see Augustine, *Confessions*, trans. Henry Chadwick (Oxford: Oxford University Press, 1998), 226, 228, 254.

causally necessitating it.[14] This view is similar to Luther's, though later writers drew different conclusions from these considerations. God is Existence itself[15] and through his pre-temporal Word (i.e. his eternity), this God as Trinity "has called us, for the Word has burst forth from eternity." By the Word existing before time, "all time was made; he was born in time, though he is eternal life; he calls temporal creatures, and makes them eternal."[16]

## Maximus the Confessor

This dynamic view of the divine life—immutability as an eternally recirculating, recalibrating rest—is also present in the Eastern Fathers. They see God in himself as unmoved, but nevertheless, the very life of creation. Thus, Maximus the Confessor (580–662 CE) remarks that God "is unmoved, complete and not subject to passion;" God is the end of all things, which itself has no beginning, the *telos* toward which they move. "For from God come both our general power of motion (for he is our beginning), and the particular way that we move toward him (for he is our end)."[17] In a sense, God is and is not creation, for he "is truly none of the things that exist, and [he], properly speaking, *is all things*, and at the same time beyond them." This is the case because God is present in the *logos* of each thing that exists and in all the *logoi* together; thus, God is the means by which all things exist.[18]

## Gregory of Nyssa

Prior to Maximus, we encounter a similar view in the writings of Gregory of Nyssa (c. 335–c. 395 CE), who says that God has true Being which is always the same, neither diminishing nor increasing, neither

---

14. See *Civ.* 5.9; English: *City of God*, 190–94; *La cité de Dieu*, 1:454–66.
15. *Conf.* 13.31.46 (CCSL 27.269–70); English: *Confessions*, 301.
16. Augustine, *Enarrat. Ps.* 2 of Ps. 101:10 (CCSL 40.1446); for English, see Augustine, *Expositions of the Psalms, 99-120*, ed. and trans. Maria Boulding and Boniface Ramsey, WSA III/19 (New York: New City, 2003), 71.
17. Maximus the Confessor, *Ambigua* 7.9–10 (PG 91.1073B–C); for English, see Maximus the Confessor, *On Difficulties in the Church Fathers: The Ambigua*, 2 vols., ed. and trans. Nicholas Constas (Cambridge, MA: Harvard University Press, 2014), 1:84–87.
18. *Ambigua* 22.2 (PG 91.1257A); ibid. 1:450–51. We shall return to this point below, pp. 167–70.

changing for the worse or the better. God as true and real Being needs nothing and is himself what is alone desirable. Everything participates in God, but God is not diminished by this participation[19] and he himself participates in nothing.[20] This Being is itself at one with its activity or power, which both remains in itself—revolving around itself so that "it never ceases its motion nor migrates into another place than that in which It is"—and yet, simultaneously maintains everything that is by itself. It permeates everything, fitting the parts together with the whole and fulfilling the whole in its parts, such that it takes the mutability of things into consideration, indeed, founding that changeableness on its self-same energies.[21] It is in everything that exists so that all things remain in existence, yet its essence is far distant from what is revealed of it in each created thing, even though it is indubitably found in those things.[22] In short, "all things depend on him Who is [Exod. 3:14 (LXX)], nor can there be anything which has not its being in him who is."[23]

The Divine Being is understood here as the radically transcendent, eternally changeless actuality of all actualities who is the self-donating infinite source and ground of all that is; God creates by bestowing finite being on that which has no existence in itself. As such, the divine actuality which births contingent creaturely actuality is absolutely immanent to all things, since God is the One in whom "we live and move and have our being" (Acts 17:8).[24] Gregory observes, in a similar fashion to Luther, that humans come to know this dynamic but immutable "Existence . . . above all" and "pervad[ing] all things" by

---

19. Gregory of Nyssa, *Vita Moysis* 25 (*GNO* 7.37); for English, see Gregory of Nyssa, *Gregory of Nyssa: The Life of Moses*, trans. Abraham J. Malherbe and Everett Ferguson (New York: Paulist, 1978), 60.
20. Cf. Thomas Aquinas, *Quaestiones de anima* 6.2ad; for English, see Thomas Aquinas, *Questions on the Soul*, trans. James Robb (Milwaukee: Marquette University Press, 1984), 96.
21. Gregory of Nyssa, *On the Soul and Resurrection*, trans. Catherine P. Roth (Crestwood, NY: St Vladimir's Seminary Press, 1993), 34 (*GNO* 15.12; PG 46.28A); compare John of Damascus, *Orthodox Faith* 1.8; 1.9ff.; for English, see John of Damascus, *St John of Damascus: Writings*, trans. Frederic H. Chase, FC 37 (Washington. D.C.: Catholic University of America Press, 1981), 183–84, 189ff.
22. Gregory of Nyssa, *On the Soul and Resurrection*, 45 (*GNO* 15.27; PG 46.44A–B).
23. Gregory of Nyssa, *The Great Catechism* 24; NPNF2 5:495 (*GNO* 3.4.63; PG 45.65).
24. For two quite different brilliant contemporary discussions, see both David Bentley Hart, *The Experience of God: Being, Consciousness, Bless* (New Haven/London: Yale University Press, 2013), 28–31, 87–151 and, in contrast, Paul S. Fiddes, *The Promised End: Eschatology in Theology and Literature* (Oxford: Blackwell, 2000), 110–47.

contemplating the "mystery of the cross." Further, Gregory comments that with the four parts of the cross Christ binds together things from all four corners of the earth: "at the hour of his pre-arranged death [he] was stretched upon it . . . who binds together all things into himself, and by himself brings to one harmonious agreement the diverse natures of actual existences."[25]

## Thomas Aquinas

Thomas Aquinas (1225-74) also endorses this unified construal of God's essence and activity, which entails a supreme dynamism of Being without, in any way, allowing mutability. God, for Aquinas, is "entirely simple"[26] and being simple, he is the perfect Being who is "most fully in being."[27] As most fully in Being, God is the best, and therefore, is essentially good.[28] He is the author of goodness by being the first origin of all activity,[29] causing all complex things[30] by the "resolution of his intellect and will."[31] Therefore, God being simple, most actualized in Being, and the origin of all activity must "of necessity" be actual and without any admixture of potentiality; God is the "unchanging first cause of change."[32] His power is coextensive with his activity, for his nature is not determined by another, but acts of itself. God's nature is unmoved by another in its own free act of knowledge[33] because his existence and essence are one,[34] so that we say that he is "sheer actuality, simply and wholly perfect, and not wanting for anything."[35] Since in his Being, God is perfectly good, truly actual, and, above all, dependent on no other but himself, and yet, causing all things, God is

---

25. Gregory of Nyssa, *The Great Catechism* 32; NPNF2 5:500 (GNO 3.4.79-80; PG 45.80D-81A).
26. Thomas Aquinas, *ST* 1.3.7co; for English, see Thomas Aquinas, *Summae Theologia: Questions on God*, ed. Brian Leftow and Brian Davies, trans. Brian Davies, Cambridge Texts in the History of Philosophy (Cambridge: Cambridge University Press, 2006), 40.
27. *ST* 1.2.3co; Aquinas, *Summa Theologia: Questions on God*, 26.
28. *ST* 1.6.3co; ibid., 67.
29. *ST* 1.4.1co; ibid., 45.
30. "The primary effective cause of all things", *ST* 1.4.2co; ibid., 47.
31. *ST* 1.19.4co; ibid., 224.
32. *ST* 1.3.1co; ibid., 30.
33. *ST* 1.18.3co; ibid., 213.
34. *ST* 1.25.1co.; ibid., 270.
35. *ST* 1.25.1co.; ibid.

said to be free, to have a free will, for "in so far as one acts voluntarily, one is said to perform any action whatever freely" because "the free is that which is its own cause and so the free has the aspect of that which is of itself."[36]

But what is it to be such a free divine Being? It is, quite simply, to "possess life in the highest degree," insofar as God in being most perfect and actual is his very own life.[37] All this results from Aquinas, under the influence of his teacher Albert the Great (1193–1280),[38] reading Pseudo-Dionysius the Areopagite's writings about the One as a productive stillness[39] in light of Aristotle's notion of "God" as a pure and complete activity which is active in its immobility.[40]

## The Modern Period: Bulgakov, Balthasar, and Barth

It is, of course, intriguing to read these ancient and medieval accounts of God's dynamically immutable Being. But this theology is not of only antiquarian interest. Rather, this trajectory continues to be developed by major modern theologians in all three of the Christian traditions.

### Sergii Bulgakov

In the modern period, the conception of God as unchanging in all his changes becomes more sensitive to history and starts to reflect on how such divine dynamism might be a form of "supra-mutability."[41] Moreover, this movement in stillness comes to be seen as the very character of the Trinitarian difference construed kenotically, or in terms of self-emptying (Phil. 2:7).

---

36. Thomas Aquinas, *SG* 1.72; for English, see Thomas Aquinas, *The Summa Contra Gentiles of St Thomas Aquinas*, trans. English Dominicans (New York: Benziger Brothers, 1924), 161.
37. *ST* 1.18.3co (citing Aristotle, *Metaph.* 12.7; 1072b); 1.18.2ad; *Summae Theologia*, 213–14.
38. See Albert the Great, *Super Dionysium de divinis nominibus*, 13, q.12 (*Utrum Deus possit nominari...*), solutio, quoted in Alexei Chernyakov, *The Ontology of Time: Being and Time in the Philosophies of Aristotle, Husserl and Heidegger* (Dordrecht: Kluwer, 2002), 128.
39. Pseudo-Dionysius the Areopagite, *Divine Names* 9.8-9 (PTS 33:212–13; PG 3.916B–D); 13.1-3 (PTS 33:226–29; PG 3.977B–81A); for English, see Pseudo-Dionysius the Areopagite, *Pseudo-Dionysius: The Complete Works*, trans. Colm Luibheid and Paul Rorem (New York: Paulist, 1987), 118–19, 127–29; cf. Plotinus, *Enn* I.7.1; I.8.2; VI.8.20 (building on Aristotle).
40. Aristotle, *Eth. nic.* 7.14, 1154b25–29; *Metaph.*12.6.2–7.9, 1071b–1072b.
41. For in-depth discussion, see Brandon Gallaher, *Freedom and Necessity in Modern Trinitarian Theology* (Oxford: Oxford University Press, forthcoming 2016).

For instance, the Eastern Orthodox theologian Sergii Bulgakov (1871–1944) argues that God is completely and radically Other than his creation. God is not an ontotheologically generalized highest Being, the temporal "first cause" in cosmic history who stands alongside other created beings in a continuous temporal series of discrete causes. Such a God would be a demiurge and does not remotely resemble the eternal God of classical theism.[42] God's being and action cannot be likened to ours in that fashion. But Bulgakov does not only regard God as radically Other. He also teaches that the wholly eternal and transcendent Trinitarian life of God can be understood in light of the revelation in Jesus Christ. Thus, the Trinity is kenotic, a perfect movement of love in which each of the divine persons lives by letting itself go, giving itself to the other and letting the other be.

Bulgakov contends, insofar as one can say anything about God, that God is in himself an Absolute "Not-is," a Divine Nothingness beyond all relations. In other words, Bulgakov affirms a properly apophatic theology where God is beyond Being (cf. chapter 6, pp. 113–15). God as Absolute Divine Nothing is "an absolute negation of all definitions", "an eternal and absolute NO to everything, to every something." "God is the NOT-something."[43] One cannot even say this NOT "exists" since "it" is beyond Being. One is left to say oxymoronically that God "is" a "NOT-is [*NE-est*]."[44]

Yet, God simultaneously is perfect personhood, which creates an antinomy to this first self-definition (further on antinomy, see chapter 5, pp. 103–7). God is absolute relation in himself (immanent Trinity); in other words, Bulgakov also affirms a properly cataphatic theology. In the eternal changeless life of God as Trinity, his absolute freedom includes moments of what we call "freedom" and what we call "necessity". To reconceive divine freedom in this fashion is to avoid a picture of God's action as a pure, groundless exertion of will,

---

42. See Hart, *Experience of God*, 19–41, 106–7.
43. Sergii Bulgakov, *Svet Nevechernii: Sozertsaniia i Umozreniia* [1917] in *Sergii Bulgakov: Pervoobraz i Obraz: Sochineniia v Dvukh Tomakh*, vol. 1 (Moscow and St. Petersburg: Iskusstvo/Inapress, 1999), 102; the quotations of this text are the translations of Brandon Gallaher. For an English version of this work, see *Unfading Light*, ed. and trans. Thomas Allan Smith (Grand Rapids: Eerdmans, 2012).
44. Bulgakov, *Svet Nevechernii*, 102.

disconnected from the God who is both the awesome, sustaining, loving creator and our self-emptying Savior who girded himself as a slave. God—as Absolute self-relation, a perfect self-realization in love—does not have to create the world to complete himself. God does not need the world. The divine life of love is God's pre-eternal divine activity (*actus purissimus*) of revealing himself to himself—the Father emptying himself completely in his begetting of the Son and the Son responding in a complete self-gift of gratitude, with the Spirit affirming them both. God is a pure act of love which is self-emptying, self-giving, and self-receiving; in the infinity of limitless eternity, this love is willing to "limit" itself in order to promote the absolute good of the other. This is the very same love we see expressed in Jesus' sacrifice on the cross. Since this pure act of love constitutes God's being and never changes, God is free to respond to his creation, to change his mind in reaction to its confused desire for him or its lack of repentance, without becoming less or more than the One who is. Such a God, in short, is more than capable of delaying the eschaton and taking creation's own actions into consideration in his economy for that creation.

Bulgakov argues that God reveals himself to humankind as economic Trinity, accepting to be in relationship to a world: "*He is*, He is ON [i.e. *ego eimi ho on*: Exod. 3:14 (LXX)], the One Who Is [*sushchii*] [Exod. 3:14], Yahweh, as he revealed himself to Moses"[45] and he came to us in Jesus Christ. Bulgakov, therefore, speaks of a cosmological antinomy between God as "Absolute self-relation in himself" (immanent Trinity) and God as "Absolute-Relative" (economic Trinity). God is perfect eternal fullness and completeness, and at the same time, creates the world out of love, putting himself in relation to it with its temporal, relative, and becoming being.

It is essential to bear in mind that the immanent Trinity is the foundation of the economic. As a consequence, God—because he is a God who in eternity exists through a boundless self-emptying love, as the Absolute-Relative—*can limit himself in the manifestation of his divinity*

---

45. Ibid., 102, 104.

*without ceasing to be absolute (changeless and eternal) in his own immanent Being.*[46] This concept is crucial to our formulation of the doctrine of God. God as Absolute-Relative enters into becoming as "a special form of the *fullness* of being,"[47] embracing change and process in the creation and redemption of the world in Christ. God even allows creation to be a necessity for himself: God becomes dependent on creation in emptying himself by taking the form of a slave in the incarnation (Phil. 2:7), but nevertheless, remains the self-same free and boundless God of love. Since God, in his limitless eternity, expresses a sort of sempiternal self-limitation in his self-emptying love, it is not impossible for him to limit himself within the bounds of temporality for love of his creation while yet remaining supremely boundless and free. For our purposes, then, God can delay the Parousia based on our lack of repentance, and can even be depicted as changing his mind by revealing himself at sundry times and in diverse manners, all the while remaining the same unchanging God.

### Hans Urs von Balthasar

For the Catholic theologian Hans Urs von Balthasar (1905–88), God is radically beyond all creaturely notions of Being; he is a free, pure act of love that can be responsive to creation without changing.[48] Indeed, for Balthasar, God is not merely *totaliter aliter* (wholly different), but, in a favorite appellation borrowed from Nicholas of Cusa (1401–64), God is *Non-Aliud* (Non- or Not-Other). Cusa's treatise "On God as Not-Other" argues that it is impossible to make God as Trinity ("Not-Other and Not-Other and Not-Other")[49] into "Other than another,"[50] and so, intellectually graspable by human understanding. God is the simple,

---

46. See Sergii Bulgakov, *Agnets Bozhii* (Paris: YMCA, 1933), 251; for English, see Sergii Bulgakov, *The Lamb of God*, ed. and trans. Boris Jakim (Grand Rapids and Cambridge: Eerdmans, 2008), 223.
47. *Agnets Bozhii*, 333; *Lamb of God*, 302.
48. Pace process theology, where (contrary to classical theism) God is mutable, develops in history (following Hegel), and is not omnipotent. This is summarized famously in Whitehead's dictum that "God is the great companion—the fellow-sufferer that understands" (A. N. Whitehead, *Process and Reality: An Essay in Cosmology* (New York: Free, 1978), 351) and defended with aplomb in Charles Hartshorne's *Omnipotence and Other Theological Mistakes* (New York: State University of New York Press, 1984). For a creative but critical appropriation of process theology in eschatology see Fiddes, *The Promised End*, 127, 168-71, 206-10.

prior, inexpressible, and unutterable Being of all beings, the Form of all forms that bestows all being in such a way that he is not any of these beings or any one form. Yet, as *Non-Aliud,* he is also simultaneously a free act of love.

For Balthasar, the free revelation that takes place in the self-emptying of God on the cross is a Trinitarian one because Christ does not show us "divinity" in the abstract; rather, he shows us the love of the Father and the gift of the Holy Spirit. In contemplating the revelation of Christ, in cleaving to his life by giving ourselves away, we come to realize that he is an historical happening that breaks through every established form of the age precisely because he is the eternal happening of love. God's immutable Trinitarian Being is, following Bulgakov,[51] a ceaseless self-emptying, self-giving, and self-receiving love. The Father, in begetting the Son, subsists by his complete self-emptying. This giving away of himself is a free letting-be of the Son. The Son exists by letting himself be generated, and hence, the Father is dependent on his Son's response. Finally, the Spirit exists by letting himself be the mutuality of the Father and the Son (their "we").[52] Balthasar expounds on Gregory of Nyssa by remarking that in the Trinity, Being and Becoming coincide:

> We believed that becoming and Being were opposites, two forms, as it were, analogous without a doubt, but irreducible. Through the Incarnation we learn that all the unsatisfied movement of becoming is itself only repose and fixity when compared to that immense movement of love inside of God: Being is a Super-Becoming. In constantly surpassing ourselves, therefore, by means of our love, we assimilate ourselves to God much more intimately than we could have suspected.[53]

---

49. Nicholas of Cusa, *De Li Non Aliud,* 2: Chap. 5, 19; for English, see Nicholas of Cusa, *Complete Philosophical and Theological Treatises of Nicholas of Cusa,* 2 vols., ed. and trans. Jasper Hopkins (Minneapolis: Arthur J. Banning, 2001), 1117.
50. *De Li Non Aliud,* 2: prop. 18, 123; *Complete Philosophical and Theological Treatises,* 1165.
51. See Jennifer Newsome Martin "The 'Whence' and the 'Whither' of Balthasar's Gendered Theology: Rehabilitating *Kenosis* for Feminist Theology," *Modern Theology,* 31, no. 2 (2015), 211–34; and *Hans Urs von Balthasar and the Critical Appropriation of Russian Religious Thought* (Notre Dame, IN.: University of Notre Dame, 2015).
52. Hans Urs von Balthasar, *TD,* 2:256, 259; 5:87.
53. Hans Urs von Balthasar, *Presence and Thought: An Essay on the Religious Philosophy of Gregory of Nyssa,* trans. Mark Sebanc (San Francisco: Ignatius, 1995), 153.

Unlike creaturely Being that needs particular essences of things in order to subsist, God *qua* divine Being does not need to go out of himself to subsist. He has no need to create the world: his existence is his essence. Nonetheless, for Balthasar as for the previously discussed writers, divine Being must never be thought of as "static", a complete state of rest; it is "a constant vitality, implying that everything is always new,"[54] since God, in his eternal hypostatic generation, is "evermore even to himself."[55] The divine Being is a "trinitarian happening." Such hypostatic pure activity is, as just noted, a Super-Becoming, but not a "becoming in an intraworldly sense" because its excess always surpasses creaturely becoming even as it includes it. It is the "inner possibility and reality of becoming."[56] The changes in the life of the Son in time reflect this dynamic: the ever-changing, but changeless eternal life ("eternal change") serves as the "eternal capacity for transformation," as expressed in God's self-emptying on the cross.[57] God is always three steps beyond the novelties of creation; therefore, creation can, in a manner of speaking, "affect" him, even if it never "changes" him. God as Father, Son, and Holy Spirit can always reveal a new face in relation to each movement of creation's life. Divine unity, then, is not rigid, but an ever-expanding circle that "comes together ever anew in love."[58] This love has a personal name: Holy Spirit.[59] This God can change his mind about coming again in response to humanity's actions and still remain the self-same Being, never increasing nor diminishing in his love since he is, as Spirit, freedom itself (2 Cor. 3:17).

## Karl Barth

This dynamic approach to the doctrine of God is also found in the Reformed Protestant Karl Barth (1886–1968). God, for Barth, is beyond

---

54. *TD*, 5:511.
55. *TD*, 5:78.
56. *TD*, 5:67.
57. *TD*, 5:515.
58. *TD*, 5:514.
59. See Hans Urs von Balthasar, *Theo-Logic: Theological Logical Theory*, 3 vols., trans. Adrian Walker and Graham Harrison (San Francisco: Ignatius, 2000-2005), 3:225-49; and Fiddes, *The Promised End*, 215.

all our conceptions and power. He is free in the negative sense that he lacks any constraints other than those he chooses in the freedom of his love. He is separated by a great gulf from humankind by his hiddenness, for he is completely "inapprehensible."[60] Once again, this has significant implications for eschatology, for one can say God is free to change the time of the second coming because he is under no external or internal constraint for it to be at a specific time or other.

But, there is a positive sense of divine freedom for Barth. Humans apprehend God in his hiddenness, know him as a mystery, in the revelation of God's own Word, Jesus Christ. Barth did not regard God as trapped in himself, unable to take flesh as Jesus Christ. As Barth says it, God must be "free also with regard to his freedom."[61] He argues, therefore, that God is love, containing true otherness in himself. As Trinity, God has the freedom to differentiate himself from himself, and his freedom consists in being a God of love. In himself as Trinity, as an eternal life of love, God includes both an eternal *prius,* a superiority of the Father to his Son and Spirit, and an eternal *posterius* or obedient subordination of the Son and Spirit to their Father.[62] Freed by this eternal and dynamic life of love, God eternally elects to be with us in Christ; he enters fellowship with us, putting himself in relation to us and creating with us what he is in himself—a pure and free fellowship of love.[63] Just as we saw earlier in Bulgakov and Balthasar, Barth argues that as God eternally contains "obedience" in the Trinitarian relations—self-emptying self-giving and a free self-limitation of the one divine person to promote the other's primacy—so too in creation and redemption, we see the free loving obedience of the Son to the Father in emptying himself and going into the far country for our salvation.

God determines himself in Christ, but we must simultaneously emphasize that this love is free since he is the "One who loves in freedom."[64] God—and this is almost a constant refrain in Barth—could

---

60. Karl Barth, *CD* II/1, 187.
61. *CD* II/1, 303.
62. *CD* IV/1, 201–2.
63. *CD* II/1, 275.

have chosen otherwise in creating and redeeming us; his free self-giving is contingent and if God chose otherwise, he would still have been the God who loves. Just as God is free in his love, so also, God is free to change his mind about the time of the eschaton without ceasing to be himself. *The unbound love of God freely binds itself*, for God has bound himself to us in Christ, and through Jesus, has revealed himself as the One who loves us in freedom. Since God binds his free love in this way, we can rely on him to keep his word by coming again in glory.

God's immutability, because it is his act of being as the One who loves in freedom, cannot be thought of as a static essence; he is rather something like a divine eternal becoming. The Lutheran Eberhard Jüngel (b. 1934), a student of Barth, famously interpreted his teacher by saying God is a Being who is in becoming.[65] Barth refers to this idea as the "holy mutability" of God where his constancy consists in the fact that "he is always the same in every change."[66] This means that he remains the same even when he takes flesh because he is "eternally new" in himself, possessing an "immutable vitality."[67]

This Barthian idea is well expressed in the writings of the Scottish Presbyterian Thomas F. Torrance (1913–2007), another student of Barth, who explains that the acts of creation and redemption are radically new works of God, "new even for himself."[68] They are such because God has an "uncreated Time" in himself—quite different from creaturely time with its beginning and end, but nevertheless, embracing it.[69] There is a direction to divine activity and life that expresses God's desire, out of free love, not to be alone.[70] His Being is an unchanging dynamism of free love, a Becoming which is:

---

64. *CD* II/1, 257.
65. See Eberhard Jüngel, *God's Being is in Becoming: The Trinitarian Being of God in the Theology of Karl Barth*, trans. John Webster, 2nd ed. (Edinburgh: T&T Clark, 2001 [1965]), 75–123, esp. 114–16.
66. Barth, *CD* II/1, 296.
67. *CD* II/1, 500, 512.
68. T.F. Torrance, *Divine and Contingent Order* (Oxford: Oxford University Press, 2000), 6; cf. *The Trinitarian Faith: The Evangelical Theology of the Ancient Catholic Faith* (London/New York: T&T Clark, 1995), 89; *The Christian Doctrine of God, One Being Three Persons* (Edinburgh: T&T Clark, 1996), 108.
69. Torrance, *Christian Doctrine of God*, 220, 241.
70. Ibid., 240.

always consistently the same in every change, and yet always new in its free spontaneous outflow unconditioned by anything beyond itself, . . . [characterized] by a total freedom from rigid immutability or inflexibility and by an infinite range of variability and mobility in which its dynamic constancy as love is brought to bear consistently and yet differentially upon every and any state of affairs beyond itself, whether it is good or bad, orderly or disorderly, rational or irrational.[71]

This should not surprise us; this is the God we meet in Jesus Christ:

> The God who has revealed himself in Jesus Christ as sharing our lot is the God who is really free to make himself poor, that we through his poverty might be made rich, the God invariant in love but not impassible, constant in faithfulness but not immutable.[72]

> This dynamic constant life of love seen in the incarnation can, therefore, include a before and after[73] allowing for distinct "moments" in the eternal life of God so that creation can exist as something new, even for God.[74]

Once again, this has great importance for eschatology: this conception of God includes space for God to change his mind. This God can take into consideration our most passionate bumblings and fumblings and can reveal himself progressively in foretastes, through stepping stones to the Parousia, while remaining the unchanging God of love in all these permutations.

To summarize: a triumvirate of modern theological giants, representatives from each of the three Christians traditions, draws on earlier Christian thinkers to elaborate strikingly similar and dynamic visions of God. We appropriate this doctrine of God for our eschatology because it is rooted in tradition, is ecumenical without being antiseptic, and is consistent with the historically-critically informed approach to prophecy found throughout the Scriptures. In other words, this doctrine of God is both supported by a diverse collection of Christianity's best thinkers and compatible with an understanding of prophecy as activation, not prognostication.

---

71. Ibid., 245.
72. T.F. Torrance, *Space, Time and Incarnation* (Oxford: Oxford University Press, 1969), 75.
73. Torrance, *The Christian Doctrine of God*, 209.
74. Ibid., 241.

In this view of deity and eschatology, human response to God is crucial for the timing of the end (not to mention our experience of it). It generates a construal of the content and a form of revelation that is utterly Christoform, and yet, progressive throughout history, in the course of which God's various theophanies "flame out, like shining from shook foil . . . gathers to a greatness, like the ooze of oil."[75] Those theophanies will finally be consummated at the end of the age, when "the city has no need of sun or moon to shine upon it, for the glory of God is its light, and its lamp is the Lamb" (Rev. 21:23).

## Divine Possibilities

God is the God of Possibility. Crucially, God is the God capable of the impossible possibility of salvation culminating in the eschaton; a God who, the more he changes, the more he remains the same. Suggesting such a vision of God presupposes that he has before him many possibilities for the divine economy which he may or may not take up. To put it crudely, it presupposes there is one possibility that the end of the age would have taken place in the first generation after Jesus' ascension and another possibility that the end would transpire at some indefinite future point. Which possibility God will take up and enact is entirely at the disposal of his divine omnipotence, wisdom, and love, employed to coax creation into union and communion with him.

The notion of divine possibilities is closely bound up with a tradition that stretches from Plato (428/27–348/47 BCE) through the Christian Fathers and onwards[76] that God has before his "mind" a pleroma of divine ideas about all the things that might be or are. Perhaps the most famous patristic example of this tradition is found in Maximus the Confessor (580–662) and his understanding of the *logoi*.[77] We mentioned

---

75. G. M. Hopkins, "God's Grandeur", ll. 2–3, in *The Poems of Gerard Manley Hopkins*, eds. W. H. Gardner and N. H. MacKenzie, 4th ed. (London: Oxford University Press, 1967), 66.
76. E.g. Plato, *Timaeus*, 29a–b, 30d–31a; Plotinus, *Enn.* V.7, V.9; Alcinous, *Didaskalikos*, 9, 16–17 (see *The Handbook of Platonism*, trans. John Dillon (Oxford: Oxford University Press, 2001), 16–17), Origen, *Princ.*, 1.2.2, 15–16 (SC 252, 92–95, ll. 25-62; for English, see Origen, *On First Principles*, trans. G. Butterworth (Gloucester: Peter Smith, 1973), 15–16), *Comm. Jo.*, 1.34.243-45 (PG 14.89B–C; SC 120, 180–83; *Commentary on the Gospel According to John: 1–10*, trans. Ronald Heine, FC 80 (Washington, D.C.: Catholic University of America Press, 1989), 83); Dionysius, *Divine Names*, 5.8 (PTS 33, 187–88).

it briefly in the last chapter (pp. 116–17, 137–38), but we now wish to focus on it at some length as a key plank in our constructive theology. The *logoi* are the innumerable "pre-existing" eternal divine reasons, or variously, ideas, principles, possibilities, intentions, and even, wills of and for each created thing that exists or may exist. As plans for created things, the *logoi* guide each thing's development, and together, the *logoi* find their coherence and are "contained" in the one creative Word (Logos) of God, described in John 1 as the God who infinitely transcends all created things:

> By his *word (logos) and his wisdom he created* and continues to create all things—universals as well as particulars—at the appropriate time. We believe, for example, that a logos of angels preceded and guided their creation; and the same holds true for each of the beings and powers that fill the world above us. A logos of human beings likewise preceded their creation, and—in order not to speak of particulars—a logos preceded the creation of everything that has received its being from God.[78]

Maximus asserts the creation of rational beings fundamentally to be creation out of nothing (ἐκ τοῦ μὴ ὄντος).[79] He states that the creative act was accomplished by God in his Wisdom and Logos (Wisd. of Sol. 9:1-2) *when* he wished: "Eternally existing as Creator, God creates when he wishes by his consubstantial Logos and Spirit out of his infinite goodness."[80] Consequently, the world has a definite moment of beginning, a *when*, at which point God brings it into existence according to his divine will. At the same time, God is said to exist *eternally* as Creator, even though the actual world is not eternal. Maximus elucidates this particular point more extensively by claiming that in his goodness, God "always and in all things" (ἀεὶ καί ἐν πᾶσιν) has an eternal desire to become "incarnated" or "embodied," as Maximus puts it, in created

---

77. But compare Augustine, *Div. quaest.* 46 and *Retract.* 1.3.2; for English, see Augustine, *Eighty-Three Different Questions*, trans. David L. Mosher, FC 70 (Washington, D.C.: Catholic University of America Press, 1982), 79–81; *Retractations*, trans. Mary Inez Bogan, FC 60 (Washington, D.C.: Catholic University of America Press, 1968), 14–15.
78. Maximus the Confessor, *Ambiguum* 7.16 (PG 91.1080A-B); English: Maximus the Confessor, *The Ambigua*, 1:94–97.
79. *Ambiguum* 7.15 (PG 91.1077C); Maximus, *The Ambigua*, 1:94–95.
80. Maximus the Confessor, *Four Hundred Chapters on Love* 4.3; for English, see Maximus the Confessor, *Maximus Confessor: Selected Writings*, trans. George C. Berthold (New York: Paulist, 1985), 75.

Being.[81] Here, the "embodied" does not primarily mean the incarnation, but the indwelling of God in the entirety of the created order: God creates with the desire to be *then* present, in some manner, within all things created. The incarnation of Christ in this respect is the pre-eminent and paradigmatic instance of God's overall embodiment in the created order. Both kinds of divine embodiment—the historical incarnation and God's more general dwelling within the created order—are part of God's *pre-eternal* plan.[82] This divine plan constitutes God's eternal activity, his ἐνέργεια.

When he creates, however, God actualizes his plan or thoughts about creation. In order to create, God brings his internal willing to create outside the sphere of his uncreated Being. He *externalizes*, as it were, his contemplation of the eternal ideas of creation. He seeds his ideas in creation, actualizes the possibilities, realizes his divine intentions. The *logoi* bridge the gap between God and the world, just like they connect God's "thinking" or "willing" to create and the actual coming into existence of beings. Through the *logoi*, creation is in God and God is in creation, but the *logoi* and created beings (God and creation) remain distinct. The multiplicity of the *logoi* accounts for the multiplicity of the universe, and, because the *logoi* are numberless, the divine freedom possesses the scope to pursue the end of love in creation. God is free to delay the eschaton, if he so chooses, based on the different "options" he has before him, that is, based on the *logoi* he seeded in creation and by which he guides it.

This patristic vision of the pleroma of creation eternally existing in the mind of God and being seeded in the world through the act of creation is described more clearly by later writers in terms of "divine possibilities," God's options for action. Here, Aquinas is the foremost source. God's will, for Thomas, is the cause of created things, but this will works in conjunction with his intellect.[83] In God's intellect, there

---

81. *Ambiguum.* 7.22 (PG 91.1084C-D); Maximus, *The Ambigua* 1:106-7.
82. Maximus the Confessor, *Ad Thalassium* 60 (CCSG 22.75ff.); for English, see Maximus the Confessor, *On the Cosmic Mystery of Jesus Christ: Selected Writings from Maximus the Confessor*, trans. Paul M. Blowers and Robert Louis Wilkens (New York: St Vladimir's Seminary Press, 2003), 124ff.
83. Aquinas, *ST*, 1.14.8co; for English, see Aquinas, *Summae Theologia: Questions on God*, 182.

exists a plurality of ideas which are the natures of things before they are created.[84] God works through his intellect (since his Being is his act of knowing) by conceiving the thing in question as a pre-existent idea; then, his will effects the thing in question,[85] like an artist who first knows his product, then effects it by his will.[86] God's wisdom is not only equal to his essence, will, and intellect, but also, to his power, and for that reason, God's wisdom encompasses the whole range of his absolute power (*potentia absoluta*). Bringing this together somewhat syllogistically, if: (a) wisdom is equal to the divine intellect, and (b) in the divine intellect are the ideas of things, and (c) God's power, which is equal to his intellect, is not restricted to the present order of things,[87] then it follows that (d) there are more ideas of things, more "possibilities", within the absolute power of God than God actually brings about by executing that power. In other words, *God could have done otherwise than he has in fact done.*

Indeed, God need not have taken flesh and become one of us for us as Jesus of Nazareth. This is the possibility God did, in fact, choose, bound himself to, actualized. But, there was no necessity for God to have chosen this particular possibility of being God for us in Christ. He had many more possibilities that—in his absolute power—were not chosen. Things in the divine economy could have been otherwise than they are. God chooses contingently to gift us graciously with himself and it is precisely because this choice need not have been the case that it is a surprising gift of the Spirit.[88]

Aquinas articulates this position by distinguishing between God's absolute power (*potentia absoluta*) and his ordinate power (*potentia ordinata*),[89] the latter of which is the divine determinate execution of

---

84. *ST*, 1.15.2; Aquinas, *Summae Theologia: Questions on God*, 202–3.
85. *ST*, 1.19.4co; Aquinas, *Summae Theologia: Questions on God*, 225.
86. *ST*, 1.14.8co; 1.19.4co; Aquinas, *Summae Theologia: Questions on God*, 182, 224–25.
87. See *ST*, 1.25.5co; Aquinas, *Summae Theologia: Questions on God*, 278–79.
88. Compare Fiddes, *The Promised End*, 169-70.
89. This key distinction is subsequently developed in both Catholicism and Protestantism. See William J. Courtenay, *Capacity and Volition: A History of the Distinction of Absolute and Ordained Power* (Bergamo: Pierluigi Lubrina, 1990); Lawrence Moonan, *Divine Power: The Medieval Power Distinction* (Oxford: Clarendon Press, 1994); Francis Oakley, *Omnipotence and Promise: The Legacy of the Scholastic Distinction of Powers* (Toronto: Pontifical Institute of Medieval Studies, 2002).

the absolute power.⁹⁰ For Aquinas, there is, in the mind of God, another possible world in contrast to what actually is—a world, for example, in which there is no Jesus of Nazareth; or, perhaps, a world in which there is a Jesus, but not Jesus the Messiah. Applying this thinking to eschatology, one can say that God has before him the possibility of a world in which Jesus returns immediately following Pentecost as well as the possibility of a world in which it may be in some distant future (and many other possibilities besides). God would be the same self-same God whether or not he returns to the world in Christ at a different time than he actually shall do because God possesses a perfectly free will, which has no necessary relation to any particular created end.⁹¹

### Narrowing the Scope of Divine Possibilities

The divine possibilities tradition was built on by many modern figures, including Barth.⁹² He argued that Christ goes into the "far country" and that God determines Godself in him through the application of a definite capacity of power (*potentia ordinata*), out of his supreme omnipotence (*potentia absoluta*), in the choice of a definite divine possibility among "an infinity of very different inward or even outward possibilities."⁹³ Thus, we are told that in Christ's obediently venturing out into the far country, there is no chance of his being controlled by caprice, a) since his freedom corresponds "to the *potentia ordinata* which is the real freedom and omnipotence of God"⁹⁴ and b) because by this ordered power, "he acts in the freedom of God, making use of a possibility grounded in the being of God," which is to be the covenanting God.⁹⁵

Nonetheless, there exists in this notion of divine possibilities—despite Barth's protests to the contrary—the danger of arbitrariness

---

90. Aquinas, *ST*, 1.25.5.1ad; for English, see Aquinas, *Summae Theologia: Questions on God*, 279.
91. Compare *ST*, 1.83.2co with 1.19.3 and 1.25.5.
92. See Barth, *CD* II/1, 539 and see II/1, 532 ff., 551–52; II/2, 606; and IV/1, 194. For discussion see Matthew J. Aragon Bruce, *Theology without Voluntarism: Divine Agency and God's Freedom for Creation*, PhD dissertation, Princeton Theological Seminary, 2013, ch. 5.
93. Barth, *CD* II/1, 539.
94. *CD* II/2, 606.
95. *CD* IV/1, 194.

(not to speak of anthropomorphism) if one conceives of the possibilities as merely abstract plans of action which God picks up and enacts according to need. Bulgakov argues that divine freedom, for God *for* himself, is not the abstract negative notion of "a void filled with limitless arbitrary possibilities"[96] upon which God has the power to apply or not apply a particular capacity of his omnipotence (so that, for example, God might or might not have enacted the eschaton at X time, depending upon factors that remain largely mysterious to us). Bulgakov sees the notion that God's will is radically *indifferent* in its freedom, that God can choose to create the world or not (or to enact the eschaton or not), based on an infinity of divine possibilities, as sheer "occasionalism." Bulgakov, therefore, rejects the scholastic distinction between *potentia absoluta* and *ordinata*. A divine *will* which can create the world or not is, he argues, "the absolute causelessness of indeterminism" whereby creation becomes a mere caprice. Such a notion is rooted in the anthropomorphism of Western theology in general, and in Aquinas, in particular.[97] Moreover, if the possibilities are limitless then clearly all of them cannot be actualized, as some will be mutually contradictory alternatives that exclude one another.[98] Something must serve as a mean upon which basis God chooses certain possibilities while he rejects others.

There is another way of conceiving of divine possibilities. In the next chapter, once again drawing on Maximus, we outline an approach that contemplates the breadth and depth of God's action in Jesus Christ through his body, the Church. Only by thinking about Christ and our co-operation with him can we see how prophecy not only exegetically, but also dogmatically must be both activation and (eventually, often through an unexpected course of events) prognostication; indeed, from this perspective, we can see how the eschaton depends upon *us*,

---

96. Bulgakov, *Agnets Bozhii*, 251; for English, see *Lamb of God*, 222.
97. Sergii Bulgakov, *Nevesta Agntsa* (Paris: YMCA Press, 1945), 37–38; for English, see *The Bride of the Lamb*, ed. and trans. Boris Jakim (Edinburgh/Grand Rapids: T&T Clark/Eerdmans, 2002), 31–32. Compare Balthasar, *Theo-Logic*, 2:147.
98. See Fiddes, *The Promised End*, 169.

how God is free in regard to his freedom, such that he can include us in the work of his coming again.

# 8

# Divine Action in Christ: The Christocentric and Trinitarian Nature of Human Cooperation with God

### Brandon Gallaher and Julia S. Konstantinovsky

In the last chapter, we argued that the divine Being of God as Father, Son, and Holy Spirit is so perfectly active, dynamically still, that God can respond to all the vagaries of human action without changing who he is. Thus, it is dogmatically plausible that God can delay the Parousia in response to human actions and still remain the immutable God of love. We also argued that God, in his freedom, possesses innumerable possibilities for creation, redemption, and the eschaton and is free to choose which possibilities to enact, at what "time" to enact them, and in what "manner."

The problem with this position, however, is its profound anthropocentricism. It runs the risk of reducing God to a capricious being, a deity who, as it were, indiscriminately chooses to delay the eschaton another thousand years. God might become an inscrutable and random will, emptied of all personhood, for the actions of which no other reason can be given except that it wills. But to assert "the divine will wills because it wills" is an unchristian voluntarism. Gone is the trustworthy God revealed through free love displayed in Jesus' crucifixion.

This is not the only option for a God of possibilities. There is a way of speaking about a divine choice that is attentive to divine love, wisdom, and justice without marginalizing human need and vulnerability.

It is our conviction that the possibilities that exist for God in the divine economy find their focus around the definitive historical reality of God's self-revelation in Jesus Christ, crucified and risen. Therefore, it is inconceivable for Christian theology to contend that God might change his mind and suddenly decide not to come again, since God has already, and henceforth, bound himself to a particular ordinate capacity of power, to be a particular sort of God, regardless of his absolute power and the existence before him of an innumerable number of possibilities. God will come again as promised because God has bound himself irrevocably to this possibility.

Simultaneously, it is necessary to recognize that although God has bound himself to this reality, God remains free to determine the ways and means of his coming again, albeit within the bounds of a determinate number of possibilities that cohere with what has already been accomplished in the life, death, resurrection, and ascension of Christ. God will not take back his word that Jesus will come again, but God can adapt the times and means of that coming because the prophecies that speak of an imminent second coming are correctly understood as ways of motivating his creation so that the day of the Lord might come soon: "what sort of persons ought you to be in leading lives of holiness and godliness, waiting for and hastening the coming of the day of God" (2 Pet. 3:11–12). Thus, the person and life of Jesus *narrows the bounds* of the potential activity of God in the economy of salvation. In short, God has freely bound himself to *this* history, though fallen, and limited his future actions toward creation in light of Christ.

Because all divine activity is now in Christ and because Christ represents humanity before the mercy seat of God, God's activity in history is intertwined with, and to a degree, limited by the actions of his creatures. Before he acts, God takes into account all human activity throughout history; God respects the inviolability of human freedom and allows it to limit the compass of his action. The locus of this recapitulation is the body of Christ, the Church as a renewed humanity. Applied to eschatology, this logic indicates that God's choice to bind himself to acting through Jesus Christ requires that he cannot now come again by a novel divine fiat; God has acted, acts, and will act only in Christ through the Church. Therefore, the eschaton is, by divine condescension, a divine–human, ecclesial, and synergistic activity in which God works together with creation in Christ and through the Church for the renewal of all things.

## In Christ

To begin to tease out these suggestions, it is first necessary to examine how Jesus Christ, the eternal incarnate Word of the Father, is *the living primordial idea of creation*. In the language of Maximus, by an unlimited free act of Being, Christ effects a perfect, preservative synthesis (σύνθεσις σωστική)—or a unity without confusion (ἕνωσις ἀσύγχυτος)[1]— of his divine nature with human nature, of uncreated with created Being. The two natures of Christ are, in the words of the Council of Chalcedon (451), "indivisibly" and "unconfusedly" united[2] in and through the divine hypostasis by their mutual indwelling or *perichoresis*, though they still retain their particularity and difference. Maximus explains that this perfect synthesis in unified tension (*coincidentia oppositorum*) of God and the world in Christ was "conceived

---

1. See Hans Urs von Balthasar, *Cosmic Liturgy: The Universe According to Maximus the Confessor*, trans. Brian E. Daley (San Francisco: Ignatius, 2003), 233.
2. DS §302, p. 108.

before the ages," and through it, "all the ages of time and the beings within those ages have received their beginning and end."³ God reveals his inner intention willed from all eternity: humanity will, with Christ, become sons and daughters of the Father, co-inheritors of the kingdom, brothers and sisters of the eternal incarnate Son, and God will never again be without the world. In short, humans are to "become partakers of the divine nature" (2 Pet. 1:4), adopted sons and daughters of God "through grace by imitation."⁴ This in no way makes us "gods" by substance, for the creature is not its Creator. God has freely chosen to be God with the world to which he has bound himself. Or, as Barth describes it, "God is not bound to the world. He binds himself! The covenant is his eternal will, but his free will."⁵

It is not surprising, since Christ is "He who is" (Exod. 3:14, LXX), that we can trace the procession of creation as an imperfect imitation of the divine nature back to him who is the "perfect image," "exemplar," "principle," and "reason" of creation.⁶ Balthasar expresses this by remarking that the Son is "the archetype," "the primordial idea," or even "the exemplary idea of the world." Jesus Christ is not only the primordial idea of the world as it will really be created in the Father's generation of him⁷—as all things are made and hold together in him

---

3. Maximus the Confessor, *Ad Thalassium* 60 (CCSG 22.75); for English, see Maximus the Confessor, *On the Cosmic Mystery of Jesus Christ: Selected Writings from Maximus the Confessor*, trans. Paul M. Blowers and Robert Louis Wilkens (New York: St Vladimir's Seminary Press, 2003), 125. On Maximus' Christology, see Ian A. McFarland, "Fleshing Out Christ: Maximus the Confessor's Christology in Anthropological Perspective," *St. Vladimir's Theological Quarterly*, 49, no. 4 (2005), 417-36.
4. Cyril of Alexandria, *Commentary on John*, I.9, 89c; critical edition: Philip Edward Pusey, *Sancti Cyrilli Alexandrini in D. Ioannis Evangelium* (Oxford: Clarendon, 1872), 133: "διὰ τῆς κατὰ μίμησιν χάριτος"; for English, see Cyril of Alexandria. "Commentary on John," in *Cyril of Alexandria*, ed. and trans. Norman Russell (London/New York: Routledge, 2000), 101. Cf. Irenaeus of Lyon, *Haer.* 5 praef. (ANF 1.526; SC 153.14-15); Athanasius, *Inc.* 54.11-12 (for English, see Athansius, *Contra Gentes and De Incarnatione*, ed. and trans. Robert W. Thomson (Oxford: Clarendon, 1971), 268-69); Gregory of Nyssa, *The Great Catechism*, 25.494-95 (GNO 3.4.63-64); Augustine, *Serm.* 192.1.1; *Enarrat. Ps.* 49.1.2 (CCSL 38.575; for English, see Augustine, *Sermons (184-229Z) on the Liturgical Seasons*, ed. John E. Rotelle, trans. Edmund Hill, WSA III/6 (New Rochelle, NY: New City, 1993), 47; *Expositions of the Psalms 33-50*, ed. and trans. Maria Boulding and John E. Rotelle, WSA III/16 (Hyde Park, NY: New City, 2000), 381); Maximus the Confessor, *Ad Thalassium* 22.115-18 (CCSG 7.137-43). For commentary, see Norman Russell, *The Doctrine of Deification in the Greek Patristic Tradition* (Oxford: Oxford University Press, 2004); for English, see Maximus, *On the Cosmic Mystery*, 115-18.
5. Karl Barth, *Karl Barth's Table Talk*, ed. John D. Godsey, Scottish Journal of Theology Occasional Papers 10 (Edinburgh/London: Oliver and Boyd, 1963), 14.
6. See Hans Urs von Balthasar, *TD*, 5:62-63.
7. See Augustine, *Tract. Ev. Jo.* 21.1.

(Col. 1:15–17); he is also the primordial cause of all possible worlds that could freely be created in that same generative act. Said differently, the divine ideas for the world that are seeded and enacted as *logoi* in creation find their coherence in and around Jesus Christ. As Aquinas writes: "For the Father, by understanding himself, the Son and the Holy Ghost, and all other things comprised in this knowledge, conceives the Word; so that thus the whole Trinity is 'spoken' in the Word; and likewise also all creatures."[8]

One might find a dramatic image for this process in Aslan's creative song in *The Magician's Nephew*.[9] Aslan, the protagonist of the story who is a lion modeled on Jesus Christ, brings the cosmos into being through singing, producing everything from the sun and stars to the earth, the trees, and the animals. It seems to the character Polly as if "all the things were coming (as she said) 'out of the Lion's head.' When you listened to his song you heard the things he was making up; when you looked round you, you saw them."[10] Once the Lion creates the earth, it begins to bubble like water in a pot from the lines of the Lion's singing; on the grassy land appear humps of different sizes "and the humps moved and swelled until they burst, and the crumbled earth poured out of them, and from each hump there came out an animal."[11] It is as if the whole of creation already contained the seeds of all that is and the song of the Lion animates these words of life into being. Finally, creation receives a rational spirit when Aslan declares, "Narnia, Narnia, Narnia, awake. Love. Think. Speak. Be walking trees. Be talking beasts. Be divine waters."[12]

Christ is the coherence of the different possibilities of the things that come into being. Once again, Maximus clarifies how all things hold together in Christ: the person of the Logos, Christ, is where the multiplicity of the *logoi* (as the uncreated divine plans) dwells. Maximus uses the image of the Logos as the center of a circle, and

---

8. Thomas Aquinas, *ST* 1.34.1ad3.
9. Beautifully described in Melchisedec Törönen, *Union and Distinction in the Thought of St Maximus the Confessor*, Oxford Early Christian Studies (Oxford: Oxford University Press, 2007), 128ff.
10. C.S. Lewis, *The Magician's Nephew* (London: Fontana Lions, 1984), 99.
11. Ibid., 105.
12. ibid., 108.

of the many *logoi* as the radii of the circle.¹³ The divine Logos is thus the center of the many *logoi*; they converge in him, and he is present in them. As the radii *coming out* of the center of the circle, the *logoi* are multiple and their multiplicity accounts for the multiplicity of the created beings. As the radii *converge toward* the center of the circle, the *logoi* are unified and their unity is reflected in the unity and harmony of the created cosmos. Maximus expresses the principle of the multiplicity-in-unity within the divine realm by stating that the "many *logoi*" in fact *are* "the one Logos":

> the many logoi are one Logos, seeing that all things are related to him without being confused with him, who is the essential and personally distinct Logos of God the Father, the origin and cause of all things, *in whom all things were created, in the heavens and on earth, visible and invisible, whether thrones or dominions or principalities or authorities: all things were created from him, through him, and return unto him.* (Col. 1:16 and see Rom. 11:36)¹⁴

The metaphor again risks falling into base anthropomorphism, but Maximus stresses the eternity of the *logoi* when he refers to them as the "pre-existing *logoi* of created beings."¹⁵ Before the ages were established, God in Christ possessed the *logoi* of what has since come into existence; this once again highlights that, while the actual created beings come into existence at a certain moment, the *logoi* of beings do not. Because the divine thoughts dwell within the divine Logos, they are eternal. Thus, Maximus maintains: "the *logoi* of our being [...] exist eternally in God."¹⁶

So, what happens at the moment of creation? God—who as uncreated Spirit is beyond the distinction of inner and outer—creates by (for lack of a better term) "externalizing" his eternal thoughts or

---

13. Maximus the Confessor, *Amb.* 7.20 (PG 91.1081C); for English, see Maximus the Confessor, *On Difficulties in the Church Fathers: The Ambigua*, 2 vols., ed. and trans. Nicholas Constas (Cambridge: Harvard University Press, 2014), 1:100–103. Cf. Pseudo-Dionysius the Areopagite, *Divine Names* 5.6 (PTS 33.185, ll. 4–11; PG 3.821A); for English, see Pseudo-Dionysius the Areopagite, *Pseudo-Dionysius: The Complete Works,* trans. Colm Luibheid and Paul Rorem (New York: Paulist, 1987), 99–100.
14. Maximus the Confessor, *Amb.* 7.20 (PG 91.1077C–80A); Maximus the Confessor, *The Ambigua*. 1:94–95.
15. *Amb.* 7.16 (PG 91.1080A); Maximus, *The Ambigua*, 1:94–95.
16. *Amb.* 7.20 (PG 91.1081C); Maximus, *The Ambigua*, 1:102–3.

wills about creation. Since the *logoi* are these divine thoughts, it follows that in Maximus' system, there must be a logical distinction between: (a) the eternal *logoi* as divine ideas within God's Being and (b) the *logoi* as they become "externalized" in the moment when God creates them as distinct realities. At *that* moment, the *logoi* appear to be transformed into God's creative activity, spilling, as it were (for we are not denying *creatio ex nihilo*), beyond God's inner Being. This idea hinges upon a technical distinction between God's Being-in-himself (the ultimately unknowable *divine essence*) and God's creative and redemptive activity (God's ἐνέργεια through which he makes himself known). God's outwardly-directed creative activity (ἐνέργεια), in fact, comprises a multiplicity of creative activities. God's creative activities are the *logoi* in their new, actualizing function. God's manifold activity through the multiplicity of *logoi* results in the creation of a diversity of beings.

Maximus goes on to introduce another distinction pertaining to his conception of the Logos of God, the Second Person of the Trinity whom Maximus very clearly identifies with Jesus Christ.[17] First, there is the transcendent divine Logos himself who, "by virtue of his infinite transcendence, is ineffable and incomprehensible, and exists beyond all creation and beyond all the differences and distinctions which exist and can be conceived of within it."[18] Second, this same Logos is "manifested and multiplied in all the things that have their origin in him, in a manner appropriate to the being of each, as befits his goodness. And *he recapitulates all things* in himself (see Eph. 1:10)."[19]

In this latter aspect, the Logos of God seems to reveal himself by dwelling or being immanent in beings and manifesting himself in various degrees through the beauty "appropriate to the being of each." The idea of the Logos of God becoming *visible* within creatures through the beauty discernible in each of them hinges upon the principle that "the one Logos of God is many *logoi* and the many are One."[20] The

---

17. E.g. *Amb.* 7.21 (PG 91.1081C–D); Maximus, *The Ambigua*, 1:102–3; and in detail: *Amb.* 2–5 (PG 91.1036D–60D); Maximus, *The Ambigua*, 1:10–59.
18. *Amb.* 7.16 (PG 91.1080A); Maximus, *The Ambigua*, 1:96–97.
19. *Amb.* 7.16 (PG 91.1080B); Maximus, *The Ambigua*, 1:96–97.
20. *Amb.* 7.20 (PG 1081B–C); Maximus, *The Ambigua*, 1:100–101.

Logos of God can be said to inhere in beings in virtue of the fact that the many *logoi*, which are the principles of being of every creature, must *also* inhere within the created things themselves. This is another way in which we can think of the many *logoi*: the *logoi* as principles of existence both concealed and revealed within the intelligible and sensible creation itself. Consequently, to summarize, the *logoi* are, first, within the mind of God in which they inhere as God's providential ideas and wills about all creatures that are to be brought into being; second, the *logoi* become God's dynamic and outwardly directed acts, whereupon God in actuality brings creatures from non-being into Being; and third and last, the *logoi* dwell within the created beings themselves. While the first two categories of the *logoi* are uncreated and divine, the third category becomes so closely associated with things as to *become* the things themselves. Consequently, it appears that in this third category, the *logoi* are modified from being divine uncreated wills into being the products of these wills.

The crucified Logos, therefore, is in all things as their very heart, and yet, totally beyond them, because as one of the holy Trinity, he is utterly transcendent of everything. He is yesterday, today, and forever (Heb. 13:8), lying at the beginning and the end of all ages, past and future.[21] Jesus is "not circumscribed by the events that occur in history, but, being active everywhere, shines forth [his] own light like the sun."[22] Maximus argues that by the potency of faith—a potency expressed dimly in the operation of the virtues in the Christian life, and indeed, supported by the *logoi* themselves, which foreshadow and conduce to future benefits—the Coming One (John 11:27) pours forth his grace to us from the future. The end of the ages, when humanity shall put on Christ and become full partakers of the uncreated divine nature (2 Pet. 1:4), is given to us now as a foretaste.[23] But, if God and God's creation in the form of the *logoi* are all spoken in Christ, who

---

21. *Ad Thalassium* 22 (CCSG 7:140); for English, see Maximus, *On the Cosmic Mystery*, 117.
22. Maximus the Confessor, *Quaestiones et Dubia*, Q. 190; for English, see Maximus the Confessor, *St. Maximus the Confessor's Questions and Doubts*, trans. Despina D. Prassas (DeKalb, IL: Northern Illinois University Press, 2010), 136.
23. *Ad Thalassium* 22 (CCSG 7.140-43).

holds all things together, then Jesus is the divine canon of the possible. Through him, what is real is realized because all possibilities exist in him, and then, are actualized in him. Thus, the whole of history, not just *Heilsgeschichte*, becomes focused in the two wills of Christ, so that by condescension, all divine action becomes divine–human action, inseparable. Thus, it must be in the light of Christ, who, with his body the Church, recapitulates the whole of creation: past, present, and future.

We are speaking of a cosmic Christ who breaks into our time from the future in certain key theophanies (what we earlier called "stepping stones"; see chapter 4, pp. 57–70). This Jesus whom God raised up is the eschatological response to the so-called delay of the Parousia. But the Christ we envision is not a dehistoricized Pantocrator glaring down from on high; rather, he is the suffering Bridegroom of the Church who, having ascended, ever bears the wounds of the nails on his hands before our Father. Indeed, the combination of Jesus' ascension and his role as the one in whom all things are created and hold together means that the life-giving sacrifice of this Lamb who was slain is written "crosswise" into the foundation of the world. In this way, history is given a cruciform shape and trajectory.[24] Christ himself, as Irenaeus of Lyons (v.130-c.202) remarks,

> was already in the world and on the invisible plane he upheld all created things and was imprinted in the form of a cross in the entire creation in as much as being the Word of God he governs and arranges all things. This is why "he came" visibly "to his own home," "took flesh" and was lifted up on the cross in order to recapitulate all things in himself.[25]

The cross of Christ shows forth visibly what has always existed on the invisible level, because Christ himself is the primordial idea of creation. The cross is the watermark of divine love imprinted on the book of

---

24. Cf. Justin Martyr, *1 Apol.* 60 (PTS 38.116–17), citing Plato, *Tim.* 36b.
25. Irenaeus of Lyons, *Haer.* 5.18.3 (SC 153.244–45 [Armenian fragment]; translation of Brandon Gallaher); cf. *Epid.* 34; for English, see *On the Apostolic Preaching*, trans. John Behr (Crestwood, NY: St Vladimir's Seminary Press, 1997), 62. One finds the same idea in Gregory of Nyssa; see above, ch. 7, pp. 155–57.

creation. Once this mark is revealed in the light of the Word of Christ, worldly being and even history itself becomes intelligible.[26]

Yet, if all divine possibilities are centered on Jesus Christ, then they are personal Trinitarian realities—divine intentions of the Father for the economy of salvation that are given to the Son in his begetting by the Father. They are given to the Son freely for him to take up and enact as he sees fit (or not). The Son freely binds himself to them, and, as Maximus explains, through his Spirit, they are then seeded and enacted in creation as God's seminal creative words (*logoi*). They are the means by which God both creates all things and then coaxes his creatures toward union and communion with himself in Christ. God the Father, therefore, does not create, redeem, and eschatologically perfect the world by turning outside himself (as if God could have an "outside"), but by eternally turning in love to his Son in begetting him. The whole activity of God is expressed in the kenotic exchange of love of the Trinitarian relations: an internal, eternal, ecstatic, self-giving, self-emptying, and self-receiving outward-going desire for creation.

This means that creation in its initial conception and in its fullest realization is sheltered within God in Christ, without effecting a change in God, since God is a pure act of love.[27] In the eternal act of creation, God wished to express his eternal internal free love for himself as a sort of "external" theophany in the world, which is actually firmly nestled in his exchange of love. Meister Eckhart (c.1260–1328) likewise identifies the very love God has for himself with his love for creatures:

> God loves Himself and His nature, His being and His Godhead. In the love in which God loves Himself, He loves all creatures, not as creatures but creatures as God. In the love in which God loves Himself, He loves all things.[28]

Put otherwise, God takes joy in himself, and in this joy, he takes joy in his creation's joy at his grace, as Maximus observed:

---

26. See Hans Urs von Balthasar, *Love Alone is Credible*, trans. D. C. Schindler (San Francisco: Ignatius, 2004), 142.
27. See *TD*, 5:100.
28. Meister Eckhart, "Sermon 56," in *The Complete Mystical Works of Meister Eckhart*, trans. Maurice O'Connell Walshe (New York: Crossroad, 1991), 293.

> God, full beyond all fullness, brought creatures into being not because He had need of anything, but so that they might participate in Him in proportion to their capacity and that He Himself might rejoice in His works (cf. Ps. 104:31), through seeing them joyful and ever filled to overflowing with His inexhaustible gifts.[29]

Although these possibilities/*logoi* are "ideas" in God, they are not bare negative abstractions. Here, we must once again retool our metaphor in order to avoid anthropomorphism. Balthasar remarks that what is realized economically is "rooted in an all-embracing divine freedom that for all eternity has been actually performing these 'possible' things."[30] A divine possibility, before it is economically expressed, is already eternally performed in the love of God. It is not a possibility in the sense of an abstract, negative (what is *not* chosen to be but could be), and empty "perhaps"; this is not T. S. Eliot's "abstraction/ Remaining a perpetual possibility/ Only in a world of speculation."[31]

Nicholas of Cusa (1401–64) is helpful here when he speaks of a divine "*possest*" (*posse est*), that is, an "Actualized-possibility"[32] or "the-actual-existence-of possibility."[33] God is the one in whom absolute actuality and absolute possibility coincide, such that all things that are created and will be created (or many which will not be created) are in and of God, who enfolds them. Cusa writes: "every creature which is able to be brought from not-being into being exists *there* [in God], where to-be-able-[to-be] is to-be, and *there* it is Actualized-possibility itself."[34] If, in God, possibility itself exists insofar as it coincides with actuality, then creatures that *will* be created are, in some sense, identical with creatures that *are* created in time when God eternally unfolds them within the divine life of the Trinity. The Father is the person of

---

29. Maximus the Confessor, *400 Chapters on Love* 3.46 (PG 90.1029C). For English, see *The Philokalia*, trans. G. Palmer, Philip Sherrard, Kallistos Ware, 4 vols. (London: Faber & Faber, 1979–95), 2:90.
30. Balthasar, *TD*, 5:509.
31. T. S. Eliot, 'Burnt Norton' in *The Complete Poems and Plays 1909-1950* (New York: Harcourt, Brace & World, 1971), 117.
32. Nicholas of Cusa, *De Possest* §14; English: Nicholas of Cusa, *Complete Philosophical and Theological Treatises of Nicholas of Cusa*, 2 vols, ed. and trans. Jasper Hopkins (Minneapolis: Arthur J. Banning, 2001), 2:921, emphasis in the English version.
33. Nicholas of Cusa, *Complete Philosophical and Theological Treatises*, 2:959 n.23.
34. Nicholas of Cusa, *De Possest* §25 Nicholas of Cusa, *Complete Philosophical and Theological Treatises*, 2:927.

"Absolute Possibility"; the Son, Jesus Christ, is Existence itself or Actuality, because he is of the Possibility of the Father; and the Spirit who is the natural love or union of them both is the actual existence of possibility.[35] The incarnate Son is the perfect figure of the substance of the Father with the Spirit resting upon him because he "is whatever [he] is able to be. The Form of God the Father [i.e., Christ] is not able to be either truer or more perfect, since it is Actualized-possibility (*possest*)."[36] Thus, all things that exist or can exist—in their possibility and their actuality—are "enfolded" in their beginning and end in the triune God in Christ, and in being created, are then "unfolded." Put otherwise, creation in both its intention from before the ages and in all its historical and temporal specificity is nestled within the eternal relations of the Father, the Son, and the Holy Spirit. This leads to the paradox that we can say equally that "as-enfolded-in-God all these things are God; similarly, as-unfolded-in-the-created-world they are the world."[37]

The possibilities of creation and redemption exist in God's own life of love in a supereminent, even "substantial", sense, which is related but not identical to their realization. Balthasar called these free quasi-substantial possibilities "all the modalities of love . . . which may manifest themselves in the course of a history of salvation involving sinful mankind."[38] This means that, upon closer examination, the anthropomorphic metaphor we used above (namely, that God contemplates *internally* the eternal *logoi* of creation and then *externalizes* them in the act of creation) begins to break down. In fact, creation in its possibility as well as in its actuality is, in some sense, contained in its Creator who, through the Spirit, is everywhere present and filling all things. But here there is an important implication for eschatology: if the world in its divine foundation as a possibility and in its creaturely external reality as an actuality is, in some sense,

---

35. De Possest §48; Nicholas of Cusa, *Complete Philosophical and Theological Treatises*, 2:939.
36. De Possest §58; Nicholas of Cusa, *Complete Philosophical and Theological Treatises*, 2:945.
37. De Possest §§6–9; Nicholas of Cusa, *Complete Philosophical and Theological Treatises*, 2:916–18.
38. Hans Urs von Balthasar, *Mysterium Paschale*, trans. Aidan Nichols (San Francisco: Ignatius, 2000), viii–ix.

sheltered within God in Christ as an actualized possibility, then its change—that is, the eternal reality of the multiple ways its free mutability may take it, the possibility of its repentance, or the embrace of the unforgivable sin against the Holy Spirit in rejecting forgiveness (Mark 3:28-29), and even its choice to rebel or not, the "No!" and "Yes!" to its Savior—is, in some sense, embraced within God. This means that the divine plan for creation, especially the Parousia, is capacious enough to take into consideration the possibility and the actuality of human actions with all their enormous multiplicity and instability.[39] This is why we affirm God's sovereign plan for creation while simultaneously espousing that what we do is absolutely crucial for the coming again of the Lord.

## With Humanity

But how can these free divine possibilities, once they have been seeded and enacted in the world, take human action into consideration? Here, we want to adapt the common notion that the eschaton is already inaugurated in the resurrection *and* the ascension of Christ—which should be taken as one complete eschatological event in, but not of, history and by which all of human history is taken up into the divine love. The eschaton is given to us as a foretaste in the ongoing Pentecost of the Church, especially in the Church's liturgy.[40] As an event, the resurrection-ascension both lies within history but also is at its end; it is the simultaneous taking up of history into God and the in-breaking of God into history. This event is retroactive in that it transforms and takes up into God the history of what went before. Yet, as an event, it is also pro-active in that it effects and transforms all that which is to come. Creation is, as it were, "proleptically conditioned" by redemption.[41] The incarnation, as Torrance observed—and here, the incarnation includes the cross, the tomb, the resurrection, and ascension—is not a "transient episode" in the interaction of God with

---

39. See Fiddes, *The Promised End*, 169-70.
40. A full discussion of this follows in ch. 9.
41. Torrance, *The Christian Doctrine of God*, 204; *The Trinitarian Faith*, 102.

the world. Rather, it has taken place once-for-all in such a fashion that it "reaches backward through time and forward through time, from the end to the beginning and from the beginning to the end."[42]

All things, then, are created through Jesus Christ and for him because he is the "central and pivotal reality of creation."[43] In him, God has "chosen to work and exercise his mighty power and sovereignty for us and our salvation."[44] The Father almighty will always act throughout all space and time "into the consummation of his purpose of love" in the way he has already acted in Jesus Christ, who is the "Kingdom of God in action."[45] It is our position, furthermore, that the resurrection-ascension, as the kingdom in action in history, in no way overwhelms creaturely activity, but rather, allows for the different possibilities that human action may take in its response to God's grace. All of the events of the life of Christ, all the stepping stones to the Parousia, from cave to grave to heaven above, become eternal events in God through the resurrection-ascension of Christ.

In being glorified, the incarnation is supratemporally extended to all time so that all of history exists in light of Christ; this is to say, salvation history is the theo-logic of history. Moreover, the hypostatic union is graciously extended to the life of God in himself, to his own self-generation as holy Trinity, in begetting and in spiration, since the glorified humanity of Christ enters the abyss of love of God the Father, Son, and Holy Spirit. Through the resurrection-ascension, creation—represented by its "epitome" in the humanity of Christ, whose body is the Church as the fullness of Christ—becomes sheltered within God.[46] As a result, we can no longer speak of God without the world, since there is no longer a world "outside" God. This formulation beginning with salvation history develops yet another way of evoking the same mystery of God lovingly holding his creation to his breast in Jesus Christ. We described it earlier, following Maximus, as the

---

42. *The Christian Doctrine of God*, 216.
43. Ibid., 204.
44. Ibid., 216.
45. Ibid.
46. See Balthasar, *TD*, 5:371–410.

"externalization" of the divine *logoi* in creation that God eternally internally contemplates and the fact that all of the *logoi* of creation find their coherence in the one Word, Jesus Christ. The world, therefore, is in God in Christ in the Church, which in him fills all things in every way according to the plan hidden in God the Father before the ages (Eph. 1:23, 3:9).[47] We have a foretaste of this reality in the experience of celebrating the Lord's Supper on the Lord's Day as a continual Pentecostal and eschatological witness to the kingdom of God with the Lamp of the Lamb at its heart (see chapter 9, pp. 121–23).

The Church, insofar as it is fully justified and renewed by the Spirit of God, and not simply a corporation of sinners *in via*, is the new creation itself embedded in God. It is the Bride of the Lamb who descends from heaven to draw all into his kingdom. Christ came down from heaven to earth and raised up, as an ancient hymn of the Church puts it, "Adam's nature which lay below in Hades' prison." By his resurrection and ascension, Jesus raises human nature to heaven so that it now sits with and in him on the "Father's throne."[48] This act both unites all things in Christ himself in God and reconciles us to God our Father. As Maximus describes it:

> By his ascension into heaven (Luke 24:51; Acts 1:9), it is obvious that he united heaven and earth, for he entered heaven with his earthly body, which is of the same nature and consubstantial with ours, and showed that, according to its more universal principle, all sensible nature is one, and thus he obscured in himself the property of division that had cut it in two. Then, in addition to this, having passed with his soul and body, that is, with the whole of our nature, through all the divine and intelligible orders of heaven, he united sensible things with intelligible things, displaying in himself the fact that the convergence of the entire creation towards unity was absolutely indivisible and beyond all fracture in accordance with its most primal and most universal principle. And finally, after all of these things, he—considered according to the idea of his humanity—comes to God himself, *appearing* as a man, as it is written, *before the face of God* the Father *on our behalf* (Heb. 9:24)—he who as Word can

---

47. See Maximus the Confessor, *Amb.* 7.36–39 (PG 91.1096A–00C); Maximus the Confessor, *The Ambigua*, 1:126–37.
48. "Kathisma/Sessional Hymn in Tone 5, Thursday Matins of the Assumption," ed. and trans. Archimandrite Ephrem Lash, 2008. http://www.anastasis.org.uk/assumpti.htm. Last accessed 27 May 2015.

never in any way be separated from the Father—fulfilling as man, in deed and truth, and with perfect obedience (see Rom. 5:19), all that he himself as God had preordained should take place (see 1 Cor. 2:7; Eph. 1:5), having completed the whole plan of God the Father for us, who through our misuse had rendered ineffective the power that was given to us from the beginning by nature for this purpose.[49]

The "place" where the world in the Church is embedded is Christ himself, who is the perfect union of the created and the uncreated. Nonetheless, as the life of God in his holy mutability (see chapter 7, p. 165) is to be forevermore, there is no "addition" to God here, even though creation has been united with its Creator and then taken up into him, for Christ has never been parted from the Father's bosom "which is uncircumscribed; and the heavenly powers accepted no addition to the thrice-holy hymn of praise, but acknowledged you, Lord, as one Son, only-begotten of the Father, even after the incarnation."[50] Even on the cross, we must speak retrospectively and retroactively in light of the resurrection-ascension of Jesus *eternally* reigning with the Father God over all creation in heaven and on earth. Thus, without any addition or diminution of God, the union and communion of God with his creation—which is the historical incarnation—is accomplished retrospectively and retroactively in the resurrection-ascension.[51]

This union of the created and the uncreated accomplished in the resurrection-ascension is gifted to us at Pentecost in the Church. The Church is, in one sense, Christ himself, his very body, eternally manifesting himself at the heart of creation in human form, perpetually being renewed and always young—the permanent extended incarnation of the Son of God himself.[52] As Augustine

---

49. Maximus the Confessor, *Amb.* 41.8 (PG 91.1309B-C); Maximus the Confessor, *The Ambigua* 2:112–13.
50. "Sticheron at the Aposticha, Tone 1, Wednesday Small Matins of the Assumption," ed. and trans. Archimandrite Ephrem Lash, 2008. http://www.anastasis.org.uk/assumpti.htm. Last accessed 27 May 2015.
51. Compare Wolfhart Pannenberg, *Jesus: God and Man*, trans. Lewis L. Wilkins and Duane A. Priebe (London, SCM, 1968), 152–53, 321; *Systemic Theology*, 3 vols., trans. Geoffrey W. Bromiley (Edinburgh: T&T Clark, 1991-97), 2:303 ff. 92, 363ff. (For discussion see Fiddes, *The Promised End*, 211–15).
52. See Johann Adam Möhler, *Symbolism: Exposition of the Doctrinal Differences between Catholics and Protestants as Evidenced by Their Symbolical Writings*, trans. James Burton Robinson, 2 vols., 2nd ed.

acknowledged, the Church is Christ's very presence with us: "For Christ is not in the head *or* in the body, but Christ is wholly in the head *and* in the body."[53]

The hypostatic union effected eternally by the resurrection-ascension has validity for all the life of Christ both before the advent of Christ by anticipation and—crucially, for our understanding that God might delay the eschaton based on human actions—*for all of history* at whose source he stands. As mentioned above, in the historical-eschatological event of the resurrection-ascension, God confirms and in confirming retroactively effects an eternal union between himself, creation in Christ, and its extension in his body, the Church. Thus, we know that God was always one with Jesus (even before his advent in the flesh) and that the Church in whom Christ dwells was foreordained from before the ages.[54] The eternal identity of God, therefore, is proven proleptically in history through the resurrection-ascension whereby the future of God consummated in the eschaton briefly breaks into history. God will only definitively demonstrate, indeed, prove to us who he is in the final consummation of the eschaton with its accompanying transformation of creation. Prior to this, the Church served as an eschatological community bearing witness to the divine identity God proleptically demonstrated in the resurrection-ascension.

The resurrection, for the German Lutheran Wolfhart Pannenberg (1928–2014), is the "locus" of the "decision" that God is "always the

(London: Charles Dolan, 1847), 2:6; Maximus the Confessor, *Amb.* 7.36–37 (PG 91.1096A–97C); *The Ambigua*, 1:126–33; Georges Florovsky, "Le corps du Christ vivant: une interprétation orthodoxe de l'Église," in *La Sainte Église Universelle: Confrontation oecuménique*, ed. Georges Florovsky et. al., Cahiers théologiques de l'actualité protestante 4 (Neuchâtel/Paris: Delachaux et Niestlé, 1948), 20–23.

53. Augustine, *Tract. Ev. Jo.* 28.1.3–13 (PL 35.1622); for English, see Augustine, *Tractates on the Gospel of John 28-54*, trans. John W. Rettig, FC 88 (Washington, D.C.: Catholic University of America Press, 1993), 3.
54. It is for this reason that the Church is sometimes described mysteriously as eternal. In *The Shepherd of Hermas* (2nd cent.), for example, the Church is portrayed as an ancient lady who "was created before all things . . . and for her sake the world was formed" (Herm. *Vis.* 2.4.1). But if we do speak of the literal "eternity" of the Church as the Body of the living Christ, then this can only be retrospectively and retroactively, in light of the resurrection-ascension, for the eternal union of God and creation in Christ was bestowed on and revealed to us in its fullness at Pentecost. The "eternity" of the Church is a gift given to us by God in Christ; it is a creaturely, spiritual mode (entailing the renewal and fulfillment of time) which needs to be distinguished from the uncreated eternity of God. See Brandon Gallaher, "Chalice of Eternity: An Orthodox Theology of Time," *St Vladimir's Theological Quarterly* 57, no. 1 (2013): 11–14.

true God from eternity to eternity." God determines to allow his eternal Being to be stated absolutely in the consummation of history in the eschaton. Thereby, he retrospectively confirms his dominion, that he is boss, the Lord of history reigning eternally, "finally and irrefutably manifested" in the last things, so that God will be what he always already is.[55] Furthermore, the "reality" of the resurrection is only "finally [*endgültig*] and irrefutably decided" in the consummation of history with the general resurrection, God's once-for-all determination for the world that he is who he is from Alpha to Omega.[56] Once the "spirit of sonship" (Rom. 8:15) is manifested in Jesus Christ, as the Son of the Father through the Spirit, it can be revealed in us as "sons of God" (8:14, 19). Thus, we are made "children of God" (8:16) and "fellow heirs with Christ" sharing in the eternal kingdom, the royal rule which is the fellowship of glory (8:17) that Jesus has with the Father through the Spirit.[57]

Reconciliation in Christ and the actualizing of the royal rule of God in Christ are "one and the same thing."[58] In Christ, the "future of God"—the eschatological rule of God—is present in the world, opening to us salvation and participation in that divine future: the kingdom.[59] Thus, Jesus' life as the revelation of his unity with God is only effected and revealed in the event which concludes and consummates that earthly life, and with it, our own total reconciliation and adoption as full participants in the divine life of the Trinity.

Pannenberg's vision of the end is highly congenial to the present authors. For us, however, the *resurrection and ascension* are treated as one divine-human event whereas it is just the resurrection which is the focus for Pannenberg. God confirms and effects retroactively (and for all time) the hypostatic union as the decisive eschatological event through the resurrection-ascension. But in the resurrection-ascension, he who breathed his Spirit on his disciples (John 20:22–23) also brings

---

55. Pannenberg, *Systematic Theology*, 1:331. For discussion see Timothy Bradshaw, *Pannenberg: A Guide for the Perplexed* (London: T&T Clark, 2009).
56. Pannenberg, *Systematic Theology*, 1:331 (translation revised).
57. Ibid., 2:138.
58. Ibid., 2:390–91.
59. Ibid., 2:390.

about Pentecost. Pentecost is both the gift and the revelation of the Church as Christ's eternal salvific body, ever given to creation in its midst until the close of the age, for the Church is an ongoing Pentecost. It is a gift in that we are given a new spiritual mode of being as sons and daughters of God in Christ through the Spirit. It is a revelation in that this identity as children of God is shown to us here in time as our eternal life in the kingdom through Christ. So, in some sense, it is a life and selfhood we have always already possessed.

We still await the completion of the Spirit's work at the return of Christ in glory, although we enjoy a foretaste of that consummation in the resurrection-ascension of Christ, which is even now at work in the world through the Church.[60] This work is the in-breaking of the "future of God."[61] Through the resurrection-ascension, the life of Christ stands at the conclusion and confirmation of history. In the resurrection-ascension, all of human history, with its free symphony of wills, is taken up into God in Christ, and we experience this ongoing reality in Christ's body, the Church. Thus, the body of Christ in God recapitulates the whole of history. The whole of history is first recapitulated in Christ's humanity in the resurrection: events prior to Christ's incarnation, co-terminous with it, and after his earthly mission. This history is then raised up to heaven in the ascension and illumined providentially by God, who infuses it with his divine life. Then, at Pentecost, through the descent of the Spirit of Christ, Jesus comes to dwell in the world in his body, the Church, which hides the glorious resurrection life of a new creation, Eden remade and reestablished in radical eternal innocence. But the history he took with him to heaven and sanctified and made eternal comes down with the Spirit of Christ and is cradled in the Church in the center of history. Through the worship of the Church, by which it is perpetually renewed as Christ's body, history is continually sanctified. History is secretly and providentially guided by God through the life of prayer of the saints until the consummation of the end of the age. At the Parousia, Christ

---

60. Ibid., 3:605.
61. Ibid., 3:627 and see 3:604.

as King of the universe will destroy the rule and authority of sin and death. He will give his Father God the kingdom and put all things under subjection to him. It is then that the Church will finally be revealed as having been all along the new eternal paradise, for it is only then that God will become all in all (1 Cor. 15:24–28).

Extending the incarnation in the Church (by the inclusion of all history and creation in the divinized and ascended humanity of Christ gifted to us by the Spirit) in no way negates the particularity and freedom of the created. The love of the Father, the Son, and Holy Spirit never constrains or coerces; it always persuades. God so greatly reverences human freedom as an image of his Trinitarian glory[62] that he respects its inviolability with a holy submission to humanity's most passionate fumbling, detours, and even sheer rebellion, drawing humanity along with cords of compassion and bands of love (Hos. 11:4). God is, as Vladimir Lossky said, like "a beggar of love waiting at the soul's door without ever daring to force it."[63]

Indeed, the peak of God's own all-powerfulness can be seen in his own all-powerlessness. He gifts man with a portion of his absolute freedom, a "space" for humanity to act freely in Christ, whose action is the quintessence and pinnacle of all human activity. This all-powerlessness consists in God's taking a sort of "divine risk" in giving his creation the possibility of love. Insofar as *free* love is the highest divine gift, God's ultimate goodness entails the risk that we may refuse his love and cause the ruin of ourselves and God's plan.[64] God takes a risk in creating the world and becomes freely dependent on "creaturely conditions" for the manifestation of the Son, as bearer of his deity.[65] This is a risk of God's love: in binding itself to creation,

---

62. See Basil of Caesarea, *Homily on Psalm 48*, 8 (PG 29b.449B–C); Maximus the Confessors *Disputation with Pyrrhus* 61 (PG 91.304C–D). For English, see *Exegetic Homilies*, trans. Agnes Way, FC 46 (Washington, D.C.: Catholic University of America Press, 1963), 324–25; Maximus the Confessor, *The Disputation with Pyrrhus*, trans. Joseph Farrell (South Canaan: St. Tikhon's Seminary Press, 1990), 25; critical edition, *Disput s Pirrom*, ed. and trans. D. Pospelov (Moscow: Khram Sofii Premudrosti Bozhiei, 2004), 170–71.
63. Vladimir Lossky, *Orthodox Theology: An Introduction*, eds. and trans. Ian and Ihita Kesarcodi-Watson (Crestwood, New York: St Vladimir's Seminary Press, 2001), 72–73 and see Fiddes, *The Promised End*, 170–75 and Irenaeus, *Haer.* 5.1.1.
64. Lossky, *Orthodox Theology*, 73.
65. Pannenberg, *Systematic Theology*, 2:7.

divine love accepts the possibility that these conditions may prove hostile to the divine economy. Creatures may deviate from God's purposes, and so, oppose his creative ends. But God will not negate human autonomy by some sort of "omnicausality"; God "risks" by giving humans independence and actively cooperating with their development, not just upholding them in being, but urging them onwards in their acts.[66] God wants creatures who are "free and independent" and can have a "free fellowship" with him, spontane-ously acknowledging him in his deity, and thereby, corresponding to the fellowship of the Son with the Father, which is realized in Jesus. But with this goal comes the divine acceptance of the "risk" that the creature may abuse its liberty by pursuing sin and evil.[67] God has, in a sense, "faith" in his creation. He freely trusts and depends upon it. Thus, God condescends to wait on man for the accomplishment of the eschaton;[68] he waits with longsuffering love in Christ. He risks everything for his creation.

## The Christoform and Ecclesial Shape of Eschatology

History has a divine–human, what one might call a Chalcedonian, logic. We elaborated this crucial Christian tradition in Maximus the Confessor earlier in the chapter, but now, we want to extend it creatively. At the heart of history stands a theandric or theoenergetic reality where two wills act in synergy with God in Christ. In this drama, the God-Man waits with an unmovable divine–human desire on human beings who, in all their woundedness and confusion, move toward him. He persuades, pulls, and nudges them forward with a "crazy love" (ἔρως μανικός) for creation "which like fire dares all things."[69]

We see this Christo-logic shining forth in the various theophanies (stepping stones; cf. chapter 4, pp. 57–70) that bind together creation

---

66. Ibid., 2:48, 52.
67. Ibid., 2:166–67 and see ibid., 2:172, 3:642.
68. See Fiddes, *The Promised End*, 171.
69. Nicholas Cabasilas, *The Life in Christ*, 6.3, 8 (PG 150.648A, 657A; SC 355, 361 *ad loc.*); for English, see Nicholas Cabasilas, *The Life in Christ*, trans. Carmino deCatanzaro (Crestwood, NY: St Vladimir's Seminary Press, 1974), 164, 172.

in Christ moving toward its fullness in his coming again. History is Christoform, and for that reason, it is open-ended. Christ's humanity, presented to us in his body the Church, summarizes and recapitulates all of a rebellious and broken creation that is even now sometimes kicking against the pricks and oft times drawing near to its Creator in sackcloth and ashes, crying mightily for mercy and turning from their evil ways and the violence in their hands (John 3:6–10). And if history is not a closed circle, pre-determined, then it is quite simply *theologically* illegitimate to say that Jesus will return at "X" point in time, as the Harold Campings and Joachim of Fiores of the world are wont to do.

This observation is crucial, because it goes well beyond a mere exegetically-based response to those announcing the imminent arrival of the end. In addition to lacking critical awareness of how prophecy as a genre functions, such interpretations misread Christian prophecy precisely because they fail to appreciate the very nature of who Jesus is and because they misconstrue the nature of divine freedom. God will not—indeed, he has bound himself so that he cannot—act alone in perfecting his creation. He has committed himself to acting in synergy with the creation which he has created and redeemed in Christ. A single divine will for creation there may have been, but there must be two wills—divine *and* human—to bring about creation's liberation and our deification into full adoption as sons and daughters of the Father. Christ's human will summarizes and recapitulates all of creation. Even now that recapitulation is ongoing in the Church. Albeit sometimes, a "wife of whoredoms" (Hos. 1:2), she is ever being sanctified, cleansed by the washing of water with the word so that she might be presented to her head as a new creation, his holy Bride without blemish (Eph. 5:25–27). Only God the Father (Matt. 24:36) can say when the full number of the gentiles will have come in, our repentance coming to fruition with the final outworking in creation of the complete removal of our sins, the banishing of all ungodliness from Jacob (Rom. 11:25–27).

This repentance, which is real and effective in the hastening of our Lord, depends also *upon us* as the Church. We are called to baptize the world, and in this way, incorporate all of creation *into* the body of the living Christ as the Lord of history. It depends on the people of God ecclesifying the world, baptizing it, drawing it to Christ and prompting a confession of Jesus' lordship so that what exists on the invisible level—his cross written into creation—might be made explicit. We make visible the reality of the Saviour crucified crosswise in creation by making the sign of the cross over it in its Christening, and in this way, we mark it as Christ's own forever. The initiative for the consummation of the age is taken by the divine will of Christ acting in conjunction with the Father and the Spirit. But Jesus' human will, in which we Christians partake as his living body, the first fruit of the new creation, follows his divine will in obedience and love, just as transpired in the garden when Christ said, "not my will, but thine, be done" (Luke 22:42 KJV). And, yes, this is most certainly another way of expressing the theological truth that the Church's mission to baptize all nations in the name of the Father, the Son, and the Holy Spirit is crucial to the coming of the end of the age, albeit with a fresh christological and ecclesiological emphasis. All this returns to a point made much earlier in our exegesis of 2 Peter: eschatology not only stimulates ethics, but ethics stimulate eschatology.

## A Cooperative Eschatology

Though it is not possible to explore in detail the ways in which humanity can and should engage in this divine–human, messianic-ecclesial collaboration to bring about the Parousia, some reflection on this issue is relevant and unavoidable here. There are at least six areas in which human action in Christ reveals the eschatological shape of Christian praxis, or as we have said, the ways in which ethics are eschatological. These are: worship, mission, ecumenism, social justice, asceticism, and contemplation.

### Worship

One way to hasten the last day is to pursue the chief and highest end of humanity: to glorify God, and in glorifying him, to love, know, and forever enjoy him by whom we were created.[70] This is what worship is—the Church's co-working with God, glorifying him as living sacrifices. In worship we are united with our God and given the grace to do his will, hastening the day by spreading the good news of his Son and by doing works to his glory. When we praise God, the Spirit graciously seizes us and empowers us to act; then in faith and love we can affirm our spiritual embrace by God. God provides us a life-saving vision for ourselves and his creation (Prov. 29:18), and in this manner, teaches us and enables us to keep the law of life, which is the ethos of love for neighbor that rules the world to come. By prompting us to keep such kingdom values, in worship, divine and human behavior converge. Owing to the crucial role that worship therefore plays in cooperation with Christ and its import for eschatology, the next chapter is devoted to the subject of Christian liturgy.

## Mission

It is a truism of sorts that mission is of the Church's essence. As Christians, we are called to proclaim the Gospel (Luke 9:60; Acts 10:42; Rom. 1:8; 9:17) and baptize all nations, bearing witness to the good news that reconciliation with God is available through Christ (Matt. 28:18–20), who makes us adopted children of the Father. If the Church does not witness to its head, then it ceases to be the body of the living Christ. Indeed, the Church fills up what is lacking in the sufferings of Christ by proclaiming this good news (Col. 1:24); that is, she creatively participates in the ongoing divine redemption of creation and furthers God's mission to become all in all (1 Cor. 15:28). The Church hastens Christ's coming by filling up the number of the late-coming gentiles (Rom. 11:25) grafted into the olive tree (11:17) until the close of the age when the whole people of God will come to salvation through faith in Christ (11:26). Then, beloved Israel will return to the arms of its lover, God in Christ (Rom. 9:25–26, Hos. 2:23; 1:10). At that time, both Jew and

---

70. See "The Westminster Shorter Catechism 1647" in *The Creeds of Christendom III*, ed. Philip Schaff, 4th ed. (Grand Rapids: Baker, 1977), 676 (question 1) and *The Catechism of the Church of Geneva* [1545], trans. Elijah Waterman (Hartford: Sheldon & Goodwin, 1815), 9 (questions 1–2).

Greek alike will inherit the full gift of God as Christ, the head of the body, breaks into history via his Church.

That said, mission is hardly a new vocation for humanity inaugurated with the existence of the Church. The work of extending the kingdom by adding to its membership takes on a new character in light of Jesus' life, death, resurrection, and ascension, but it remains consistent with the tasks given to humanity at creation. The command to "be fruitful and multiply, and fill the earth and subdue it" (Gen. 1:28) is a directive to proclaim the goodness of God and God's creation in word and deed, thereby incarnating God's kingdom. From a different angle, proclaiming the good news of reconciliation to God and the coming of the kingdom is a particularly Christian manifestation of the persistent Old Testament exhortation to love neighbor and stranger. To proselytize is an act of loving neighbor not only because it may reconcile a person to God, but also because it may hasten the Parousia, setting creation free "from its bondage to decay" and bringing "the freedom of the glory of the children of God" (Rom. 8:21).

## Ecumenism

But how can the Church cooperate in bringing about the fullness of God's inheritance through its mission to the world if it itself is riven by divisions? The disunity of the churches (i.e. schism) is a deep sin of the Church. It is disobedience to its Master's direct injunction that the world may know of the love of the Father for his Son, their common bond through the Spirit, by the love (John 13:35) and unity of the Church:

> I do not pray for these only, but also for those who believe in me through their word, that they may all be one; even as thou, Father, art in me, and I in thee, that they also may be in us, so that the world may believe that thou hast sent me. (John 17:20-21, KJV)

Disunity among Christians quite simply prevents the coming of our Lord and his full transformation of the Church into the Bride of the Lamb, and the sanctification of all matter. God cannot witness to his coming kingdom through a body that is known for its mutual hatred, suspicion, enmity, and judgment. Who will join a body which is divided by its constant back-biting and which cannot even agree on what the Gospel means for all of creation? Ecumenism, then, is absolutely necessary as the drive to obey the Lord's command that we all may be one. In view of the schisms between and within the various Christian bodies, the principal place for the people of God to demonstrate the ethical discipline of forgiveness, repentance, and reconciliation is within the Church itself. Indeed, in co-authoring this book, which is an ecumenical act, we hope to contribute in some small way to our corporate work of hastening the coming of the Lord through seeking greater unity among Christians, and ultimately, the reunion of the churches.

By no means do we disregard that there is between the churches, as Georges Florovsky (1893-1979) observed, a "deep disagreement about the Truth."[71] Future progress on the road to unity will only come from supplementing the necessary "ecumenism in space" (the discovery and registry of the various agreements and disagreements among the churches) with an "ecumenism in time," a common return to the tradition ever ancient and ever new, which is the Church itself.[72] This tradition is witnessed to in the teachings of the Faith of the Church of the first millennium, with its Ecumenical Councils and creeds. We have attempted to show some ways in which those traditional formulations persist in Church teachers in both the East and the West, Roman Catholic, Protestant, and Eastern Orthodox, right down until the present day.

Ecumenism is an eschatological work aimed at bringing the kingdom of God ever nearer. Therefore, it is a foretaste of what is to be accomplished in Christ, yet hidden in his body until he appears with us in glory. Christian reunion is an epicletic act of Christ, who invokes the healing balm of his Spirit upon his battered Body, the scarlet woman being transformed into his radiant Bride (Eph. 5:25-27). This

---

71. Georges Florovsky, "The Challenge of Disunity," *St Vladimir's Seminary Quarterly*, 3, no. 1-2 (1954-55): 35.
72. Ibid., 36.

appearance of the Bride of the Lamb, the *Una Sancta,* the woman clothed with the sun, will only be realized on earth in the last days. We are given a helpful image of this in the short "Tale of The Anti-Christ" (1899–1900) by the Russian Orthodox philosopher and poet Vladimir Solov'ev (1853–1900). At the end of the age, the reunited Church—Orthodox, Roman Catholic, and Protestant—gathers in the waste places and marches toward a vision of the woman clothed with the sun as it shines above God's Holy Mountain, Sinai. In the tale, through this divine gift and divine-human work of reunion, all of Israel is restored by uniting with the Church, since God's chosen people return to him "in the hope and strength of its eternal faith in the Messiah," seeing then "Christ coming towards them in royal apparel, and with the wounds from the nails in his outstretched hands."[73]

## Social Justice

The mission of the Church, however, is hardly exhausted in the ministry of word and sacrament and the pursuit of ever-greater unity with other Christians. Her mission cannot be separated from the pursuit of *justice* and the practice of *mercy*. Any attempt to privilege the spiritual side of Christianity at the expense of the social side is a docetic distortion of the gospel. Jesus' proclamation of the good news, the εὐαγγέλιον, was that "The kingdom of God has come near" (Mark 1:15). In other words, the encapsulation of the gospel is that the anointed King, the Messiah, has come to exercise God's reign over the entire world, not just over souls. Accordingly, the Church's prayer is that God's will might come to be done on *earth* as it is in heaven (Matt. 6:10; see chapter 5, p. 84).

God's reign can no more be reduced to the establishment of orthodoxy and faithful weekly (or even daily) worship than can Jesus' Messiahship be reduced to theological teachings about the forgiveness of sins. The Gospels depict Jesus pardoning sins *and* proclaiming good

---

73. Vladimir Solov'ev, *War, Progress and the End of History: Three Conversations Including a Short Story of the Anti-Christ,* trans. Alexander Bakshy and Thomas R. Beyer (Hudson, NY: Lindisfarne, 1990), 190–93.

news to the poor (Luke 4:18-19). He teaches his disciples to free those oppressed by demons (see e.g. Luke 9:1-2) and to liberate those oppressed by poverty (see e.g. Luke 12:33; 16:19-31; 18:22). Likewise, the earliest Church was characterized by common worship *and* by the sharing of possessions with such liberty that "there was not a needy person among them" (Acts 4:34; cf. Acts 2:43-47).[74]

When Jesus announced that this all-encompassing "kingdom of God has come near," his corresponding imperative, the very next word in the Gospel text, was to "repent" (Mark 1:15). We have already shown that repentance is key to the timing of the Parousia.[75] But repentance cannot be reduced to mere emotional contrition. Repentance entails a commitment to turn away from evil and to practice what is good; it requires *fruit*. And beginning at least with John the Baptist's preaching, "fruits worthy of repentance" (Luke 3:8) have been understood to include the abjuration of injustice and the proactive commitment to self-sacrificial generosity (Luke 3:10-14).[76] Thus, during this time while God's patience brings us to repentance (2 Pet. 3:9), we "hasten the coming of the day of God" through "godliness" (2 Pet. 3:12), imitating the justice and mercy of the God who is merciful (Luke 6:36; cf. 1:50-53; 10:37).[77]

## Asceticism

Repentance is not just crucial to our acting justly and mercifully toward the poor, downtrodden, persecuted, and to those who are our enemies; it is also the key mode of the Christian life as a "science" to

---

74. See Christopher M. Hays, "Provision for the Poor and the Mission of the Church: Ancient Appeals and Contemporary Viability," in *Sensitivity towards Outsiders: Exploring the Dynamic Relationship between Mission and Ethics in the New Testament and Early Christianity*, ed. Jacobus Kok, et al., Wissenschaftliche Untersuchungen zum Neuen Testament 2.364 (Tübingen: Mohr Siebeck, 2014), 569-602.
75. Acts 3:19-21; Rom. 2:4; 2 Pet. 3:8-13; see ch. 5, pp. 87-99.
76. Jesus picks up and confirms precisely this message in Luke 13:1-9; as the culmination of his discourse in Luke 12:1—13:9, the requisite fruits of repentance clearly include the care for the needy (12:32-34, 42-48); see further Christopher M. Hays, "Slaughtering Stewards and Incarcerating Debtors: Coercing Charity in Luke 12:35-13:9," *Neotestamentica* 46, no. 1 (2012): 41-60.
77. See further Christopher M. Hays, *Luke's Wealth Ethics: A Study in Their Coherence and Character*, Wissenschaftliche Untersuchungen zum Neuen Testament 2.275 (Tübingen: Mohr Siebeck, 2010), 116.

cultivate the virtues: growth in humility, wisdom, holiness, and above all, love. It is quite simply what the celebrated Russian spiritual teacher and monastic Seraphim of Sarov (1754-1833) called "the acquisition of the Holy Spirit."[78] The providential mission of the Church we have described cannot come about except through allowing and seeking that our whole being become conformed to the mystery of the cross. We must decrease and Christ must grow in us (John 3:30) until we attain to mature humanity, to the "measure of the stature of the fullness of Christ" (Eph. 4:13): "I have been crucified with Christ; it is no longer I who live, but Christ who lives in me; and the life I now live in the flesh I live by faith in the Son of God, who loved me and gave himself for me" (Gal. 2:20). We are speaking of a spiritual discipline that Church tradition calls "asceticism."[79]

Asceticism has sadly become associated for many with "works righteousness" due to its abuse by censorious, austere, and legalistic men, such as Fyodor Dostoyevsky's character in the novel *The Brothers Karamazov*: the "ascetic" monk Father Ferapont, who persecutes the holy monk, the Elder Zossima.[80] Such people as Father Ferapont have forgotten the essential presupposition of all asceticism—love that drives away all fear (cf. 1 John 4:8). As Zossima puts it famously, "If you love each thing, you will perceive the mystery of God in things":[81]

> Do not be afraid of anything, never be afraid and do not grieve. Just let repentance not slacken in you, and God will forgive everything. There is not and cannot be in the whole world such a sin that the Lord will not forgive one who truly repents of it. A man even cannot commit so great a sin that exceeds God's boundless love. How could there be a sin that exceeds God's love? Only take care that you repent without ceasing, and

---

78. See Seraphim of Sarov, "On the Acquisition of the Holy Spirit," in *Little Russian Philokalia: Vol. I: Seraphim of Sarov*, ed. and trans. Seraphim Rose (Platina, CA: St. Herman of Alaska Brotherhood, 1983), 62-112. For discussion, see Helen Kontzevitch, *Saint Seraphim: Wonderworker of Sarov and His Spiritual Inheritance*, trans. Saint Xenia Skete (Wildwood, CA: Saint Xenia Skete, 2004); Lazarus Moore, *St Seraphim of Sarov: A Spiritual Biography* (Blanco, TX: New Sarov, 1994).
79. For an easily accessible discussion of the spiritual disciplines in the contemporary Christian life, see Richard J. Foster, *Celebration of Discipline: The Path to Spiritual Growth* (San Francisco: HarperSanFrancisco, 1988); Tito Colliander, *The Way of the Ascetics* (Crestwood, NY: St Vladimir's Seminary Press, 1985); Thomas Merton, *Contemplative Prayer* (Garden City, NY: Image, 1971).
80. See Fyodor Dostoyevsky, *The Brothers Karamazov*, trans. Richard Pevear and Larissa Volokhonsky (London: Vintage, 2004), 163-71.
81. Ibid., 319.

chase away fear altogether. Believe that God loves you so as you cannot conceive of it—even with your sin and in your sin he loves you. There is more joy in heaven over one repentant sinner than over ten righteous men. If you are repentant, it means that you love. And if you love, you already belong to God. With love, everything is bought, everything is saved. Love is such a priceless treasure that you can buy the whole world with it, and redeem not only your own but other people's sins. Go, and do not be afraid.[82]

For us, asceticism is the science of the soul's cleaving in love to God by which it becomes virtuous, or lives wholly in, by, and through Christ. Through exercise/training—English equivalents of the Greek word ἄσκησις—like an athlete (1 Cor. 9:24–26), one can cleave to God in Christ, and in cleaving to him, bring the kingdom nigh. In this way, we enter into new life in his kingdom that is to come, but we do so here, right now in history, as sons and daughters of God not motivated by fear as are slaves, but by love, since we are God's children (Rom. 8:14–17). But this faithful cleaving that brings about the kingdom requires real work on our part, upheld by the Spirit of God (James 2:17–26), so that we can develop watchfulness of the mind, purification of our passions, and cultivation of the virtues. Here, we commend with discernment the use of the traditional tools (all Scriptural, but later developed in monastic literature) of the "scientific" work of repentance, of the soul's cleaving to God in love: ceaseless prayer, confession, vigils, fasting, and charitable works (cf. above, p. 201).

At the heart of this ascetic work is the requirement of our *kenosis*, or sacrificial self-emptying, a *sine qua non* condition of morality. Becoming true persons in Christ, cleaving to him in love, is not a gentle hyperbole, but a radical moral U-turn from one's present sinful condition to a new virtuous one in God. Following the Apostle, we can characterize this transformation using metaphors of extreme sacrifice, warfare, crucifixion, and death in the spirit of his theology of the cross. A life of stillness and knowing God (Ps. 46:10) is founded on radical sayings: "Go and sell all you have and give to the poor" (Matt. 19.21) and "deny yourself, taking up your cross" (Matt. 16:24). "Let the dead

---

82. Ibid., 52.

bury their dead", says the Lord, "but come, follow me" (cf. Matt. 8:22); "the sufferings of this present time . . . are not worthy to be compared with the glory which shall be revealed in us" (Rom. 8:18); and "seek the kingdom of God and his righteousness, and all these things as well will be given to you" (Matt. 6:33). Christian εὐδαιμονία may be the enjoyment of the kingdom, yet this kingdom is not to be confused with the pleasures "of this world" (cf. John 18:36), such as the prosperity and political success Plato and Aristotle might emphasize; it is, rather, the kenotic εὐδαιμονία of the beatitudes (Matt. 5:3-10).

Asceticism is not entirely about denial and loss; it contains an important aspect of freedom. Perhaps, this is expressed most clearly in the exhortation of Heb. 12:1 to "throw off everything that hinders and the sin that so easily entangles" so that the Christian can run the race "marked out for us." In other words, asceticism is equally about excising those things that delay or disrupt the attainment of a goal. It is no stretch to say, then, that the discipline of asceticism—the practice of repenting of those things that encumber and distract us—frees up a person to love others: physically, emotionally, financially, and spiritually.

## Contemplation

Finally, we cooperate with Christ in order to bring about his return through "contemplation." By contemplation, we mean prayerful study of God's Word. Additionally, in light of and trained by the Bible, this "word of life" (Phil. 2:16), we also turn to the "book of creation" to look for the traces of its Creator Jesus Christ (Rom. 1:19-20, Ps. 19). With the lamp of the Word (in Scripture and in creation) shining as a light upon our path, we can walk in God's ways, according to his precepts; by so living, we can come to know him, and in seeing him, become as he is.

Through the Holy Spirit, the identity, work, and teaching of Christ are revealed in all Scripture, known to the Church as the Old and New Testaments. The Father makes the Son known by the "Spirit of truth" (John 15:26) in all Scripture, even though much of what one can know about Jesus Christ from the Old Testament is shadowy and anticipatory, only made explicit in the apostolic proclamation of the Gospel preserved in the New Testament and gifted to the Church in tradition (understood as an "inherited hermeneutics"). Christ revealed the Trinitarian rule of faith[83] to the apostles, and through them, he gave this wisdom to the Church. By this canon of faith or hypothesis of truth, we can see in Scripture that God is one as Father, Son, and Holy Spirit, and that in Christ, God has created and redeemed us for himself. Jesus Christ is made known in the "concise word"[84] of the Gospel that clearly sums up all of the Law and the Prophets into the command to "love the Lord your God with all your heart, and with all your soul, and with all your mind" and to "love your neighbor as yourself" (Matt. 22:37-39). Moreover, in the gospel of Jesus Christ, we have a short and clear form of the "gift of paternal grace,"[85] that is, the gift of our new calling to adoption, whereby in loving God and our neighbor, we are made godly, righteous, and good. This gift of Christ himself was formally made known in Scripture as a "treasure hidden in a field" (Matt. 13:44); in Scripture, it was "signified by means of types and parables,"[86] but after his resurrection, Christ unlocked to his disciples, revealing how it spoke of him (Luke 24:25-32, 44-48).

We not only come to know and to draw nearer to our Lord in Scripture, but also, in what Augustine called the "book of created nature."[87] The entire creation, embodied and bodiless, comprises the book of God. Through contemplation, the mind purified by God's grace, after meditation on the revelation of Christ as witnessed to in Scripture, comes to know the rich multiplicity of the universe focused on the one Word, in whom and through whom and for whom, all things were created (Col. 1:16). One cultivates this awareness of how all things hold together (Col. 1:17) in Jesus through constantly calling on his name in prayer (1 Thess. 5:17). Then, through God's grace, the mind

---

83. See Irenaeus, *Epid.* 6; for English see Irenaeus of Lyons, *On the Apostolic Preaching*, trans. John Behr (Crestwood, NY: St Vladimir's Seminary Press, 1997), 43-44.
84. *Epid.* 87; Irenaeus, *On the Apostolic Preaching*, 93.
85. *Haer.* 4.36.4 (ANF 1.516; SC 100.894-95).
86. Ibid., 4.26.1 (SC 100.712-13; translation of Brandon Gallaher).
87. Augustine, *Serm.* 68.6 (CCSL 41Aa.443); English translation from Augustine, *Sermons (51-94) on the Old Testament*, ed. John E. Rotelle, trans. Edmund Hill, WSA III/3 (Brooklyn, NY: New City, 1991), 225.

which calls on the Lord descends into the heart, that is, the depths of our person before God. Thus, one may become a pure prayer with the Word of God always holding one close to his breast as one ever embraces him at one's core. In doing so, there is a sense in which the mind's own true spiritual identity becomes known and realized.[88] It appears that, by contemplating prayerfully the *logoi* of beings, the mind comes to an understanding of the principles of divine providence and judgment about them and how they find their coherence in Christ. God's providence and judgment is God's self-manifestation to creation. Just as with Scripture, in the book of creation, God has left traces of his acts and we can come to know him through them by prayerful contemplation.

To be sure, there is an individual element to this discipline of contemplating both general and special revelation. But, lest one get the notion this is an entirely individual process, it is necessary to stress that this contemplation must be done in community, through dialogue and even debate with others, but especially, in shared prayer and praise in the Spirit with our brothers and sisters in Christ. This communal aspect of the discipline is even modeled in Scripture: take, for example, Job's exploration of suffering and meaning in dialogue with his friends before God and with God. Likewise, the corporate reading of Scripture and the practice of prayerfully studying it together as an act of worship are ways in which we are taught not only by the Holy Spirit, but also, by our sisters and brothers in Christ who serve us as the hands and feet of our Savior himself.

The objects of this *theoria* are the objective immaterial goods locked in beings, the *logoi*, which the divine Logos, Jesus Christ, implanted in the universe at its creation. The *logoi* manifest God's creative and sustaining action, what Evagrius Ponticus (c. 345–99) calls God's "finger" upon the universe[89] and the principles of his providence and

---

88. See *The Philokalia*, trans. G. Palmer, Philip Sherrard, Kallistos Ware, 4 vols. (5th forthcoming) (London: Faber & Faber, 1979-). More popularly see Kallistos Ware, *The Orthodox Way* (Crestwood, NY: St Vladimir's Seminary Press, 1995); *The Power of the Name: The Jesus Prayer in Orthodox Spirituality* (Oxford: SLG Press, 2014).
89. Cf. Evagrius Ponticus, *Letter to Melania* 64; for English, see M. Parmentier, "Evagrius of Pontus and the 'Letter to Melania'," *Bijdragen, tijdschrift voor filosofie en theologie* 46 (1985): 9.

judgment for beings. God manifests himself through his glory in the universe and in history, and the *logoi* reflect it. The knowledge of the glory of creation and of God is the key to the personal flourishing of the moral agent and is the basis for the early Christian doctrine of deification (2 Pet. 1:4), where one develops into the moral agent one is meant to be by modeling oneself on the prototype Christ, who, in his incarnation, assimilated himself to the human condition. In a reciprocal process, contemplation assimilates one to the Creator and to his kingdom that is to come.

The glory that is in all things also reflects the *logoi* of creation in the mind of God. The Creator performs the work of creating by referring to these *logoi* in an act of his own primordial contemplation. Consequently, in contemplating the created universe, the agent learns contemplation from the Creator himself. Since God's creation is contemplation, and humans, who are in the divine image, are called to contemplate, they are required to become micro-creators. Virtuous contemplative creativity, in particular, is our re-creating the universe and ourselves through progressively uncovering the glory of God in beings and in us, and then, offering this glory back to him as a sacrifice of praise. This is an eschatological work, a co-creation with God of the kingdom that is to come in glory in the eschaton.

### Christ Within and Before Us

The cooperative vision of eschatology we have just outlined is far from abstract. Our point in this chapter is really very simple: only through divine–human action in Christ will the day of the Lord draw near. Eschatology, if it is to be ethical, and ethics, if they are to be eschatological, must begin with our co-operation as Christians, members of the body of the living Christ, in the divine–human cosmic drama of the two wills of Christ. This is a drama written into Scripture, and indeed, into the foundation of creation. In the more emotive language of a hymn:

Christ be with me, Christ within me,
Christ behind me, Christ before me,
Christ beside me, Christ to win me,
Christ to comfort and restore me.
Christ beneath me, Christ above me,
Christ in quiet, Christ in danger,
Christ in hearts of all that love me,
Christ in mouth of friend and stranger.[90]

---

90. "St Patrick's Breastplate," trans. Cecil Frances Alexander, in *An Annotated Anthology of Hymns*, ed. J. R. Watson and Timothy Dudley-Smith (Oxford: Oxford University Press, 2002), 61.

# 9

# Liturgy: Partial Fulfillments and the Sustaining of God's People

## C.A. Strine, Richard J. Ounsworth OP, and Brandon Gallaher

Though the topics have ranged from New Testament exegesis to apophasis and the nature of time to the doctrine of God proper, one aim has unified our argument since chapter 3—to apply and explore the ramifications of the insight that Jesus' eschatological proclamations are predictive prophesies, which, therefore, have their future fulfillment conditioned by human response to them. Chapter 3 provided an ancient foundation for this insight; chapter 4 explained how adducing partial fulfillments complements this idea; and then, chapter 5 demonstrated its explanatory power in the New Testament. An investigation of the ways in which this interpretative approach cascades into various areas of doctrine began in chapter 6. There, we drew on the resources of apophatic theology to explain how the known and unknown aspects of the Parousia correspond well with the necessary balance between positive affirmations and negative conscriptions of all doctrinal statements about God. Next, chapters 7 and 8 established the precedent for this approach to eschatology in both ancient and modern theologies of God that span denominational boundaries. This long discussion culminated at the end of chapter 8 with an outline of six ways in which the people of God cooperate with God to establish the kingdom on earth: worship, mission, ecumenism, social justice, asceticism, and contemplation.

In this chapter, we aim to expand the discussion of how worship serves both to sustain the Church until the Parousia and, at the same time, to effect the arrival of the eschaton by arguing that liturgy—the corporate service God's people in which they offer a gift of praise to God in cooperation with Jesus—embraces humanity's primordial vocation as priests. The New Testament, our argument will show, appropriates liturgical ideas from the Old Testament and later Jewish literature in order to explain that symbolic re-enactments of cardinal moments in salvation history—embodied in the Christian liturgy of worship—enables the people of God to look back and to see how history is *salvation* history. At the same time, the Christian liturgy of worship offers stepping stones that support and guide the Church's efforts to live as the wounded hands and feet of Jesus that incarnate the ethical vision outlined in the New Testament.

## Past to Present, Present to Future: Horizontal Typology

It is neither distinctively Christian nor, by any means, new to claim that liturgy is a sustaining force that shapes a community, expresses its conviction that God is active in the world, and conveys a teleological view of history. It is, in fact, a pattern one can trace back to the earliest periods of ancient Israel, and even to cultures that precede it historically. The present discussion is the logical conclusion of the argument begun in chapter 2, which has built upon a foundational insight about the provisional nature of predictive prophecy to show the implications of that rebalancing of prophetic hermeneutics through New Testament exegesis and Christian doctrine. It is now time to explore the ways in which Christian practice, specifically liturgical praxis, serves as perennial encouragement for the Church while it seeks to hasten the Parousia.

### Historical Background of the Major Israelite Festivals

To begin, a brief exploration of religious celebrations from ancient Israel and Second Temple Judaism that inform Christian liturgy is necessary.

> Three times a year you shall hold a festival for Me: You shall observe the *Feast of Unleavened Bread*—eating unleavened bread for seven days as I have commanded you —at the set time in the month of Abib, for in it you went forth from Egypt; and none shall appear before Me empty-handed; and the *Feast of the Harvest*, of the first fruits of your work, of what you sow in the field; and the *Feast of Ingathering* at the end of the year, when you gather in the results of your work from the field. Three times a year all your males shall appear before the Sovereign, the LORD. (Exod. 23:14–17, *JPS*)

These words, perhaps some of the oldest prescriptions in the Hebrew Bible,[1] enumerate the three high points of the ancient Israelite year. Certainly, by the Second Temple period, the religious, economic, and social worlds of Judaism (if one can even speak of them as distinct spheres) depended upon these three festivals.

Although the ancient Israelite calendar included other festivals and celebrations (cf. Leviticus 23), Passover in the spring, the Feast of Weeks forty-nine days later, and the Feast of Booths in the autumn (Deut. 16:16) stood above all others. Historical-critical scholarship has

---

1. While there remain wide discrepancies in scholarly views about precisely when the so-called Covenant Code in Exodus 20–23 was written, there is a strong consensus that it predates the Deuteronomic Code (Deuteronomy 12–26) and the Holiness Code (Leviticus 17–26), both of which appear to be aware of the Covenant Code. The chronological relationship between the Covenant Code and the Priestly Code (Exodus 25–40, Leviticus 1–16) is less clear and more debated. For further discussion, see, *inter alia*, Jeffrey Stackert, *Rewriting the Torah: Literary Revision in Deuteronomy and the Holiness Legislation*, FAT I/52 (Tübingen: Mohr Siebeck, 2007) and Bernard M. Levinson, *Deuteronomy and the Hermeneutics of Legal Innovation* (Oxford: Oxford University Press, 1997).

shown that each festival related to the annual agricultural cycle; indeed, the earliest forms of the festivals probably derived from similar religious celebrations in adjacent societies. In order to understand the later Christian theological and liturgical appropriation of the festivals, it is necessary first to sketch their historical origins, and afterwards, to outline the theological and eschatological significance subsequently ascribed to each festival in Judaism.

## Passover

What is commonly called Passover today is actually the combination of two distinctive rites: the sacrifice of the Passover lamb with the accompanying Seder meal and the seven-day Feast of Unleavened Bread (*Maṣṣot* in Hebrew). Scholars differ in their assessment of whether these two traditions were always connected to one another or whether the combined celebration of the two represents a fusion of an originally nomadic, pastoralist ritual (the lamb sacrifice) with an agrarian custom (a defined period of eating unleavened bread).[2] Whatever the case, in the biblical texts, the combined Passover-Unleavened Bread ritual is so thoroughly entwined with the Egyptian exodus tradition that it is impossible to say with any degree of certainty what prehistory the ritual had. It is simply the annual celebration of YHWH's redemption of Israel and a memorialization of YHWH's victory over opposing powers.

## Weeks

The second annual festival is known by a pair of names: Weeks (based on its Hebrew name *Shavuot*) and Pentecost (coming from the Greek term denoting the fifty days between Passover and this celebration).[3] There is no doubt about its connection to the agrarian cycle: this

---

2. For instance, Jacob Milgrom, *Leviticus 23-27: A New Translation with Introduction and Commentary*, AB 3B (Doubleday, New York, 2000), 1972, and Gerhard von Rad, *Deuteronomy: A Commentary* (Westminster: Philadelphia, 1966), 112, argue that the two were originally separate while A.D.H. Mayes, *Deuteronomy* (Grand Rapids: Eerdmans, 1981), 254-57, concludes the two were always connected.
3. This term first appears in Tob. 2:1 and 2 Macc. 12:31-32.

festival considers divine blessing upon the harvest to be indicated by the first fruits of that activity.[4] The event is based upon a straightforward logical deduction: one can extrapolate from the initial yield of the harvest to the total crop. If the early reaping is copious, then one may reasonably expect that a full season's labor will produce an abundant return. Of course, the inverse logic is operative if the first fruits are meager: the Feast of Weeks may well be a time to appeal for an extraordinary divine blessing on the remainder of that year's crops.[5]

## Booths

The Israelite liturgical calendar culminated in the autumn with the Festival of Booths (from the Hebrew *Sukkoth*; sometimes translated as "Tabernacles"), which marks the end of the harvest season. Whereas Weeks inaugurates the harvest and anticipates its fullness, Booths observes its completion. The seven-day event is designed to be a grand celebration of divine blessing as manifested in an abundant harvest.[6] The texts prescribe sacrifices and a communal gathering that provide a great banquet at which a numerous host of people rejoice in YHWH's provision. "It is most natural," remarks Jacob Milgrom, "that only after the ingathering of all the crops and before the advent of the rainy and sowing season," such a celebration was possible.[7]

While Booths is a celebration of the completed agricultural cycle, it is simultaneously the first appeal for divine blessing on the next harvest, specifically by entreating God's favor upon the rainy season that is about to begin. The biblical precedent for this idea is Zech. 14:16–17, which enjoins all the nations to come to Jerusalem in order to celebrate *Sukkoth*, lest YHWH Sabaoth withhold rain from them. "The rabbis were fully cognizant that the theme that unites all these rituals [of Sukkoth] is a supplication for rain," writes Milgrom.[8] Indeed, the

---

4. Exod. 34:22; cf. Deut. 16:9–15, where it is the harvest of the first of several crops. For further discussion of Weeks as a celebration of the first fruits, rather than the end of the harvest, see Milgrom, *Leviticus 23–27*, 1991–92.
5. Milgrom, *Leviticus 23–27*, 1985; cf. the rabbinic explanation in t. *Suk.* 3:18.
6. Lev. 23:34–36, 39; Deut. 16:13–15; cf. Exod. 23:16b, which calls the same event a "feast of ingathering".
7. Milgrom, *Leviticus 23–27*, 2027–28, commenting on Lev. 23:34.

rabbis specified that water should be brought from the pool of Shiloah (*t. Sukkah* 3:18) to be used in the ritual "so that your rains this year may be blessed" (*b. Roš Haš.* 16a).[9] In subsequent practice, prayers for rain were made specifically on the eighth and final day of the festival.[10]

Thus, *Sukkoth* functions as a Janus in the agrarian cycle: it is the occasion both to celebrate what has happened during the past year and to anticipate all that may come in the next one.

### Salvation-Historical Meaning of the Major Israelite Festivals

In time, Passover, Weeks, and Booths each accrued a theological significance that resulted from being paired with an event in the narrative of YHWH's salvation of and providential care for Israel.

Passover, it is well-known, commemorates the exodus from Egypt and the transition from bondage as slaves to freedom in the service of YHWH. Perhaps this theological—one might even say soteriological—significance was not always connected to Passover, but the biblical texts give no indication that Passover ever existed without this associated significance. The exodus is, bluntly, *the* paradigmatic event in Israel's salvation history.[11]

In contrast to Passover, both Weeks and Booths evince a clear transition from agrarian festival to theological commemoration. Weeks, occurring shortly after Passover in the calendar year, developed into a memorial for YHWH's bestowal of the Torah on Mt. Sinai. It is impossible to say when this association began, but it developed because the date of Weeks' celebration—fifty days after the Passover (Lev. 23:15–16; Deut. 16:9–10), or the fifteenth day of the third month after the exodus—corresponds to the date on which the book of Exodus indicates the Israelites arrived at Sinai (Exod. 19:1; cf. *Jub.* 1:1).

Alongside Weeks' connection to the giving of Torah, the festival is also linked to covenant renewal. This association develops because

---

8. Ibid., 2043.
9. For further discussion, see ibid., 2043–44.
10. Merja Merras, *Origins of the Celebration of the Christian Feast of Epiphany* (Joensuu: Joensuu University Press, 1995), 32–33.
11. Cf., *inter alia*, Jer. 16:14–15; 23:7–8; Ezekiel 20; Psalm 106.

of another chronological detail in the biblical text: the story of King Asa's covenant renewal celebration (2 Chron. 15:10–14) occurs on the fifteenth day of the third month of the year. There is no evidence of when this link emerged either, but it existed by the time Jubilees was written in the second century BCE (cf. *Jub.* 6:17–19).[12]

The theological significance of Booths develops similarly, and, by the time the book of Leviticus reached its final form, a link had been established between Booths and the wilderness wanderings (Lev. 23:39–43, *JPS*):

> Mark, on the fifteenth day of the seventh month, when you have gathered in the yield of your land, you shall observe the festival of the LORD to last seven days: a complete rest on the first day, and a complete rest on the eighth day. On the first day you shall take the product of *hadar* trees, branches of palm trees, boughs of leafy trees, and willows of the brook, and you shall rejoice before the LORD your God seven days. You shall observe it as a festival of the LORD for seven days in the year; you shall observe it in the seventh month as a law for all time, throughout the ages. You shall live in booths seven days; all citizens in Israel shall live in booths, in order that future generations may know that I made the Israelite people live in booths when I brought them out of the land of Egypt, I the LORD your God.

Booths acquires a connection to covenant renewal as well, which in time grows even stronger than the Feast of Weeks' association with covenant renewal. Not only does Deut. 31:10–11 prescribe the septennial reading of Torah to all Israel during Booths, Nehemiah 8 places the post-exilic community's rededication to YHWH in its celebration of Booths.

In short, Booths represents YHWH's presence with Israel on its long journey to the promised land, divinely administered providential care for Israel during that time, and Israel's enduring (albeit faltering) commitment to serve YHWH.

---

12. James Kugel, *A Walk through Jubilees: Studies in the Book of Jubilees and the World of Its Creation*, VTSup 156 (Leiden: Brill, 2012), 61–63. Interestingly, this connection does not appear again in extant Jewish literature prior to the Babylonian Talmud (*b. Meg.* 31a), but is common from that point onward.

By the time that Christianity emerged, all three of the major Jewish festivals possessed an agricultural and salvation-historical meaning that informed their celebration and colored their religious significance. Those characteristics can be charted in this fashion:

| | Agricultural Meaning | Salvation-History Connection |
|---|---|---|
| **Passover** | Appeal for an abundant harvest | Egyptian exodus, release from bondage to foreign powers |
| **Weeks** | Celebration of the first fruits of the harvest | Giving of the Torah on Mt. Sinai |
| **Booths** | Celebration of the completion of the harvest, supplication for rain in the coming year | Sustenance in the wilderness wanderings, covenant renewal |

Now it is time to examine the ways these highpoints of the Jewish liturgical calendar are adopted and adapted in Christian theology and practice.

## Christian Appropriation of the Salvation-Historical Interpretation

Rather than offer a general discussion of Christian theology with respect to these three Jewish festivals, it is more constructive to look at one concrete example of their reappropriation. Perhaps no text in the New Testament provides a better example than the Gospel of John, where the Jewish festivals play a prominent role.[13] Indeed, the Gospel of John shows how early Christianity adopted the agricultural and salvation-historical associations of these festivals into its eschatological expectation, and thereby laid a foundation for their later use in ecclesial liturgical praxis.

---

13. Johannes Beutler, *Judaism and the Jews in the Gospel of John*, Subsidia Biblica 30 (Rome: Editrice Pontificio Instituto Biblico, 2006), 7–14.

### Passover

Passover remains the central salvation-historical celebration in Christianity, as a consequence of its transformation into Easter or Pascha, as it is known in Eastern Orthodoxy, according to the Greek term for the Passover (Exod. 12:48 LXX). It is the first festival mentioned in John (2:13-21). While Passover's initial appearance in the Gospel serves as little more than an occasion for Jesus to be at the Jerusalem temple, when Passover occurs again in John 6, the Evangelist draws significantly on the festival's theological meaning in order to frame Jesus' discourse.

The whole of John 6, explicitly linked to Passover in v. 4, portrays Jesus establishing new connotations for the exodus and Passover. Without rehearsing all the evidence for how Passover adumbrates the Christian Eucharist, it is worth noting two points. First, the feeding of the 5,000, which generates a discussion between Jesus and the crowds about seeking food, ends with Jesus proclaiming, "I am the bread of life" (6:35). Here, Jesus is depicted as a new manifestation of the manna from heaven (6:50), the source of sustenance for God's people during their journey from Egypt to the Promised Land. Second, Jesus claims that "my flesh is true food and my blood is true drink" (6:55). The clear but unspecified referents of these two elements are the unleavened bread and wine that are essential to the Seder meal. Of course, bread and wine also evoke the earlier form of the Unleavened Bread celebration, where it relates directly to the agricultural cycle that underlies the annual liturgical cycle.

At the same time, John 6 adapts Passover's salvation-historical significance as a commemoration of Israel's redemption from bondage by linking Jesus' claim to be the true food and drink to receiving eternal life. There is, for instance, an unmistakable soteriological and eschatological significance in the pronouncement, "those who eat my flesh and drink my blood have eternal life, and I will raise them up on the last day" (6:54; cf. 6:35-40, 51, 58). Victory over death (the so-called

## Pentecost

Pentecost is never explicitly mentioned in the Gospel of John. Still, scholars recognize that the otherwise unspecified festival in John 5 is probably Weeks. Raymond Brown, for instance, notes that the location of the events in Jerusalem and "the references to Moses in the discourse" can be best explained by this calendrical setting.[14] Indeed, this liturgical background also explains the role given to both "the scriptures" mentioned in 5:39 and the claim that Moses (a metonymy for Torah) is the one who accuses the audience (vv. 45–47). It is no surprise, therefore, when Jesus maintains that "anyone who hears my word and believes him who sent me has eternal life, and does not come under judgment, but has passed from death to life" (6:24). Testifying about God and guiding the believer into life is precisely the role of Torah in Judaism (e.g., Pss. 19:7–14; 119:1–2).

Should any doubt remain that the early Christians utilized the link between Pentecost and the giving of Torah, the evidence from Acts 2 settles the matter. The Lukan account of Pentecost famously describes the outpouring of Holy Spirit upon a great crowd, after which Peter's sermon persuades 3,000 to be baptized in the name of Jesus. With its emphasis on Holy Spirit as the divine power that guides believers (e.g. Acts 1:2; 13:2; 20:23; 21:4, 11 *et passim*), the Lukan account allusively capitalizes upon the way in which Judaism viewed the Torah as a manual for thought and life.[15] Furthermore, the Lukan portrait can illumine the Johannine perspective if one takes note of their pneumatological commonalities: for Acts, the arrival of Holy Spirit represents a new manifestation of Torah, the repository of divine instruction for life; this is analogous to the Johannine assertion that Holy Spirit will "guide you into all truth" (John 16:13).

---

14. Raymond Brown, *The Gospel According to John (i-xii)*, AB 29A (Garden City, NY: Doubleday, 1966), 206; cf. Beutler, *Judaism*, 10.
15. Cf. J.W. Rogerson, *The Holy Spirit in Biblical and Pastoral Perspective* (Sheffield: Beauchief Abbey, 2013), 69–74.

The Lukan account of Pentecost also alludes to the agricultural background of its precursor, the Feast of Weeks. Recall that Weeks celebrates bringing in the first fruits of the harvest. Furthermore, it invites people to extrapolate from that early gathering: if the first fruits are copious, then one may reasonably expect that a full season's labor will produce an abundant harvest. The festival praises YHWH for this blessing before it is fully realized. This agricultural imagery occurs a number of times in Jesus' parables, where a common metaphor presents the arrival of the kingdom and the abundance of believers as a "harvest" (Matt. 9:37-38//Luke 10:2-3; John 4:35; Matt. 13:30, 39; 21:34, 41; Mark 4:29). In this light, it is unsurprising but significant to observe that Acts 2 capitalizes upon the logic of Weeks in a similar way: if at the celebration of the first fruits, the apostolic proclamation reaps 3,000 new believers, then the full harvest of this mission will surely be a vast community.

### Booths

The festival of Booths is specified as the context for John 7 (v. 2), where Jesus' comments recall the agricultural significance of Booths. Booths serves as the Janus event that simultaneously celebrates the previous harvest and also appeals for divine blessing upon the one to come. In its future orientation, the festival petitions God to provide ample rain. This request dominated the final day of the festival when water was brought from the pool of Shiloah and poured out on the altar to accompany prayers for rain.[16] That practice is likely the background for Jesus' comments in John 7:37-39, which occur "on the last day of the festival" (v. 37a). When Jesus claims to be the living water that people should seek, the context of his comments lie within the forward-looking agricultural meaning of Booths; the clear intent is to depict Jesus as the power capable of fructifying the world and providing life for the people of God.

---

16. Merras, *Epiphany*, 32-33.

A degree of the salvation-historical import of Booths is present in the claims of John 7 as well. Notably, Jesus explains his ability to quench a person's thirst with reference to "the scripture" that says "out of the believer's heart shall flow rivers of living water" (7:38). This statement alludes to Ezek. 47:1-12 and Zech. 14:8, both of which describe the eschaton as a time when a miraculous river will flow from the Jerusalem temple into the land of Israel to provide abundant life. At a minimum, this allusion gives the passage an undercurrent of eschatological expectation that exhibits an interest in the future arrival of God's kingdom in its fullness. This evidence suggests that Booths does not receive an immediate realization, but is reappropriated in a manner that capitalizes upon its future-oriented implications. Invoking Booths provides a means by which to build anticipation for the future completion of the eschatological harvest and for the unmistakable sign of that time, the Parousia of the risen Jesus.

This interpretation also aligns with the Feast of Booths' traditional association with the wilderness wanderings. Just as there was an extended time between YHWH's initial soteriological act (the Egyptian exodus and victory at the sea) and Israel's arrival in the promised land, so also is there a prolonged period between the inauguration of the kingdom in the resurrection and ascension of Jesus and the arrival of the kingdom in its fullness at his Parousia. The length of the journey from inaugurated kingdom to its full arrival, which we have argued might have been less than a single lifetime, is extended by the failure of God's people to heed the divine commands they are given, a synopsis that fits the wilderness wanderings equally well (cf. Numbers 13-14).

One might map all this onto the earlier chart of Jewish understanding in this way:

|  | Agricultural Meaning | Jewish Salvation-Historical Link | Christian Eschatological Connotation |
|---|---|---|---|
| Passover | Appeal for an abundant harvest | Egyptian exodus, release from bondage to foreign powers | Release from bondage to death |
| Weeks | Celebration of the first fruits of the harvest | Giving of the Torah on Mt. Sinai | Arrival of Holy Spirit, 3,000 new believers as the first fruits of a great "harvest" |
| Booths | Supplication for rain in the coming year | Sustenance in the wilderness wanderings | Future orientation, anticipation of "harvest" to come |

This is, of course, only an examination of the way that *one* Christian text appropriated the Jewish feasts for distinctly Christian theological purposes. One can, no doubt, adduce a wide array of ways that other early Christians (and ancient Jews and modern scholars) have understood these feasts. Nevertheless, the Johannine approach anticipates neatly the ways in which subsequent Christian liturgies capitalize on the Jewish theological connotations of the feasts in order to enrich the life and worship of the Church.

### Liturgy: Stepping Stones to Sustain the Church

Each of these three festivals plays a role in both the Christian calendar and its liturgy. Easter, it goes almost without saying, is the high point of the Christian calendar. Pentecost, though less prominent, remains widely known, not least for its association with so-called charismatic or Pentecostal Christianity. The role of Booths remains elusive; while there is a rationale to link it to Christmas and Epiphany as a celebration of the incarnation,[17] the preceding discussion has explained that there is a greater emphasis on its anticipatory function.

---

17. Ibid., 35–38, 41–46, 55–57, 190–92. The connection to Christmas and Epiphany provides an interesting past-oriented complement to the eschatological view outlined above. There is good textual warrant for this view, which can be anchored in the Johannine prologue that describes the incarnation as the "tabernacling" (ἐσκήνωσεν) of the Word among humanity (John 1:14). In the Eastern Orthodox tradition, these themes feature in the feasts of the Transfiguration and the Theophany (the feast of the baptism of Jesus and the revelation of the Trinity, which falls at the same time as the Western Epiphany; on the Transfiguration, see ch. 4, p. 72).

Both Passover-Easter and Weeks-Pentecost have a role in the more quotidian liturgical practice of the Church. Baptism unites the symbol of water with the presence of Holy Spirit and the outward manifestation of the community's growth, a constellation of ideas shown to be central to the message of Acts 2 in the preceding section. Still, the preeminent liturgical act in Christianity is the Eucharist, the sacrament that recalls Passover-Easter. Since its inception, the Eucharist, saturated with symbolic allusions to the agricultural and salvation-historical meanings of Passover, served both a commemorative and a proleptic role. These roles are encapsulated in the instructions St. Paul gives to the Corinthian church (1 Cor. 11:23–26):

> For I received from the Lord what I also handed on to you, that the Lord Jesus on the night when he was betrayed took a loaf of bread, and when he had given thanks, he broke it and said, "This is my body that is for you. Do this *in remembrance of me*." In the same way he took the cup also, after supper, saying, "This cup is the new covenant in my blood. Do this, as often as you drink it, *in remembrance of me*." For as often as you eat this bread and drink the cup, you proclaim the Lord's death *until he comes*.

The first time that each element of the Eucharist is prescribed, St. Paul specifies that the sacrament commemorates the salvific death of Jesus. Yet, when he summarizes the Eucharist, St. Paul is explicit that there is a proleptic component to this sacrament: the Eucharist is done *until the Parousia*. Christians throughout time have, therefore, rightfully understood that this liturgical meal corresponds to both the Last Supper, and also, to the great eschatological banquet that will accompany Jesus' return in glory.

This proleptic or eschatological element is strongly emphasised in the Catholic tradition. The *Catechism of the Catholic Church*, referring to 1 Cor. 15:28, states that "by the Eucharistic celebration we already unite ourselves with the heavenly liturgy and anticipate eternal life, when God will be all in all" (*CCC* 1326). Moreover, the connection between this eschatological anticipation and the Christian fulfilment of the Old Testament rites is strongly emphasized: "By celebrating the Last Supper with his apostles in the course of the Passover meal, Jesus gave the Jewish Passover its definitive meaning. . . [The Eucharist] fulfils the Jewish Passover and anticipates the final Passover of the Church in the glory of the kingdom" (CCC 1340). This bipolar chronological understanding, with its concomitant ethical aspect, is captured clearly in the liturgical texts, e.g.:

> ...For at the Last Supper with his Apostles,
> establishing for the ages to come
> the saving memorial of the Cross,
> he offered himself to you...
> that the human race... may be enlightened by one faith
> and united by one bond of charity.
> And so we approach the table of this wondrous Sacrament, that...
> we may pass over to the heavenly realities here foreshadowed.[18]

A similar theme occurs in the Eastern Orthodox liturgical tradition, which begins with an eschatological reading of Scripture: Christ asks those present at the Last Supper to eat the bread and wine, symbolizing his body and blood broken and shed for the life of the world, *in remembrance of him prior to the actual sacrifice*.[19] In other words, memory is not merely retrospective—looking back at a life of sacrifice—it is simultaneously prospective, appropriating the sacrifice of the cross before it happens. For this reason, at the anaphora, the priest proclaims a retrospective and prospective truth all at once:

> Remembering this saving commandment *and all those things which have come to pass for us*: the Cross, the Tomb, the Resurrection on the third day, the Ascension into heaven, the Sitting down at the right hand, and *the second and glorious Coming*.[20]

This statement emphasizes that Christians must remember the future life to come and that the liturgy compels the people of God to gather together all the moments of salvation history, to ponder at once how salvation is present now and still to come. The call to *anamnesis*, to

---

18. *Preface II of the Most Holy Eucharist* in *The Roman Missal: English Translation according to the Third Typical Edition* (London: Catholic Truth Society, 2010), 523.
19. Luke 22:19 (οὗτο ποιεῖτε εἰς τὴν ἐμὴν ἀνάμνησιν); cf. Matt. 26:20–30 and Mark 14:17–26.
20. *The Liturgy of St. John Chrysostom* in *The Divine Liturgy According to St. John Chrysostom with appendices*, 2nd ed. (South Canaan, PA: St. Tikhon's Seminary Press, 1977), 29–87; quote from 65.

continually recalling past and future, does not destroy the past as past or the future as future; rather, as Nikolai Berdyaev says, "[i]mmortality is memory made clear and serene."[21]

Early Christians often expressed this notion by speaking of Sunday as the eighth Paschal day, a day without end.[22] The Orthodox hymnography of Easter/Pascha, thus declares that "[t]his is the chosen and holy day, first of Sabbaths, king and lord of days, the feast of feasts, holy day of holy days. On this day we bless Christ forevermore."[23] Furthermore, the *Liturgy of St. John Chrysostom* alludes to the same concept when it exclaims "O Christ! Great and Holy Pascha! O Wisdom, Word and Power of God! Grant that we may more perfectly partake of Thee in the never-ending Day of Thy Kingdom."[24] Christians, thus, explain their practice to worship on Sunday (called both the "Lord's Day" and "a Little Pascha") and not the Jewish Sabbath day (i.e. Saturday) because it more explicitly connects that act with the resurrection, the event in which all things are and will be made new. Or, as the author of the *Epistle of Barnabas* states in explaining the condemnation of new moons and Sabbaths in Isa. 1:13:

> Not the Sabbaths of the present era are acceptable to me, but that which I have appointed to mark the end of the world and to usher in the eighth day, that is, the dawn of another world. This, by the way, is the reason why we joyfully celebrate the eighth day—the same day on which Jesus rose from the dead.[25]

The liturgy, therefore, facilitates participation in that which is eternal so that it carries both an ascendant and descendant aspect—the faithful are elevated toward the kingdom of God as it presently exists in

---

21. Nicolas Berdyaev, *The Divine and the Human*, trans. R. M. French (London: Geoffrey Bless, 1949), 158.
22. The scheme in which there is *one* eternal day outside of the ordinary time scheme of seven days originates in *2 En.* 33:1–2 (cf. 28:5). The notion may be a Christian interpolation (cf. Jean Daniélou *The Bible and Liturgy* (London: Darton, Longman & Todd, 1951, 1960), 256), positing that seven ages of 1,000 years are followed by an eighth, 1,000-year Messianic age without end, where "1,000" is a symbolic number pointing to perfection.
23. *Matins of Pascha*, Canon, Ode VIII, Irmos in *The Paschal Service*, eds. John Erikson and Paul Lazor (n.p.: Department of Religious Education, Orthodox Church in America, 1997), 36.
24. *The Liturgy of St. John Chrysostom*, 82.
25. *Barn.* 15.59–60; translation of James A. Kleist, *The Didache, The Epistle of Barnabas [etc.]*, ACW 6 (Westminster, Maryland/London: Newman/Longmans, Green and Co., 1961), *ad loc.* The numerous patristic texts on the octave are given in Jean Daniélou, *The Bible and Liturgy*, 255ff.

heaven[26] at the same time as the power of Christ in the Spirit descends to make the liturgy a genuinely divine act.[27] Each individual liturgical act of the Church, all the celebrations of its sacraments, exhibits both the vertical and the horizontal dimensions. They are acts of divine power carried out by human beings, and this is possible because those human beings are united to Christ; thus, they are the body of Christ. At the same time, the sacraments are true acts of remembrance that also point us forward and lead us forward to the eschaton. By the divine power of the sacraments, we are united ontologically to the efficacy of the paschal mystery and prepared for its final consummation at the end of time.

### Stairway to Heaven: Liturgy as Vertical Typology

So far, the discussion has focused on the role of the Eucharist in recalling what has already been done to inaugurate the kingdom of God and in encouraging Christians to look forward with anticipation for the consummation of that kingdom on earth as it is in heaven. It is also worth highlighting that 1 Corinthians 11 ties the Eucharist to the ethical domain: "Whoever, therefore, eats the bread or drinks the cup of the Lord in an unworthy manner will be answerable for the body and blood of the Lord. Examine yourselves, and only then eat of the bread and drink of the cup" (1 Cor. 11:27–28). Thus, the Christian reception of the Jewish liturgical calendar functions as a series of "stepping stones," sustaining both hope and an eschatologically driven ethic of repentance.

In addition to this temporal dimension—recalling the past and longing for the future, what we have called a "horizontal" typology (see above, p. 212)—the liturgy also directs us upwards to the heavenly source of the promises. Many Christian traditions understand their liturgy to be principally a divine act: it is the divine power breaking

---

26. In the Orthodox tradition, one finds this sentiment expressed in the *Liturgy of St. John Chrysostom* through the prayer said by all prior to receiving the bread and wine, which wonders how the worshipper, who is unworthy to enter into God's presence because she is not clothed in a "wedding garment," can yet enter the splendor of God's saints.
27. See, *inter alia*, CCC 1083 and *The Liturgy of St. John Chrysostom*, 82.

forth from heaven and irrupting into the earthly realm that makes the liturgical life of the Church so much more than a gathering of like-minded worshipers. For instance, in the *Liturgy of St. John Chrysostom*, the deacon says quietly to the priest before the liturgy commences, "It is time for the Lord to act" (Ps. 119:126a), stressing that all which follows is a divine act and a human deed at once. Just as the horizontal dimension oscillates between past and future, with the present-day Christian sustained in a creative tension between remembrance of the past and hope in the future, so there is an analogous movement on this "vertical" axis: the actors in the liturgy, while caught up in a divine act that "descends" to earth from heaven, are not puppets mindlessly acting out a divine drama on a human stage, but free and rational creatures, making (under grace) an authentic sacrifice of praise that "ascends" to be heard on high. Central to our argument is the fact that these two typological axes, though distinct, are far from contradictory. Rather, they tend to intertwine, especially in biblical texts dealing with the liturgical life of God's people. It is undoubtedly the case that the emphasis of Scripture is on horizontal rather than vertical typology; the Bible speaks far more frequently in the temporal than the spatial mode. There are, moreover, few places where the vertical mode occurs without mention of the horizontal. Still, in those places where the biblical text invokes vertical typology, there is an explicitly liturgical focus.

This feature results, in part, because eschatological hopes that appeal to the consistency of God's action in salvation history establish typological links between past and future, but not simply to past *historical* events, but also to *primordial* ones. In other words, the age to come will have the features not of past human history, but of the primeval milieu of the creation. Such, for example, is the promise of Isa. 65:17-25, but the idea is already present in first Isaiah (11:6-9). Isaiah 51 and Psalms 74, 78, and 89 similarly draw a link between the creative power of God manifested before the ages and the power of God to redeem Israel that will be manifested at the end. Isaiah 11:15 portrays the deliverance of Israel from her enemies by comparison to God smiting the sea. This last passage exemplifies the *mediating* function of types, which is crucial when applying typology to the liturgy: given the preceding section of Isaiah 11, in which the future is portrayed in terms of a return to Eden, we are justified in supposing that the smiting of the sea is a creation motif, drawing on the common ancient Near Eastern mythology of creation as the victory of God or his agent (Baal, Marduk et al.) over the sea deity or monster (Tiamat, Leviathan). The reference to God's *ruaḥ*, his wind or spirit, brings to mind Gen. 1:2, and Isaiah's division of the waters into seven streams suggests that the parallel is not directly with the parting of the Red Sea; and yet, there clearly is reference to the latter event in the mention of passing over the river dry-shod. Isaiah's depiction does not evoke *just* creation or *only* exodus, but *both*. There is parallelism to *Endzeit* and *Urzeit*, the evocation of a salvation-historical event that interprets the exodus in terms of primordial and eschatological apocalyptic events.[28] Salvation history is the stage upon which the eternal drama of God's creative and redemptive power plays out; it is this power that gives the historical type its strength to mold human history and to propel it to its eschatological conclusion.

The Old Testament also gives us examples of purely spatial typologies, what one may call *Heilsgeographie*. Like other typologies, these tend to center on the temple and often look back to Eden, the primordial garden. Psalm 46, for example, attributes to Jerusalem the life-giving river characteristic of Eden (Gen. 2:10). In the exilic and post-exilic periods, this typology really develops, especially in eschatologically-directed typologies: Isa. 51:2 and Ezek. 36:35 explicitly portray the land to which the people will return as a new Eden.[29] Similar ideas can be found in Joel 2:3 and Zech. 14:8–11. Particularly important is the fact that the vertical typologies of the Old Testament consistently

---

28. We might, perhaps, go so far as to say that the account of the original exodus itself appeals to creation motifs, so that the Isaiah passage is correctly understanding the protological nature of the exodus and then re-applying it eschatologically.
29. Ezekiel 37—the subsequent chapter that describes the prophet raising up the dry bones into living humans—may continue the theme by implicit reference to the creation of Adam in Eden. The Orthodox tradition draws on this interpretation by reading the chapter at the matins of Holy Saturday to look forward to Christ's resurrection on Easter Sunday, whereby he liberates Adam and Eve (representing humanity) from the jaws of death.

take the Jerusalem temple as their focal point. A similar approach occurs in the New Testament; consider, for instance, that the letter to the Hebrews (8:5) appeals to Exod. 25:40 (and cf. v. 9) in order to explain that the heavenly divine sanctuary is the model for the earthly dwelling place of God. Conversely, then, the earthly temple constitutes a reliable image of the heavenly reality. The eternal and supernal sanctuary stamps its mark into earthly space to create a sacred geography, a *Heilsgeographie*.

The same claim to a formative relationship between the heavenly sanctuary and the temple of Solomon occurs in 1 Chron. 28:19 and is strongly implied in Ezekiel's vision of the reconstructed temple (Ezek. 40–48). The description of heaven as the temple or sanctuary of God is also common in the poetic and prophetic texts of the Old Testament (e.g. Pss. 11:4; 18 *et passim*, Hab. 2:20, Mic. 1:2). This approach does not cease when the biblical authors escape the influence of their Canaanite and Babylonian neighbors; rather, the notion becomes all the more pervasive in the Persian and Hellenistic periods (cf. *1 En.* 14.10-20, *T. Levi* 3:2-4, *Wisd. of Sol.* 9:8, *2 Bar.* 4.5). The Songs of Sabbath Sacrifice among the Dead Sea Scrolls (4Q400, 403, 405 *et passim*) seem to imply some simultaneity between the worship at the temple and the eternal heavenly liturgy. This notion does not even disappear after the destruction of the temple in 70 CE, according to the testimony of rabbinic texts such as *b. Hag.* 12b, *Gen. Rab.* 55:7, and *Midr. Cant.* 4.4.

The most sophisticated effort to relate the heavenly and earthly sanctuaries appears in the Jewish book *Jubilees*. This text is of particular interest because it concerns itself not only with liturgy, but especially with the liturgical calendar. In *Jubilees,* the calendar expresses a heavenly order that must be reflected in the earthly temple services, so that the harmony between the worlds above and below may be maintained. Throughout, *Jubilees* typologically relates the feasts and sacrifices of the temple to the events of the past; for instance, *Jubiliees* combines the Feast of Weeks celebration, the celebration of the harvest, and also, a commemoration of the promises made to Noah and to Abraham into a single moment. As *Jubilees* remarks, "the feast is twofold and of two natures" (*Jub.* 6:21). Failure to observe the feasts properly and in a timely way debases Israel, fails to recognize their history and identity, and deprives them of their "holiness"—a powerful echo of Leviticus's "Holiness Code" (see e.g. *Jub.* 16:18; 33:20). The purpose of the covenant is to conform Israel to the angelic host whose service to God in heaven they echo on earth; this covenant is epitomized by circumcision (*Jub.* 15.24-26), a feature that the male Israelites share with the angels of the presence and the angels of sanctification (*Jub.* 15.27-28). Liturgical mistakes prevent Israel from representing to the world the eternal patterns in the cosmos established at creation (see, especially, *Jub.* 6:32-34). Keeping of the feasts is no mere temporal phenomenon: "It is an eternal decree and engraved upon heavenly tablets for all the children of Israel. . . . And there is no limit of days because it is ordained forever" (*Jub.* 6:14). Levi and his successors re-enact the eternal liturgy of the heavens (*Jub.* 30.14; cf. 31.18) at the same time as they re-enact the events of salvation history. The levitical priests—indeed, all Israel—do the whole world a vital service in sustaining the stability of the universe.[30]

Are we in danger of abandoning the authentically biblical view of history (linear and directed toward a soteriological endpoint) in favor of a circular view of history that owes more to Athens than to Jerusalem?[31] It is true that the *Book of Jubilees* purports to reveal the workings of the heavens to the privileged seer, and perhaps, does have a circular view of history. This feature would be a concern if our appeal to liturgy maintained a strict division between the vertical and the horizontal. However, it is crucial to say again that the Scriptures rarely invoke vertical typology (i.e. in respect of the tent/temple) purely on its own. The vertical dimension is intertwined with the historical, especially the eschatological, as Ezekiel clearly shows: the Prophet sees a heavenly vision of the new temple while "on a very high mountain" (40:2) that he, like Moses on Mount Sinai, must relate to the people.

---

30. Jubilees associates this particularly with the daily *Tamid*, a sentiment that echoes ideas found also in Sirach 50.
31. See also Brandon Gallaher, 'Chalice of Eternity: An Orthodox Theology of Time', *Saint Vladimir's Theological Quarterly* 57.1 (2013): 5-35.

Thus, Ezekiel functions as a new Moses and this envisioned temple becomes a type of the heavenly sanctuary. The vision is at once a horizontal and a vertical typology that casts the future in terms of the past and portrays the earthly temple as a projection into the world of eternal, heavenly realities. Ezekiel's temple is, furthermore, infused with both Eden and Sinai associations; Eden here represents the primordial pre-history and Sinai represents both the founding moment of Israel's history as a covenant people and the heavenly dwelling of the Most High.

In view of all of this, we must agree with Fishbane:

> [T]he phenomenon of typological exegesis requires a modification and reconsideration of the common view that the Israelite apprehension of history is linear only and never cyclical. . . . [T]he issue cannot be easily polarized into a juxtaposition of a "mythic ahistorical paradigm", in which fundamental patterns recur cyclically, and a "biblical historical paradigm", in which new and unique events unfold linearly.[32]

It is worth noting that this combination of the cyclical and the linear (which are often seen as mutually incompatible) is really only problematic if we equate eschatology with *imminent* eschatology (a frequent but often implicit correlation). But, as Barton points out in his book *Oracles of God*, an eschatological view of history only specifies that history is going somewhere, without making any claims as to the imminence of this destination.[33] Indeed, one can go further to say that history is shaped both by its origin (i.e. by creation) and by its destination (i.e., its τέλος), so that protology and eschatology determine the trajectory of history. Still, this does not preclude the possibility, even the likelihood, than the intervening period will show repeated patterns. On the contrary, it is predictable that the protological and eschatological shaping of history emerges through a repeated patterning, through a perennial inscribing of the forms of the creation and the eschaton into salvation history. What is a more

---

32. Michael Fishbane, *Biblical Interpretation in Ancient Israel* (Oxford: Clarendon, 1985), 357.
33. Barton, *Oracles of God*, 218.

natural place for such repeated patterning than the liturgical life of the people of God with its daily and yearly rhythms?

It is necessary to underscore that it is above all in the eschatological writings that the primarily vertical temple typology becomes interwoven with horizontal typology. This interweaving forms a distinctive tapestry that depicts the eternal through the history and future of the people of God. That picture, furthermore, is habitually exhibited to the people of God in their liturgical praxis, in their sacramental recollection of the past, and in their longing for the future. This is certainly in the case in the New Testament, in which typology is so often related to baptism and/or the Eucharist. Take just the most obvious examples: 1 Peter 3 and 1 Corinthians 10. In the former case, there is a correspondence (ἀντίτυπον; 1 Pet. 3:21) between the salvation of those who found refuge in the ark and the salvation now to be found through Christian baptism. The latter example is more transparent: the events of the exodus, the subsequent wilderness wanderings, and the provision of supernatural food and drink all took place τυπικῶς, foreshadowing the provision of spiritual food and drink in the Eucharist.

Yet the best example of the interrelationship between the horizontal and the vertical axes occurs in Hebrews 9, with its elaborate (and again explicitly typological) consideration of the significance of the layout of the sanctuary. The contrast between the first/outer tent and the second/inner tent is simultaneously one between Holy Place and Holy of Holies, between earthly and heavenly sanctuaries, and between "the present age" (Heb. 9:9) and the "end of the ages" (Heb. 9:26). Thus, while the overt typology is vertical (Heb. 8:5, cf. 9:23), two things make the vertical typology distinctive: first, it is directed to an eschatological purpose; and second, the vertical aspect is combined with a two-fold horizontal aspect that embraces both space and time, *Heilsgeschichte* and *Heilsgeographie*.

The New Testament invokes typological relationships both horizontal and vertical in various ways to denote correspondences that are both formative and mediating. These typologies are formative because they explain that it is the "*Urbild*"—that is the prototype, be it Christ, the heavenly sanctuary, or some other thing—that is the source of power for the earthly or historical reality. And, these typologies are mediating because—whether relating two past events, or the past to the present, or the past/present to the eschatological future—they manifest the repeated pattern of God's dealing with humanity in grace and for salvation. The repetitive nature of these things, occurring in slightly varied ways over and over again throughout time and place, demonstrate that it is the unchanging God who dwells in heaven making a mark upon history in this way. Typological similarities, bordering on tedious in their reprisal, are anything but stale. Their recurrence, their similarity depends directly upon the consistent character of God. It is because God does not change that history unfolds in ways that can appear cyclical. Those similarities are, nevertheless, indications of an ageless pattern that resides in the heavenly realm. The patterns the people of God discern in history bespeak that the "father of lights with whom there is no variation or shadow due to change" (James 1:17) is at work.

It is in the eschaton, however, where the horizontal and vertical dimension reach the pinnacle of their interweaving. The end of history is portrayed as the *descent* of the Son of Man with the heavenly Jerusalem at the same time that it is the *ascent* from earth to heaven of the righteous. Corporately and cosmically, the world is set to rights. The veil between heaven and earth is at last definitively removed. The eschaton is, we might say, the apotheosis of the whole of creation. For the individual believer too, the end—that is, the τέλος—of her life simply *is* heaven. For both individual believer and the whole Church, the future, in a real sense, already exists in heaven. Thus, "our citizenship is in heaven, and it is from there that we are expecting a Savior, the Lord Jesus Christ" (Phil. 3:2); so also, Col. 1:5 speaks of "the hope laid up for you in heaven." The ultimate fulfillment of Christ's promises is the final fusion between the two dimensions, as history itself culminates, time climaxes, and the people of God enter into eternity.

The New Testament appropriates the liturgical ideas developed in the Old Testament and later Jewish literature in order to explain that symbolic re-enactments of cardinal moments in salvation history conform the people of God to the eternal realities they make manifest. Until the Parousia, the liturgical acts of the Church, particularly celebrating the sacraments, serve to teach and to highlight the vertical and horizontal dimensions of the New Testament's typologies. The sacraments are acts of divine power carried out by human beings made possible because those human beings are united to Christ, and are, thus, the body of Christ.

Christian liturgies are true acts of remembrance that carry the power to *propel* us toward the eschaton. The liturgy allows the people of God to look back and to see how God has irrupted from above into the earthly realm. The liturgy enables the Church to see how history is *salvation* history. It sustains us, it leads us forward.

The liturgy also carries us upwards, and, in a real but difficult to comprehend way, it brings us to Christ already enthroned in heaven. So enthroned, Jesus mediates his supernal power to us through the sacraments so that the people of God to continue his ethical work here on earth. The liturgy contains stepping stones that support and guide our often faltering efforts to live as the wounded hands and feet of Jesus that incarnate the ethical vision outlined in the New Testament, the pursuit of which 2 Peter 3 reminds us will hasten the final consummation of all salvation history in the Parousia.

In the Lord's Prayer—not coincidently, at the heart of all liturgies for the Eucharist—the world is reminded that the kingdom of God already exists in heaven. Because the consummation of all things is already laid up for the people of God in heaven, the liturgy leads us forwards and upwards, directing the feet that walk in Jesus' ways not only a "path" of stepping stones, but a stairway to heaven.

## Liturgy in Eschatological Action

Finally, it is crucial not to overlook the ethical and eschatological effectiveness of liturgy. Though mentioned briefly in the final section of chapter 8 (p. 198), this issue demands further attention here. Liturgy—because it is above all participation and cooperation with Christ in our true vocation as "priests of creation"[34]—incarnates the kingdom of God and speeds the day of the Lord.

### The Liturgical Priesthood of All Believers

Liturgy is, simply defined, the corporate, public work or service (λειτουργία; e.g. Luke 1:23) of God's people in which they offer up a gift to God in cooperation with Jesus. The Church—the communion of people united to God in Christ and through the Holy Spirit—collaborates with Jesus in his high-priestly mediation when they worship. Liturgy is, therefore, a substantial fulfillment of humanity's primordial vocation as priest of creation.[35] Likewise, it is not trivial to recognize that the notion of liturgy, as a public, corporate act of the body of Christ, is natural to God. If it seems odd to say that God in Godself is a "liturgy," it is crucial to keep in mind that liturgy is the corporate work of offering up a gift. And this is a key characteristic of the Christian, Trinitarian understanding of God. The Trinity, as outlined in chapter 7 (pp. 158–67), is self-giving and self-receiving love: God the Father eternally begets His one-and-only Son, and in this begetting, the Father offers up his whole life in an eternal sacrifice—an act which is the very essence of self-gift. This is emblematic of a process repeated in the second and third persons of the Trinity, who are not haughty about this gift, but in distinctive ways, imitate the self-sacrificial giving of themselves to another. Son and Spirit receive the gift from the Father, make it their own, and, in gratitude, confer it on another. The very being of God, one can say from this perspective, is the perpetual work of offering up a gift.

---

34. See John Zizioulas, *The Eucharistic Communion and the World*, ed. Luke Ben Tallon (London: T&T Clark, 2011), 133–41 and Brandon Gallaher, "Creativity, Covenant and Christ: The Dignity and Task of Humankind within God's Creation" in *Human Action within Divine Creation: Christian and Muslim Perspectives*, eds. Lucinda Mosher and David Marshall (Washington D.C.: Georgetown University Press, forthcoming).

35. This role is implicit in the depiction of Adam in Gen. 2:15, where the command to "till" it (עבד) and to "keep" it (שמר) corresponds to the terms often used for explaining the Levites duty to oversee proper worship at the tabernacle/temple (e.g. Lev. 18:5; Num. 3:7–8; 4:23–24, 26); cf. Gordon Wenham, *Genesis 1–15* (Nashville: Thomas Nelson, 1987), 67, 87, 90.

## LITURGY: PARTIAL FULFILLMENTS AND GOD'S PEOPLE

If liturgy is part of God's character, then humanity is called to conform itself to this feature of the divine being (e.g. Rom. 12:1; Eph. 5:2; Heb. 13:15-16). Said otherwise, humanity is obliged to live liturgically as priests of creation. Thus, one message of Genesis 2-3 is that humanity turns from its priestly vocation: shunning the command of God, neglecting to appreciate the abundance provided for human sustenance and the gift-giving worship of God, humanity instead turned to the world and fed on it, greedily and resentfully partaking of it as if its life depended entirely upon it. Genesis 2-3 depicts humans who are no longer living through contemplation and communication with God, but as people delusionally convinced that their role in the world comprises self-interested lordship over it, even to the extent of liberation from dependence on God. In other words, Genesis 2-3 represents a humanity that fails to participate in liturgical activity. Adam and Eve do not use what is gifted to them by God to build God's kingdom, to bring forth order (or one might say "the image of God") from chaos, to conform creation more and more into the likeness of the Trinity. They do not, as one author wrote, take the opportunity to "share of [the very same] being"[36] that is the substance of the divine hypostases; they refuse to become partakers of the divine essence (2 Pet. 1:4), to be, as an ancient Christian writer said, a "portion of God."[37]

Jesus Christ reopens the path of our priestly vocation. Humanity's priestly garment, once lost through disobedience, is offered again in Jesus Christ as the eternal high priest of our salvation in whom we have not merely a means to partake of the divine life, but true God in human form. As high priest, Christ fulfilled the Law by cleansing the lepers, healing the sick, interceding for us before the Father, and, finally, as

---

36. Origen, *Princ.* 1.3.6 (for English, see *On First Principles*, trans. G. Butterworth (Gloucester: Peter Smith, 1973), 35); and see Pseudo-Dionysius, *Divine Names* 5.6.17-21 (PTS 33.184; for English, see *Pseudo-Dionysius: The Complete Works,* trans. Colm Luibheid and Paul Rorem (New York: Paulist), 99); Thomas Aquinas, *SG* 3a.20 (for English, see *The Summa Contra Gentiles of St Thomas Aquinas,* trans. English Dominicans (New York: Benziger Brothers, 1924), 38).
37. Maximus the Confessor, *Ambiguum* 7, pref.; (PG 1068D; for English, see *On the Cosmic Mystery of Jesus Christ: Selected Writings from Maximus the Confessor,* trans. Paul M. Blowers and Robert Louis Wilkens [Crestwood, NY: St Vladimir's Seminary Press, 2003]). Here, Maximus is exegeting Gregory Nazianzen, *Or.* 14.7 (PG 35.865C; for English, see Brian Daley, ed., *Gregory of Nazianzus,* Early Church Fathers [London/New York: Routledge, 2006], *ad loc*).

the pinnacle of his own self-offering, dying as the paschal lamb slain so that humans who were exiled from paradise might return to face God without condemnation and to receive the inheritance for which they were created. This inheritance, this adoption as God's sons and daughters, is not only a privilege, but also a responsibility. Adoption requires, as Irenaeus puts it, that one embrace the "Lord's levitical substance."[38] Like the Levites, the tribe that lacks a parcel of land in the trans-Jordan, the Christian has no inheritance but the Lord. Thus, the Christian accesses their inheritance at the altar, where Jesus is experienced in worship. Christ empowers humanity for its vocation of gratitude, opening a way though his cross by which suffering can be creatively transformed by the prayers of the Church, making possible once more the union and communion God had wished to lavish upon creation by pouring it out into a people dedicated to glorifying God. This is, in no small measure, what it means that the Church is "a chosen race, a royal priesthood, a holy nation, God's own people" (1 Pet. 2:9; cf. Rev. 5:10), a task that begins at Baptism, when Christians receive the Holy Spirit to seal (σφραγίζειν) them in this role and to enable them to offer their "bodies as a living sacrifice, holy and acceptable to God" (Rom. 1:12). Said simply, the corporate act of worship, in which the body of Christ gives thanks for its inheritance, also declares the body's share in Christ's priesthood to the wider world.

Translated into an image, when Christians worship as a community, when the body of Christ engages in liturgy, when believers do a public work or service in which they offer up a gift to God in cooperation with Jesus, they epitomize the broken, bloody hands and feet of Jesus interceding before the throne of God for all of creation (Rom. 8:34; cf. 8:26–27). Indeed, the Apostle Paul speaks of such offering as "reasonable worship (τὴν λογικὴν λατρείαν)" (Rom. 12:1). Thus, the whole of the divine economy of salvation promotes the participation of humans in the life of God; such participation occurs in the locus the kingdom of Christ made manifest in our midst—the Church as an assembly of the living and departed saints. Liturgy joins the Church in

---

38. *Haer.*, 4.8.3 (PG 7.995C), translating *Domini leviticam substantiam*; ANF 1.470 ft. 11.

both content and form with the departed saints (Rev. 5:6-14) to stand before God in corporate worship and prayer and hasten the Coming of our Lord.

### Remembering and Hastening the Future through the Liturgy

Christ is the coming one (Matt. 11:3). Said differently, the Eucharist recapitulates the saving act of Jesus Christ as the paschal lamb, gathering together the whole economy of God expressed in the cross. It is, in this way, not merely an act in history, but an act in God. When Christ ascended to the Father, he took with him all of history, every act before his incarnation and every act to come. These actions are all recapitulated in his human nature. This mystery depicted in the Eucharist, as described above, is both an act of remembrance and an enactment of hope for the full presence of God's kingdom. This is an ἀνάμνησις (Luke 22:19, 1 Cor. 11:24-25); this recollection includes not only historical recall but, perhaps more importantly, remembrance of the future. Liturgy invites the trinitarian God to ponder the promise that Jesus, the second person of that Trinity, will come again in glory. Because of Jesus' role, this prospective remembrance is a divine-*human* one in which Christians share, for its locus is the incarnate deity. God's promise of salvation for all creation is revealed in Jesus' body, which resides beyond our vision at the right hand of God and within our vision as the Church in its worship, its liturgy.

In offering all of our selves, our souls, and our bodies back to God in Christ via the Church's worship, we announce the union and communion of flesh and the Spirit for which creation was designed. But worship and liturgy—certainly, as we have defined it here—include other efforts to incarnate the kingdom of God. To return to a key thought from earlier (see chapter 8, pp. 201-5), this is encapsulated in the Sermon on the Mount and explicated throughout the Gospels in various ways when Jesus calls believers to ethical action. Eschatology motivates and manifests itself in ethics. God will not come again without the Church's cooperation in Christ to hasten the day of the Lord's coming. Creation exhibits its cruciform shape by our ecological care, by our building of a society that is Christ-like in its concern to feed the hungry, by welcoming the stranger and protecting the outcast, by seeking justice through a fair distribution of goods and services in society, through protecting the most vulnerable in the world, and, no doubt, by spreading the good news of Jesus' life, death, resurrection, and impending return.

Cooperation with Christ in this self-giving to others hastens his coming. Liturgy, in both its corporate, ceremonial form and also in its self-sacrificial provision for others is, therefore, an embodied form of the prayer "Amen. Come, Lord Jesus!" (Rev. 22:20b). It is the "liturgy after the liturgy."[39]

---

39. Ion Bria, 'The Liturgy after the Liturgy', *International Review of Mission* 67, no. 265 (1978): 86–90.

# 10

# Our Method: Reflections on Our Hermeneutical Principles and Collaborative Practices

## Christopher M. Hays and C.A. Strine

It may seem odd for the penultimate chapter of a book to address its method. Why wait this long to discuss the theological hermeneutics that guide our thesis and the research practices that produced this text? After all, most theological monographs prefer to dedicate their first twenty pages to methodological prologue. The authors of this book, however, did not approach the guiding question of this volume with a method already in mind. Rather, our hermeneutic emerged from our work as much as it generated our results. It seems disingenuous, therefore, to place this chapter anywhere other than at the end of our argument.

This brief chapter on hermeneutics is not a rear-guard attempt to defend our approach, but instead, an effort to represent our view of how theology might be done better in community than by individuals. Because the process of developing our argument on the delay of the Parousia has been so illuminating to us with regard to the possibility of collaborative theology, we want to be explicit about our method in the hope that other groups might attempt similar work in the future. Here, we shall meander through the various theological and methodological considerations that gave shape to this work; this requires briefly visiting subjects as wide-ranging as historical criticism, Christocentric theology, ecumenism, and Christian worship. Subsequently, we will describe the logistics of how we moved from guiding question to initial proposal to polished prose. Since theologians seldom imitate the collective-authorial methods of scientists, perhaps these reflections on the nuts-and-bolts of our process will help others.

## A Communal & Theological Hermeneutic

### Historical Criticism

This book starts with a historical-critical problem: how does one explain New Testament texts widely understood as unfulfilled prophecy, specifically the non-fulfillment of Jesus' prophesied second coming? Historical Jesus studies made this issue prominent; it is a crucial historical-critical topic because it poignantly captures the dissonance between the affirmations of Scripture and the events of time and space.

Our desire has always been to accept and even foreground that this constitutes a real historical-critical problem (chapters 1–2). It was our aim, accordingly, to give an answer that employed historical criticism. Thus, our argument lays its foundation upon a historical-critical approach to how Jewish prophecy works (chapter 3) in order to offer a fresh interpretation of the problem of Jesus' non-return (chapter 5). Upon retrospective reflection, it is clear that this was an attempt to embrace the tensions raised by historical-criticism, following an instinct that this method could also stimulate innovative ways to answer those same dilemmas.

Contrary to any suspicion that this might merely be an effort to remain "respectable academics" to the scholarly community, it is the character of Scripture as inspired text created in history that makes historical-critical investigation a needful expression of deference to the method of revelation God chose. Since God deigned to speak to humanity in particular times and places, it may be taken as a matter of necessity to consider the historical particularities of that ancient time and place in an effort to apprehend that divine revelation.[1]

One should not think, however, that our approach was exclusively historical-critical. Quite the contrary. Despite the notion that historical-criticism is an academic juggernaut that marginalizes all other methods, we take it to be one component of a multifaceted effort to grapple with divine revelation and to know God. The Catholic tradition has felt more at peace with this interplay than have conservative Protestants and Orthodox in recent history,[2] and Catholics have by and large avoided animosity toward historical criticism.[3] We adopted a hermeneutic in which historical-criticism is not viewed as an enemy to theological interpretation, but rather, as a tool by which one may see text, history, and guiding question framed in a novel way. Our approach seeks to express humility by refusing to subject Scripture to our own autonomous standard of perfection, but that we must instead seek "the perfection Scripture has in a historically *a posteriori* act of discipleship."[4] By remaining convinced that God can, and indeed does, reveal truth through this undeniably more-complex mode of revelation, the scholar gains access to

---

1. Christopher M. Hays and Christopher B. Ansberry, "Faithful Criticism and a Critical Faith," in *Evangelical Faith and the Challenge of Historical Criticism*, ed. Christopher M. Hays and Christopher B. Ansberry (Grand Rapids: Baker Academic, 2013), 213–15.
2. Consider, for example, the Pontifical Biblical Commission's 1993 document *The Interpretation of the Bible in the Church*; for further detail, see Benedict Thomas Viviano, "The Normativity of Scripture and Tradition in Recent Catholic Theology," in *Scripture's Doctrine and Theology's Bible: How the New Testament Shapes Christian Dogmatics*, eds. Markus Bockmuehl and Alan J. Torrance (Grand Rapids: Baker, 2008), 125–40.
3. Cf. Hays, "Towards a Faithful Criticism," 1–10.
4. Christopher B. Ansberry et al., "Pseudepigraphy and the Canon," in *Evangelical Faith and the Challenge of Historical Criticism*, eds. Christopher M. Hays and Christopher B. Ansberry, 155.

possibilities not available to earlier theologians.[5] This may—and it is necessary to stress this is only a possibility—enable more persuasive responses to old and new interpretive problems.

## Typology

Historical criticism and typology may seem strange bedfellows: the former often is used to desacralize putatively divine events, while the latter highlights the revelatory significance of many events that are not self-evidently transcendent. Still, our group embraced the possible contributions of typological interpretation with the logic that "Nobody is more likely to do something theologically symbolic than is God."

Because Christians believe that all history is *God's* history, we inquire into typology (chapters 4 and 9), sensitive to the resonances, reoccurrences, and rhythms of the events of sacred history. The recapitulation of themes and motifs follows from the continual direction of a God who does not change, even as that God authors history through and with humans. Christians justifiably anticipate typological correspondences between the celestial and the terrestrial, for the God who rules heaven is committed to ensuring that the divine will be done on earth too. No doubt, we have formulated our typologies in ways that sometimes differ from earlier approaches in Judaism and Christianity, but we endeavored to remain faithful to the concept and the content of those earlier contributions whenever possible.

In a similar way that Christians have always found resonances, reoccurrences, and rhythms in history, so also have they found them in Scripture. Typology is one way of expressing the fact that various themes and images run like threads throughout the Bible, tying

---

5. Some representative examples focusing on Genesis are: Walter Moberly, *The Theology of the Book of Genesis* (Cambridge: Cambridge University Press, 2009); John E. Anderson, *Jacob and the Divine Trickster: A Theology of Deception and YHWH's Fidelity to the Ancestral Promise in the Jacob Cycle*, Siphrut 5 (Winona Lake, IN: Eisenbrauns, 2011); and Christoph Levin, "Genesis 2–3: A Case of Inner-Biblical Interpretation," in *Genesis and Christian Theology*, eds. Nathan MacDonald, Mark W. Elliot, and Grant Macaskill (Grand Rapids: Eerdmans, 2012), 85–100. Moberly offers helpful methodological reflections (ch. 1, 'What Is a "Theology of Genesis"?); a similar discussion with more emphasis on the German scholarly tradition is Jan Christian Gertz, Angelika Berlejung, Konrad Schmid, and Markus Witte, *T&T Clark Handbook of the Old Testament: An Introduction to the Literature, Religion, and History of the Old Testament* (London: T&T Clark, 2012), 767–92.

together the entirety of the Christian canon. Typology, hackneyed though it may now be in many circles, always remained a reasonable and logical consequence of our attempts to read both history and Scripture carefully.

## Canon

Even though high regard for the Christian canon comports with typology, it will seem discordant with historical-critical research to many. Indeed, a hallmark of historical criticism is underscoring at each turn ways in which one biblical book is distinct from and in tension with another. Critical attentiveness to the diversity of the biblical witness might strike some as a liability for Christian theology, but this presumes that each dissonance represents an insuperable problem. Dissonance between texts, however, may be complementary, or barring that, reflect an antinomy that appropriately describes a transcendent God (see chapter 5, pp. 103–7). Instead of seeing prophecy as either predictive or conditional, our work indicated that prophecy is predictive *and* conditional, according to the interplay between genuine human responsibility and the freedom of an omnipotent God (cf. chapter 8, pp. 187–95). Different parts of the canon accentuate the various sides of this antinomy, with the occasional text (such as 2 Pet. 3:8–15) explicitly stating the mystery in order to offer Christians surer footing on which to grapple with the implications of such indeterminacy.

## Ecclesial Christocentric Trinitarianism

A key observation of this volume is that the dynamics of conditional prophecy—which entail that history comprises an irreducible cooperation and interaction between both God and human agents—mirror the dynamics of the hypostatic union (see chapter 8, pp. 223–27). In Christ, who is fully divine and fully human in nature, a divine will and a human will cooperate,[6] and those two wills in one person conducted Jesus through the key events of the world's redemption. So too, the course of history: though the vicissitudes of human volition may make it seem haphazard, history is a macrocosm for the cooperative dynamics of divine and human wills in Christ in his living body, the Church. We term our approach to the problems of eschatology *Christocentric*[7] because it sees the hypostatic union of Christ as undergirding the logic of the delay of the Parousia. Likewise, we classify the method *ecclesial*, first, because the universal and confessing Church is the site where Christian theology is properly done, and second, because, being Christ's body, the Church is the locus of the cooperation between God and his people.

Our approach is also *Trinitarian* since Jesus Christ is, in his person, the self-interpretation of the Trinity. Christ's life of self-sacrificial cooperation provides a glimpse of the collaboration between the persons of Father, Son, and Spirit. Such self-sacrificial cooperation is not limited to this sphere, but also characterizes the interaction between the Trinity and humans in their collaborative work of forming history. Just as Christ's incarnation, suffering, and death bear witness to the willingness of the Trinity to give of itself for the redemption of the human, so also the entire scope of history reflects the cruciform sacrifice of the Trinity's forbearance, in which the triune God patiently waits to consummate all history in judgment and glory, choosing a selfless deferral of the salvation-historical denouement in order to redeem more of the rebellious creation.

The give-and-take of the Trinitarian cycle of self-surrender is innate to the character of God and to the mystery that is the divine kenosis on behalf of humanity; therefore, it is also essential to the unfolding of history. Though the notion of an *ecclesial, Christocentric,* and *Trinitarian* theology surely would have appealed to our group before this project, the process of embracing the conditionality of prophecy, working out its implications, and finding all this deeply fitting to the God depicted in the Bible provided definition to those potentially ambiguous terms.

---

6. Although the levels of their causality are incommensurate, just as the two natures of Christ are incommensurate but inseparable.
7. While "Christocentrism" in sometimes used as a way to reduce to the Old Testament to a sort of *preparatio evangelica*, that is far from the manner in which we engage the term.

They encapsulate for us that concerted reflection on God—what theology seeks to be—will always recognize the reciprocal self-sacrificial relationships within the Trinity and of the triune God with humanity, especially in the church. Prophecy remains conditional and human decisions have driven history beyond where Jesus' prophecy indicated the end might lie because the self-giving God who prophesied to us in the self-emptying Christ is committed to drawing his people out of our rebellion and into the life of the Trinity.

This means, then, that the conditionality of prophecy is not a convenient excuse or special pleading for the delay of the Parousia; it is a theological answer rooted in the core attributes of the creator God who is our redeemer. Neither were the chapters on divine will and action (chapters 6-8) needless doctrinal window-dressings for a critical, exegetical argument. Quite the contrary: historical-critical findings help frame the cruciform divine reality on display in salvation history.

## Worship

Perhaps it will seem obvious to say that an ecclesial, Christocentric, and Trinitarian approach places high value on Christian worship in developing its arguments, since worship is the preeminent instance of humans cooperating with God in Christ.[8] It is important to specify, nevertheless, that when we refer here to worship, we do not exclusively mean collective prayer and partaking of the sacraments together (though both were part of our collaboration). Neither is it sufficient to say that our work led to doxology (though all faithful theology should indeed do that). Rather, in this book, our recourse to worship denotes a sustained effort to use varieties of both Jewish and Christian liturgies and practices (especially in chapter 9, but also throughout the volume) to develop an answer to our guiding question. This was not done in an effort to drum up a modicum of rhetorical

---

8. See ch. 8, pp. 197-208, for more on worship and other aspects of human cooperation with Christ, such as missions, contemplation, asceticism, and the pursuit of social justice and Christian ecumenism.

verve amidst dry exegetical niggling, but it followed from a conviction that liturgies are revelatory as well.

The longstanding practice of *lex orandi lex credendi* presumes that Christian worship is Christian theology. Liturgical verbiage is not just useful because it communicates theology to those who might not receive formal religious education; through centuries of reflection and refinement, the liturgy has become a distillation the most poignant expressions of what Christians regard as true. Ascribing theological value to the Christian liturgical tradition is a consequence of believing that God's Spirit remains active in God's Church, especially when it gathers as a community. These ancient traditions, preserved and cultivated throughout the history of Christianity, are valuable resources for apprehending the self-revelatory activity of God.

## Ecumenism

These comments on the revelatory potential of Christian tradition lead to the next key to our approach: proactive theological ecumenism. Naturally, Christian tradition comprises a diverse range of practices across time and place. Diversity may, at times, be an obstacle to clarity, but we found the variation resulting from theological ecumenism to be a benefit and not a hindrance.[9] As a collaboration of one Catholic, two Orthodox, and two Protestant scholars (a mixture of ordained persons, laypersons, and even a missionary), at every stage we endeavored to query theologians and texts from all of our denominational homes, and others besides.

The composition of the group, furthermore, was not accidental, but a choice based upon a sense that no single tradition or academic subdiscipline would provide a truly robust response to the delay of the Parousia. That premonition seems to have been vindicated, as this volume draws vital insights from a range of thinkers such as Dale

---

9. Ecumenism here does not represent the notion that all Christians should exist within one massive church (though we are not ashamed to confess our desire for that and our confidence in its reality at the consummation of history; cf. ch. 8, pp. 199–201). Rather, ecumenism reflects our efforts to proactively interrogate all our theological traditions without hoping to vindicate one at the expense of the other.

Allison, Pseudo-Dionysus, Thomas Aquinas, Karl Barth, and Vladimir Lossky; our argument would have been significantly impoverished without that diversity of contributions. The differences between our particular traditions did create impediments at some points, though none that entirely obstructed our progress. Indeed, the wide variations proved both provocative and productive, to the extent that we are all pleased—if a bit surprised—by just how much we agree.

### Ethics

Finally, it was one of our initial instincts in addressing this topic that ethics would be involved in our answers, since, after all, Jesus' eschatological teachings are almost always tilted toward paraenesis (repent, be alert, store up treasures in heaven, etc.) and since his kingdom ethics are consistently eschatological in orientation. This hunch did not derive from a supposition of praxiological primacy of the sort one sees vaunted in liberation theology,[10] though there was a certain praxiological presupposition. Consequently, from the early days of our collaboration, an eye was kept on the entailments of our eschatology for our ethics, believing that orthodoxy and orthopraxy should not be isolated one from another.

This conviction manifested itself most decisively as we grasped that the conditionality of prophecy is, in fact, rooted in ethical contingency. The New Testament depicts the Parousia of Jesus as intimately connected with human repentance and morality (*à la* 2 Pet. 3:8–15), so that by extension, human responsibility forms a crucial part of the cruciform dynamic of God's governance of history.

Ethics not only proved to be the lynchpin for our *explanation of* the delay of the Parousia; ethics also emerged as the necessary *faithful response to* and *engagement with* that delay (what chapter 8 calls a "cooperative eschatology"; see p. 197). Seeking to live according to Jesus' ethical teachings is the reply of faith and hope to present worldly realities. Adopting a kingdom ethic means rejecting the apparent

---

10. Gustavo Gutiérrez, *A Theology of Liberation: History, Politics, and Salvation*, trans. Sister Caridad Inda and John Eagleson, rev. ed. (Maryknoll, NY: Orbis, 1988, 1973), 5–11.

hegemony of the terrestrial and unredeemed, liberating the Christian to contribute to the divine redemption that is and will be (Heb. 12:1). Morality, the sustained effort to live by kingdom values, is the way in which human hands pray *Thy kingdom come, thy will be done, on earth as it is in heaven.*

Predictably, but reassuringly, one might summarize all this with Augustine's hermeneutical dictum that a proper interpretation of Scripture is one which builds up love.[11] Therefore, ethics became the acid test of our eschatological proposal. And it seems to us that the same criterion must play a key role in future theological proposals that deal with any number of topics besides the doctrines of the last things.

## Collaborative Authorship

It has been our practice to refer to this book as a "collectively authored monograph," which may strike some as an oxymoron. Potential confusion notwithstanding, the nomenclature aptly expresses that this volume is not a compilation of essays. It is, insofar as possible, a book with one voice and with a single, progressive line of argument, albeit one that traverses often-separated theological sub-disciplines.

## Method of Composition

Our five authors include an Old Testament scholar, a systematic theologian, a patristics expert, and two New Testament scholars from different Christian traditions. It was said more than once that this interdisciplinary team passably approximated the academic breadth of one decent thirteenth-century theologian.[12] This was never interdisciplinarity for its own sake—ever so vogue in the contemporary university—but an effort to ensure that the constituent parts of our work would be appreciated by experts in each respective field. Still,

---

11. "Anyone who thinks that he has understood the divine scriptures or any part of them, but cannot by his understanding build up this double love of God and neighbor, has not yet succeeded in understanding them." Augustine, *On Christian doctrine* 1.36.40 (CCSL 32.53); translation of R.P.H. Green, *De Doctrina Christiana* (Oxford: Clarendon, 1995), 49.
12. Taking into account that a good deal more books are on shelves today than there were in the thirteenth century.

to balance that ideal with those of readability and coherence to non-experts in each sub-discipline, we tended to value poignancy, clarity, and brevity over comprehensiveness. Because no single reader could have expertise in each discipline represented in the volume,[13] we sought to write with a learned but not necessarily specialist audience in mind.

When we began this project, we did not have even a fuzzy idea of whither we would go to find a solution; we had little more to go on than a nasty question and a box of biscuits. Publication of our work was not a goal to begin with, though it became one as we grew in the conviction that we had something to say. Because most of us were sustained by postdoctoral fellowships, the clock was not a tyrant. So, we took time: each month, one group member presented on a relevant idea from her or his own area of expertise. The steady rhythm of our meetings allowed ideas to percolate, and as a thesis emerged, we began to write and present conference papers together. Intentionally, our presentations always involved two or more members of the group. It would be wrong to say we never worked as individuals, but even in those moments, we consciously labored as part of a community.

To transform conference papers into a collectively authored monograph, it was necessary to assign component tasks to various people. Each chapter has a "lead author." The lead authors typically structured the chapter and drafted the majority of the prose in the first draft, though nearly every chapter contains subsidiary sections, paragraphs, and footnotes written by other group members. Chapter drafts were then repeatedly circulated to the entire group, with each member offering feedback for revision by the lead author for that section. Finally, a single editor (Hays) revised the whole volume to smooth out the prose and style. It will no doubt remain clear that the voice of, e.g. Casey Strine is not the same as the voice of Julia Konstantinovsky, but the collaborative and editorial efforts provide

---

13. We also appreciated that few would have the patience to read exhaustive treatments of each sub-discipline's take on the delay of the Parousia!

continuity, and we would venture to say more coherence than one finds in even the best-planned collections of essays.

## Final Comments

These reflections on our working practice are not a methodological memoir, or much less, a manifesto. It seemed necessary, nevertheless, to give some account of why we approached this project in a manner that is rather different from most publications in our various fields.

Ambitiously, we have sought to weave historical criticism, typology, canonical consciousness, ecclesial Christocentric Trinitarianism, liturgy, ecumenism, and ethics into a coherent thesis. Perhaps a single volume is simply too small for this effort; perhaps, it will strike readers more as a cacophony than a symphony. Our judgment is for the latter, and we are more convinced now than when we started that such diverse methodological concepts can get along rather splendidly. In hindsight, we believe that this accords with Augustine's exhortation that "a good and a true Christian should realize that truth belongs to his Lord, wherever it is found."[14] Excluding any one of the disciplines represented in our group in order to provide greater space or weight to another sub-discipline would, we are convinced, have impoverished our conversation. That said, there is no denying the value of specialist works, and each member of our group will continue to produce such monographs.

And yet, the process of writing this book has persuaded us all that some issues are better handled by a team. Or by a Church.

---

14. Augustine, *On Christian doctrine*, 2.18.28 (CCSL 32.29); translation of Green, *De Doctrina Christiana*, 91.

# 11

# Conclusion: A Fourfold Response to the Delay of the Parousia

## Christopher M. Hays

### What Do We Say about the Delay of the Parousia?

It may be that Jesus' words "There are some standing here who will not taste death until they see that the kingdom of God has come with power" (Mark 9:1) caused consternation among his listeners when they were first uttered. After all, the disciples seem to have expected that the eschatological war would kick off almost immediately (see Luke 9:54; 19:11; 22:49–50). To such a zealous audience, Jesus' indication that only *some* would see denouement of the kingdom may have been rather dispiriting.

The disciples' confidence possibly faltered in the initial decades of the apostolic church as the persecution of the Jerusalem community scattered most of them into the surrounding regions (Acts 8:1–4).[1] But Jesus had foretold that as much would happen (Mark 13:9–13), so even bad news could be seen as good news; these events vindicated Jesus' words. Still, it was probably in the 60s of the first century, as the Neronic persecution cut down the two greatest apostles of the age, that some Christians really *worried* about whether or not Jesus was correct. It is likely in this context—when Christian bodies served as torches for the imperial gardens—that Mark the Evangelist penned his Gospel, urging the Church to stay the course, "For those who want to save their life will lose it, and those who lose their life for my sake, and for the sake of the gospel, will save it" (Mark 8:35).

Then, hope-inspiring tragedy struck! Roman armies besieged Jerusalem, raiding, plundering, and burning. In that awful moment, these early Christians must have taken heart, for Jesus predicted that precisely this would happen (Mark 13:1–26). Glorious prophetic fulfillment! The branch of the fig tree had become tender and put forth leaves; summer was near (Mark 13:28). No doubt, the vindication of Jesus' prophecy buoyed the Christians for another decade, maybe two.[2] But then Domitian's reign turned malevolent in the 90s,[3] and the last apostle died, the one who (it was rumored) would remain until Jesus returned (John 21:20–23). What could these Christians reply when their pagan neighbors scoffed, "Where is the promise of his coming?"

Scripture and history indicate they responded in four ways. They said: Jesus is already with us; Jesus Christ is coming again; perseverance in holy and godly living can hasten that day; and, finally, they exclaimed '*Maranatha!*'

What about twenty-first-century Christians? What does one say today, when Jesus has tarried far longer than anybody expected in those first decades, when the ebb and flow of history has seen Christians rise from ignominy to imperial supremacy, and, now it

---

1. Most of Paul's letters were written in the 40s and 50s, and they give minimal evidence that people were wavering in the expectation of the second coming (excepting perhaps 1 Cor. 15). Cf. ch. 2, pp. 34–35.
2. In this context, the Gospels of Matthew and Luke were penned.
3. Contributing to the composition of the book of Revelation.

seems, descend into a pluralistic cacophony? How does one act when those who most ardently predict Jesus' return are the eccentric, the fundamentalist, the perpetually mistaken and the constantly recalculating? Does one adopt the complacent eschatology of some Christians in the comfortable West? How does one react when Christians continue to be cast into prison, beaten, and beheaded in numbers equal to or greater than during the Roman Empire? Perhaps most pointedly for the present question, when the suffering Christian cries out "Come, Lord Jesus" and the self-satisfied Christian says "Take your time," how does one respond to a scholarly community that mutters with exasperation, "Can't we just forget about this nonsense and move on?"

If you have read this far, you will know that this book argues Christians living in the third millennium since Jesus' ministry should meet this challenge with the same four responses as the apostolic church: Jesus is already with us; Jesus Christ is coming again; perseverance in holy and godly living can hasten the arrival of that day; and, above all, we should exclaim '*Maranatha!*'

## Jesus is Already with Us: Eternity in Historical Time

Discussions of the delay of the Parousia often veer toward speaking as if the kingdom did not come at all, as if Jesus left his people Fatherless. But the New Testament writers firmly refused to interpret the non-consummation of the kingdom as the absence of the kingdom.

### Stepping Stones and the Presence of the Kingdom

The New Testament authors saw the kingdom breaking into their present situation in the form of discrete events of God's presence and reign that provided *stepping stones* toward the final consummation (see chapter 4, pp. 68–76). They first recognized these stepping stones in Jesus' transfiguration; second, in his resurrection; third, in his ascension and celestial reign; fourth, in the imparting of the Holy Spirit; and fifth (though far from finally), in the making disciples of all nations, vindicating Jesus' promise "Lo, I am with you always, even unto the end of the world" (Matt. 28:19, *KJV*; cf. Acts 1:8).

John's Gospel explains with particular tenderness that the departure of Jesus does not amount to his absence (cf. chapter 4, pp. 74–76).

> I will not leave you orphaned; I am coming to you. In a little while the world will no longer see me, but you will see me; because I live, you also will live. On that day you will know that I am in my Father, and you in me, and I in you." (John 14:18–21, *NRSV*)

The Fourth Gospel argues that Jesus comes already in the presence of the Paraclete. While the disciples who remain in the world are, to the eyes of outsiders, alone, through the Spirit they are joined to the Son who is united with the Father. Jesus proclaims to the suffering Church longing for his Parousia that he is present with those who suffer (cf. Acts 7:54–59); no discussion of the delay of the kingdom's culmination justifies God's people speaking as though God is absent. God is present even in the suffering and loneliness of his people. As Julian of Norwich lay at the door of death, Jesus came near to her and he

> gave me spiritual insight into the unpretentious homely manner of His loving. I saw that for us He is everything that is good, comforting and helpful; He is our clothing, who, for love, wraps us up, holds us close; He entirely encloses us for tender love, so that He may never leave us.[4]

## Apophatic Theology and Our Limited Understanding of Divine Time

Julian's mystical encounter with Christ, her apprehension of Jesus' presence in advance of his return, points us toward the more paradoxical lessons expounded in the contemplative experiences of Dionysius and Gregory Nazianzen: just as Christians should not doubt the kingdom's presence (its non-culmination notwithstanding), neither should God's people think *time* is the linear juggernaut it seems to be. Here, apophatic theology is immensely valuable. Theological

---

4. Julian of Norwich, *The Revelation of Divine Love*, trans. M.L. Maestro (Tunbridge Wells, Kent: Burns & Oates, 1994), 67.

*apophasis* denies the arrow of time's apparent hegemony. Human linear temporality is not the measure of God's non-linear eternality; rather, things are quite the opposite (see chapter 6, p. 140).

Put simply, *humans do not understand or experience time in the way God does*. For this reason, 2 Pet. 3:9 stresses the difference between divine and human time in order to articulate the relevance of it for the delay of the Parousia: "With the Lord one day is like a thousand years, and a thousand years are like one day. The Lord is not slow about his promise."

To some, this verse initially appears a desperate attempt to save Jesus from his infelicitously specific statements. Nonetheless, apophatic reflection on the nature of divine time indicates that 2 Peter's observation is a good deal more profound than a stubbornly modernist perspective will admit. Humans are the material, time-bound creations of an immaterial and eternal Creator; by dint of our existence within time and space, and compounded by our nature as fallen beings, humans are essentially incapable of fathoming the operations of the deity who is beyond time and space. Accordingly, brazen judgments about the inadequate timing of the eternal Logos' "return", reckoned according to our solar calendar, need to be severely chastened (cf. chapter 6, pp. 129–31).

### The In-Breaking of the Divine Time into Human Time

Still, Christians should not think that the disjunction between created time and divine time is permanent. It is already passing away. The incarnation and resurrection of the eternal Logos begin the restoration and elevation of chronological time. When one speaks of the inauguration of the kingdom, or describes the in-breaking of the eschaton, one conveys that the arrow of fallen time is being overruled. Somehow, God's eternity subsumes and subverts linear, human time. Inaugurated eschatology does not advocate living *as if* the kingdom were here; far more radically, it maintains that kingdom time *has already* deposed fallen time as a result of the victory of the Logos and through the ongoing operation of the Holy Spirit (cf. chapter 6, pp. 118–21).

The Spirit pierces the fabric of human time and knits us into the eschatological eternal Now (see chapter 6, p. 137). In the words of John Zizioulas, the Church "has its roots in the future and its branches in the present."[5] Christian liturgy, properly understood and appropriated, instantiates this reality. When believers gather in Christ's name, Jesus is present (Matt. 18:20); in the breaking of bread, he is there. When the people of God employ the sacramental elements to proclaim "the Lord's death until he comes" (1 Cor. 11:26), the vertical typology of the liturgy literally brings heaven and earth together. By making the eschaton proleptically present to us, the liturgical life of the Church functions like stepping stones, sustaining the people of God as they travel towards the eschaton (cf. chapter 9, pp. 227–35).

Likewise, the social ministries of God's people—feeding of the poor and clothing the naked—serve Christ (Matt. 25:34–40) and manifest his reign, for "in fact, the kingdom of God is among you" (Luke 17:21) (cf. chapter 6, p. 140 and chapter 8 p. 201). These are the practical ways in which the people of God follow the greatest commandment: "You shall love the Lord your God with all your heart, and with all your soul, and with all your strength, and with all your mind; and your neighbor as yourself" (Luke 10:28; cf. Matt. 22:37–39//Mark 12:29–31). It is with all this in mind, that we assert that *liturgy and ethics are eschatological*.

That said, it remains necessary to bear in mind the balance between apophasis and cataphasis: whatever the limitations of our understanding of time, however much the eschatological Spirit may be breaking into the present, it remains both possible and necessary to insist on the future completion of what God has begun. Christians can still affirm the clear statements of Scripture and tradition that the King and the kingdom are yet to come in their fullness. The Spirit marks the in-breaking of God's eternity into fallen time in order to *activate* God's people, granted a foretaste of the kingdom, to live in a way that realizes

---

5. John Zizioulas, *Being as Communion: Studies in Personhood in the Church* (Crestwood, NY: St Vladimir's Seminary Press, 1997), 59.

the total restoration of time and the consummation of God's eternal reign.

## Jesus Christ Will Come Again: Non-Fulfillment Does Not Falsify Fulfillment

The later writings of the New Testament remain quite unabashed in their affirmation that, despite the delay in Jesus' return, he would indeed come again (2 Pet. 3:10; Rev. 22:20). Some will still consider this a truculent refusal to accept that Jesus' prophecy was false, but we have demonstrated that the non-fulfillment of prophecy does not falsify the prophecy because prophecy is, by its nature, *conditional*. Prophetic fulfillment interacts with and frequently is governed by the response of the hearers to the prophet's exhortation. It does not just *prognosticate* future events; it *activates* righteous living (cf. chapter 3, p. 57).

### The Conditionality of Prophecy and the Delay of the Parousia

The conditional and hortatory nature of prophecy explains a great deal of the non-fulfillment of the prophesied kingdom of God. The Messiah arrived preaching that the people of Israel should repent (Mark 1:15) in order that they might serve the kingdom of God that drew near. But the vast majority of his hearers, including the nation's leaders, rejected him so emphatically that they put him to death. One can fairly infer that this qualified as an inadequate response to the prophetic summons to repentance!

Yet, even the treason of God's people offered an occasion for divine grace. While the Lord could well have returned in those first months or years, seized his rebellious slave Israel, "cut him in pieces, and put him with the unfaithful" (Luke 12:46), he chose *not to do so*, "not wanting any to perish, but all to come to repentance" (2 Pet. 3:9; cf. Rom. 2:4). The final vindication of God's people was delayed, yes, but so was the final castigation, which would have fallen on a great many more souls.

And so the apostles and the Church of God persisted in urging people to:

> Repent therefore, and turn to God so that your sins may be wiped out, so that times of refreshing may come from the presence of the Lord, and that he may send the Messiah appointed for you, that is, Jesus, who must remain in heaven until the time of universal restoration that God announced long ago through his holy prophets. (Acts 3:19–21; cf. chapter 5, pp. 98–99)

God's people, nevertheless, persisted in rebellion. Of the seven churches addressed in Revelation 2–3, only two escape censure; even a cursory glance at the letters of Galatians, Corinthians, Peter, and Jude confirm the impression that the church convulsed between holiness and rebellion. The first decades of the Church lacked idyllic orthodoxy and orthopraxy; the ensuing ones followed suit. So it remained the case in subsequent centuries that the Church Fathers identified the delay of the Parousia as God's forbearance toward an unworthy but loved people (cf. chapter 5, pp. 99–101). For all this, though, they did not shrink from their conviction about the return of Jesus. Indeed, they confidently enshrined that confession in their creeds: *He will come again in glory to judge the living and the dead, and his kingdom shall have no end.*

For anyone who read past chapter 5 of this book, it should be clear that our case does not stop at a historical-critical observation regarding the complex nature of prophetic prediction. We do not employ the conditionality of the ancient prophetic genre only to get Jesus "off the hook." Neither do we find it sufficient to observe that multiple New Testament authors explained the delay of the Parousia in these terms (see chapter 5, pp. 87–99)—although for many readers, this fresh approach to the witness of the New Testament will satisfy their discomfort. Rather, this book advances an additional series of theological arguments that corroborate the exegetical and critical ones, building on top of this exegetical foundation a doctrinal case that God's forbearance corresponds neatly to the character of the Triune God revealed in Jesus Christ, in accordance with the theologies of the three major traditions spread across the last two millennia.

## God's Being as a Pure Act of Love and God's Responsiveness to Human Action

*Prima facie*, the theological challenge to our construal of prophecy as conditional claims that it is incompatible with the doctrine of divine immutability: how can God change his mind about something prophesied under divine inspiration if God does not change? On the contrary, the assumption that a change in God's mind would entail a change in God himself is, in fact, rather facile.

From the patristic period through the modern era, and crucially, across all three Christian traditions that have developed in those two millennia, the outstanding theologians of Christianity elaborate a dynamic Trinitarian theology that describes a God whose essence is one of pure act—namely, the pure act of love. God's being consists of the perichoretic love between the persons of the Trinity; from before eternity, God has never had any existence that is not composed of the dynamic loving between the persons of the Trinity. Out of the abundance of this love, God chose freely to create the world, and thus, to enter relationship with beings that change. And yet, because the intra-trinitarian love in God's essence never changes, God is capable of interacting with his creation without compromising his immutable essence. God can react to what creation does without that interaction and response connoting a change in God's loving life as Trinity. This means God may even "change his mind" on the basis of the unruly decisions and actions of his people, and *yet, he will remain the selfsame God*.[6]

This raises the question of why an absolute and unchanging God would choose to interact with and react to an inconstant and perfidious creation. But this decision flows directly from God's essence as the act of love too. Freely-given love is the greatest good, for it is constitutive of the divine life. It only stands to reason, then, that the creation God generates as the overflow of the intra-trinitarian

---

6. Exod. 32:14; 2 Sam. 24:16; 1 Chron. 21:15; Jer. 26:13; Amos 7:3, 6; Jon. 3:10; cf. ch. 3, pp. 42–52; ch. 7, pp. 153–67.

love would itself be governed by freely-given love. But creation of this sort entails risk, insofar as freedom to love entails freedom not to love. Furthermore, God, whose nature includes free love, refuses to oblige his creation to love unfreely (cf. chapter 8, pp. 194–95). Human decisions may resist the aims God lovingly set in motion for their good. But God has the freedom to react lovingly to humanity's rebellion (i.e., their self-sabotage) by dynamically shaping his response in a way that will still achieve his goals through other historical means. In other words, *we can still put our confidence in the second coming of Christ, despite the delay of the Parousia*; far from being evidence of God's unreliability, the deferral of Jesus' return is an expression of his love for and commitment to us.

Since God's essence consists of intra-trinitarian love, the adaptability in God's behavior does not amount to a change in God's being; God is *immutable*, but he is not *incapable* of responding to us. In fact, insofar as God's reactions to humans enable an expression of love for them, in many situations *not* reacting, not responding to human actions, would amount to a departure from God's essence as freely giving love. God's flexibility with respect to the prophesied timing of the Parousia is more than something that the Trinitarian God *could* do because of the contingency native to the prophetic genre and the divine freedom to react to his creation. It is the case, more accurately, that God's willingness to "change his mind" about the timing of the Parousia in order to enable more people to repent is something that the Trinitarian God *would* do (cf. chapter 7, pp. 158–67 and chapter 8, pp. 195–97).

## Pro-Chalcedonian Christology and God's Commitment to Involve Humans in Eschatology

This discussion likely raises the specter of divine arbitrariness or caprice for some readers. While we have affirmed that God created the world under no compulsion and that he could have done otherwise, we have correspondingly denied that God's freedom continues to entail an unbounded set of possibilities (for example, *not* returning in Christ to judge the living and the dead). God has *bound himself* in Jesus Christ to a particular outcome for salvation history (cf. chapter 7, pp. 163–65). While God remains free to react to creation in that history, God has ceded the freedom to abandon the salvation-historical outcomes described in the eschatological promises (cf. chapter 7, pp. 171–73).

Conversely, this affirmation does not entail determinism, for the reality to which God has bound himself in Christ is one in which God cooperates freely with humanity. The pro-Chalcedonian dynamics of dyotheletism of the Sixth Ecumenical Council (i.e. the Third Council of Constantinople, 680–81) capture the aspects of this situation: the divine will and the human will in Christ cooperate; neither one dominates the other.[7] This situation is sensible, insofar as the Logos reconciled creation to the Godhead *by becoming* fully human while remaining fully divine. God created the world *without* human contributions, yes, but he has chosen to consummate it in cooperation *with* humanity.

Although this book treated the issues in the inverse order, there is also a logical progression from these aspects of the doctrine of God proper and Christology to the doctrine of eschatology. It stands to reason that a deity who bound himself to cooperate with creation as Jesus of Nazareth will, in similar fashion, bind himself to an eschatology that reflects the same dynamics. God has committed himself to bringing all things to completion by means of Christ and through Christ's body, the Church. The eschatological consummation is, by divine decision, something that God will bring about in cooperation with the Church. This entails that God will engage with and react to the decisions, actions, and even shortcomings of the Church.

In other words, the timing of history's consummation *must be open ended*, because it requires both a fully divine and also a fully human will. Thus, *eschatological prophecy must be conditional*. It is theologically (not to mention exegetically) erroneous to claim to know *when* God will bring about the eschaton, and it would remain so even if the prophetic

---

7. DS §§553–59, pp. 185–89.

texts had fixed a date. *God can and has changed his mind about the timing of the eschaton in response to the work and shortcomings of the Church* (cf. chapter 8, p. 196).

## Hastening the Day: Eschatology is Ethical

There is a joke in some seminarian circles in which the speaker (often a befuddled student prepping for an exam) decries premillennialism, postmillennialism, and amillennialism, asserting instead that he or she is a "panmillenialist, because it will all 'pan out' in the end." In the joke's theological favor, it does apprehend the ultimate sovereignty of God in salvation history: God will have his own way, regardless of how one exegetes Rev. 20:1-6. But behind the joke's cavalier punchline rests the flip assumption that one's eschatology does not really matter for the life of the Church or her mission to the world. In this, the joke merits censure, for the apostles understood human commitment to and participation in the eschaton to be of grave importance. The delay of the Parousia is wrapped up with human indolence. Ideas matter. Doctrine matters. It is not simply desirable for Christians to call for and to call forth the coming of the day of the Lord through both prayer and action. It is an absolute necessity.

It is neither theologically nor morally sufficient to operate simply with the knowledge that Jesus will return. The refrain of Jesus' and the apostles' teaching on the Day of the Lord and the coming of the Son of Man is "Be alert."[8] Alertness entails more than doctrinal conviction of the second coming and requires far more that scanning the heavens anxiously for the first peek of Jesus' celestial warhorse. "Being alert" necessitates activity. As Anthony Thiselton explains,

> The practical or existential currency of these two future events [i.e. resurrection and universal judgment] during the present period of "waiting" is not psychological intensity, but *living as those counted righteous in advance of the final public confirmation of this, at the Last Judgment, and living as those who belong to Christ as slaves to their Lord*.[9]

---

8. Matt. 24:42-44; 25:13; Mark 13:23, 33-37; Luke 12:27-38; 1 Thess. 5:6; Rev. 3:2-3.

# CONCLUSION

It is precisely the Christoform way in which God elects to cooperate in human history that compels Christians to respond to the delay of the Parousia with the utmost moral and missiological earnestness. Jesus' deferral of the second coming corresponds to the Church's moral half-heartedness and her anemic repentance. Several times, we have highlighted that 2 Peter 3 highlights the virtue of the Parousia's delay, enabling "all to come to repentance" (2 Pet. 3:9; cf. 3:15). That said, 2 Peter is not shy about reaffirming that "the day of the Lord will come like a thief" and "the heavens will be set ablaze and dissolved, and the elements will melt with fire" (2 Pet. 3:10, 12). It is in light of this fact that one reads the crucial text: "what sort of persons ought you to be in leading lives of holiness and godliness, waiting for and hastening the coming of the day of God?" (2 Pet. 3:11-12; cf. chapter 5, pp. 87-103).

A.C. Ainger reiterated 2 Peter's question in the hymn *God is Working His Purpose out*:

> What can we do to hasten the time,
> The time that shall surely be,
> When the earth shall be filled
> With the glory of God
> As the waters cover the sea?[10]

The answer to Ainger's query is plain from the broader context of 2 Peter: Christians are to lead lives of holiness and to call for repentance where it is lacking (both in and out of the Church); Christians are to serve in ways that recognize the presence of the kingdom and incarnate it through worship, mission, ecumenism, justice, asceticism, and contemplation (see chapter 8, pp. 197-208). In these ways, historical time ceases to be the sinister linear force capable of driving all life down a path of moral corruption leading ultimately to death.

---

9. Anthony C. Thiselton, *The Last Things: A New Approach* (London: SPCK, 2012), 66, emphasis original. See further pp. 53-67 for the full scope of Thiselton's masterful argument on the implications of the New Testaments injunctions about "waiting" and "expecting".

10. *The English Hymnal*, (Oxford: Oxford University Press, 1926), 524; this hymn was brought to my attention by the marvelous book of Michael Lloyd, *Café Theology: Exploring Love, the Universe, and Everything*, 3rd ed. (London: Alpha International, 2012), 96-97, wherein Lloyd continues "There *is* a contribution for us to make, but our (feeble and contradictory) contributions are not all there is: 'All we can do is nothing worth unless God blesses the deed.' It is a partnership." (Emphasis original.)

Quite the contrary, transformed time becomes a means of not only stopping, but even healing the corruption fallen time abets (see chapter 6, p. 131). As a result of the incarnation, the space created by the Parousia's delay becomes a seed-bed for the germination of new life which will blossom into eternity. As we have said repeatedly throughout this book: *eschatology is ethical, and ethics are eschatological.*

### Last Words: Come, Lord Jesus

It has been tempting, throughout the course of this study, to delineate neat trajectories in salvation history, even (or especially) against a narrative of meaninglessness that might emerge from a strict existentialism (see chapter 6, pp. 127–28). If one wants to explain God's decision to delay the Parousia, one might do so in terms of postmillennial optimism: God delayed the judgment so that God and humans could together make heaven of earth. Or, one might paint the delay in darker, amillennial shades: God deferred the judgment so that the final few souls might repent even as most of the world plunges into diabolical rebellion.[11]

The realia of human history, nonetheless, resist both such reductionist narratives. Rome persecutes and then repents; it becomes decadent and then falls; it rallies and splits with Constantinople; indeed, Rome sparks the Reformation and reforms itself. The Church wends its way around continents and in and out of centuries, reviving and necrotizing, suffering heinous persecution and inflicting it, ascending into great heights of love and generosity and hypocrisy. This untidy narrative parallels the complexity of God's interaction with specific humans. God engages with us individually, and the flux of salvation history represents the aggregate of God's bespoke relationships with each of us.

The Christian Church will likely persist in this nonlinear oscillation between high and low, *iustus et peccator*, day and dark, dark night. But the lack of a single trajectory neither belies the reality that Jesus will

---

11. This narrative certainly fits better with apocalyptic literature's pessimism about human affairs than does the postmillennial narrative.

come again, nor the truth that he is already with us. Through the Holy Spirit, the people of God are united with him in sacrament and service, in theophany and *theoria*; because the incarnation of the eternal Logos changed our time, it is always capable of opening onto the eternal Now, each moment a stepping stone bearing us along in hope. So it will be for as long as we see in a mirror dimly (1 Cor. 13:12). As Julian of Norwich said, "I saw him and I sought him. I had him and I lacked him. And this is, and should be, our usual way"[12] That is, at least, until we see him face to face. So we cry, *Maranatha*.

In the twenty-first century, when indifference masquerades as learnedness and where earnest expectation is all too often the domain of the deranged and fundamentalist, it is a hortatory necessity to underscore the human side of the eschatological deferral, especially in a scholarly book like this. Indeed, the divine–human cooperative dynamics of sacred history, epitomized in the hypostatic union of Christ, bespeak the eternal significance of human action, under the Spirit, in salvation history. For all that, however, one cannot lose sight of the undeniable biblical and Christian conviction that the final arbiter of history's perpetuation and climax is God himself. It is God's sovereignty that extends humanity more time, that births new generations of people to love and serve him, that is present in sustaining the faith and progress of the Church. It remains God alone who will decree history's consummation. Only God decides how human actions will impact upon the fulfillment of a prophecy (2 Sam. 12:7-23); God alone knows when the fullness of the gentiles has come in (Rom. 11:25); only the Father knows the hour and the day (Matt. 24:36). For all that humans can do to hasten the day or to obstruct our reception of eschatological beatitude, only God can finally put an end to all our wanderings.

It is for this reason that the Scriptures implore, "Come, Lord Jesus" (1 Cor. 16:22; Rev. 22:20). Likewise, this is why the second petition of the Lord's Prayer is "Your kingdom come" (Matt. 6:10). Ultimately,

---

12. Jean Furness, *Love is His Meaning: Meditations on Julian of Norwich*, trans. Sheila Upjohn (Great Wakering, Essex: McCrimmon, 1993), 10.

God must act, must chose to come again in Christ. It is because God is committed not just to *react to* humans, but rather, to *cooperate with* us, that we have hope that he might come *soon*. Were it not for God's commitment to bring his work to completion, the moral contingency of the prophesied Parousia might be a crushing burden instead of a consolation. However much our flickering moral lights can illuminate this present darkness through the help of the Spirit, the darkness shall only be finally expelled by the Lamb who is the lamp of the New Jerusalem (Rev. 21:23). Then, as Christ said to Julian, "all shall be well, and all shall be well, and all manner of thing shall be well."[13]

> The one who testifies to these things says, "Surely I am coming soon." Amen. Come, Lord Jesus!
> The grace of the Lord Jesus be with all the saints. Amen. (Rev. 22:20–21)

---

13. Norwich, *Revelation*, 102.

# Bibliography

Adams, Edward. "The Coming of the Son of Man in Mark's Gospel," *Tyndale Bulletin* 56, no. 1 (2005): 39–61.

———. *The Stars Will Fall From Heaven: Cosmic Catastrophe in the New Testament and its World*. Library of New Testament Studies. Vol. 347. London: T&T Clark, 2007.

———. "Where is the Promise of his Coming? The Complaint of the Scoffers in 2 Peter 3.4," *New Testament Studies* 51, no. 1 (2005): 106–22.

Adler, William. "The Apocalyptic Survey of History Adapted by Christians: Daniel's Prophecy of 70 Weeks," in *The Jewish Apocalyptic Heritage in Early Christianity*, edited by James VanderKam and William Adler, 201–38. Compendia Rerum Iudaicarum ad Novum Testamentum (Minneapolis: Fortress Press, 1996).

Alcinous. *The Handbook of Platonism,* translated by John Dillon (Oxford: Oxford University Press, 2001).

Allison, Dale C. *Constructing Jesus: Memory, Imagination, and History*. London: SPCK, 2010.

———. *Jesus of Nazareth: Millenarian Prophet*. Minneapolis: Augsburg Fortress Press, 1998.

Anderson, John E. *Jacob and the Divine Trickster: A Theology of Deception and YHWH's Fidelity to the Ancestral Promise in the Jacob Cycle*. Siphrut 5. Winona Lake, IN: Eisenbrauns, 2011.

Anderson, Robert A. *Signs and Wonders: A Commentary on the Book of Daniel*. International Theological Commentary. Grand Rapids: Eerdmans, 1984.

Ansberry, Christopher B., Casey A. Strine, Edward W. Klink, and David Lincicum. "Pseudepigraphy and the Canon," in *Evangelical Faith and the Challenge of Historical Criticism*, edited by Christopher M. Hays and Christopher B. Ansberry (Grand Rapids: Baker Academic, 2013), 125–57.

Aristotle. *The Complete Works of Aristotle: The Revised Oxford Translation*. 2 vols, edited by Jonathan Barnes. Bollingen 71.2 (Princeton: Princeton University Press, 1984).

———. *The Works of Aristotle: Vol. 9: Ethica Nicomachea, Magna Moralia and Ethica Eudemia*, translated by W. D. Ross (Oxford: Oxford University Press, 1925).

Athanasius of Alexandria. *Contra gentes and De Incarnatione*, edited and translated by Robert W. Thomson (Oxford: Clarendon Press, 1971).

Augustine. *Concerning The City of God against the Pagans*, translated by Henry Bettenson (London: Penguin, 1987).

———. *Confessions*, translated by Henry Chadwick (Oxford: Oxford University Press, 1998).

———. *Eighty-Three Different Questions*, translated by David L. Mosher, FC 70 (Washington, D.C.: Catholic University of America Press, 1982).

———. *Expositions of the Psalms, 33-50*. WSA III/16, edited and translated by Maria Boulding and John E. Rotelle (Hyde Park, NY: New City, 2000).

———. *Expositions of the Psalms, 99-120*. WSA III/19, translated and edited by Maria Boulding and Boniface Ramsey (New York: New City, 2003).

———. *La cité de Dieu: Livres I-V*, edited by Bernhard Dombart and Alfons Kalb, translated by Gustave Combes (Bibliothèque augustinienne 33. Paris: Institut d'Études Augustiniennes, 2012).

———. *Retractations*. FC 60, translated by Mary Inez Bogan (Washington, D.C.: Catholic University of America Press, 1968).

———. *Sermons (51-94) on the Old Testament*. WSA III/3, edited by John E. Rotelle, translated by Edmund Hill (Brooklyn, NY: New City, 1991).

———. *Sermons (184-229Z) on the Liturgical Seasons*, WSA III/6, edited by John E. Rotelle, translated by Edmund Hill (New Rochelle, NY: New City, 1993).

———. *Tractates on the Gospel of John 11-27*, translated by John Rettig. FC 79 (Washington, D.C.: Catholic University of America Press, 1988).

———. *Tractates on the Gospel of John 28-54*, translated by John W. Rettig. FC 88 (Washington, D.C.: Catholic University of America Press, 1993).

_____. *The Trinity,* edited and translated by Edmund Hill. WSA I/5 (New York: New City, 1996).

Aune, David E. *Prophecy in Early Christianity and the Ancient Mediterranean World.* Grand Rapids: Eerdmans, 1983.

_____. *Revelation 17-22.* Word Biblical Commentary 52C. Dallas: Word, 1998.

Ayres, Lewis. *Nicaea and Its Legacy: An Approach to Fourth-Century Trinitarian Theology.* Oxford: Oxford University Press, 2004.

Balthasar, Hans Urs von. *The Cosmic Liturgy: The Universe According to Maximus the Confessor,* translated by Brian E. Daley S.J. (San Francisco: Ignatius, 1989, 2003).

_____. *Love Alone is Credible,* translated by D. C. Schindler (San Francisco: Ignatius, 2004).

_____. *Mysterium Paschale,* translated by Aidan Nichols (San Francisco: Ignatius, 2000).

_____. *Presence and Thought: An Essay on the Religious Philosophy of Gregory of Nyssa,* translated by Mark Sebanc (San Francisco: Ignatius, 1995).

_____. *Theo-Drama: Theological Dramatic Theory,* translated by Graham Harrison. 5 vols (San Francisco: Ignatius Press, 1988-98).

_____. *Theo-Logic: Theological Logical Theory,* translated by Adrian Walker, Graham Harrison. 3 vols (San Francisco: Ignatius, 2000-2005).

Barth, Karl. *Church Dogmatics,* edited by T. F. Torrance and G. W. Bromiley, translated by G. W. Bromily. 13 vols (Edinburgh: T&T Clark, 1936-77).

_____. *Karl Barth's Table Talk,* edited by John D. Godsey. Scottish Journal of Theology Occasional Papers 10 (Edinburgh/London: Oliver and Boyd, 1963).

Barton, John. *Joel and Obadiah: A Commentary.* Old Testament Library. Louisville, KY: Westminster John Knox, 2001.

_____. *Oracles of God: Perceptions of Ancient Prophecy in Israel after the Exile.* London: Darton, Longman and Todd, 1986.

Basil of Caesarea. *De Spiritu Sancto = Über den Heiligen Geist,* edited and translated by Hermann Josef Sieben. Freiburg im Breisgau: Herder, 1993.

_____. "Homily 2 on Hexaemeron," in *Basilius von Caesarea: Homilien zum Hexaemeron,* edited by Emmanuel Amand de Mendieta and Stig Y. Rudberg. GCS n.f. 2. Berlin: Akademie-Verlag, 1997.

_____. "Homily on Psalm 48," in *Exegetic Homilies*, edited and translated by Agnes Way, 311–31. FC 46. Washington, D.C.: Catholic University of America Press, 1963.

_____. *On the Holy Spirit*, translated by Stephen M. Hildebrand. Yonkers, NY: St. Vladimir's Seminary Press, 2011.

_____. *St. Basil of Caesarea: Against Eunomius*, translated by Mark Delcogliano and Andrew Radde-Gallwitz. Washington, D.C.: Catholic University of America Press, 2011.

Bauckham, Richard. *2 Peter, Jude*. Word Biblical Commentary. Vol. 50. Dallas: Word, 1998.

_____. "The Delay of the Parousia," *Tyndale Bulletin* 31 (1980): 3–36.

_____. *Jesus and the Eyewitnesses: The Gospels as Eyewitness Testimony*. Grand Rapids: Eerdmans, 2006.

Bauer, Walter. *Orthodoxy and Heresy in Earliest Christianity*. London: SCM, 1972.

Beale, G. K. *The Book of Revelation: A Commentary on the Greek Text*. New International Greek Testament Commentary. Grand Rapids: Eerdmans, 1999.

Beckett, Samuel. *Waiting for Godot*. London: Faber and Faber, [1956] 1988.

Beckwith, Roger T. *Calendar and Chronology, Jewish and Christian: Biblical, Intertestamental and Patristic Studies*. Arbeiten zur Geschichte des antiken Judentums und des Urchristentums 33. Leiden: Brill, 1996.

Berdyaev, Nicolas. *The Divine and the Human*, translated by R. M. French. London: Geoffrey Bless, 1949.

Berry, R. J., and T. A. Noble. *Darwin, Creation and the Fall: Theological Challenges*. Nottingham: Apollos, 2009.

Beutler, Johannes. *Judaism and the Jews in the Gospel of John*. Subsidia Biblica 30. Rome: Editrice Pontificio Instituto Biblico, 2006.

Bigg, Charles. *A Critical and Exegetical Commentary on the Epistles of St. Peter and St. Jude*. International Critical Commentary. Second edition. Edinburgh: T&T Clark, 1902.

Blowers, Paul. "The Dialectics and Therapeutics of Desire in Maximus the Confessor," *Vigiliae Christianae* 65 (2011): 425–51.

Bockmuehl, Markus. *The Remembered Peter: In Ancient Reception and Modern Debate*. Wissenschaftliche Untersuchungen zum Neuen Testament 262. Tübingen: Mohr Siebeck, 2010.

———. *Seeing the Word: Refocusing New Testament Study.* Studies in Theological Interpretation. Grand Rapids: Baker Academic, 2006.

Borg, Marcus J. *Jesus in Contemporary Scholarship.* Valley Forge, PA: Trinity Press International, 1994.

———. "An Orthodoxy Reconsidered: The 'End-of-the-World Jesus,'" in *The Glory of Christ in the New Testament: Studies in Christology,* edited by L. D. Hurst and N. T. Wright, 207–17. Oxford: Clarendon, 1987.

Borger, Rykle. *Die Inschriften Asarhaddons, Königs von Assyrien.* Graz: Im Selbstverlage des Herausgebers, 1956.

Bradshaw, Timothy. *Pannenberg: A Guide for the Perplexed.* London: T&T Clark, 2009.

Bria, Ion. "The Liturgy after the Liturgy," *International Review of Mission* 67, no. 265 (1978): 86–90.

Brinkman, J. A. "Through a Glass Darkly: Esarhaddon's Retrospects on the Downfall of Babylon," *JAOS* 103 (1983): 35–42.

Brown, Raymond E. *The Gospel According to John: Introduction, Translation, and Notes.* Anchor Bible 29. 2 vols. London: G. Chapman, 1971.

Brownlee, William H. *The Midrash Pesher of Habakkuk: Text, Translation, Exposition with an Introduction.* Society of Biblical Literature Monograph Series 24. Missoula, MT: Scholars, 1979.

Bruce, F. F. *1 and 2 Thessalonians.* Word Biblical Commentary 45. Dallas: Word, 1998.

Bruce, Matthew J. Aragon. *Theology without Voluntarism: Divine Agency and God's Freedom for Creation.* PhD dissertation. Princeton Theological Seminary, 2013.

Bulgakov, Sergii. *Agnets Bozhii.* Paris: YMCA, 1933.

———. *The Bride of the Lamb,* translated and edited by Boris Jakim. Edinburgh/Grand Rapids: T&T Clark/Eerdmans, 2002.

———. *The Lamb of God,* translated and edited by Boris Jakim. Grand Rapids: Eerdmans, 2008.

———. *Nevesta Agntsa.* Paris: YMCA Press, 1945.

———. *Svet Nevechernii: Sozertsaniia i Umozreniia* [1917] in *Sergii Bulgakov: Pervoobraz i Obraz: Sochineniia v Dvukh Tomakh.* Vol. 1 of 2. Moscow/St Petersburg: Iskusstvo/Inapress, 1999.

———. *Unfading Light,* translated and edited by Thomas Allan Smith. Grand Rapids: Eerdmans, 2012.
"Byzantine Matins of Lent," in *The Lenten Triodion,* translated by Mother Maria and Kallistos Ware. London and Boston: Faber and Faber, 1978.
Cabasilas, Nicholas. *The Life in Christ,* translated by Carmino deCatanzaro. Crestwood, NY: St Vladimir's Seminary Press, 1974.
Caird, G. B. *A Commentary on the Revelation of St. John the Divine.* Black's New Testament Commentaries. London: Adam & Charles Black, 1966.
Calvin, John. *Calvin's Commentaries.* 22 vols. Baker: Grand Rapids, 1984.
Camping, Harold. *1994?* New York: Vantage, 1992.
———. "What Happened on May 21?" http://www.familyradio.com/x/whathappened.html.
Camus, Albert. *The Myth of Sisyphus,* translated by Justin O'Brien. Harmondsworth: Penguin Books, 1975.
Carroll, John T. *The Return of Jesus in Early Christianity.* Peabody, MA: Hendrickson, 2000.
Carroll, R. P. *When Prophecy Failed: Reactions and Responses to Failure in the Old Testament Prophetic Traditions.* London: SCM, 1979.
Carson, D. A. *The Gospel According to John.* The Pillar New Testament Commentary. Leicester: Intervarsity, 1991.
Chernyakov, Alexei. *The Ontology of Time: Being and Time in the Philosophies of Aristotle, Husserl and Heidegger.* Dordrecht: Kluwer, 2002.
Childs, Brevard S. *Isaiah.* Old Testament Library. Louisville, KY: Westminster John Knox, 2001.
Clement of Alexandria. *Stromateis,* translated by John Ferguson. Washington, D.C.: Catholic University of America Press, 1991.
Colliander, Tito. *The Way of the Ascetics.* Crestwood, NY: St Vladimir's Seminary Press, 1985.
Collins, John J. *Daniel: A Commentary on the Book of Daniel.* Hermeneia. Minneapolis, MN: Fortress Press, 1993.
Courtenay, William J. *Capacity and Volition: A History of the Distinction of Absolute and Ordained Power.* Bergamo: Pierluigi Lubrina, 1990.
Crenshaw, James L. "The Expression Mî Yôdēa' in the Hebrew Bible," *VT* 36 (1986): 274–88.

———. *Joel: A New Translation with Introduction and Commentary.* Anchor Bible 24C. New York: Doubleday, 1995.

Crossan, John Dominic. *The Historical Jesus: The Life of a Mediterranean Jewish Peasant.* San Francisco: HarperCollins, 1991.

Cyril of Alexandria. "Commentary on John," in *Cyril of Alexandria*, edited and translated by Norman Russell, 96–129. London/New York: Routledge, 2000.

Daley, Brian E., ed. *Gregory of Nazianzus.* Early Church Fathers. London/New York: Routledge, 2006.

Daniélou, Jean. *The Bible and Liturgy.* London: Darton, Longman & Todd, 1951, 1960.

de Jong, Matthijs. "Biblical Prophecy—A Scribal Enterprise. The Old Testament Prophecy of Unconditional Judgment considered as a Literary Phenomenon," *VT* 61 (2011): 39–70.

———. "The Fallacy of 'True and False' in Prophecy Illustrated by Jer 28:8–9," *JHS* 12.10 (2012): 1–29.

Dionysius the Areopagite. *Corpus Dionysiacum,* edited by Beate Regina Suchla, Günter Heil, and Adolf Martin Ritter. 2 vols. (Berlin: Walter de Gruyter, 1990–1991).

———. *Pseudo-Dionysius: The Complete Works,* translated by Colm Luibheid (New York: Paulist, 1987).

Dostoyevsky, Fyodor. *The Brothers Karamazov,* translated by Richard Pevear and Larissa Volokhonsky (London: Vintage, 2004).

Dunn, James D. G. *Jesus Remembered.* Christianity in the Making 1. Grand Rapids: Eerdmans, 2003.

———. *Romans 9–16.* Word Biblical Commentary 38B. Dallas: Word, 1998.

Dysinger, Luke. *Psalmody and Prayer in the Writings of Evagrius Ponticus.* Oxford Theological Monographs. Oxford: Oxford University Press, 2005.

Eddington, Arthur. *The Nature of the Physical World.* Cambridge: Cambridge University Press, 1928.

Ehrman, Bart D. *Jesus: Apocalyptic Prophet of the New Millenium.* Oxford: Oxford University Press, 1999.

Eliot, T. S. "Burnt Norton," in *The Complete Poems and Plays 1909-1950*, 117–22. New York: Harcourt, Brace, 1971.

Erikson, John, and Paul Lazor, eds. *The Paschal Service.* n.p.: Department of Religious Education, Orthodox Church in America, 1997.

Evagrius Ponticus. *Évagre le Pontique: Sur Les Pensées,* edited and translated by Paul Géhin. SC 438. Paris: Cerf, 1998.

———. *Les Six Centuries des 'Képhalaia Gnostica'd'Évagre le Pontique,'* edited by A. Guillaumont. Patrologia Orientalis 28.1, no. 134. Paris: Firmin-Didot, 1958.

Evans, Craig A. *To See and Not Perceive: Isaiah 6:9-10 in Early Jewish and Christian Interpretation.* JSOTSup 64. Sheffield: JSOT, 1989.

Fiddes, Paul. *The Promised End: Eschatology in Theology and Literature.* Oxford: Blackwell, 2000.

Fishbane, Michael. *Biblical Interpretation in Ancient Israel.* Oxford: Clarendon, 1985.

Fitzmyer, Joseph A. *The Acts of the Apostles: A New Translation with Introduction and Commentary.* Anchor Bible 31. New York: Doubleday, 1998.

———. *First Corinthians: A New Translation with Introduction and Commentary.* Anchor Bible 32. New Haven: Yale University Press, 2008.

Florovsky, Georges. "The Challenge of Disunity," *St Vladimir's Seminary Quarterly* 3, no. 1-2 (1954-55): 31-36.

———. "Le corps du Christ vivant: une interprétation orthodoxe de l'Église," in *La Sainte Église Universelle: Confrontation oecuménique,* edited by Georges Florovsky, Franz J. Leenhardt, Regin Prenter, Alan Richardson, and Celsus Spicq, 9-57. Cahiers théologiques de l'actualité protestante 4. Neuchâtel/Paris: Delachaux et Niestlé, 1948.

Foster, Richard J., *Celebration of Discipline: The Path to Spiritual Growth.* San Francisco: HarperSanFrancisco, 1988.

France, R. T. *The Gospel of Mark.* New International Greek Testament Commentary. Grand Rapids: Eerdmans, 2002.

———. *The Gospel of Matthew.* New International Commentary on the New Testament. Grand Rapids: Eerdmans, 2007.

Funk, Robert W. *Honest to Jesus: Jesus for a New Millennium.* San Francisco: HarperSanFrancisco, 1997.

Furness, Jean. *Love is His Meaning: Meditations on Julian of Norwich,* translated by Sheila Upjohn. Great Wakering, Essex: McCrimmon, 1993.

Gallaher, Brandon. 'Chalice of Eternity: An Orthodox Theology of Time,' *St Vladimir's Theological Quarterly* 57, no. 1 (2013): 5–35.

———. "Creativity, Covenant and Christ: The Dignity and Task of Humankind within God's Creation," in *Human Action within Divine Creation: Christian and Muslim Perspectives,* edited by Lucinda Mosher and David Marshall. Washington D.C.: Georgetown University Press, forthcoming.

———. *Freedom and Necessity in Modern Trinitarian Theology.* Oxford: Oxford University Press, forthcoming.

Gertz, Jan Christian, Angelika Berlejung, Konrad Schmid, and Markus Witte. *T&T Clark Handbook of the Old Testament: An Introduction to the Literature, Religion, and History of the Old Testament.* London: T&T Clark, 2012.

Goldingay, John E. *Daniel.* Word Biblical Commentary 30. Dallas: Word, 1998.

Golom, Jacob. *In Search of Authenticity: Existentialism from Kierkegaard to Camus.* New York: Routledge, 1995.

Green, Gene L. *Jude & 2 Peter.* Baker Exegetical Commentary on the New Testament. Grand Rapids: Baker Academic, 2008.

Green, R. P. H. *De Doctrina Christiana.* Oxford: Clarendon, 1995.

Greene, Brian. *The Fabric of the Cosmos: Space, Time, and the Texture of Reality.* London: Penguin, 2005.

Gregory of Nazianzus. "Concerning His Own Life," in *Autobiographical Poems,* edited and translated by Caroline White. Cambridge Medieval Classics 6. Cambridge: Cambridge University Press, 1996.

———. *Gregoire de Nazianze: Lettres théologiques.* Text and French translation by P. Gallay with M. Jourjon. SC 208. Paris: Cerf, 1974.

———. *On God and Christ: The Five Theological Orations and Two Letters to Cledonius,* translated by Frederick Williams and Lionel Wickham. Crestwood, N.Y.: St. Vladimir's Seminary Press, 2002.

Gregory of Nyssa. *The Easter Sermons of Gregory of Nyssa: Translation and Commentary,* edited by Andreas Spira and Christoph Klock. Cambridge, MA: Philadelphia Patristic Foundation, 1981.

———. *Gregory of Nyssa: Homilies on the Song of Songs,* translated by Richard A. Norris Jr. Writings from the Greco-Roman World 13. Atlanta: Society of Biblical Literature, 2012.

———. *Gregory of Nyssa: The Life of Moses or Concerning Perfection in Virtue*, translated and edited by Abraham J. Malherbe and Everett Ferguson (Kalamazoo, MI: Paulist, 1978).

———. *On the Soul and Resurrection,* translated by Catherine P. Roth. Crestwood, NY: St Vladimir's Seminary Press, 1993.

Gregory Palamas. "Topics of Natural and Theological Science," n *The Philokalia*, vol. 4, 346-418, translated and edited by G. E. H. Palmer, Philip Sherrard, and Kallistos Ware. London: Faber and Faber, 1995.

Gutiérrez, Gustavo. *A Theology of Liberation: History, Politics, and Salvation*, translated by Sister Caridad Inda and John Eagleson. Revised edition (Maryknoll, NY: Orbis, 1988).

Haenchen, Ernst. *The Acts of the Apostles: A Commentary,* translated by Bernard Noble, Gerald Shinn and R. McL. Wilson. Oxford: Basil Blackwell, 1971.

Hagner, Donald A. *Matthew 14-28.* Word Biblical Commentary 33B. Dallas: Word, 1998.

Hallo, W. W., ed. *Canonical Compositions from the Biblical World.* The Context of Scripture 1. Leiden: Brill, 1997.

Harnack, Adolf von. *Dogmengeschichte.* Tübingen: Mohr Siebeck, 1905.

Harrison, Peter. *The Fall of Man and the Foundations of Science.* New York: Cambridge University Press, 2007.

Hart, David Bentley. *The Experience of God: Being, Consciousness, Bless.* New Haven/London: Yale University Press, 2013.

Hartshorne, Charles. *Omnipotence and Other Theological Mistakes.* New York: State University of New York Press, 1984.

Hays, Christopher M. *Luke's Wealth Ethics: A Study in Their Coherence and Character.* Wissenschaftliche Untersuchungen zum Neuen Testament 2.275. Tübingen: Mohr Siebeck, 2010.

———. *Sensitivity towards Outsiders: Exploring the Dynamic Relationship between Mission and Ethics in the New Testament and Early Christianity,* edited by Jacobus (Kobus) Kok, Tobias Nicklas, Dieter T. Roth, and Christopher M. Hays, 569-602. Wissenschaftliche Untersuchungen zum Neuen Testament 2.364. (Tübingen: Mohr Siebeck, 2014).

———. "Slaughtering Stewards and Incarcerating Debtors: Coercing Charity in Luke 12:35-13:9," *Neotestamentica* 46, no. 1 (2012): 41-60.

―――. "Towards a Faithful Criticism," in *Evangelical Faith and the Challenge of Historical Criticism*, edited by Christopher M. Hays and Christopher B. Ansberry, 1–23 (Grand Rapids: Baker Academic, 2013).

Hays, Christopher M., and Christopher B. Ansberry. "Faithful Criticism and a Critical Faith," in *Evangelical Faith and the Challenge of Historical Criticism*, edited by Christopher M. Hays and Christopher B. Ansberry, 204–22 (Grand Rapids: Baker Academic, 2013).

Hays, Richard B. *Echoes of Scripture in the Letters of Paul*. New Haven, CT: Yale University Press, 1993.

Heil, Günter and Adolf Martin Ritter, eds. *Corpus Dionysiacum*. PTS 33/36. Berlin: de Gruyter, 1990–91.

Heschel, Abraham J. *The Prophets*. New York: Harper & Row, 1962.

Hopkins, G. M. "God's Grandeur," in *The Poems of Gerard Manley Hopkins*, edited by W. H. Gardner and N. H. MacKenzie, 66. Fourth edition. London: Oxford University Press, 1967.

Horsley, Richard A. *1 Corinthians*. Abingdon New Testament Commentaries. Nashville: Abingdon, 1998.

Irenaeus of Lyons. *On the Apostolic Preaching*, translated by John Behr. Crestwood, NY: St Vladimir's Seminary Press, 1997.

Jewett, Robert. *Romans: A Commentary*. Hermeneia. Minneapolis: Fortress Press, 2007.

John of Damascus. *St John of Damascus: Writings*, translated by Frederic H. Chase. FC 37. Washington D.C.: Catholic University of America Press, 1981.

John Paul II. *Sign of Contradiction*. Strathfield NSW, Australia: St. Paul, 1979.

Judaken, J., and R. Bernasconi, eds. *Situating Existentialism: Key Texts in Context*. New York: Columbia University Press, 2012.

Julian of Norwich. *The Revelation of Divine Love,* translated by M. L. Maestro. Tunbridge Wells, Kent: Burns & Oates, 1994.

Jüngel, Eberhard. *God's Being is in Becoming: The Trinitarian Being of God in the Theology of Karl Barth,* translated by John Webster. Edinburgh: T&T Clark, 2001.

Justin Martyr, *Iustini martyris apologiae pro christianis,* edited by M. Marcovich. PTS 38. (Berlin/New York: De Gruyter, 1994).

Käsemann, Ernst. *Commentary on Romans*, translated by Geoffrey W. Bromiley (London: SCM, 1980).

Kelly, J. N. D. *A Commentary on the Epistles of Peter and of Jude*. Black's New Testament Commentaries. London: Adam & Charles Black, 1969.

Kirk, Alexander N. "Yes, 'A Human Figure Flying Downwards on a Cloud': A Response to N. T. Wright and R. T. France on Mark 14:62." Paper presented at the Society of Biblical Literature International Meeting, London, June 2011.

Kirk, G. S., J. E. Raven and M. Schofield, eds. *The Presocratic Philosophers: A Critical History with a Selection of Texts*. Second edition. Cambridge: Cambridge University Press, 1993.

Kleist, James A., ed.*The Didache, The Epistle of Barnabas [etc.]*. ACW 6. Westminster, Maryland/London: Newman/Longmans, Green and Co., 1961.

Kloppenborg, John S. *Excavating Q: The History and Setting of the Sayings Gospel*. Edinburgh: T&T Clark, 2000.

Konstantinovsky, Julia S. *Evagrius Ponticus: The Making of a Gnostic*. Ashgate New Critical Thinking in Religion, Theology, and Biblical Studies. Farnham: Ashgate, 2009.

Kontzevitch, Helen. *Saint Seraphim: Wonderworker of Sarov and His Spiritual Inheritance*, translated by St Xenia Skete. Wildwood, California: Saint Xenia Skete, 2004.

Köstenberger, Andreas J. *John*. Baker Exegetical Commentary on the New Testament. Grand Rapids: Baker Academic, 2004.

Kugel, James. *A Walk through Jubilees: Studies in the Book of Jubilees and the World of Its Creation*. VTSup 156. Leiden: Brill, 2012.

Ladd, George Eldon. *The Presence of the Future: The Eschatology of Biblical Realism*. London: SPCK, 1974.

_____. *A Theology of the New Testament*. Revised edition. Grand Rapids: Eerdmans, 1993.

Lash, Ephrem, trans. and ed. "Kathisma/Sessional Hymn in Tone 5, Thursday Matins of the Assumption." 2008, http://www.anastasis.org.uk/assumpti.htm. Last accessed 27 May 2015.

―――. "Sticheron at the Aposticha, Tone 1, Wednesday Small Matins of the Assumption." 2008, http://www.anastasis.org.uk/assumpti.htm. Last accessed 27 May 2015.

Leichty, Erle. *Royal Inscriptions of Esarhaddon, King of Assyria (680-669 BC)*. RINAP 4. Winona Lake: Eisenbrauns, 2011.

Leuchter, Mark. *Josiah's Reform and Jeremiah's Scroll: Historical Calamity and Prophetic Response*. Hebrew Bible Monographs 6. Sheffield: Sheffield Phoenix, 2006.

Levin, Christoph. "Genesis 2-3: A Case of Inner-Biblical Interpretation," in *Genesis and Christian Theology*, edited by Nathan MacDonald, Mark W. Elliot, and Grant Macaskill, 85-100 (Grand Rapids: Eerdmans, 2012).

Levinson, Bernard M. *Deuteronomy and the Hermeneutics of Legal Innovation*. Oxford: Oxford University Press, 1997.

Lewis, C. S. *The Magician's Nephew*. London: Fontana Lions, 1984.

Lloyd, Michael. *Café Theology: Exploring Love, the Universe, and Everything*. Third edition. London: Alpha International, 2012.

Lossky, Vladimir. *The Mystical Theology of the Eastern Church*, translated by the Fellowship of St. Albans and St. Sergius. Crestwood, NY: St Vladimir's Seminary Press, 1976.

―――. *Orthodox Theology: An Introduction*, edited and translated by Ian and Ihita Kesarcodi-Watson. Crestwood, NY: St Vladimir's Seminary Press, 2001.

Louth, Andrew. *Denys the Areopagite*. London and New York: Continuum, 1989/2002.

―――. *Maximus the Confessor*. London: Routledge, 1996.

―――. "St Maximos' Doctrine of the Logoi of Creation," in *Studia Patristica: Volume XLVIII*, edited by Jane Ralls Baun, Averil Cameron, Mark J. Edwards, and Markus Vinzent, 77-84. Leuven and Paris: Peeters, 2010.

Loux, Michael J., "The World of Universals," in *Metaphysics: Contemporary Readings*, edited by Michael J. Loux. Contemporary Readings in Philosophy. New York: Routledge, 2001.

Luther, Martin. *D. Martin Luthers Werke: kritische Gesamtausgabe, Weimarer Ausgabe*. 127 vols. Weimar: Hermann Böhlaus Nachfolger, 1883-1993.

―――. "Heidelberg Disputation, 1518," in *Luther: Early Theological Works*, 47-61, translated by James Atkinson. Philadelphia: Westminster, 1962.

———. *Luther's Works*. 55 volumes, edited by J. Pelikan and H. Lehman. St. Louis: Concordia, 1955–75.

Mantzaridis, Georgios. *Time and Man*, translated by Julian Vulliamy. Waymart, PA: St. Tikhon's Seminary Press, 1996.

Martin, Jennifer Newsome. *Hans Urs von Balthasar and the Critical Appropriation of Russian Religious Thought*. Notre Dame, IN: University of Notre Dame, 2015.

———. "The 'Whence' and the 'Whither' of Balthasar's Gendered Theology: Rehabilitating *Kenosis* for Feminist Theology," *Modern Theology* 31, no. 2 (2015): 211–34.

Maximus the Confessor. "400 Chapters on Love," in *The Philokalia*, vol. 2, 52–113, translated by G. Palmer, Philip Sherrard and Kallistos Ware. London: Faber & Faber, 1995.

———. *Ambigua to Thomas; Second Letter to Thomas*. Turnhout: Brepols, 2009.

———. *Disput s Pirrom*, edited and translated by D. Pospelov. Moscow: Khram Sofii Premudrosti Bozhiei, 2004.

———. *The Disputation with Pyrrhus*, translated by Joseph Farrell. South Canaan, PA: St. Tikhon's Seminary Press, 1990.

———. *Maximus the Confessor*, translated by Andrew Louth. CCSG 48. London: Routledge, 1996.

———. *Maximus Confessor: Selected Writings*, translated by George C. Berthold. New York: Paulist, 1985.

———. *On the Cosmic Mystery of Jesus Christ: Selected Writings from Maximus the Confessor*, translated by Paul M. Blowers and Robert Louis Wilkens. New York: St Vladimir's Seminary Press, 2003.

———. *On Difficulties in the Church Fathers: The Ambigua*. 2 vols., edited and translated by Nicholas Constas. Cambridge, MA; London: Harvard University Press, 2014.

———. *St. Maximus the Confessor's Questions and Doubts*, translated by Despina D. Prassas. DeKalb, IL: Northern Illinois University Press, 2010.

Mayes, A. D. H. *Deuteronomy*. Grand Rapids: Eerdmans, 1981.

McFadden, Robert D. "Harold Camping, Dogged Forecaster of the End of the World, Dies at 92," *New York Times*, December 17, 2013.

McFarland, Ian A. "Fleshing Out Christ: Maximus the Confessor's Christology in Anthropological Perspective," *St. Vladimir's Theological Quarterly* 49, vol. 4 (2005): 417–36.

Meier, Sam. "2 Peter 3:3-7: An Early Jewish and Christian Response to Eschatological Skepticism," *Biblische Zeitschrift* 32, no. 2 (1988): 255–57.

Meister Eckhart. "Sermon 56," in *The Complete Mystical Works of Meister Eckhart*, edited and translated by Maurice O'Connell Walshe, 292–94. New York: Crossroad, 1991.

Melito of Sardis. *On Pascha: With the Fragments of Melito and Other Material Related to the Quartodecimans*, translated by Alistair Stewart-Sykes. Crestwood, NY: St Vladimir's Seminary Press, 2001.

Merras, Merja. *Origins of the Celebration of the Christian Feast of Epiphany*. Joensuu: Joensuu University Press, 1995.

Merton, Thomas. *Contemplative Prayer*. Garden City, NY: Image, 1971.

Michaels, J. Ramsey. *The Gospel of John*. New International Commentary on the New Testament. Grand Rapids: Eerdmans, 2010.

Milgrom, Jacob. *Leviticus 23-27: A New Translation with Introduction and Commentary*. Anchor Bible 3B. Doubleday, New York, 2000.

Moberly, Walter. *The Theology of the Book of Genesis*. Cambridge: Cambridge University Press, 2009.

Möhler, Johann Adam. *Symbolism: Exposition of the Doctrinal Differences between Catholics and Protestants as Evidenced by their Symbolical Writings*, translated by James Burton Robinson. 2 vols. Second edition. London: Charles Dolan, 1847.

Moonan, Lawrence. *Divine Power: The Medieval Power Distinction*. Oxford: Clarendon Press, 1994.

Moore, A. L. *The Parousia in the New Testament*. Supplements to Novum Testamentum 13. Leiden: Brill, 1966.

Moore, Lazarus. *St Seraphim of Sarov: A Spiritual Biography*. Blanco, TX: New Sarov, 1994.

Moyise, Steve. *Evoking Scripture: Seeing the Old Testament in the New*. London: T&T Clark, 2008.

Nicholas of Cusa. *Complete Philosophical and Theological Treatises of Nicholas of Cusa*. 2 vols., edited and translated by Jasper Hopkins. (Minneapolis: Arthur J. Banning, 2001.

Oakley, Francis. *Omnipotence and Promise: The Legacy of the Scholastic Distinction of Powers*. Toronto: Pontifical Institute of Medieval Studies, 2002.

Origen. *Commentary on the Gospel According to John: 1-10*, translated by Ronald Heine. FC 80. Washington, D.C.: Catholic University of America Press, 1989.

\_\_\_\_\_. *On First Principles*, translated by G. Butterworth. Gloucester: Peter Smith, 1973.

Pannenberg, Wolfhart. *Jesus: God and Man*, translated by Lewis L. Wilkins and Duane A. Priebe. London: SCM, 1968.

\_\_\_\_\_. *Systematic Theology*. 3 vols., translated by Geoffrey W. Bromiley. Edinburgh: T&T Clark, 1991-97.

Parmentier, M. "Evagrius of Pontus and the 'Letter to Melania'." *Bijdragen, tijdschrift voor filosofie en theologie* 46 (1985): 2-38.

Pascal, Blaise. *Pensées*, translated by A. J. Krailsheimer (London: Penguin, 1966).

Patterson, Stephen J. "The End of Apocalypse: Rethinking the Eschatological Jesus," *Theology Today* 52 (1995): 29-58.

Perrin, Nicholas. "Recent Trends in *Gospel of Thomas* Research (1991-2006): Part 1, The Historical Jesus and the Synoptic Gospels," *Currents in Biblical Research* 5, no. 2 (2007): 183-206.

Pervo, Richard I. *Acts: A Commentary*. Hermeneia. Minneapolis: Fortress Press, 2009.

Philo. *The Works of Philo: Complete and Unabridged*, translated by C.D. Yonge. Revised edition. Peabody, MA: Hendrickson, 1993.

Plass, Paul. "Transcendent Time and Eternity in Gregory of Nyssa," *Vigiliae Christianae* 34, no. 2 (1980): 180-92.

Pouderon, B., and M. J. Pierre. *Aristide: Apologie*. SC 470. Paris: Cerf, 2003.

Pratt, Richard L., Jr. "Historical Contingencies and Biblical Prediction," in *The Way of Wisdom: Essay in Honor of Bruce K. Waltke*, 180-203. Grand Rapids: Zondervan, 2000.

Price, R., ed. *The Acts of the Council of Constantinople of 553 with Related Texts on the Three Chapters Controversy*. 2 vols. Translated Texts for Historians 51. Liverpool: Liverpool University Press, 2009.

Pseudo-Dionysius the Areopagite. *Corpus Dionysiacum*, edited by Günter Heil, Adolf Martin Ritter, PTS 33/36. Berlin: De Gruyter, 1990-91.

———. *Pseudo-Dionysius: The Complete Works*, translated by Colm Luibheid and Paul Rorem. New York: Paulist, 1987.

Pseudo-Macarius. *Die 50 Geistlichen Homilien des Makarios*, edited by H. Dörries, E. Klostermann, and M. Kroeger. PTS 4. Berlin: De Gruyter, 1964.

———. *Pseudo-Macarius: The Fifty Spiritual Homilies and the Great Letter*, translated and edited by George A. Maloney S.J. New York: Paulist, 1992.

Pulliam Bailey, Sarah. "Harold Camping, Radio Host who Predicted World's End, Dies at 92," *Religion News Service*, 2013.

Pusey, Philip Edward. *Sancti Cyrilli Alexandrini in D. Ioannis Evangelium*. Oxford: Clarendon, 1872.

Ramelli, Ilaria L. E. *The Christian Doctrine of Apokatastasis: A Critical Assessment from the New Testament to Eriugena*. Supplements to Vigiliae Christianae 120. Leiden: Brill, 2013.

Rogerson, J. W. *The Holy Spirit in Biblical and Pastoral Perspective*. Sheffield: Beauchief Abbey, 2013.

Rondeau, M. -J. "Le commentaire sur les Psaumes d'Évagre le Pontique," *Orientalia Christiana Periodica* 26 (1960): 307–48.

Rowland, Christopher. *The Open Heaven: A Study of Apocalyptic in Judaism and Early Christianity*. London: SPCK, 1982.

Russell, Norman. *The Doctrine of Deification in the Greek Patristic Tradition*. Early Christian Studies. Oxford: Oxford University Press, 2004.

Sakharov, Sophrony. "Foreword," in *Wisdom from Mount Athos: the Writings of Starets Silouan, 1866-1938*, edited by Archimandrite Sophrony Sakharov, translated by Rosemary Edmonds (London: Mowbrays, 1974).

———. *Podvig Bogopoznaniia. Pis'ma s Afona (k Bal'furu)*. Moscow: STLT, 2010.

Schweitzer, Albert. *The Quest of the Historical Jesus: A Critical Study of its Progress from Reimarus to Wrede*, translated by W. Montgomery. London: A&C Black, 1910.

———. *The Quest of the Historical Jesus: First Complete Edition*, translated by W. Montgomery, J. R. Coates, Susan Cupitt, and John Bowden. Minneapolis: Fortress Press, 2001.

Seraphim of Sarov. "The Acquisition of the Holy Spirit," in *Little Russian Philokalia: Vol. I: Seraphim of Sarov*, edited and translated by Seraphim Rose, 62–112. Platina, CA: St. Herman of Alaska Brotherhood, 1983.

Solov'ev, Vladimir. *War, Progress and the End of History: Three Conversations Including a Short Story of the Anti-Christ*, translated by Alexander Bakshy and Thomas R. Beyer. Hudson, NY: Lindisfarne, 1990.

Sorabji, Richard. *The Philosophy of the Commentators: 200-600 AD: A Sourcebook: Volume 2: Physics*. Ithaca, NY: Cornell University Press, 2005.

Soskice, Janet M. *The Kindness of God: Metaphor, Gender, and Religious Language*. Oxford: Oxford University Press, 2007.

Sprigge, T. L. S. "The Unreality of Time," *Proceedings of the Aristotelian Society* n.s. 92 (1992): 1–19.

"St Patrick's Breastplate," translated by Cecil Frances Alexander, in *An Annotated Anthology of Hymns*, edited by J. R. Watson and Timothy Dudley-Smith, 60–62. Oxford: Oxford University Press, 2002.

Stackert, Jeffrey. *Rewriting the Torah: Literary Revision in Deuteronomy and the Holiness Legislation*. FAT I/52. Tübingen: Mohr Siebeck, 2007.

Stone, Michael E. *Fourth Ezra: A Commentary on the Book of Fourth Ezra*. Hermeneia. Minneapolis: Fortress Press, 1990.

Strine, C. A., *Sworn Enemies: The Divine Oath, the Book of Ezekiel, and the Polemics of Exile*. BZAW 436. Berlin: Walter de Gruyter, 2013.

Strobel, August. *Untersuchungen zum eschatologischen Verzögerungsproblem: Auf Grund der spätjüdisch-urchristlichen Geschichte von Habakuk 2,2 ff*. Supplements to Novum Testamentum 2. Leiden: Brill, 1961.

Stuhlmann, Rainer. *Das eschatologische Maß im Neuen Testament*. Forschungen zur Religion und Literatur des Alten und Neuen Testaments 132. Göttingen: Vandenhoeck & Ruprecht, 1983.

Swinburne, Richard. *Providence and the Problem of Evil*. Oxford: Oxford University Press, 1998.

Talbert, Charles H. "II Peter and the Delay of the Parousia," *Vigiliae Christianae* 20, no. 3 (1966): 137–45.

Theissen, Gerd, and Annette Merz. *The Historical Jesus: A Comprehensive Guide*, translated by John Bowden. London: SCM, 1998.

*The Catechism of the Church of Geneva* [1545], translated by Elijah Waterman. Hartford: Sheldon & Goodwin, 1815.

*The Divine Liturgy According to St. John Chrysostom with appendices*. Second edition. South Canaan, PA: St. Tikhon's Seminary Press, 1977.

*The English Hymnal.* Oxford: Oxford University Press, 1926.

"The liturgy of St. John Chrysostom," in *The Orthodox Liturgy,* translated by the Stavropegic monastery of St. John the Baptist. Essex: Stavropegic Monastery of St. John the Baptist, 1982.

*The Philokalia.* Translated by G. Palmer, Philip Sherrard, and Kallistos Ware. 4 vols. London: Faber & Faber, 1979-.

*The Roman Missal: English Translation according to the Third Typical Edition.* London: Catholic Truth Society, 2010.

"The Westminster Shorter Catechism 1647," in *The Creeds of Christendom III,* edited by Philip Schaff, 676–704. Fourth edition. Grand Rapids: Baker, 1977.

Thomas Aquinas. *De ente et essentia opusculum S. Thomae Aquinatis. Ad octo codicum manu scriptorum saec. XIII et XIV nec non editionis Pianae fidem in usum scholarum,* edited by L. Baur. Opuscula et Textus: Series Scholastica et Mystica 1. Aschendorff: Münster, 1926.

———. *Liber de veritate catholicae fidei contra errores infidelium seu Summa contra Gentiles.* vols. 2–3, edited by P. Marc, C. Pera, and P. Caramello. Taurini and Rome: Marietti, 1961.

———. *On Being and Essence,* edited and translated by Armand Maurer. Second edition. Toronto: Pontifical Institute of Mediaeval Studies, 1968.

———. *Questions on the Soul [Quaestiones de Anima],* translated by James Robb. Milwaukee: Marquette University Press, 1984.

———. *The Summa Contra Gentiles of St Thomas Aquinas,* translated by the English Dominicans (New York: Benziger Brothers, 1924).

———. *Summa Theologiae, Questions on God,* edited by Brian Leftow and Brian Davies, translated by Brian Davies. Cambridge Texts in the History of Philosophy. Cambridge: Cambridge University Press, 2006.

Thomas, Stephen. *Deification in the Eastern Orthodox Tradition: A Biblical Perspective.* Piscataway, NJ: Gorgias, 2008.

Tiemeyer, Lena-Sofia. "Prophecy as a Way of Cancelling Prophecy – The Strategic Uses of Foreknowledge," *ZAW* 117 (2005): 329–50.

Thiselton, Anthony C. *The Last Things: A New Approach.* London: SPCK, 2012.

Törönen, Melchisedec. *Union and Distinction in the Thought of St Maximus the Confessor.* Oxford Early Christian Studies. Oxford: Oxford University Press, 2008.

Torrance, T. F. *The Christian Doctrine of God, One Being Three Persons.* Edinburgh: T&T Clark, 1996.

_____. *Divine and Contingent Order.* Oxford: Oxford University Press, 2000.

Turner, Denys. *The Darkness of God: Negativity in Christian Mysticism.* Cambridge: Cambridge University Press, 1995.

_____. *Space, Time and Incarnation.* Oxford: Oxford University Press, 1969.

_____. *The Trinitarian Faith: The Evangelical Theology of the Ancient Catholic Faith.* London: T&T Clark, 1995.

Viviano, Benedict Thomas. "The Normativity of Scripture and Tradition in Recent Catholic Theology," in *Scripture's Doctrine and Theology's Bible: How the New Testament Shapes Christian Dogmatics,* edited by Markus Bockmuehl and Alan J. Torrance, 125–40. Grand Rapids: Baker Academic, 2008.

von Allmen, Daniel. "L'apocalpytique juive et le retard de la parousie en II Pierre 3:1-13," *Revue de theologie et de philosophie* 16 (1966): 255–74.

von Rad, Gerhard. *Deuteronomy: A Commentary.* Westminster: Philadelphia, 1966.

Ware, Kallistos. *The Orthodox Way.* Crestwood, NY: St Vladimir's Seminary Press, 1995.

_____. *The Power of the Name: The Jesus Prayer in Orthodox Spirituality.* Oxford: SLG, 2014.

Weiss, Johannes. *Jesus' Proclamation of the Kingdom of God,* translated by Richard Hyde Hiers and David Larrimore Holland. Scholars Press Reprints and Translations. Chico, CA: Scholars, 1985.

Wenham, Gordon. *Genesis 1-15.* Word Biblical Commentary 1. Nashville: Thomas Nelson, 1987.

Werner, Martin. *The Formation of Christian Dogma: An Historical Study of its Problem.* London: Adam & Charles Black, 1957.

Whitehead, A. N. *Process and Reality: An Essay in Cosmology.* Gifford Lectures Delivered in the University of Edinburgh during the Session 1927-1928. Corrected edition by David Ray Griffin and Donald W. Sherburne. New York: Free, [1929] 1978.

Williams, Rowan. *On Christian Theology.* Oxford: Blackwell, 2000.

Williamson, H. G. M. *Ezra; Nehemiah.* Word Biblical Commentary 16. Waco: Word, 1985.

Wilson, Gerald. *The Editing of the Hebrew Psalter*. SBLDS 76. Chico, CA: Scholars, 1985.

Winkle, Ross E. "The Jeremiah Model for Jesus in the Temple," *Andrews University Seminary Studies* 24, no. 2 (1986): 155–72.

Wolff, Hans Walter, *Joel and Amos*. Hermeneia, translated by W. Janzen, S. D. McBride, and C. A. Muenchow. Philadelphia: Fortress Press, 1977.

Wright, N. T. *Jesus and the Victory of God*. Christian Origins and the Question of God 2. London: SPCK, 1996.

_____. *The New Testament and the People of God*. Christian Origins and the Question of God 1. London: SPCK, 1992.

_____. *Paul and the Faithfulness of God*. Christian Origins and the Question of God 4. London: SPCK, 2013.

Zachhuber, Johannes. *Human Nature in Gregory of Nyssa: Philosophical Background and Theological Significance*. Leiden: Brill, 2000.

Zamfir, Korinna. "Jeremian Motifs in the Synoptics' Understanding of Jesus," in *Prophets and Prophecy in Jewish and Early Christian Literature*, edited by Jozef Verheyden, Korinna Zamfir, and Tobias Nicklas, 139–76. Wissenschaftliche Untersuchungen zum Neuen Testament 286. Tübingen: Mohr Siebeck, 2010.

Zizioulas, John. *Being as Communion: Studies in Personhood in the Church*. Crestwood, NY: St Vladimir's Seminary Press, 1997.

_____. *The Eucharistic Communion and the World*, edited by Luke Ben Tallon. London: T&T Clark, 2011.

# Index of Names

Adams, Edward, 9–14, 74, 87–88
Adler, William, 33
Allison, Dale C., 7–8, 13–20, 41, 70, 248–49
Anderson, John E., 244
Anderson, Robert A., 30
Ansberry, Christopher B., 243
Aune, David E., 36, 52
Ayres, Lewis, 133

Balthasar, Hans Urs von, 127–28, 135, 148, 161–64, 172, 177–78, 184–86, 188
Barth, Karl, 127, 148, 163–67, 171–72, 178, 249
Barton, John, 14, 48, 68
Bauckham, Richard, 81–82, 88–90, 92–93, 95–96, 99
Bauer, Walter, 133
Beale, G. K., 96
Beckett, Samuel, 128, 144
Beckwith, Roger T., 33, 71
Berdyaev, Nicolas, 226
Berlejung, Angelika, 244

Berry, R. J., 125
Beutler, Johannes, 218, 220
Bigg, Charles, 88
Blowers, Paul, 126, 144
Bockmuehl, Markus, 81
Borg, Marcus J., 22
Borger, Rykle, 45
Bradshaw, Timothy, 192
Bria, Ion, 240
Brinkman, J.A., 46
Brown, Raymond E., 74–75, 220
Brownlee, William H., 31
Bruce, F. F., 35
Bruce, Matthew J. Aragon, 171
Bulgakov, Sergii, 124, 127, 148, 158–62, 164, 172

Cabasilas, Nicholas, 195
Caird, G. B., 36
Calvin, John, 123, 125, 127
Camping, Harold, 1–3, 33, 80, 196
Camus, Albert, 128, 129
Carroll, John T., 98
Carroll, Robert, 44

Carson, D.A., 74–75
Childs, Brevard S., 49
Colliander, Tito, 203
Collins, John J., 29–30, 32
Courtenay, William J., 170
Crenshaw, James L., 48
Crossan, John Dominic, 7–8
Cusa, Nicholas, 117, 161–62, 185–87

Daniélou, Jean, 226
De Jong, Matthijs, 44–45, 47
Dostoyevsky, Fyodor, 143, 203
Dunn, James D. G., 35, 69–70
Dysinger, Luke, 116

Eddington, Arthur, 119
Ehrman, Bart D., 4, 8, 15–20, 41
Eliot, T. S., 185
Evans, Craig A., 49

Fiddes, Paul S., 156, 161, 163, 170, 172, 187, 190, 194–95
Fishbane, Michael, 30, 232
Fitzmyer, Joseph A., 34, 98
Florovsky, Georges, 190, 200
Foster, Richard J., 203
France, R. T., 9–10, 73
Funk, Robert W., 7–8
Furness, Jean, 267

Gallaher, Brandon, 130, 141, 150, 158, 191, 231, 236
Gathercole, Simon J., 135
Goldingay, John E., 29, 32

Golom, Jacob, 129
Green, Gene L., 87, 91–92
Greene, Brian, 119, 128
Gertz, Jan Christian, 244
Gutiérrez, Gustavo, 249

Haenchen, Ernst, 98
Hagner, Donald A., 73, 86
Harnack, Adolf von, 133
Harrison, Peter, 111
Hart, David Bentley, 156, 159
Hartshorne, Charles, 161
Hays, Christopher M., 202, 243
Hays, Richard B., 53
Heschel, Abraham J., 57
Hopkins, G. M., 167
Horsley, Richard A., 34

Jewett, Robert, 35, 94
John Paul II, 140
Jüngel, Eberhard, 165

Käsemann, Ernst, 35
Kelly, J. N. D., 91–93
Kirk, Alexander N., 10–11
Kirk, G. S., 153
Kloppenborg, John S., 7–8
Konstantinovsky, Julia S., 116
Kontzevitch, Helen, 203
Köstenberger, Andreas J., 74–75
Kugel, James, 217

Ladd, George Eldon, 69–70
Leichty, Erle, 45

# INDEX OF NAMES

Leuchter, Mark, 42
Levin, Christoph, 244
Levinson, Bernard M., 213
Lewis, C. S., 179
Lloyd, Michael, 265
Lossky, Vladimir, 113–14, 120, 194, 249
Louth, Andrew, 114, 124, 138
Loux, M. J., 112
Luther, Martin, 123, 150–51, 155–56

Mantzaridis, Georgios, 130
Martin, Jennifer Newsome, 162
Mayes, A. D., 214
McFadden, Robert D., 2
McFarland, Ian A., 178
Meier, Sam, 89
Meister Eckhart, 184
Merras, Merja, 216, 221
Merton, Thomas, 203
Merz, Annette, 69–70
Michaels, J. Ramsey, 74–75
Milgrom, Jacob, 214–15
Moberly, Walter, 244
Möhler, Johann Adam, 190
Moonan, Lawrence, 170
Moore, A. L., 87
Moore, Lazarus, 203
Moyise, Steve, 53

Oakley, Francis, 170

Palamas, Gregory, 120, 122
Pannenberg, Wolfhart, 190–95
Parmentier, M., 207
Pascal, Blaise, 124
Patterson, Stephen J., 7–8
Perrin, Nicholas, 8
Pervo, Richard I., 98
Plass, Paul, 122
Pratt, Richard L. Jr., 41, 58
Pulliam Bailey, Sarah, 2

Ramelli, Ilaria L. E., 130
Raven, J. E., 153
Rogerson, J. W., 220
Rowland, Christopher, 14
Russell, Norman, 126, 178

Schmid, Konrad, 244
Schofield, M., 153
Schweitzer, Albert, 4–6, 15, 19
Solov'ev, Vladimir, 201
Sorabji, Richard, 126
Soskice, Janet M., 143
Sprigge, T. L. S., 145
Stackert, Jeffrey, 213
Stone, Michael E., 32
Strine, Casey A., 55
Strobel, August, 87, 90, 92, 94
Stuhlmann, Rainer, 96
Swinburne, Richard, 125

Talbert, Charles H., 87
Theissen, Gerd, 69–70
Thomas, Stephen, 126
Tiemeyer, Lena-Sofia, 46–47

Thiselton, Anthony C., 11, 13, 73, 264–65
Törönen, Melchisedec, 141, 179
Torrance, T. F., 165–67, 187–88

Viviano, Benedict Thomas, 243
von Allmen, Daniel, 89
von Rad, Gerhard, 214

Weiss, Johannes, 4–6
Wehnam, Gordon, 236
Werner, Martin, 88
Whitehead, A. N., 161

Williams, Rowan, 144
Williamson, Hugh G. M., 29, 64
Wilson, Gerald, 90
Winkle, Ross E., 25, 86
Witte, Markus, 244
Wolff, Hans Walter, 56
Wright, N. T., 7, 9–15, 41, 52–53, 69, 72–73

Zachhuber, Johannes, 114
Zamfir, Korinna, 52
Zizioulas, John, 236, 257–58

# Index of Subjects

apocalyptic, 1–19, 33, 95, 106, 229, 266
apophasis, 21, 106, 109–31, 134, 137, 140–45, 147, 159, 211–12, 256–58
ascension, 10–11, 13, 21, 23, 72–76, 90, 114, 134–35, 150–51, 167, 176, 183, 187–94, 199, 222, 225–26, 228, 234, 239, 255
Asceticism, 93, 127, 197, 202–5, 212, 247, 265

cataphasis, 111–21, 147–48, 159, 258
Christology, 105–6, 132–45, 148–52, 164–66, 169–70, 177–97, 207–8, 237–40, 245–47, 263–64
cooperation, 21–22, 58, 76–77, 92–93, 111, 145, 149, 172, 177, 195–99, 205, 208, 212, 236, 238–40, 245–47, 249, 263, 265, 267–68

Easter, 219, 223–24, 226, 229
ecumenism, 93, 166, 197, 199–201, 212, 242, 247–49, 252, 265

ethics, 19, 55, 58, 71, 83, 92–93, 140, 147, 153, 197, 200, 209, 212, 225, 227, 235, 239, 249–50, 252, 258, 264–66

incarnation, 21, 58, 71, 105, 110, 120, 127, 131–33, 136, 138, 161–62, 166, 168–69, 177–78, 186–88, 190, 193–94, 199, 208, 212, 223, 235–36, 239, 246, 257, 265–67

justice, 11, 63, 66–68, 93, 103, 176, 197, 201–2, 212, 240, 247, 265

*kenosis*, 22, 120, 137, 144, 151, 158–59, 162, 184, 204–5, 246–47

liturgy, 211–15, 218–20, 223–40, 247
*logoi*, 116–17, 138, 155, 167–69, 179–82, 184–86, 188–89, 207–8

missions, 76, 93, 102, 197–99, 201–3, 212, 221, 247–48, 264–65

Parousia, 1–4, 9–10, 15, 23–24, 34–37, 40–41, 56, 60, 70, 73–75, 86, 88, 98, 103, 110, 115, 120–21, 125, 132, 142, 145, 148, 152, 164, 166, 187–88, 193, 202, 212, 222, 224, 235, 249, 253, 256, 262, 268; delay of, 4, 20–21, 24, 38, 39, 56, 60–61, 80–81, 92, 95, 100–101, 103–4, 109, 112, 127, 134, 138, 144, 161, 175, 183, 222, 242, 246–49, 255, 257, 260, 262, 264–66; hastening of, 72, 101–3, 145, 197, 199, 213, 235; imminence of, 3, 9–11, 16–17, 34–35

pascha (see also Easter), 152, 219, 226–27, 238–39

Pentecost, 17, 73–74, 148, 171, 187, 189–93, 214, 220–21, 223–24, 266

possibilities, 138, 145, 147–49, 152, 167–73, 175–76, 179, 183–88, 262–63

prophecy: conditional, 20–21, 46–48, 52, 54–55, 57, 60–63, 66, 82–86, 90, 102, 211, 245–49, 259–63; contingent, 20–21, 57–58, 71, 77, 83–87, 103, 249, 262, 268 (see also prophecy: conditional); failure, 20–21, 24–38, 60–66, 82; Jeremianic, 3, 24–31, 42–43, 47, 52–53, 57, 59–60, 62–68, 71, 85–86, 104–5 (see also prophecy: conditional); majority hermeneutic (see prophecy: predictive); minority hermeneutic (see prophecy: conditional); mosaic, 23, 40, 56–57, 62–63, 82, 104–5 (see also prophecy: predictive); non-fulfillment, 20–21, 24–33, 87, 92, 103, 242, 259; partial fulfillment, 17, 20–21, 56, 60–70, 72–76, 102, 211; predictive, 3, 34, 40–43, 46–51, 53–58, 61, 63, 66, 211, 213, 245, 260

repentance, 6, 18, 37, 42, 49–51, 55, 66, 69–70, 74, 85–86, 89–100, 102–4, 110, 148, 151, 160–61, 187, 196, 200, 202–5, 227, 249, 259, 262, 265–66

resurrection, 4, 10–11, 13–14, 16, 20–21, 72–73, 75–76, 88, 102, 133–35, 139, 142, 176, 187–93, 199, 206, 222, 225–26, 229, 240, 255, 257, 264

second coming. See Parousia

stepping stones, 20–21, 56, 60, 66–70, 72–74, 76, 79–80, 102, 110, 115, 121, 131, 166, 183, 188, 195, 212, 227, 235, 255, 258, 267

time, 9–10, 21, 34, 50, 83, 89–94, 100, 111, 113, 118–19, 122, 127–31, 133, 136, 138–39, 142–43, 145, 149–50, 152, 155, 165, 176 183, 185, 188, 191–93, 196, 200, 211,

227, 233–34, 242, 248, 256–58, 265–67

Trinity, 21–22, 75, 109, 117, 122, 137, 151, 154–55, 158–65, 179, 181–83, 185, 188, 192, 194, 206, 223, 236–37, 239, 246–47, 252, 261–62

typology, 89, 113, 115, 124, 178, 208, 227–35, 244–45, 252, 258

# Index of Ancient Writings

**OLD TESTAMENT**

*Genesis*
1:2......229
1:5......129
1:28......126, 199
2—3......237
2:10......229
2:15......236
3......123
6:6–8......150
6:6......150
6:9–8:13......89

*Exodus*
3:10......136
3:14......149, 152, 156, 160, 178
12:48......219
19:1......216
20—23......213
23:14–17......213
23:16b......215
25—40......213
25:9......230
25:40......230
32:14......261
34:6–7......91
34:22......215

*Leviticus*
1—16......213
17:26......213
18:5......236
23......213
23:15–16......216
23:34–36......215
23:34......215
23:39–43......217
26:14–26......65

*Numbers*
3:7–8......236
4:23–24......236
4:26......236
13–14......222

*Deuteronomy*
12—26......213
13:2-6 (ET 13:1–5)......40, 43

13:6 (ET 13:5)......40
16:9–15......215
16:9–10......216
16:13–15......215
16:16......213
18......47
18:15–22......40, 43, 56–57
18:15–17......23
18:20......24, 40
18:22......24, 40
30:11–14......151
31:10–11......217
32:36......50

*2 Samuel*
11—12......54
11:3......54
12:1–4......54
12:7–23......267
12:7......54
12:21–23......55
12:22......48
24:16......261

*1 Chronicles*
21:15......261
28:19......230

*2 Chronicles*
15:10–14......217
36:2–23......27
36:20–23......63
36:20–21......27
36:22–23......66

*Ezra*
1:1–3......63
1:1......27
1:2–4......27
2:1–65......28
4:1–23......27
5:1–6:11......27
6:15......27, 63
7:11–28......28
8:1–20......28, 63
9—10......64
9:10–15......64
10:7–8......64

*Nehemiah*
1:1–11......28
1:3......28
2:1–10......28, 63
5:1–13......64
5:14–15......28
8......216
9......64
9:36......29
13......64
13:1–3......64
13:4–9......64
13:10–14......64
13:14–22......64
13:23–29......64

*Job*
28:20–28......136

## Psalms
11:4......230
11:18......230
19......205
19:7-14......220
42—89......90
46:10......204
74......228
78......228
82:6......126
89......228
89:49......90
90......90
90:4......89-90
90—106......90
93—99......90
93:1......90
96:10......90
97:1......90
99:1......90
106......216
119:1-2......220
119:126a......228
120—132......90
138:16......116
145—150......90

## Proverbs
8:22-31......136
8:22-30......136
29:18......198

## Ecclesiastes
1:2......128

1:4-9......136
24:3-22......136

## Isaiah
1:13......226
5:8-13......64
6:9-10......49
11:6-9......228
11:15......228
13:10......73
19:22......49
29:15-24......42
34:4......73
44:28-45:1......27
45:9-13......42
51......228
51:2......229
53:5......49
55:8......115
57:18......49
58......133
59:20......51
60:22......50, 92
62:1-5......98
64:7-11......42
65:17-25......228
65:17......98
66:22......50, 98

## Jeremiah
7......43
7:1-15......25, 85
7:11......85
16:14-15......216

18......47, 57
18:1–11......42
18:1–10......42
22:5......85–86
23:7–8......216
25:8–14......25
25:8–9......25
25:11–12......25, 28
26......43–44, 53, 57
26:2–3......43
26:7–9......43
26:12–15......85–86
26:12......43
26:13......86, 261
26:15......86
26:17–19......43
29:10–14......25–26, 28, 59, 63
29:11......28

*Ezekiel*
18......42
20......216
27:32......95
32:7......9
33......42
36:35......229
37......229
40—48......230
40:2......231–32
47:1–12......222

*Daniel*
7:1–28......32
7:13......9–11, 73

7:24......67
8:14......31
9......29–31, 33, 65, 71
9:1–19......65
9:1–27......29
9:1......30
9:16......65
9:20–27......65
9:24......30, 66
12......31, 36

*Hosea*
1:2......196
1:10......198
2:23......198
11:4......194

*Joel*
1:2–4......48
1:8–15......48
2......73
2:1–11......48
2:3......229
2:10......73–74
2:11b–14......48–49
2:13......95
2:14......48–49
2:28–32......73–74
4:15–16......73

*Amos*
2:6–8......64
7:3......261
7:6......261

8:4–6......64
8:9......9

*Jonah*
1:2......47
3:9......47–49
3:10......47, 261
4:2–3......47–48

*Micah*
1:2......230
3:12......43

*Habakkuk*
2:2–3......52
2:3......31
2:15......32
2:20......230

*Zephaniah*
1:15......9

*Zechariah*
1:7–17......63
1:7......26, 63
1:12–17......26–27
7–8......27, 63
7:1–8:23......27
7:4......27
7:8–11......64
7:9–14......67
8:14–17......67
14:5......10
14:8–11......229

14:8......222
14:16–17......215

*Malachi*
3:7......95
4:6......98

ANCIENT NEAR EASTERN TEXTS
*Shamash Hymn*
ll. 127–29......46
ll. 151–52......46
ll. 163–64......46

DEUTEROCANONICAL BOOKS
*Tobit*
2:1......214

*Wisdom of Solomon*
5:1–7......11
7:25–37......136
9:1–2......168
9:8......230
11—12......97
11:23–24......90
11:23......90, 97
12:2......97
12:10......90, 97

*Sirach*
36:6 LXX (36:10 ET) ......92
50......231

*2 Maccabees*
12:31–32......21

PSEUDEPGIRAPHA

*1 Enoch*
1:3–9......12
14:10–20......230
37—71......10
60:4–6......90
60:25......90
62:1–3......11
83:3–10......52
83:3b–5......13
83:3–4......52
83:8......52
102:1–4......12
102:1–3......13

*2 Enoch*
28:5......226
33:1–2......226

*Sibylline Oracles*
3.669–701......12
4:136......51
4:162–70......51
4:175–78......13

*Apocalypse of Zephaniah*
12:5–8......13

*4 Ezra*
3:30......90
7:33......90
7:72–74......90
7:134......90
11—12......12, 33

11:1–46......32
11:46......98
12:10......32
13......10

*2 Baruch*
4:5......230
12:3–4......90
20:1–2......92
21:20–21......90
24:2......90
32:1......13
35—40......12
48:29......90
54:1......92
59:6......90
83:1......92
85:8......90

*Testament of Judah*
23:5......99

*Testament of Moses*
10:1......12
10:3–5......12

*Testament of Levi*
3:2–4......230

*Jubilees*
1:1......216
6:14......231
6:17–19......217
6:21......231

6:32–34......231
15:24–26......231
15:27–28......231
16:18......231
30:14......231
31:18......231
33:20......231

*Liber antiquitatum biblicarum*
19:13......92

DEAD SEA SCROLLS
*1 QH*
11:19–36......13

*1 QpHab*
VII 1–14......32
VII 7–8......32

4Q400......230
4Q403......230
4Q405......230

PHILO OF ALEXANDRIA
*Legum allegoriae*
2:86......136
3:34......91

*Quod deterius potiori insidari soleat*
115–18......136

JOSEPHUS
*Bellum Judaicum*
6.288–300......12

NEW TESTAMENT
*Matthew*
3:1–12......16, 69, 99
3:17......151
4:13–17......70
5:3–10......205
6:10......84–85, 96, 101, 201, 268
6:33......205
8:22......205
9:37–38......221
10:19–20......83
10:23......4, 9, 15–16, 81
10:32–33......83
10:34–36......15
11:3......239
12:50......151
13:1–9......70
13:2–9......16
13:18–23......70
13:24–30......16
13:24......70
13:30......221
13:31–32......18, 70
13:33......70
13:39......221
13:44......206
13:47–50......16
16:14......86
16:24–26......144
16:24......204
16:27......72
16:28......9, 15, 72, 81, 83
17:1–13......72
18:8......127

18:11......132
18:20......258
19:21......204
21:13......85
21:34......221
21:41......221
22:36–40......127
22:37–39......206, 258
23:13–36......15
23:34–39......86
24:3......11, 88
24:14......83, 85, 99
24:20......85
24:27......11
24:29......81
24:32–34......80
24:34......9, 15, 81
24:36......3, 80, 196, 267
24:37......11
24:39......11
24:42–25:13......16
24:42–45......83
24:42–44......264
24:43......92
24:44......11
24:48......80
24:50–51......11
25:1–46......8
25:1–13......80, 83
25:5......80
25:13......80, 264
25:31......11
25:34–40......258
26:20–30......225

26:64......73
28:18–20......198
28:19......255

Mark
1:1–8......69
1:2–8......99
1:14–15......69
1:15......18, 201–2, 259
3:28–29......187
4:1–9......70
4:2–9......16
4:13–20......70
4:29......221
4:30–32......70
8:34......144
8:35......254
8:38–9:1......8
8:38......10–11, 13, 83
9:1......3, 9, 11, 15–16, 72, 74, 81, 83, 253
9:2–13......72, 120
12:29–31......258
12:30–31......127
11:17......85
13......73
13:1–37......8
13:1–26......254
13:1......85
13:5–23......13
13:9–13......253
13:10......83
13:11......83
13:18......85

13:23......264
13:24–37......9
13:24–27......12–13, 73
13:24......81
13:26–27......9
13:26......11
13:28......254
13:30......4, 9, 15–16, 81
13:31......13
13:32–37......9
13:32......3, 80
13:33–37......4, 83, 264
13:33–35......80
14:17–26......225
14:61–62......73
14:62......11, 17

Luke
1:23......236
1:50–53......202
2:34......140
2:35......98
3:1–17......16
3:1......69
3:3–17......99
3:3–14......69
3:8......202
3:10–14......202
4:16–21......69
4:18–19......202
6:24–26......15
7:20–23......69
8:4–8......16, 70
8:11–15......70

9:1–2......202
9:18......132
9:23......144
9:27......9, 16, 72, 74, 81, 83
9:28–36......72
9:54......253
9:60......198
10:2–3......221
10:27......127
10:28......258
10:37......202
11:2......84
11:42–52......15
11:49–51......86
12:1–13:9......202
12:14–15......83
12:32–34......202
12:33–38......264
12:33......202
12:35–59......8
12:35–48......16
12:35–40......80
12:38......80
12:39......92
12:40......11
12:42–48......202
12:45–46......11
12:45......80
12:46......80, 259
12:51–53......15
12:54–56......16
13:6–9......85
13:18–19......70
13:20–21......70

307

16:19–31......202
17:21......76, 258
18:7–8......11
18:8......11
18:22......202
19:11......17, 80, 89, 253
19:41–44......86
19:46......85
21:25–26......73
21:32......9, 81
21:34–36......80
22:19......225, 239
22:42......197
22:49–50......253
22:69......, 88
24:25–32......206
24:44–48......70, 206
24:51......189

*John*
1:1......142
1:14......223
2:13–21......219
2:19–22......80
3:6–10......196
3:30......203
4:35......221
5:28–29......8
5:39......220
5:45–47......220
6......219–20
6:24......220
6:40......151
7:2......221

7:37–39......221
7:37a......221
7:38......222
8:58......136
10:18......135
10:28......134
11:27......182
13:35......199
14......74–76
14:3......74
14:6......76
14:16–17......75
14:16......75
14:18–21......256
14:18–20......75
14:20......75
14:21......76
14:23–27......75
14:23–26......75
14:24......76
14:28......74
15:26......205
16:13......220
17:20–21......199
18:36......205
19:28......135
19:30......110
20:19......75
20:22–23......192
20:26......75
21:20–23......254
21:22–23......17, 74, 88

## Index of Ancient Writings

*Acts of the Apostles*
1:2......220
1:7......80
1:8......255
1:9......189
2:16–38......70
2:17–21......73
2:37–40......74
2:43–47......202
3:19–21......98–99, 101, 202, 260
3:19–20......98
3:22......23–24
4:34......202
7:37......23–24
7:54–59......256
7:55–56......17
8:1–4......253
10:40–41......75
10:42......198
13:2......220
15:17......98
17:8......156
20:23......220
21:4......220
21:11......220
28:22......140

*Romans*
1:8......198
1:12......238
1:17......145
1:19–20......205
2......95
2:3–4......93–95, 99, 101

2:4–6......95
2:4......202, 259
2:5......94
5:19......190
7:24......125
8:14–17......204
8:14......192
8:15......192
8:16......192
8:17......192
8:18......205
8:19......192
8:21......199
8:23......144
8:26–27......238
8:34......238
9......95
9:17......198
9:19–33......42
9:22–24......94, 101
9:22–23......149
9:25–26......198
10:5–8......151
10:12–17......137
11:17......198
11:25–27......196
11:25......94, 198, 267
11:26......198
11:36......180
12:1......237–238
12:2......151
13:11–12......34–35
16:20......35

*1 Corinthians*
1:18–2:16......136
2:7......190
1:23......140
3:19......120
7:29–31......16, 34–35
8:6......137
9:24–26......204
10......233
11:23–26......224
11:24–25......239
11:26......258
11:27–28......227
13:12......267
15......253
15:23–24......88
15:24–28......194
15:28......198, 224
16:21......84, 101
16:22......267

*2 Corinthians*
3:17......163
4:14......35

*Galatians*
2:20......120, 203
4:4......136

*Ephesians*
1:5......190
1:10......181
1:23......189
3:9......189
3:10......118
4:13......203
5:2......237
5:16......131
5:25–27......196, 200

*Philippians*
2:7......158, 161
2:16......140, 205
3:2......234
4:5......34

*Colossians*
1:5......234
1:15–17......178–79
1:16......180, 206
1:17......206
1:24......150, 198

*1 Thessalonians*
4:13–18......8, 16
4:15......35, 88
5:1–2......80
5:2......92
5:4......92
5:6......264
5:17......206

*2 Thessalonians*
2:1......88
2:8......88
2:19......88
3:13......88
5:23......88

## Hebrews
8:5......230, 233
9:9......233
9:23......233
9:24......189
9:26......233
12:1......250
13:8......143, 182
13:15-16......237

## James
1:17......147, 234
2:17-26......204
5:7-8......88
12:1......205

## 1 Peter
2:9......238
3:9......100
3:12......101
3:20......90
3:21......233

## 2 Peter
1:4......178, 182, 208, 237
1:16......88
3......87-93
3:3-4......37, 87-88
3:4......87-89
3:5-7......89
3:7......94
3:8-15......245, 249
3:8-13......202
3:8-10......37
3:8-9......89
3:8......4, 89, 90
3:9......90, 92, 101, 202, 256, 259, 265
3:10......92, 259, 265
3:10-12......92
3:11-12......92, 176, 265
3:12......84, 92, 101, 202, 265
3:13......88
3:14......93
3:15-16......93
3:15......92-93
3:16......39

## 1 John
1:14......133
3:2......121
4:8......203

## Revelation
1:7......152
1:8......138
2—3......83
3:2-3......264
3:3......92
5:10......238
5:6-14......238
6—7......95-97
6:8......96
6:9-11......96
6:10......85, 96
6:10-11......96
6:11......96
7:9-17......96
8—9......96

8:12......96
9......95–97
9:20–21......97
15:1–16:21......96
15:1......96
16:15......92
17......36
17:1–4......36
17:9–11......36
17:15–18:24......36
19:11–21......36
20:1–6......264
21:5......138, 141
21:23......167, 268
22:20......16, 84, 101, 132, 240, 259, 267
22:20–21......268

RABBINIC WORKS
Mishnah
'Abot
4:17......98
5:2......90
Yoma
8:8......50–51

Tosefta
Sukkah
3:18......215–16

Babylonian Talmud
Yoma
86b......51, 92
Sanhedrin
97b......50, 92
98a......50, 92
Megillah
31a......217
Roš Haššanah
16a......216
Ḥagigah
12b......230

Midrash Rabbah
Gen. Rab.
55:7......230
Qoh. Rab.
7:15......

Other Midrashim
Midr. Cant.
4.4......230

EARLY AND MEDIEVAL CHRISTIAN WRITINGS
Albert the Great
*Super Dionysium de divinis nominibus*
13, q.12......158

Aristides
*Apologeticus*
16:6......100

Athanasius of Alexandria
*Against the Gentiles*
8.1......124
*On the Incarnation*
54.11–12......178

# INDEX OF ANCIENT WRITINGS

Augustine
*De trinitate*
5.1.3......154
7.3.10......154
8.1.2......154
*De civitate dei*
5.9......155
8.6......154
11.10......154
*Confessiones*
11.7.9......154
11.10.12......154
12.15.18......154
13.31.46......155
*Enarrationes in Psalmos*
49.1.2......178
101.10......155
*De diversis quaestionibus 83*
46......168
*Retractationes*
1.3.2......168
*Sermons*
68.6......206
192.1.1......178
*Evangelium Johannis tractatus*
21.1......178
28.1.3–13......191
*De doctrina christiana*
1.36.40......250
2.18.28......252
*Barnabas*
4:3......92
15:59–60......226

Basil of Caesarea
*On the Holy Spirit*
27.66......129
*Homilies on Hexaemeron*
2.4.28–29......129
*Against Eunomius*
1.21......131
*Homily on Psalm 48*
8......194

*1 Clement*
23:3–5......88–89

*2 Clement*
11:2–12:1......88
12:6......92

Clement of Alexandria
*Quis dives salvetur*
36......101

Cyprian of Carthage
*De mortalitate*
18......54, 84, 101
*De bono patientia*
4......95
*Testimonia ad Quirinum*
35......95

Cyril of Alexandria
*Commentary on John*
I.9, 89c......178

Pseudo-Dionysius the Areopagite
*Mystical Theology*
1......118
1.3......114
*Divine Names*
2.10......114
5.6......180
5.6.17–21......237
6......116
9.8–9......158
*Epistle of Diognetus*
9:1......94

Eusebius
*Historia ecclesiastica*
3.39.4......81

Evagrius Ponticus
*Scholia*
8......116
*Gnostic Chapters*
2.47......122
*On the Thoughts*
3......127
*Letter to Melania*
64......207

*Gospel of Thomas*
3......8
9......16
18......8
37......8
57......16
113......8

Gregory of Nazianzus
*Concerning His Own Life*
1947–49......109
*De oratione*
14.7......237
28.4......114

Gregory of Nyssa
*Against Eunomius*
10......114
*Vita Moysis*
25......156
230......126
*Homilies on the Song of Songs*
15.449......127
*De mortuis*
III. 521AB......128
*Easter Sermon*
1......141
*De hominis opificio*
XVII.2......142
*On the Soul and Resurrection*
34......156
45......156
*The Great Catechism*
24......156
25.494–95......178
32......157

Ignatius of Antioch
*To the Ephesians*
11.1......91, 94

## Irenaeus of Lyon
*Adversus haereses*
4.26.1......206
4.36.4......206
5......178
5.18.3......183
*Epideixis*
6......206
34......183
87......206

## John Damascene
*The Orthodox Faith*
1.4......115
1.8......156
1.9ff. ......156

## Justin Martyr
*Dialogue with Trypho the Jew*
61......133
*1 Apologia*
28......91, 100
60......183
*2 Apologia*
7......100
*Clementine Homilies*
9.19.1......91
16.20......91

## Maximus the Confessor
*Ambigua*
2.112–13......190
5.13......139
5.14......139
5.15......135
7......123, 237
7.9–10......155
7.15......123, 168
7.16......137–38, 168, 180–81
7.20......180–81
7.21......181
7.22......169
7.36–39......189
7.36–37......190
8......124
10......123
22.2......155
71.5......132
*Epistula*
2......124
*Ad Thalassium*
22......178, 182
60......138, 141, 169, 178
*Four Hundred Chapters on Love*
3.46......185
4.3......168
*Quaestiones et dubia*
Q.190......182
*The Disputation with Pyrrhus*
61......194

## Melito of Sardis
*Peri Pascha*
103–05......152

## Nicholas of Cusa
*De li non aliud*
5.19......162

*De possest*
6–9......186
14......185
25......185
48......186
58......186

Origen
*De principiis*
1.2.2......167
1.3.6......237
*Commentarius in Johannis*
1.34.243–245......167

Shepherd of Hermas
*Similitudes*
8.11.1......91
9.14.2......88
10.4.4......88
*Visions*
2.4.1......191
3.9.9......88

Tertullian
*De oratione*
5......53–54, 84–85, 96, 101
*Apologeticus*
32......100–101
39......100

Thomas Aquinas
*De ente et essentia*
4......122
5.2......122

*Summa contra gentiles*
1.26......122
1.72......158
3a.20......237
*Quaestiones de anima*
6.2ad......156
*Summa Theologica*
1.2.3......157
1.3.1......157
1.3.7......157
1.4.1......157
1.4.2......157
1.6.3......157
1.14.8......169–70
1.15.2......70
1.18.2......158
1.18.3......157–58
1.19.3......171
1.19.4......157, 170
1.25.1......157
1.25.5......170–71
1.25.5.1......171
1.34.1......179
1.83.2......171

GRECO-ROMAN LITERATURE
Aeschylus
*Suppliants*
599......92

Alcinous
*Didaskalikos*
9......167
16–17......167

# INDEX OF ANCIENT WRITINGS

Aristotle
*Ethica nichomachea*
7.14......158
*Metaphysica*
9.6......126
12.6.2–7.9......158

Euripides
*Iphigenia among the Taurians*
201......92

Homer
*Iliad*
236......92

Herodotus
1.38......92

Plutarch
*Moralia*
511B–D......91

Plato
*Timaeus*
28c......114
29a–b......167
30d–31a......167
36b......183

Pseudo-Macarius
*Collection*
II.15.38......121

Plotinus
*Enneads*
I.7.1......158
I.8.2......158
V.7......167
V.9......167
VI.1.16......126
VI.8.20......158

www.ingramcontent.com/pod-product-compliance
Lightning Source LLC
Chambersburg PA
CBHW071148070526
44584CB00019B/2713